An Introduction to Language

Linguistics in the World

Linguistics in the World is a textbook series focusing on the study of language in the real world, enriching students' understanding of how language works through a balance of theoretical insights and empirical findings. Presupposing no or only minimal background knowledge, each of these titles is intended to lay the foundation for students' future work, whether in language science, applied linguistics, language teaching, or speech sciences.

What Is Sociolinguistics?, by Gerard van Herk
The Sounds of Language, by Elizabeth Zsiga
Introducing Second Language Acquisition: Perspectives and Practices, by Kirsten M. Hummel
An Introduction to Language, by Kirk Hazen

An Introduction
to Language

Kirk Hazen

WILEY Blackwell

This edition first published 2015
© 2015 John Wiley & Sons, Inc

Registered Office
John Wiley & Sons Ltd, The Atrium, Southern Gate, Chichester, West Sussex, PO19 8SQ, UK

Editorial Offices
350 Main Street, Malden, MA 02148-5020, USA
9600 Garsington Road, Oxford, OX4 2DQ, UK
The Atrium, Southern Gate, Chichester, West Sussex, PO19 8SQ, UK

For details of our global editorial offices, for customer services, and for information about how to apply for permission to reuse the copyright material in this book please see our website at www.wiley.com/wiley-blackwell.

The right of Kirk Hazen to be identified as the author of this work has been asserted in accordance with the UK Copyright, Designs and Patents Act 1988.

Wiley also publishes its books in a variety of electronic formats. Some content that appears in print may not be available in electronic books.

Designations used by companies to distinguish their products are often claimed as trademarks. All brand names and product names used in this book are trade names, service marks, trademarks or registered trademarks of their respective owners. The publisher is not associated with any product or vendor mentioned in this book.

Limit of Liability/Disclaimer of Warranty: While the publisher and author have used their best efforts in preparing this book, they make no representations or warranties with respect to the accuracy or completeness of the contents of this book and specifically disclaim any implied warranties of merchantability or fitness for a particular purpose. It is sold on the understanding that the publisher is not engaged in rendering professional services and neither the publisher nor the author shall be liable for damages arising herefrom. If professional advice or other expert assistance is required, the services of a competent professional should be sought.

Library of Congress Cataloging-in-Publication Data

Hazen, Kirk.
    An introduction to language / Kirk Hazen. – First Edition.
        pages cm – (Linguistics in the world)
    Summary: "An Introduction to Language helps shape readers' understanding of what language is, how it works, and why it is both elegantly complex and yet essential to who we are" – Provided by publisher.
    Includes bibliographical references and index.
    ISBN 978-0-470-65895-6 (hardback) – ISBN 978-0-470-65896-3 (paper)   1. Linguistics.
    I. Title.
    P121.H449 2014
    410–dc23
                                                                            2014007435

A catalogue record for this book is available from the British Library.

Cover image: Close-up of conkers. @ Andrew Masters/IStockphoto
Cover design by Nicki Averill

Set in 11/13 pt MinionPro by Toppan Best-set Premedia Limited
Printed and bound in Singapore by Markono Print Media Pte Ltd

1   2015

For their willingness to tune me out, for their five-second attention spans, for their exasperation at my efforts to teach them all the same, and for their continued love no matter how aggravating I am, I dedicate this book to the three people who most challenged me to become a better teacher.

For Keegan, Coleman, and Madara

Brief Contents

Contents

Companion Website

This text has a comprehensive companion website which features a number of useful resources for instructors and students alike.

For Instructors
Instructor's manual
Answer keys for the end of chapter exercises

For Students
Interactive sample quizzes
Flashcards of key concepts
Annotated web links and video clips

 Visit http://quizlet.com/_puhix to access the flashcards, and www.wiley.com/go/hazen/introlanguage for all other materials

Acknowledgments

Writing a book is something like walking down a crowded city street. You might be doing the walking by yourself, but you are not alone. Your effort might be in your walking, but you did not build the sidewalk or the city around you. You might be walking to a certain spot, but there are lots of diversions that alter your path. As walks go, writing this book has been a good one.

My two Wiley Blackwell editors deserve many thanks. The person who started me off on this trip was Danielle Descoteaux, and I want to thank her for her persistence with me (she first asked in 2006, but I did not sign up until 2010): Her vision, voluminous knowledge of publishing, avalanche-like emails, and support throughout made this project possible. Julia Kirk, my other primary editor at Wiley Blackwell, was able to carry me through with patience and sage advice.

Locally at West Virginia University, I would like to thank the students I have taught in an introduction-to-language course, vaguely enough titled *The English Language*. I have had the good fortune to teach this course 30 times since 1998, and it is my experience from that class and those students that forms the foundation for this book. I still enjoy teaching this class, and it is the students who make it valuable and enjoyable.

The students who have helped me the most are those who have worked with the West Virginia Dialect Project. From the lab managers to the teaching assistants, we have had amazing folk, and I am immensely grateful to have worked with them. For assistance with this book, I would like to specifically thank the WVDP technical writers/copy editors/indexers: Isabelle Shepherd, Jaclyn Daugherty, Lily Holz; team MCQ: Margery Webb, Kiersten Woods, Emily Vandevender; and the teaching assistants who contributed to quizzes, glossary terms, and homework answers: Allison Eckman, Jordan Lovejoy, Emily Greene, Emily Justiss, Shannon Goudy, Caleb Stacey, Khali Blankenship, and M'lyn Gibson.

I would like to thank my mentor, Walt Wolfram, for marking so many trails for me to follow. I want to thank Patrick Conner for hiring me at WVU and working with me on the Old English examples at WVU. I thank Julia Davydova for helping me with Russian examples and discussions of language variation, and Jim Harms and Mary Ann Samyn for their assistance with poetry and genre. Janet Holmes taught me a great deal about producing a book while we edited *Research Methods in Sociolinguistics*, and this book benefited from that experience. I want to thank the Department of English and the Eberly College at WVU for providing me with so many opportunities and so much freedom to work.

The reviewers for this book were invaluable for its development. Their advice was clear and direct, and I incorporated it in every section. I thank them for their astute reading and precise comments.

I especially want to thank my family for their love and support. My parents, Barbara and Al Hazen, provided me with a wonderful childhood and set me on firm educational ground, entrenching in me the idea that parents are the first teachers. My mother-in-law, Janet Coleman, and my entire extended family have kindly brought me into their lives. Above all, I want to thank Kate Hazen for working with me for the last 24 years to build the beautiful life we have and loving me all the way through.

Note to Instructors

Early introductions to language have included Saussure's *Cours de Linguistique Générale* (1916), Bloomfield's *Language* (1933), and Hockett's *A Course in Modern Linguistics* (1958). In these works, the authors aimed at slightly different audiences and wrote from different sociocultural contexts. Saussure lectured in an age of European language scholarship where linguistic study was the study of historical linguistics, and his lectures turned generations of students away from the concrete and historical and towards abstract systems. Bloomfield wrote as an American scholar surrounded by exciting work in dialectology, anthropological linguistics, and the study of mental systems created by students of Saussure. Both of those scholars developed material aimed at a small percentage of the population. Both of their books are works of scholarship. The difference between Saussure's work and Bloomfield's is that Saussure's was his collected lectures about how the study of language should play out. Bloomfield wrote a tremendous scholarly work about language which elucidated the state of knowledge at the time. Additionally, Bloomfield's book was a greatly expanded revision of his *Introduction to the Study of Language* (1914), incorporating the previous decades of work in linguistics.

For the editions I own, Saussure's *Cours de Linguistique Générale* is 317 pages with 30 chapters (in five parts), Bloomfield's *Language* is 564 pages with 28 chapters, and Hockett's *A Course in Modern Linguistics* is 621 pages with 64 chapters. A few modern textbooks have the same length, but these earlier works are vastly more dense. In terms of writing style, both Bloomfield's and Hockett's works are very readable for modern scholars and impressively expansive. Yet for most teachers of students who are not majoring in linguistics, the approach they take is daunting.

Hockett (1958:vii) clearly designates his book for "those college students who take an introductory course in linguistics," but he did not write a "popularization" and warns the potential readers accordingly. As a Professor of Linguistics and Anthropology at Cornell University, Hockett (1958:viii) considered that the university "with a magic seemingly unique, makes itself a congenial home for the scholar in linguistics."

Saussure, Bloomfield, and to a great extent Hockett, directed their work towards audiences prepared for scholarly engagement with detailed language facts. With the opening up of universities in the United States after the advent of the GI Bill, many different kinds of students entered the university, including those from blue-collar and poor families who may never have been exposed to the expectations of twentieth-century scholarship. Both of my parents fit that description, and I have wondered how my parents, from working-class Pittsburgh and poverty-stricken rural Florida, would have dealt with Hockett's morphophonemics or the distinction between internal and external sandhi. I do not imagine that it would have worked well, and I am not sure Hockett wrote for such students – those who were not budding scholars.

Since 1958, most of the textbooks have been openly designed for introductory linguistics courses and have followed Hockett's model, but rarely with the ambition needed to cover all 64 of his chapters. This book crafts a different path. This book is for people who will probably not study linguistics as scholars. It is designed for college students, and specifically for college students of the twenty-first century.

In an introductory biology course for humanities majors (an "intro to life" course), you would deal with evolution and concepts like natural selection. The general public has heard about evolution, but might not know how natural selection actually works. There would be some challenge in getting students to know how these concepts interact, plus time spent disabusing people of misconceptions. In an introductory biology course for majors, you would learn how biologists actually study natural selection and more detailed descriptions of how it works. You would have a clue about how research projects are conducted to test ideas. But natural selection would be part of both courses because it is an important concept for biology.

For this book, one foundational concept is that our species has a specific ability to acquire a highly complex communication system. That concept should be part of both intro to linguistics and intro to language classes. The intro to linguistics course might provide research studies by linguists that investigate that concept; the intro to language course would just fit it into the story about how language works. The key difference between the biology example and the linguistic example is that very few people in the college educated public realize in any explicit way the complexity human language has. When I do public talks, people overwhelmingly believe that language clearly has two forms (good and bad) and that it is a human invention; rarely does anybody start with the distinction between language and writing. I really hope that with this book, some of its basic tenets of linguistics become the norm for college-educated understanding.

The difference between what high school biology now teaches and what my parents' generation knew is dramatic. My father-in-law did not understand what a cell was when he was diagnosed with stage 4 cancer; my wife, with a BS in zoology, had to explain how cells worked. My children's high school biology classes are on the same level (with updated facts and concepts) with my intro to biology college class from 1988. Linguistics has made no such gains with general public knowledge or high school education. I want us to do so.

Preface: About the Book

the scope of the book

This book explores the nature of language primarily through an explanation of English, drawing on examples from other languages to illustrate similarity and diversity in human language.

As a result of the expansion of the British Empire, English is now a global language. With all the people who have learned English over the last 200 years, the language is in a different state than it used to be. We might be able to imagine a possible universe where language does not change, but as we will explore in this book, humans have a natural instinct to understand and produce language variation. A product of that daily variation is language change. Over time, our natural ability for variation has created many varieties of English.

At times, I refer to these different varieties as *Englishes*. It is more concise than *dialects of English*. Plus, the term *dialect* carries with it a great deal of social baggage, which will be explained throughout the book. Although speakers of many different Englishes can understand each other, the social differences and language characteristics of these varieties of English are widely recognized. As we talk about the qualities of language throughout this book, the examples will come from Englishes around the world.

intro classes

A note is needed on the general approach to teaching about language in this textbook.

The world would be a better place if everyone were required to take (and pass) two linguistics courses. People would be more likely to demand rational arguments and empirical evidence, and we would be better able to provide those things. The field of linguistics, important to both academia and industry, would also benefit from the increased interest. The reality is that a graduate degree in linguistics is not an easy task, and few people become professional linguists. Yet everyone should know about language. It is one of our most important human qualities, and something all of us talk about. If people learned about the basic qualities of human language, we would better understand ourselves.

The training to become a linguist is specialized in the same way that the training to become an ornithologist (bird scientist) is specialized: A lot has to be learned about the material, and the methods for analysis are particular to the kinds of data under study. Yet, for nonspecialists to learn about birds, they do not have to learn genetics. For nonspecialists to learn about how wonderful language is, they do not have to train to be linguists and learn about acoustic phonetics. Most other introduction-to-language books adopt the same model, the same chapter set-up, as do books for linguistic majors. This book does not. With this difference between linguists and normal people in mind, the traditional book divisions, which mirror the traditional subfields in linguistics, were modified in this book. Instead, we move from small parts to larger parts.

In writing this book, I have attempted to maintain the distinction between a textbook working as an introduction to linguistics and this textbook, which is an introduction to language. Although this book will not teach you how to do the science of language, known as *linguistics*, it will use knowledge from linguistics to explain language. For a comparison, *biology* is the study of life, and an introduction to *life* would use knowledge from biology. An introduction to biology itself, as a field of academic study, would be a different book than an introduction-to-life textbook. In many ways, an introduction-to-life textbook would work in a biology class for nonbiology majors. This textbook is an introduction to language for nonlinguistic majors.

Just like human biology or human society, language is more complex than most people realize and more complex than any one book can explain. This particular book introduces modern ideas about language. I sincerely hope you continue to study language after reading this book, but certainly not all readers will analyze language in scientific ways. With those expectations in mind, this book maintains different goals than books which introduce the academic field of linguistics. It relies on your knowledge as language users to help you discover the wondrous skills you already have. The book does not, however, train you to be a linguist, and it keeps at reasonable levels the linguistic jargon borrowed from that professional training.[1]

Throughout your life as language users, you will have debates about the meaning of words, the history of phrases, and how appropriate certain bits of language might be for certain situations. Eventually, some readers become parents, and they will want to know how their children develop language as babies and why they sound so different as teenagers. Debates about language are regular events in religion, government, and legal systems all over the world. When all these people talk about language, it is extremely helpful for them to understand how language actually works (in contrast to the many myths about language that float through the world). In this book, I attempt to lead you to an understanding of what language is and why it is both beautiful and essential to who we are.

this book's structure

This book has numerous, digestible subdivisions for every chapter. Understanding language is not a simple task, and a subdivided structure allows students to focus on the important information bit by bit. All chapters have the following sections plus chapter specific topics:

Chapter overview: This section provides a clear and concise description of each topic in the chapter. It is intended to orient the student to the area of language study.

Textboxes with Words to the Wise *and* Word Play: These sidebars provide interesting topics related to the main focus of the chapter. These side topics can provide ideas for undergraduate research studies.

Chapter summary: This section reiterates the main topics to offer the student another opportunity to step back and consider the entire area of study.

Key concepts: These keywords and concepts, which serve as the foundational vocabulary for each chapter, should be the primary focus for the students.

Further reading: Featuring both popular and academic titles, the further reading sections provide suggestions for the most accessible language research. These suggestions are accompanied by summaries of each work.

Exercises: These questions, instructions, and sample data will help the student actively engage and work with the concepts in the chapters.

Study questions: Although not exhaustive, these questions provide the basics for the concepts in the chapters. If the students can answer these questions fully and provide detailed examples with each one, they should be on their way to performing well in the class.

Most chapters will also address the following themes:

Meaning
Structure
English and other languages
Variation through time
Variation today

These topics bring together many different areas of research and translate them into larger pools of interest. Throughout the chapters, certain themes are more prominent than others. In some chapters, *meaning* will be a larger theme of focus; in other chapters, *structure* will require more explanation. For example, Chapter 3, on the patterns of sounds, contains more stories about *variation today* than does Chapter 8, which is about building sentences. Since the nature of human language restricts variation for building sentences but allows abundant variation with sounds, there are simply fewer examples of variation for building sentences within English at the present time.

The discussions of language variation bring a grand opportunity to this book. Language is an important part of our personal and social identity, and the construction of these identities is carried out by our innate ability to play with and produce language variation. Since language variation is a natural vehicle for expressing social qualities, discussion of sociolinguistic topics will not be segregated from linguistic topics. Instead, social qualities of language variation are integrated with linguistic qualities. In many books of this type, one chapter would talk about how suffixes are added to words, such as *-ing* added to the verb in *I am walking*, and a different chapter would talk about how people use variation in language to mark social differences: To use *-in'* rather than *-ing* is more informal. This book discusses the social and linguistic qualities of variation together to illustrate the rich texture of language for students.

exercises

The exercises in this book are designed to help students engage the concepts presented in each chapter. Some of the main points in this book are abstracted away from many observations of language, and to make those points real, students must play with language to observe its patterns. The exercises help students discover their own language, its basic qualities, its social nuances, and its inherent variation. The exercises are divided into two sets: those for individual work and those for in-class group work. With the individual exercises, students develop analytical skills through the close examination of data sets and their own personal language variation. In these studies, students pursue the ancient goal of knowing oneself. With the group exercises, the collective work of a small group develops a body of shared (socio)linguistic knowledge for group analysis while also building camaraderie within the class.

One of the most important steps students can make to successfully learn about language is to take the time in these exercises to account for the language knowledge and language beliefs in their own heads. When students approach topics such as physics or economics, they may not have many explicit beliefs about how things work in those branches of scholarship. In contrast, all students approach the study of language with long-standing beliefs about their languages, others' languages and dialects, and the judgments made about them. Unfortunately, some of those beliefs are factually wrong. To learn about how language works, most people have to unlearn things they already believe.

Englishes and other languages

Discussion of Englishes and other languages will compare what happens in the many varieties of English to the even wider expanse of languages on Earth, over 6,900 of them. The biggest downside to learning about language through just one of them is that the range of language diversity cannot be accurately displayed. For example, English has a fairly rigid order to its sentences, and this order affects meaning: *The coach hit the ball* and *The ball hit the coach* have two different meanings. Yet, many other languages do not work this way, allowing instead a freer word order. Such alternative realities are presented in these sections.

Language variation and varieties of English are part of many different sections of this book. In Chapter 2, for example, the words used to exemplify certain sounds are presented with regular spelling to represent those sounds (as spoken by someone from the state of Michigan). Although some other varieties share the same words to represent those vowels, not all do. Speakers from Alabama and New Zealand might well have different words to best represent those vowels. The course instructor can help negotiate these paths of variation.

the limits of this book

Language itself is complex, yet language is not all there is to human communication. For many linguists, body language and clothing choices are not considered language, though they are certainly part of communication. This division between *language* and *communication* will be maintained throughout this book. The study of meaning overall is called *semiotics*, but that includes a really large group of activities, including how you dress, when you cross your arms, and whether you are smiling or frowning. All those clues let people know information about you. They all fall into the category of communication and can all be examined with semiotics. Communication is a broader range of human skills than just language, and an introduction to human communication would be a different kind of book. This book focuses on language.

analogies for language

In order to explain how language works, linguists have tried to make comparisons between language and many different things. None of them are perfect, but with some of these analogies, decent explanations are provided for parts of what language does. Analogies provide a comparison between two unlike things. Better analogies compare something the audience knows well to something the audience knows less well: "Walking in outer space is like walking on smooth ice without skates." In that analogy, the qualities of lack of control and very little friction are conveyed. For anyone who has been on smooth ice, it is difficult to get going without a push. As with any analogy, this one fails in several ways. Outer space is frictionless on every dimensional plane, not just where your feet are located; outer space also presents many more dangers, including deathly cold and no atmosphere. So, admittedly, analogies are not perfect, but they remain an effective teaching tool.

This book will use analogies throughout to relate certain qualities of language, although some of the most common analogies are not used. One of the most common comparisons not used in this book is between language and clothing. The analogy works something like the following: Language is like clothing in that it comes in styles, certain parts go in and out of fashion, and you can use clothes for a while and then change them for different occasions. This is a decent analogy in some ways, but it is wrong in many other ways. For example, you can consciously choose to "wear" some words and not others, but patterns of pronunciation and grammar are not fully open to that kind of choice. Words certainly do go in and out of fashion, but dialects are not things which can be put on and taken off like a coat; they cannot be packed up for the winter once the last leaf falls. When providing analogies in this book, I explain in what ways they apply to language, and at times, in what ways they do not apply.

a prescriptive guide for social trends

Everyone has vast experience with language. From the day you are born, language is all around you. It is one of the essential things we do every day, and it is difficult to imagine life without at least one language. Unfortunately, most people's experiences with language in school are unpleasant. When people think about school and language together, they think about teachers who correct their writing or tell them specific words *not* to use. If you were one of the lucky ones who learned the school rules easily, you may have taken it upon yourself to correct your classmates. If you were one of the many who did not conform so easily to the school rules, you may have wondered why you were being picked on for your language. This book will not judge you by those kinds of rules. We will make distinctions between the kinds of rules used in writing and the other types of rules people use in every human language. This book will not tell you how to pronounce any certain word nor will it tell you to place your periods inside or outside of quotes. It will, however, explain what language is and how it works.

a path to education: confusion

In reading this book, there may be points where you are confused. That is OK. Although it may not always be a comfortable feeling, confusion is a necessary step towards learning. The world is more complex than we can imagine; we should learn about that complexity. To understand more of that complexity, we must engage it, considering the connections and the layers of interacting parts, be they molecules, cities, or nations. In studying language, it is also more complex than we can imagine.

As students, when you begin to consider that complexity, your normal understanding of *how language works* gets challenged. Everyone has some implicit explanation for how language works, whether or not they have ever written it down or said it out loud. The explanation (the model) you hold at the start of the course cannot handle the complexity of information presented in this introductory book. That mismatch, between the simplicity of your starting model and complexity of language, creates *confusion*. That confusion is a good thing. Yes, in the education business, confusion is an important early by-product of learning. It is physical evidence that you are trying to learn and that you have engaged the material. If you are not confused at some point in an introduction to language course, you are not trying hard enough. Leading yourself out of the fog of confusion is where the education happens. To actually achieve education, you must revise your model to accommodate the complexity of language. Well beyond providing you information about language, this book should help you revise your model of how language works.

for instructors

The theories of how language works in this book are not the only ones out there. In writing this book, I had to choose a coherent set of theories to explain how language works. One way to teach from this book is to challenge its explanations of how language works and provide alternative hypotheses. For example, in Chapter 6 there is the *assumption of composition*, a term that allows us to break apart words like *renationalization* into subparts (e.g. re-nation-al-iz-ation) and assume that those subparts are in the lexicon. The challenging question to ask would be something like: "If we do not adopt the assumption of composition, how does that affect our lexicon?" Students and teacher could then explore the implications of that model of language. Challenging and arguing well are important skills in language study.

note

1   Linguists reading this book might be dismayed at how much jargon is missing, but I hope to have carried through the essential meanings in the absence of the terms. Teachers can always add additional terms.

 Visit the book's companion website for additional resources relating to this chapter at http://www.wiley.com/go/hazen/introlanguage

1 Introduction

Chapter outline

An Introduction to Language, First Edition. Kirk Hazen.
© 2015 John Wiley & Sons, Inc. Published 2015 by John Wiley & Sons, Inc.

chapter overview

This chapter introduces you to human language, but that is a huge thing to study. Some brave linguists catch words from the last speaker of a dying language while others study subtle changes in a language spoken by millions. Although we use knowledge gathered from such studies, we take a broader look at how language works. To do this, we narrow our focus to specific topics about language, including the many different parts that make up language. We tour the small, medium, and large parts of language to explain their qualities and how the language factory in your mind fits them together, like so many nuts, bolts, metal forms, and plastic widgets assembled together to make a car. To prepare for this tour, we must first understand what *language* and *grammar* mean, how a language can be living or dead, and the differences between languages and writing. Importantly, you must also face the language judgments you make on a daily basis: If you consider yourself part of the Grammar Police, be forewarned, many of your assumptions are overturned in this book.

language, languages, and the people who speak them

There are more people on earth than ever before, and every place we find humans, we find language. In large cities like Singapore, many languages are spoken, and most people speak more than one. As with most humans, Singaporeans are **multilingual**. In rural areas of some countries, like the state of West Virginia, almost everyone speaks only one language and is **monolingual**. Regardless of the number, we naturally develop language, and even in those communities where people only speak one language, there will be different pronunciations, different words, and different styles of language.

One of the difficult parts of learning about language is that language is so normal and natural for us: We take it for granted. Like eating or breathing, we language every day.[1] Most of us focus our attention on talking or listening, not on dissecting how we speak. But like the biology of eating and breathing, the machinery behind language is complex. For language, what we produce and consume is beautifully complex.

There are about 6,900 languages currently spoken on Earth. Those languages can be grouped by similarities into around 128 different families.[2] A wide range of language topics will be considered in this book, primarily with English as the example language. For good or for bad, and most likely for both, English has become a dominant world language. There are at least 350,000,000 speakers of English who learned it as babies. Depending on how you restrict the label *English*, there are probably 1,000,000,000 speakers of some kind of English. With that many speakers, a lot of variation is introduced into English every day, and that diversity provides us with opportunities to examine how language works.

The idea of **language variation** will come up a lot in this book. For example, people in the United States usually call a small, movable room that rises and falls between floors in a building an *elevator*. In England, the same object would be called a *lift*. We say that there is variation in the words because we note the differences in form. Having different sounds for the same object may not happen in any other species, but it is a basic feature of human language. Language variation tells us important information about human language. The chapters in this book often use variation in language to teach about its qualities.

In order to illustrate what is *fully* possible in language, this book would need to use examples from several hundred languages. Such a book would be a daunting task for any reader. With at least a billion speakers, English has a lot of variation. The goal in this book is to understand how language works through illustrations of what humans do with language, and there is enough variation in the Englishes around the world to provide many examples.

what is language?

Language is the discrete combinatorial system humans use most for communication. *Discrete* means 'separate' here, and *combinatorial* means 'ability to add together.' We take small separate parts, push them together in specific combinations, and create larger parts of language. For spoken languages, we store collections of sounds together with their associated ideas. We call them words, and they can be short (e.g. *I*) or long (e.g. *Mississippi*), but they are all sets of sounds connected to a meaning. With those words, we build larger phrases such as noun phrases (e.g. *most squids*), verb phrases (e.g. *crushed the daisies*), and prepositional phrases (e.g. *on the kangaroo*). The phrases themselves are discrete parts

in larger constructions such as sentences (a larger kind of phrase) and conversations. Phrases and sentences are discussed in Chapters 7 and 8.

It is important to understand that language is not a thing. It is important, but a difficult task for all of us. Despite the word *language* being a noun, it is not an object: Instead, it is a set of relationships. We produce and consume language naturally, and we do it quite well. Yet, language is a complex activity, and in that complexity is beauty.

Since language itself is not an object but is instead a natural human ability to communicate, it may seem odd to hear about **living languages** and **dead languages**. The label *living language* refers to any language which is used by a community of native speakers; the label *dead language* refers to any language which is not used by a community of native speakers. Living languages like English, Arabic, Spanish, and Mandarin Chinese have many native speakers. Dead languages like Natchez, Kitanemuk, and Wappo were all North American languages, but they no longer have native speakers. Ancient Latin has no native speakers and is also considered a dead language, even though its modern descendants now thrive as Spanish, Italian, French, and Portuguese. You can even get modern texts translated *into* Latin, such as Dr. Seuss's *Cat in the Hat* (*Cattus Petasatus*), but Latin is still a dead language. A small number of languages have actually been revived. Modern Hebrew is a revived language, brought back starting at the end of the nineteenth century from the dead language of Classical Hebrew (which was still used for religious ceremonies). The Celtic language Manx last had a native speaker in 1974, but revival efforts by local enthusiasts are underway to bring it back to living status.

what are language sounds?

Humans can make a lot of different noises. With our hands, feet, or mouths, we are a noisy species. When you consider all the other tools that make noise, such as guitars, hammers, and dump trucks,, our communities contain multitudes of

Word Play: Sounds and meaning

In languages like English, there are some sets of sounds that do come up in words with similar meanings. Consider the combination <gl> [ɡl]. What kinds of meanings get associated with <gl> words? How many counter examples can you come up with?

Try to make a language where each sound represents one meaning. Perhaps a <p> represents 'water' and an <o> represents 'horse,' so that <po> would be a decent form for 'seahorse.' Choose ten sounds and ten basic meanings. Can you come up with at least 25 words for your invented language? When does it start breaking down?

sounds. Yet, only some of those are used as small parts in the discrete combinatorial system called language. Sounds of clapping are used in different cultures, but clapping is not used as a language sound. Only some of the sounds that humans make are used as language sounds, and some of these language sounds are used in most languages. For example, the first sound of *pea* is used in many of the world's languages, along with the first sounds of *tea* and *key*. Other sounds are more rare, such as making a short, sharp sound with your mouth, normally called a *click*. Clicking is used meaningfully in numerous cultures, and clicks are used as consonant sounds in several African languages, including Khoisan and Bantu. Despite the enormous diversity of human language, we share a limited set of language sounds.

For these small language parts, we do not connect them directly to meaning. We could imagine a world where every sound had a primitive meaning and both the meaning and form of words were constructed from those meaningful sounds. Take the word *tea*, for example, which has the phonetic transcription of [ti]. The initial [t] sound of *tea* could mean 'wet,' and the vowel sound [i] could mean 'leaves': In this hypothetical construction, the word *tea* might then mean 'wet from leaves.' Good enough for that word, but one of the troubles would be that we would need a lot more sounds to represent all the meanings we have. Plus, think of all the words with [t] that do not have any relation to wetness. In human language, individual sounds are not themselves connected to meaning.

what are words?

The letter *a* can represent the sounds in *bake* and *nap*, but the letter *a* in <u>*a*</u> *pencil* represents both a sound and a word. Certainly, the *a* vowel in *bake* does not mean anything like the *a* vowel in the phrase *a pencil*. How do sounds differ from words?

Words to the Wise: Sounds and the fury

Phonetic symbols like [t] and [k] are different from letters like <t> and <k>. The differences are fully explored in Chapter 2, but for now, just consider the square brackets around [t] and [k] to mean *sound*. The [t] sound is what most English speakers have as the first letter in <top>. The angled brackets indicate regular spelling.

The <t> letter has a name, Tee, but we do not use the *name* Tee when pronouncing a word like <top> unless we are *spelling* the word out loud: Tee- Ow- Pee.

A **word** is a language package containing both form and meaning. For a spoken language like English, the forms of words are sounds; for signed languages like American Sign Language (ASL), the forms are signs.

In either case, the form by itself does not make a word: The form *skrackleblit* is not associated with any meaning at the time of this writing, and it is not therefore a word. It is the combination of the form and the meaning which makes a word. How can a single sound be a word, like the *a* vowel? In the history of English, speakers pared down the word *one* until it was simply a vowel with the function of an indefinite determiner (e.g. *an* eye; *a* book). It is a word because that sound is paired in a relationship with a specific meaning. In Chapters 4, 5, and 6, we discuss the nature of those relationships.

what are phrases?

Phrases are combinations of words in structured patterns. As young children, we figure out from the language around us what patterns are used to make certain phrases. For English, we learn that determiners like *the* and *a* come before the noun (e.g. *the squid*) as do most adjectives (e.g. *the calm squid*), but prepositional phrases come after the noun (e.g. *the squid in the tank* rather than *the in the tank squid*). These phrases work like templates which we populate with words. For every type of phrase, there is a different template. Some phrases are sentences, but most are not. This sentence

The belligerent fan in the stands hit the ref with the water bottle

has eight phrases inside of it and is also ambiguous. How phrases work is taken up in Chapters 7 and 8.

what is discourse?

As you may have noticed, we have been building up here from small to big. We started with small parts (sounds), moved to larger yet discrete combinations (words), and then put those together to form phrases. Is there any kind of organization beyond phrases? Yes, there are patterns such as conversations, monologues, arguments, and any type of talking which uses multiple phrases in a context, all of which can be labeled **discourse**. The times you have most likely noticed the structure of discourse is in turn-taking, where people in a conversation tradeoff who has the floor so that everyone is not talking at once. Turn-taking is most obvious in its absence, when someone in the conversation is messing it up, either by not taking their turn (remaining completely silent) or by not giving up their turn (continuing to talk over other peoples' turns). The structures of discourse are discussed in Chapter 9.

language differences

The variety of language seems baffling to most of us. With nearly 7,000 languages, there are hugely diverse vocabularies. Think of it: There are thousands of words for what we call a tree. Some of them sound similar to each other, such

Figure 1.1 Arbitrariness also works for sign languages. In this *Girls with Slingshots* comic, the signs are conventionally connected to their meanings, just like the forms of spoken words. Rollover text: (ASL does not always mean what it looks like it means!): http://www.girlswithslingshots.com/ comic/gws-1058/. © Danielle Corsetto/www.girlswithslingshots.com

as *el árbol*, *l'arbre*, and *l'albero* for 'tree' in Spanish, French, and Italian. Others are thoroughly different, such as *osisi*, *puu*, and *ki* in Igbo, Finnish, and Japanese. The words do not always identify the same parts. In some languages, such as Igbo spoken in Nigeria, one word, *aka*, covers the body parts referred to in English as *hand* and *arm*. With all these differences goes the sheer number of words. While no one has a clear estimate of the upper bounds of Earth's vocabulary, it is safe to assume that for the 6,900 languages around today, each one might average 10,000 words, so the lowest limit we can figure is 69,000,000. The connection between the form of a word like *tree* and its meaning in the mind is a cultural convention. Yet the natural relationship between form and meaning is considered arbitrary, and this quality is called arbitrariness. The quality of **arbitrariness** allows for all the possible sound combinations to be possibly paired with all the possible meanings, yielding a mind-boggling amount of variation. It allows for humans to create so many different words through cultural choices.

language similarities

With all the differences between languages, it might surprise you to learn that languages actually have many similarities. One language quality humans share appears to be nouns and verbs. We are not born with words in our heads, but we are most likely born with empty baskets for word types like nouns and verbs. As children, we learn words quickly and continuously, at least 10 a day in our younger years. While we pick up these new words, we sort them for faster retrieval into baskets for nouns, verbs, and other word types.

Another quality which all languages share is structure in how words and phrases are built. Even when the specific structures differ, they do so in highly constrained ways. With word order, two patterns account for 87% of the world's

languages. As Mark C. Baker describes in *The Atoms of Language,* the organization of phrases is not random. Languages do not have exactly the same patterns, but they do come in definite sets. Languages like English, Edo (spoken in Nigeria), and Indonesian each have a word order of subject-verb-object.

For example: The child   kicked   the ball
                 subject   verb   object

The majority of languages have subject-object-verb as the word order, including Japanese, Turkish, and Quechua (a native South American language).

For example: The child   the ball   kicked
                 subject   object   verb

For any two languages, differences exist between them. The vocabularies do not match, and their inventories of sounds are not exactly the same. But, those qualities spread from contact with other languages, and historically none of these languages have enjoyed extensive contact with each other. Patterns of how speakers build sentences are not spread through contact, but instead the genetic blueprints provide either/or choices for word order.

Such choices of how to organize phrases appear to be biologically constrained. Languages like English, Edo, and Indonesian have followed the path where verbs come *before* objects (e.g. *eat the food*), position markers (called *pre*-positions) come *before* nouns (e.g. *in the house*), and auxiliaries come *before* main verbs (e.g. *I will run*). In languages like Japanese, Turkish, and Quechua, the opposite is true: verbs come *after* objects, position markers come *after* nouns (called *post*-positions), and auxiliaries come *after* main verbs.

As humans, our biological blueprints allow us to acquire language by building a **mental grammar**. The mental grammar is the part of the mind that *does* language. It languages. For each language we acquire as a child, we develop a mental grammar to understand and produce that language. To be clear, we are not born *with* language, but we are born with the ability to acquire any language (by building a mental grammar for that language). Not too mysteriously, we end up acquiring the ones we encounter and practice. However, the biological blueprints to build a mental grammar are the same for all of us.

variation through time

Living languages change. No exceptions have ever been found. English, in its roughly 1,500 year history, has changed dramatically. In the beginning, the first varieties of English were a collection of West Germanic dialects spoken by invaders to Britain. Those varieties, be they spoken or written, are completely unintelligible to untrained audiences today. Yet, as a living language, English is now spoken by vast numbers of people. The language has been altered over that 1,500 year history. Throughout this book, we explore how the language has changed, from changes in sounds to changes in how sentences are built.

variation today

For those languages not on the verge of extinction, language variation is part of daily life. Englishes vary across region, ethnicity, social class, gender, sexual orientation, and many other human boundaries. Since language is an important part of how we identify ourselves, people systematically mark themselves as different with various levels of language, from sounds to sentences. British speakers pronounce *schedule* with the same initial sound as in *shed*; US speakers use the initial sounds as in *skip*. Whether these differences are "consciously" chosen or not, they are part of the language variation patterns found in all living languages.

understanding the world of language

Learning would be simpler if the world were simpler. If there were only a few types of objects in the world, it would be easier to understand how it all works. Instead of the periodic table containing over 100 chemical elements, it could have four: Earth, Water, Air, and Fire. That would certainly be simpler to remember, but working with only those four elements would not allow us to understand any of our modern technology or even life itself.

Speaking of life, instead of our massively complex modern understanding of the human body, we could return to the older understanding of health that was common through much of the history of Western society. The basic idea was that the human body was controlled by four humors: black bile, yellow bile, blood, and phlegm. Those four humors were seen as the key controlling elements in human health from the time of Hippocrates (400 BCE) until the 1800s, when modern medical practice was developed. There was no variation in the humors or room for growth that would allow there to be a fifth humor. Every kind of sickness had to be explained with those humors. During that 2,200 year period, patients underwent all kinds of horrible practices doled out by well-meaning healers. One of these was blood-letting, where a person was drained of some of their blood to balance out their humors. From this simple yet wildly wrong understanding of the human body, untold thousands of people were further injured and killed.

The scientific community eventually improved their understanding of life throughout the 1800s, and medical practice became both safer and more effective. Outside the scientific community, a lot of false information still persists about how the body works, but health education has improved greatly since the 1950s.

A close analogy can be made between our understanding of the human body and our understanding of human language. Since the 1850s, the scientific community has improved their understanding of language, but they have only had partial success in replacing the myths most people hold about language. Some positive steps have been taken in Europe and the United States: It used to be believed that some languages (e.g. Latin) were inherently superior to others (e.g. English). That belief has faded from many people's minds. In contrast, most people still believe that some varieties of any given language are structurally superior to other varieties: that English in the Midwest of the United States is superior to English from the US South, or that British RP[3] simply works better than a Liverpool variety. That belief is also a myth, but the language science community has turned few people away from that one.

the complex nature of language

One of the most important and most daunting qualities of language is its complexity. It would be simple if everything in language were uniform: if there were only one language in the world with one set of vocabulary, one pronunciation for each word, only one meaning for each word, and one way to arrange every sentence. It would be even simpler if this one language were perfectly stable over time, with pronunciations and meanings never changing. It would be a simpler world, but the idea is fantasy. If this imaginary scenario were true, we would be a different species and our societies would be completely different. {Future Mad Scientists reading this book may take this imaginary, simpler language as a personal challenge, but what would it be like if we *were* genetically engineered to have a different communication system?} The reality is that our brains create and interpret language variation and complexity as essential qualities. To get rid of language variation, we would need to genetically reengineer our brains so they produced or received a limited set of signals.

How extensive is human language variation? We have approximately 6,900 languages, many of which have numerous dialects, and all of which have wide-ranging sets of vocabulary. A safe guess is that we have at least 10,000 varieties of human language, but that is probably a ridiculously low estimate. All these varieties are changing, either in the pronunciation, in their meanings, or in the ways they put together words and phrases; for example, the Russian language in 2050 will be different from Russian in 2000. At any one time, there is variation between dialects of a language, and across time, there is variation between different stages of the same dialect.

Within any one language, some parts vary more than others. In English, more variation exists between pronunciations than in how sentences are built. To parallel that pattern in this book, there is more discussion about variation within English in the chapters on sounds and more discussion about variation between languages in the chapters on building phrases.

judging language

One thing all people do with language is use it to judge other people. Judging people by the language they use is so automatic that it must be part of our basic genetic code, perhaps as a safety mechanism to distinguish in-group from out-group.

There are two basic ways people judge language, either prescriptively or rhetorically. The **Prescriptively Correct Perspective** assumes that one certain form of the language always works better at all times. It also assumes that this unitary correct form must be protected from variation, which is seen as corruption and decay. The **Rhetorically Correct Perspective** judges language as good or bad based on how well that language works for that speaker in that context: Does the speaker's language accomplish the speaker's goals for that situation? In other words, this form of judgment is based on a classic sense of rhetoric as *the art of persuasion.*

Both the prescriptive viewpoint and the rhetorical viewpoint allow all of us to judge any kind of language. Take the two verbs *shall* and *will*. Prescriptively, *shall* should appear with subjects like *I* and *we* (e.g. *I shall leave*), and *will* should appear with subjects like *you*, *she*, *they*, and regular nouns like *wombats* (e.g. *The wombats will dig up the garden*). In regular, modern English usage, the two verbs are often switched, and when contracted, they are indistinguishable (e.g. *You'll be going soon*). Prescriptively, that common modern usage is wrong, no matter when it is used. Rhetorically, it depends. If you are giving a formal speech, it might serve you well to impress your audience with your knowledge of the *shall/will* distinction, as you may persuade your audience you are well educated. If you are at a party, dropping *shall* in a sentence like *I shall drink that* will probably get you stares and give people the impression that you are snooty. The modern usage of *who* and *whom* is much the same story, in that *who* is the common form, but prescriptively the *who~whom* distinction is still made.

For this book, the important difference is that the rhetorical approach works well with linguistic analysis, but the prescriptive approach flounders by denying so much of what language scientists have learned over the last century. The only way to understand how language works is to set the prescriptive approach aside. If you are unable to take up the rhetorical approach to language judgment, you will find it difficult to learn how language works.

Another fundamental difference between the Rhetorically and Prescriptively Correct Perspectives is that the latter does not allow for language variation and change. As you will read throughout this book, language variation and change is part of human language. It is fundamental to who we are. The Rhetorically Correct Perspective can handle that fact, but the Prescriptively Correct Perspective cannot. This conflict will be illustrated throughout the book.

When studying language, the first step is to describe. What is going on with the language, and how does it all work? For this reason, linguists have a firm belief in the descriptive approach to language study in which all judgment is suspended. In looking at an utterance like "I ain't going," the descriptive approach allows the linguist to describe the negative present-tense conjugation of *be*. The prescriptive approach simply says, "*ain't* is wrong," since it is out of fashion in modern times. The rhetorical approach would judge the phrase depending on the context: It would be wrong in more formal context but works well in many casual contexts.

All of the language knowledge presented in this book was gathered by many linguists using the descriptive approach. If you want to judge other peoples' language, the rhetorical approach is the only one which allows you to understand how language works and make your judgment.

standard Englishes and vernacular Englishes

Dictionaries are fascinating books, but they are not divinely generated. Whether they are general dictionaries of a language or specialty dictionaries for medicine or law, dictionaries are surveys of usage. It is important to realize that as usage changes, so do dictionaries. Dictionaries survey how people use words, checking the context of the word to see what meanings are intended.

The printing press came to England in 1476, and after that point the perception of English began to change. In previous centuries it had been a "local" language, used in everyday life but kept out of legal and educational contexts where French or Latin were used. With England's increasing power during the centuries after the printing press, writers and leaders wanted to make English a more respected language. The result was a self-help industry where people followed advice to improve their supposedly sick language. Dictionaries had begun to appear for English after 1600, and people began to view English as a tool for business and literature. The first modern dictionary was published in 1755: Samuel Johnson's *A Dictionary of the English Language*. In that dictionary, Johnson used quotes to illustrate his meanings and provided pronunciation and usage guides.

Most dictionaries survey the usage of words in **writing**, but some specialize in spoken English. Online, contributor-based, dictionaries, such as Urbandictionary.com and Wiktionary.org, work off the same idea. The difference with them is that no editor comes along and condenses all the opinions. Not all dictionaries are equally well built, but all dictionaries provide a snapshot of the language and society. With the hordes of speakers we have in our modern time, we also have thousands of dictionaries which survey their usage.

From the previous discussion of Rhetorically vs. Prescriptively Correct Perspectives, what do we do with the idea of standard English? Most who have considered the idea of standard English have assumed the idea of an either/or choice: There is or there is not a standard English. For language scholars, the only accurate description is quite different from the one-or-none choice: There are numerous standard Englishes. Most people new to the study of language are baffled by the idea that there is not just *one* standard English, but *many*. The easiest illustrations are the numerous varieties of national Englishes: American English, Australian English, British English, Irish English, New Zealand English, and Singaporean English, to name a few. Those standards can all be found at the present time. As we look back over time, we realize that different time periods had different standards, so that the standard for any one region has changed over time. Standard English in 1800 in Massachusetts is different from standard English in 2000 in Massachusetts.

There is a **standard∼vernacular continuum** for language variation. The term *standard* exists in contrast to the term *vernacular*. They are opposite ends of the scale of language judgment. A standard variety receives no social stigma; a vernacular variety receives social stigma. The term *vernacular* is also used to mean several different things in regards to language, but we only work with one specific meaning in this book: By virtue of being at different ends of the same continuum, **vernacular** means *not standard*. In some ways, that might seem too obvious, but it is accurate for our needs. A vernacular dialect feature, like *ain't* in most places, or a vernacular variety, like Southern US English, is *vernacular* because it is not considered to be standard.

For a language example in the standard∼vernacular continuum, consider the language variation of R-dropping. This pattern can happen when a word has a potential R near the end of it, e.g. *part*, but the R sound is turned into a vowel instead of a consonant, something like <paht>. Many Australian, English, and New Zealand speakers have R-dropping as a regular part of their speech. R-dropping is also in a few regions of the United States, including the Boston area of Massachusetts and areas of the US South. What is different for all these regions is the cultural evaluation of R-dropping. In the British varieties, R-dropping is the prestigious form and can be considered standard. In the US South, it is vernacular because it is seen as nonstandard.[4] The mechanics of R-dropping is exactly the same in every region, but the social evaluation differs because it is associated with different social groups in the different regions.

For North American English, the most reliable scale is the standard∼vernacular continuum. Other languages' speakers use one prestige variety as the ideal form and then judge all deviations from that prestige form. For US English speakers, the definition of standard English is simple, if not a bit unsatisfying. Standard English is defined by what it is not: It is not vernacular. What is vernacular? Anything that is stigmatized. In the US South, *y'all* is the normal pronoun for second person plural: *Y'all should go to the museum.* Outside the US South, *y'all* is stigmatized as vernacular; it is seen as bad. The linguistics of *y'all* is not relevant for judging *y'all* along the standard∼vernacular continuum, since that is simply a range of social judgment. Whether any bit of language is vernacular or not is a social judgment. It depends on what the audience thinks of it.

Word Play: Along the continuum

Rate along a standard~vernacular continuum dialect features you know well. The dialect features could include sounds or whole phrases, such as bir[f]day, *yous guys* vs. *y'all*, *between you and I, the car needs washed.*

Standard--Vernacular

Have the class vote where each feature falls in this continuum. Which dialect features have the largest range of votes (i.e. the largest estimated standard deviation)?

grammars

Perhaps the most common word used when the topic of *language* comes up in school is *grammar*. Like a jilted lover, the term *grammar* has quite a history and carries a lot of baggage. It started as an ancient Greek term for the *art of writing*, and the term maintained that meaning for centuries. Many beginning schools have been called *grammar schools* because of a medieval tradition of teaching the *trivium*, a collection of three basic topics: grammar (the art of writing), rhetoric (the art of persuasion), and dialectic (the art of logical debate). Within that art of writing, the study of language and comparison of languages became more common. In the Middle Ages, the study of grammar mostly meant the study of languages like Greek and Latin, the dominant languages of medieval Europe. During these earlier times, the study of grammar was often connected to magic, and several related words were split from the term, including the French *grimoire* and English *glamour* (think of modern vampires who *glamour* their victims). In the twentieth century, the study of grammar was carried on by those who taught Latin, and it eventually landed in English departments where linguists now usually perform that duty. Its connection to the art of writing was lost at this point in the United States, since a separate field of composition studies exists today, although in Europe there continues a connection to the much broader study of philology.[5] For modern linguists, the study of grammar became a study of how languages work, mostly focused on how words and phrases were built by native speakers.

From this long history, the word *grammar* has hooked up with lots of different words and suffixes. The *Oxford English Dictionary* lists 13 different entries for *grammar* related terms, and in the main entry for the word, there are 24 sub-entries for words like *grammar-rule*, *grammar-lad*, and *grammar-monger*. Although we do not need to work through all the *grammar* terms, we do need to distinguish between different types of grammar. Here, we will focus on five kinds of grammars: teaching grammars, prescriptive grammars, descriptive grammars, mental grammars, and Universal Grammar.

teaching grammars

Learning a second or third language as an adult is much more challenging than learning it as a child. Children have a natural ability to acquire a language, but this ability gets lost around puberty. To compensate for that lost skill, many people take formal classes and buy books explaining the language they are trying to learn. Those books are **teaching grammars**. They are big business, especially for a language like English, which is the focus of a billion-dollar-a-year industry. Teaching grammars explain language regulations like "adjectives come before their nouns" and "objects come after their verbs," as well as supplying a limited vocabulary and exercises to practice. Teaching grammars include many regulations that no native speaker had to formally learn in a classroom; native speakers knew those rules before they started school. Yet, teaching grammars assume you have knowledge of at least one language. If you were to use only the information in a teaching grammar to help children learn their first language, it would not be enough.

prescriptive grammars

Medical professionals write prescriptions for medicine. Such medicine is intended to make sick patients better. Those who give **prescriptive grammar** advice also intend for people's language to get better by virtue of taking their advice. However, the people prescribing medicine are licensed professionals, whereas the people giving prescriptive grammar advice are not. There is no institutional authority for prescriptive grammar.

The foundational assumption with prescriptive grammar is that language can be sick. Variation is often seen as a symptom of this sickness. For example, advice such as "don't end your sentence with a preposition" attempts to enforce a pattern from Latin on to English. Yet, prepositions in English have always been free words and have appeared in different positions throughout its history (e.g. Middle English, Layamon's *Brut* (§88), *Þenne he Þe treoweðe alre best on* 'Then he you trusts all best on'). Despite the disapproval of variation, prescriptive grammar advice itself does vary over time. Prescriptive grammar advice follows social fashion, and will change over time. Jonathan Swift (1667–1745) disliked the word *mob*, meaning a group of people, because it was a clipping of *mobile*. Today, this meaning of *mob* is a well-accepted part of English.

One of the basic facts of modern language study is that writing is a human invention. Language is not a human invention. Writing is a method of representing language, and we can experience language through the technology of writing the same way we can experience language through the technology of audio recordings. Writing systems have been invented in different cultures using various techniques, such as systems of hieroglyphs, cuneiform, logographs, syllabaries, and alphabets. Writing systems have been invented as a helpful technology, and they are an essential part of modern society. In many

Word Play: Judging the verbs

Read through the following sentences and figure out your judgment of where they would fall along the standard~vernacular continuum.

- *If this be to your liking, please sign below.*
- *I would buy that bike if I were rich.*
- *I will do it so I can go.*
- *It is important that our rights be upheld.*
- *What if she was the last one on Earth?*
- *He be laughing all the time.*

countries, literacy is a necessity for success. As a widely used technology, learning to read and write follows from prescriptive advice. Capital letters at the start of sentences and periods at ends are part of the prescriptive repertoire for the English alphabetic system. Paragraphs, introductions, conclusions, and all other regulations of writing are part of prescriptive grammar advice. Prescriptive grammars are not inherently evil, but they are restrictive, and all too often people give prescriptive grammar advice with an air of self-righteousness.

If we were to train an infant with only the knowledge in a prescriptive grammar book, that infant would be in bad shape. Most of these works assume you are already a native speaker of the language and have full literacy skills. As an example of prescriptive grammar advice, *me* is used as an object form and *I* is used as a subject form. Native speakers, however, have started to reshuffle the deck with *I* and *me* in phrases such as *The athletic director fired Rich and I.* Were the combined phrase *Rich and I* a subject, it would prescriptively be correct: *Rich and I could not beat Ohio State.* People have begun to assume that *and I* is prescriptively correct in every situation, even when the *and I* is working as an object. So some people will see *Divide the candy between her and me* as wrong, despite it being prescriptively correct.

With the importance placed upon literacy in our modern world, too many people are tempted to fan the flames of self-righteousness when discussing genre conventions. Plus, prescriptive grammar advice is used to chide students. Chapter 10 explains how a different approach can accomplish all the beneficial educational goals of prescriptive grammar while fostering an understanding of human language. It would be most efficient if this modern approach were delivered with accurate information about how language works. In this book, I hope to provide a detailed portrait of language to allow for better teaching of genre-specific rules for writing.

descriptive grammars

A **descriptive grammar** is a book about a language. Such books are not written for students learning the language (teaching grammars), nor are they written for natives who want to follow the writing fashions of the language (prescriptive grammars). Descriptive grammars are written for linguists who want to learn how a certain language works. Does the language allow multiple suffixes or any suffixes? Can a syllable start with only one consonant or two, or even three? How many types of vowels are there in the language? These kinds of questions are answered in a descriptive grammar. They are highly technical books. With those technical details, an attempt is made to document the inner workings of a language. For most descriptive grammars, the vocabulary of the language would need to be delimited and described in a separate dictionary. With a descriptive grammar and a dictionary for a language, we could program a computer to generate grammatical sentences in that language. Descriptive grammars are more complete than teaching grammars or prescriptive grammars.

Descriptive grammars describe the workings of a language, but they do not judge speakers' usage of that language. A descriptive grammar of English should note that a common negative present-tense form of *be* is *ain't*, and that *ain't* also functions as a replacement for *have* or *do* in some varieties of English. This descriptive grammar should also note that *ain't* is stigmatized by many speakers, but describing social judgments is different from exercising them.

The difference between descriptive and prescriptive grammars has caused a lot of confusion and a fair bit of anger. For many people, a "grammar" is supposed to tell you how to use your language, such as when to use "which" or "that" in front of a clause (e.g. *I lost the book [which/that] I bought*). Descriptive grammars do not give advice: They detail the ways in which native speakers use their language. A descriptive grammar is a survey of a language. For any living language, a descriptive grammar from one century will differ from a descriptive grammar of the next century because the language will have changed. This textbook follows the path of descriptive grammars. As **linguistics** is the scientific study of language, this book presents information from linguistic studies.

mental grammars

The first three grammars can come in books and have a tangible form. These next two kinds of grammar, mental grammar and Universal Grammar, are more abstract. The **mental grammar** is the place in the mind where language happens. When you are speaking or writing, your mental grammar is producing language. When you are listening or reading, your mental grammar is dissecting language and making the meaning real for you.

When we talk about the mind, we make a subtle but worthwhile distinction between the brain and the mind. The brain is the squishy part which sloshes

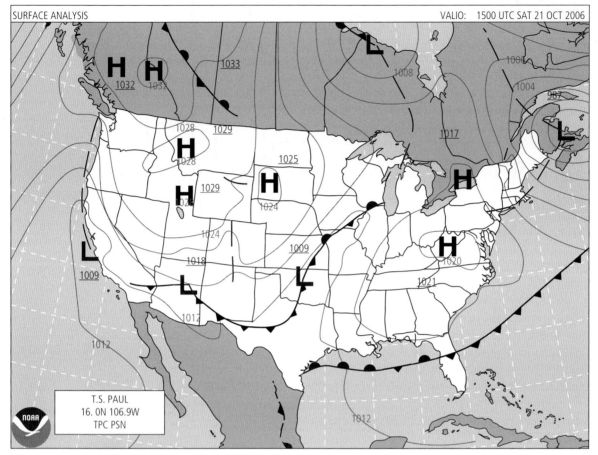

SURFACE ANALYSIS

Figure 1.2 A standard weather map representing billions of small happenings. From the National Oceanic and Atmospheric Administration. www.noaa.gov

around in your skull. It is an object, and you can touch it, but you probably should not try to. The mind is an abstraction, not an object; no one has ever touched a mind. Yet, this concept of the mind has been really useful for the study of humans because it is a model of what happens in the brain. One good analogy to explain the distinction between minds and brains is the comparison of weather maps and weather itself.

On a weather map like the one above, from the US National Oceanic and Atmospheric Administration, there are symbols for different weather forma- tions, such as high and low pressure systems. These maps are a common part of modern life, and we interpret them as *models* for the weather. Yet, from looking at this map, no one will walk outside and expect to see a giant H in the sky. New Brunswick, Canada should be safe from the giant L floating overhead because they know there is no giant L. The map is not the weather, only a model of the weather. But, there are billions of molecules interacting with each other over large patches of space, and trying to explain all of those interactions just to tell someone whether it is going to rain or not would be silly. Accordingly, all of those interactions are abstracted into a model we can more easily understand. Like weather maps, the mind is a simplified abstraction for the billions of molecular interactions in the brain.

In the model called the mind, the mental grammar is the language module. It is that unit which *does* the language. It languages, both producing and receiving. In this book, we will discuss what role the mental grammar plays at every level of language. As with models in many scientific fields, linguists do not agree on what the best model should be. Establishing that is one of the goals of modern linguistics. The model presented in this book is one of several which vary in how the parts are configured. For example, a lot of ink has been spilled in linguistics over whether or not to include our mental dictionary, the **lexicon**, as part of the mental grammar or not.

Universal Grammar

Universal Grammar is even more of an abstraction than the mental grammar. Our discussion of the mental grammar of English generalizes from as many as a billion people, characterizing what qualities of English are in their heads. Universal Grammar generalizes to the entire species, but it is not the grammar in an adult's head, it is the template for grammar we are born with. The **Universal Grammar** is the biological endowment for building a mental grammar. It in itself is not a mental grammar of any particular language, but it is the set of genetic instructions we use as infants to acquire languages.

The Universal Grammar is something of a holy grail in linguistics. Although some argue against its possible existence, a lot of linguistic effort has gone towards describing it. It most likely contains instructions for building a lexicon with arbitrariness as a basic tenet, along with a module to put together words and phrases. The lexicon instructions might also direct the construction of slots for nouns and verbs. In Chapter 8, we discuss some other qualities the Universal Grammar might contain.

---

meaning

Meaning is the goal for language and for all forms of communication. To communicate is to *mean* something. For humans, many different ways to convey meaning are used every day. If two people approach a doorway at the same time, and one pauses, the other person might take that pause to mean "permission to go first." Language is a subset of human communication, but it is a special subset. As far as linguists know, the ability to acquire and use language is a genetically-endowed, species-specific trait. Only humans do it. In the evolution of this ability, meaning must have been one of the first components, since we find meaning to be part of all animal communication systems.

Words to the Wise: Unambiguating language

There has been a long-standing desire to eliminate ambiguity from human language. Some mathematicians and philosophers have tried over the years to create a more logical system of communication. The polymath Gottfried Leibniz (1646–1716) wanted to create a communication system which would disallow the normal confusions of human language so that philosophers could argue about law and ethics as precisely as mathematicians argue about space and time. Modern computer languages are also designed to prohibit ambiguity. At the level of hardware, computers need clear, step-by-step instructions to allow operations to flow smoothly. Ambiguity would make a computer stop, but humans work around such problems every day.

Meaning in language is not always clear. There are many ways in which a speaker's intended meaning does not become the same as the received meaning. Several important traits of language allow for these twists in meaning.

First, it is important to recognize that meaning is not *transferred* between speaker and hearer. Language is not a pipe that carries meaning from one person to another. Language is a discrete combinatorial system. Small parts are put together into packages and sent off (by speaking or signing) to an audience. Those packages are broken apart on the receiving end, triggering meanings in the audiences' minds. The sounds of <bat> combine to form the word, which itself fits inside of sentences (parts within larger parts). How the receiver interprets <bat> depends on other factors, such as the context of the word: *the wooden bat* vs. *the flying bat*.

Meaning can be confounded because of **ambiguity**. Ambiguity can happen when multiple meanings are attached to some bit of language. When two or more meanings are associated with the form of a word, the word is potentially ambiguous. For example, the form *set* could be connected to 'a group of things' or to 'place something somewhere'; the form *bat* could be connected to 'a flying mammal' or to 'a stick used to hit.' When sentences are ambiguous in their phrases, the collection of words can be seen to make up different meanings. For example, in *the child kissed the toddler with the puppet*, two meanings arise: either the child used the puppet to kiss the toddler or the child kissed the toddler who was holding the puppet. Some sentences can contain both word and phrase ambiguity. How many meanings can you pull out of this sentence: *Umberto turned on the TV* (Consider how "on the TV" could be a prepositional phrase or how "turn on" can be a verb). These kinds of ambiguity are a natural part of every language. They are also absent from other animals' communication systems.

Perhaps the most important quality related to meaning itself is arbitrariness. To explain this quality, let us begin with the idea that a word is a pairing of form and meaning. For sounded languages the form is one or more sounds; for signed languages, the form is a gesture. The meaning is whatever is *conventionally* associated with that form.

There is no meaning assigned by nature to any certain form, because the relationship between form and meaning is arbitrary. That quality of arbitrariness distinguishes us from many other species.

If speakers use the form *pop* in the Northern United States, but Southerners use *coke*, they may have the same meaning, but arbitrariness allows for different forms to be connected to that meaning. Arbitrariness refers to any form's lack of inherent meaning. There is nothing in the meaning of 'artificial, packaged, sweetened beverage' which is naturally affiliated with either the forms *pop* or *coke* or *soda*. On the flip side, there is nothing in the form *pop* which requires it be associated with that meaning. *Pop* also means 'to hit someone' or 'the sound of hitting someone' in many English varieties.

If language were not arbitrary, then forms would be naturally connected to certain meanings. The form <bow> [bo] would mean one and only one thing in all the world's languages. Perhaps that meaning would be 'a certain kind of knot' (English, <bow>) or 'beautiful' (French, <beau>) or 'stay' (Norwegian, <bo>), all with similar pronunciations, but perhaps not. As a quality of language, arbitrariness has received its share of complaints over the years, but it is one of the basic qualities that make us human.

standard Englishes and different world views

Treating "standard English" as a single entity with coherent and solid boundaries is an empirical mistake. What might be standard English gets defined both today and over time by shifting social standards. There are standard Englishes throughout North America and the world, but there is no single set of features that is "standard English." There never was just one, and there are numerous standard Englishes now.

Yet for many people, the common belief about language is that some supremely correct form exists for all contexts and times. In previous centuries, this belief extended to the superiority of some languages, such as Latin, to all other languages. We are currently in the transition from such older concepts to improved, modern ones. Two signs of this transformation are the following trends: (1) People more readily accept that no one language is inherently supreme, and (2) people more readily accept that language change is not decay. Both of those ideas used to be the norm. Were other tenants of modern linguistics, such as the legitimacy of language variation, to be taken up by educational professionals, then the educational goals of literacy and writing would be accomplished more thoroughly and efficiently.

Many teachers, speech pathologists, and other educational professionals have transitioned from a foundational assumption of language having only correct and incorrect forms to an assumption of language having multiple, linguistically legitimate forms. It is important for all of us to understand that the linguistic evaluation of language can be separate from the social evaluation of language.

structure

Words are some of the most noticeable parts of language. They are the bricks and mortar used to build language. But, buildings are more than just a pile of raw materials. Buildings are structures. They have certain qualities which link their parts together and allow them to be useful. Language also has structure, at many different levels. A significant portion of this book is dedicated to explaining that structure.

Sounds make up words and are arranged in specific orders. In phonetic script, the word *blue* has three sounds [blu], and the first two are sounds which cannot be reversed in English. The combination [lbu] is not something English speakers do, and this ordering of sounds is part of the structure of English.

As parts, words are combined together to make up phrases, some of which are short, and some of which are long. Some phrases are sentences, but most are not. A noun phrase like *the whale* is short, but it can be combined with other units to form larger phrases. Perhaps the most literary whale is *the sperm whale*, which is a noun phrase that has an adjective phrase inside of it. But, that phrase can be used as a single unit in yet a larger phrase. Herman Melville writes of "the sperm whale's vast tail" in *Moby Dick*, positioning that noun phrase in yet a longer phrase: "let me assure ye that many a veteran who has freely marched up to a battery, would quickly recoil at the apparition of the sperm whale's vast tail, fanning into eddies the air over his head" (Chapter XXIV, 107).

Layers of structure such as these are explained throughout the book, starting with the smallest parts and building to larger and larger combinations.

a tour of language

Human language is a natural phenomenon and demonstrates the diversity of human culture while illustrating our shared humanity as members of the same species. Some scientists study language to better understand how it works in the human mind. The scientific study of language is called linguistics, and this book provides a modern linguistic description of human language.

Consider this book to be your tour guide to the "language factory" inside your head. You do amazing things with language every day. I hope you enjoy your tour and learn to appreciate how special language is.

chapter summary

This chapter explains that human language is diverse in its vocabulary but similar in its sounds and sentence patterns. To analyze language, we must first understand that it is a natural biological development of being human, like vision, and that writing is a technological innovation, like photography. A language like English has basic parts we combine into patterns. The parts include sounds, words, and phrases. Words are built by connecting sound forms to meanings; those connections are culturally determined because no natural relationship exists between sound and meaning. With all these parts, we often judge other people's language, either from a Rhetorically or Prescriptively Correct Perspective. The Rhetorically Correct Perspective is based on the appropriateness of an utterance for a certain speaker in a certain context, and it makes the most sense given how language works. The Prescriptively Correct Perspective is based on the mythical assumption of one correct form. Teaching grammars and descriptive grammars are different kinds of books; the first helps students learn another language, and the second describes how a certain language works. The mental grammar is not a book at all; it is the factory in your mind where the parts get assembled to make language. To build that factory requires special instructions, and the Universal Grammar is the genetically coded blueprint babies use to build mental grammars. In this book, there are many terms that might seem familiar to students, but though terms such as *word* and *vowel* will be familiar from everyday speech, they are technical terms in this book and have distinct definitions. A term like accent can mean different things to different people. What does it mean in this *Natalie Dee* comic: http://www.nataliedee.com/021210/?

key concepts

- Ambiguity
- Arbitrariness
- Dead languages
- Descriptive grammar
- Discourse
- Language
- Language variation
- Lexicon
- Linguistics
- Living languages
- Mental grammar
- Monolingual
- Multilingual
- Phrases
- Prescriptively Correct Perspective
- Prescriptive grammar
- Rhetorically Correct Perspective
- Standard-vernacular continuum
- Teaching grammars
- Universal Grammar
- Word
- Writing

notes

1. For some teachers of linguistics, using *language* as a verb is as normal as using *table*, *pen*, *mind*, *box*, or *cup* as verbs. John E. Joseph (2002) has written about the usage, rationale, and history of *language* as a verb, which dates back to at least 1628.

2. Lewis, M. Paul (ed.). 2009. *Ethnologue: Languages of the World*, Sixteenth edition. Dallas, TX: SIL International. Online version: www.ethnologue.com/

3. British RP is a prestige variety in England. The RP stands for *received pronunciation*, supposedly received from the monarchy itself.

4. R-dropping used to be prestigious in the US South, but since World War II, it has become increasingly seen as vernacular as it has become more of a rural and non-upper-class language variation pattern.

5. Philology is the study and comparison of classical texts, usually ancient Greek and Latin. Modern language study now takes place in most European philology departments. Friedrich Nietzsche was perhaps the most famous classical philologist, although his fame was more for his philosophical writings than his philology.

references

Dee, N. www.nataliedee.com/021210

Joseph, J.E. (2002) "Is language a verb? Conceptual change in linguistics and language teaching." H. Trappes-Lomax and G. Ferguson, eds. *Language in Language Teacher Education*: 29–48.

Lewis, M.P. (ed.) (2009) *Ethnologue: Languages of the world*. 16th edition. Dallas, TX: SIL International. Online version: www.ethnologue.com/

Melville, H. (2011) *Moby Dick*, Harper Perennial Classics (Chapter XXIV, 107).

further reading

The Language Instinct. Steven Pinker. 2007. Penguin.

For linguists, this book is now a classic and shining example of introducing language to public audiences. For most readers, this book is a quick read packed with humorous stories and memorable examples. *The Language Instinct* covers the sound system, the construction of words and phrases, and the workings of language in the mind. Although originally published in 1994, it is still relevant, accurate, and highly readable today.

Doctor Dolittle's Delusion: Animals and the Uniqueness of Human Language. Stephen R. Anderson. 2004. Yale University Press.

Anderson takes on Hugh Lofting's fictional character of Doctor Dolittle, the British doctor who could speak to animals. The key arguments are that all animals have communication systems, but only humans have language. Anderson works through discussions about animal communication, including the dances of honeybees and the warning calls of vervet monkeys. He also addresses the sign-language gestures learned by primates. Additionally, Anderson makes clear the distinction between language and communication.

Language Matters: A Guide to Everyday Questions About Language. Donna Jo Napoli and Vera Lee-Schoenfeld. 2010. Oxford University Press.

In *Language Matters,* the authors explain *why* language matters to all of us and the most pressing language matters which arise in our society. The authors write chapters on questions such as "Is Ebonics really a dialect or simply bad English? Do women and men speak differently? Will computers ever really learn human language? Does offensive language harm children?" These and many other questions come up regularly in discussions about education, parenting, and society in general. From their linguistic background, Napoli and Lee-Schoenfeld answer them directly and clearly for the widest possible audience.

exercises

individual work

1. Pet peeves are things other people do which drive you crazy. Everyone has them.
   a. What language pet peeves do you have?
   b. Are your pet peeves about written or spoken language?
   c. Which pet peeves deal with sounds, which with words (apart from sounds), and which with how phrases are built?
   d. Are any of them about spelling?
2. When do meanings not work as intended? Provide an example of a misinterpreted meaning in a conversation you have had or in a movie.
3. Using a dictionary which provides the etymology of words (their history), write up a description of the following types of words, complete with how the word or phrase is used:
   a. What is the most old-fashioned word you know? When did it actually come into the language?
   b. What is the most modern-sounding word you know? When did it actually come into the language?
   c. Find three words with a Latin history.
   d. Find three words with an Anglo-Saxon history.
   e. How do these words differ in how they are used? Sometimes, words such as *beautiful* (Latin) and *pretty* (Anglo-Saxon) compete against each other for certain styles of speaking.

group work

1. The longest word:
   a. What is the longest (nontechnical & nonplacename) English word in terms of sounds your group can remember?
   b. What is the longest (nontechnical & nonplacename) English word in terms of letters your group can remember?
   c. How many units does each one have (sounds or letters), and which one is longer?
2. Judging language:
   a. Consider these two sentences:

      The cabin in which we stayed burned down yesterday.
      The cabin we stayed in burned down yesterday.

   b. From the prescriptive perspective, judge these two sentences on a scale of good and bad.
   c. From the rhetorical perspective, what contexts would make either sentence better than the other?
3. Prescriptive perspective vs. rhetorical perspective:
   a. Develop two sentences which would satisfy the prescriptive perspective, and provide two contexts where those same sentences would not work rhetorically.
   b. Develop two other sentences which would not satisfy the prescriptive perspective, and two contexts where those same sentences would work rhetorically.
   c. Develop two more sentences which satisfy neither the prescriptive nor rhetorical perspectives, regardless of context.
7. Meaning in language:
   a. Develop a skit where a couple is having a verbal fight. The fight builds in the skit until one says to the other, "What do you mean by that?" At that point the skit ends, and the audience then must figure out not only what was "meant by that," but also how they are able to discern what the speaker meant. Additionally, why *did* the second member of the couple ask, "What do you mean by that?"
   b. Develop a single sentence with as many meanings as possible. The context for the sentence can be changed as many times as you like (e.g. change the decade, the place, the speaker, or audience), but the sentence itself cannot change. The group with the sentence which can yield the most meanings wins. It is best to let the class as a whole be the judge as to how legitimate the meanings might be.

8. Language diversity:
   a. With your group, try to develop what you know about languages other than English. How many other languages does your group know?
   b. With your group, how many different dialects have you encountered?

9. Debate between groups (in front of the class) whether or not the following are myths about language:
   a. Some languages are primitive and do not perform the same functions as others.
   b. Some people speak dialects, but others do not.
   c. Some languages have only three vowels.
   d. Some writing systems have symbols which represent syllables, some represent sounds, and some represent words.
   e. Our languages are the basis for our thought.
   f. English is the hardest language to learn.
   g. In Appalachia, people speak Elizabethan English.
   h. Some languages have no grammar.
   i. Everyone has an accent.
   j. Humans can communicate with other species.
   k. Other animals also have language.
   l. Children cannot speak or write properly anymore.

10. Language play:
   The following information came from one of those endlessly forwarded emails. The main question for you is the following: Which statements deal with language, which with spelling, and which ones deal with both?

   Learn this info if you intend to try out for "Jeopardy":
   A. The longest one-syllable word in the English language is "screeched."
   B. "Dreamt" is the only English word that ends in the letters "mt."
   C. The word "set" has more definitions than any other word in the English language.
   D. "Underground" is the only word in the English language that begins and ends with the letters "und."
   E. There are only four words in the English language which end in "-dous:" tremendous, horrendous, stupendous, and hazardous.
   F. Los Angeles's full name is "El Pueblo de Nuestra Senora la Reina de los Angeles de Porciuncula" and can be abbreviated to 3.63% of its size: "L.A."
   G. There is a seven letter word in the English language that contains ten words without rearranging any of its letters. This word is

"therein," and the words within it are: the, there, he, in, rein, her, here, ere, therein, herein.

H.   "Stewardesses" is the longest English word that can be typed with only the left hand.

I.   The combination "ough" can be pronounced in nine different ways; the following sentence contains them all: "A rough-coated, dough-faced, thoughtful ploughman strode through the streets of Scarborough; after falling into a slough, he coughed and hiccoughed."

J.   The only 15 letter word that can be spelled without repeating a letter is "uncopyrightable."

K.   "Facetious" and "abstemious" contain all the vowels in the correct order, as does "arsenious," meaning "containing arsenic."

Some points to ponder for these statements are the following: What does *longest* mean in statement A? How could you reword statement I so that it takes into account that writing is a representation of language? What does *correct order* mean in statement K? How many vowel sounds are there in the English language? In contrast, how many vowel letters? How would some of these work if we replaced *sound* for *letter*? What does *word* mean in statement G?

study questions

1.   Are most humans multilingual or monolingual?
2.   What is language variation?
3.   How are language and writing not the same thing?
4.   Why is Latin considered a dead language?
5.   Are individual language sounds connected to meaning?
6.   What is a word?
7.   What are phrases?
8.   What are the two most common word order patterns?
9.   What must infants build to acquire a language?
10. Approximately how many varieties of human language do we have?
11. What is something that all varieties of language have in common?
12. How is language variation seen in the prescriptive perspective?
13. What is the rhetorical perspective?
14. How is standard English defined for US English speakers?
15. How has the meaning of the term *grammar* changed?
16. What basic assumption is the foundation for prescriptive grammar advice?

17.   What is a descriptive grammar, and how do linguists use them?
18.   In the mind, what is the mental grammar's job?
19.   What is the lexicon?
20.   What is Universal Grammar?
21.   How is the Universal Grammar related to a mental grammar?
22.   What is ambiguity, and how does it relate to meaning?
23.   How is arbitrariness related to meaning?
24.   What goes into making a word?

Visit the book's companion website for additional resources relating to this chapter at: http://www.wiley.com/go/hazen/introlanguage

2 Sounds

An Introduction to Language, First Edition. Kirk Hazen.
© 2015 John Wiley & Sons, Inc. Published 2015 by John Wiley & Sons, Inc.

chapter overview

You have been using sounds to do English for years, but few students know much about those sounds. This chapter provides many opportunities to learn about the sounds of English. One of the trickiest things for students is making the distinction between letters and sounds. Every student reading this book has had extensive training with letters. Yet here, the focus is on sounds. The main topics for this chapter are the qualities for producing language sounds in the mouth. For consonants, these include where in the mouth the sound is made, how the air is shaped, and whether or not your throat vibrates while making the sound. For vowels, we mark the vowels with coordinates, like on a map. We also explore how vowels and consonants vary from dialect to dialect. For all these sounds, they combine to form words, and the patterns of those combinations are the focus of the next chapter.

learning about what you already know

I like books, but sometimes books are not the best way to learn about a topic. Some realms of knowledge require more than a book. Learning about language sounds is one of those realms. That is where you, the reader and *speaker*, come in. To do it well, you will need to do more than just passively *read* this chapter: You must work through your own repertoire of language sounds. This chapter by itself can only teach you so much. When you work through the chapter, analyzing the knowledge of sounds already in your head, you will learn a great deal about language sounds.

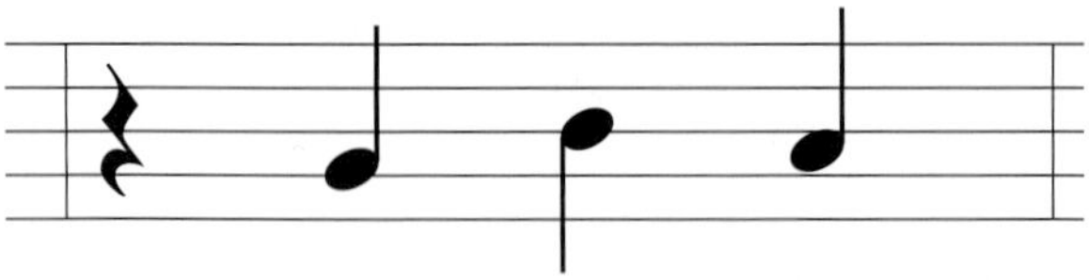

Writing about sounds is somewhat disingenuous. It is like writing about music, but only showing musical notes. If I want to write about The Beatle's song "Let it Be," I can cite the line

Figure 2.1   A quarter rest, G, B, and A on the treble clef.

with musical notes on a staff. The notes are black marks pressed on a white frame, measured by even divisions of horizontal lines. They sit on the page, and they do not make a sound. Not a squeak nor a growl nor a sigh. Those notes must be made into music. On the page, the notes are separate, tied at times, but divided in general. In the air, the music of the notes flows, with one note blended into the next, forming complex eddies and currents of sound waves. On the page, the notes are named by their position relative to other notes: The treble clef note A on the staff is below B on the staff yet above G. In the air, musicians can *name* a note, but the sound the note makes is different from its name. For all these reasons and more, writing about musical notes is a different activity than performing or listening to music. In the same way, writing or reading about language sounds is a different activity than performing or listening to them.

letters and phonetic symbols: a mismatch

In both hearing and speaking languages, as well as seeing and signing languages, there is variation in what people do. As we explore below, the sounds of language might or might not correspond to how words are spelled in English. In countries like Italy and Spain, there are no spelling bees: Who would lose when the spelling so closely matches the pronunciation? For such languages, the written letters correspond closely with the sounds they represent. For English, it is a different story.

It is important to remember that language was part of human life long before writing and that writing is a human invention which incompletely reflects what language does. The English spelling system is partially phonetic, meaning there is some correspondence between symbol and sound, but the relationships are far from simple. Although the letter <k> normally represents a [k] sound, as in *kit*, sometimes it does not, as in *knit*. The reason here is that historically, the [k] before [n] was lost, but the spelling did not change. It was still useful to visually distinguish <knit> from <nit>. Throughout this chapter, you will learn how English sounds have diverged over time from the written letters used to represent them.

To mark on the page the difference between a written letter and a spoken sound, different kinds of brackets are used. For written letters (also called **orthographic symbols**), the angled brackets are used in this book, like <photo>. For **phonetic symbols**, which represent spoken sounds, the square brackets are used, like [foto]. For those symbols, we follow the International Phonetic Alphabet, crafted by the International Phonetic Association. Their website might help you figure out what is what, but be aware that this book only uses a subset of all the symbols available: http://www.langsci.ucl.ac.uk/ipa/.

The semi-phonetic English spelling system has many connections between symbols and sounds. At times, a single spelling represents multiple sounds. For example, the digraph <th> represents three sounds in English. The <th> in *thin* has a non-vibrating voice box, the <th> in *there* has a vibrating voice box, and the <th> in *Thomas* has a [t] sound. If you put your hand lightly on your throat, you can feel the voice box vibrate when you talk. If you do not whisper, it should vibrate during the <th> of *there*.

phonetic symbols: a convenient lie

In 2006, the award-winning documentary *An Inconvenient Truth* was released to draw attention to climate change (www.climatecrisis.net/). The gist of the title is that despite the troublesome nature of the problem, we cannot avoid the facts of the situation. To invert that phrase, consider the idea of *a convenient lie*. The gist of that phrase is that a certain situation is false, but it is useful regardless of its known falsehood. When writing about sounds in language, scholars use written symbols to represent sounds. These are phonetic symbols, like [foto] for *photo*. They are useful when discussing sounds in written texts like this one. Unfortunately, they are a convenient lie.

Take the word *feed*. With the symbol system used in this book, the International Phonetic Alphabet, the word *feed* could be represented as [fid]. Like musical notes, these are black marks in a white frame; they are separated and evenly spaced left to right and aligned evenly to the bottom of the line, but this symmetry and separation is not there when the sounds are pronounced. Additionally, the [i] in [fid], the [i] in *feet* [fit], and the [i] in *fiend* [find], appear to be the same on the page, but they have some subtle physical differences. For example, the [i] in *feed* is slightly longer in time than the [i] of *feet*, although it might be hard to tell without a computer program like Praat (www.praat.org) where we can measure the sounds. For the [i] in *fiend* [find], it is pronounced with some air coming out of the nose, whereas the other two instances of [i] do not have that trait. There are other symbols we can use to add these distinctions, but in general, we will be keeping things simple.

Phonetic symbols have been extremely helpful tools for language sciences and humanities. Scholars have used them to document thousands of languages over the last 125 years. Especially before portable recording devices, phonetic symbols provided reliable means of keeping a long-term record of speech. In those early days, phonetic symbols were even used as parlor tricks to entertain people, who would make a wide variety of sounds so that an off-location actor could later replicate the sounds from the written phonetic symbols.

So, phonetic symbols are a convenient means of learning about sounds and describing sounds. This book uses them extensively. Just remember that there is more information packaged in the sounds of human language than phonetic symbols allow.

meaning, ambiguity, and arbitrariness

The most important issue in this subsection is whether sounds *mean* anything. At first glance, it seems like a ridiculous question. If sounds did not mean anything, how could we have language?

How about a better set of questions: Does any sound mean one thing in all languages? Does any one sound mean only one thing in English? How do sounds mean anything for us?

sound symbolism

When people examine language, one desire that comes up again and again is to have a particular sound connected to some specific meaning. This set up is often referred to as *sound symbolism*. The hope is that through a natural connection, perhaps the force of the sound, or the way it flows or stops, the sound functions as the meaning. In English, several different contenders arise. The most noticeable is <gl>, which is associated with some terms for light and seeing in English: *glimmer, glow, glisten, gleam, glimpse, glance, glair*. Yet, other <gl> words are out there with no vision or light connection: *glamour, glaze, glory, glad, glee, glue*, and *globe*. And there are plenty of words with the meanings of light and vision which do not start with <gl>: *light, vision, eye, sight, see, scope, behold, discern*. Around 2,400 years ago, Plato wrote the dialogue *Cratylus* where Socrates discusses the nature of language. At one point, Socrates argues that the ideal language would have a sound for every sense, and he even tries his hand at figuring out where the meaning of words came from. Today, it is clear that individual sounds do not carry as much meaning as words.

Yet, different sets of sounds which may seem similar actually represent the same meaning. *Tomato, tomatah*; *potato, potater, tater*. How slight can the change be and still be noticeable? A small shift in a single vowel can make people notice. In parts of the United States, a raised [æ] in words like *bag* and *mad* can signal the speaker's home region. The vowel sound itself does not *mean* anything in particular. People from around Chicago, Detroit, and upstate New York generally pronounce the [æ] vowel in *bat* as raised to the mid-front part of the mouth, so that it sounds more like *bet*. Because this raised pronunciation of the [æ] vowel is connected with people from those areas, it picks up the social attributes usually associated with those people.

With consonants, the difference between pronouncing them with an initial *th-* or *d*-sound can be seen as marking social class, but it is not the [d] sound itself which people judge. No club exists to eliminate *d*-sounds from the language in general (The D-Haters Club of America?), but this particular replacement of *d* for *th* is associated with lower-status speakers in most of the Western world. Accordingly, all of the stigma levied against those speakers is transferred to this morsel of language variation.

mergers

Some sound differences are stable and can last for centuries. Other differences between sounds are less stable. The qualities of the sounds begin to resemble each other, and the sounds begin to be heard as the same sound, even if there remain some distinctions between them. In general, consonants are more stable sounds in language than vowels. Consonants can take centuries to change, but vowels can transform in decades.

There are many qualities to sounds. The language sounds we produce are packed with clues so listeners can tell them apart. This book is not the place to explain all the clues, but, for example, vowels differ in several acoustic qualities discussed below. When those qualities grow more similar, the vowels are perceived more often as the *same* vowel.

Even when English speakers produce what they consider to be the same vowels, often those pronunciations differ in some way. In baseball, a batter might hit three line-drives for runs in a game, but it is unlikely that he will hit the ball to the same spot with the same speed every time. Ponder how difficult it would be to get the physics just right to hit a line-drive to the same spot with the same speed every time (and during game conditions). The same lack of control goes with moving your tongue around your mouth. When you produce the vowel in *bud*, note that it is mid-height and more toward the center of your mouth. Now try to move it back and say the word again (out loud, without whispering). Does it still sound like *bud*? Now try to move your vowel in *bud* toward the high front part of your mouth. How far forward can you move it without the word becoming *bead*?

A vowel merger happens when pronunciations that have previously been considered to belong to different vowels begin to be heard as the *same* vowel. Throughout numerous English-speaking communities, such as New Zealand and the US South, the vowels in the words *pit* and *pet* are often merged, especially before nasal sounds in words like *windy* and *Wendy*.

When different words sound the same they are called **homophones**. Homophones can be found in all the world's languages and appear to be a normal condition for us. In English, language change has left us with some interesting homophone sets: for example, *right*, *rite*, *write*, and the obsolete form *wright*. As their spellings indicate, these words were originally pronounced differently. Because of various language changes, the pronunciations of these four words have all ended up to be the same.

For the homophone sets which are widely accepted, such as *there/their* or *four/for* or *dear/deer*, no social judgments are made. For others though, social judgments are sometimes attached to the speakers who have them. Depending on where the students grew up, they may or may not have the following sets of words as homophones: *which/witch*; *death/deaf*; *cot/caught*; *pin/pen*. The pronunciation difference between words like *which* and *witch* used to be normal for all dialects of English, but some dialects no longer make this distinction. If you have a difficult time making a distinction in these two, try pronouncing the original spelling of <which>, namely <hwich>. This kind of language change is called a merger: two distinct sounds have become one. In this case, the <hw> sound became the same as the <w> sound, and as a result the word pairs *which/witch*, *where/wear*, and *whine/wine* became homophones. Where we find spelling differences but similar sounds, we can make a safe guess that a merger has occurred between previously distinct sounds. An important side lesson here is that spelling preserves older forms. In looking into the spelled forms of words, we are often looking into their history. Practicing and understanding spelling might be easier for all involved if the historical nature of spelling were an open issue.

For much of the western United States and some areas east of the Mississippi river, the two words *cot/caught* most likely are homophones. For many people in the south-eastern United States, the pair *pin/pen* may also be homophones. Take a look at some of the words implicated in these mergers:

Table 2.1 Some mergers in English

cot/caught *merger*		pin/pen *merger*		No merger in the United States but some merger in New Zealand and Australia	
bot (robot)	bought	pin	pen	pit	pet
don	dawn	wind	wend	bid	bed
knot	naught	tin	ten	Jeff	gif
cot	caught	din	den	slipped	slept
hock	hawk	gin	Jen	pig	peg

For those with the *cot/caught* merger, the words in each pair in that list are pronounced the same. For those with the *pin/pen* merger, it only occurs with some kinds of words: When the vowels come before <n> sounds, they are pronounced the same; however, when the vowels are before other sounds, they are pronounced differently. For those with this merger, *pin/pen* are homophones but *pit/pet* would not be. For those with the Southern *pin/pen* merger, they have a specific pronunciation rule which details when the merger can and cannot occur. Unfortunately, for all too many people, the *pin/pen* merger has been stigmatized, even though it is, in fact, a normal, rule-governed part of the English language.

two related kinds of meaning with sound

The foundation for any communication system is the combination of a signal and a meaning. Be it a porpoise looking for a mate or a woman selling baskets in a market, signals and meanings get tied together. What kinds of meaning can be tied to sounds? Two types of meaning are connected with sounds: **social meaning** and **reference meaning**.

The social meaning of sounds concerns what social traits are attributed to the sounds. For some communities, a distinction exists between pronouncing *wh*-words (e.g. what, which, when) as [ʍ][1] or [w] initially. If you pronounce *which* and *witch* the same, then you do not have a difference. Earlier in English, the [ʍ] pronunciation in words like *which* was the normal thing to do, but over time, [w] has become more normal. Once variation between the forms exists,

Word Play: In-class writing

- Why might vowels be less stable than consonants? Contrast two consonants and two vowels to prove your point.
- Which consonants are more vowel-like?
- List out eight words, four of which sound like they are spelled orthographically, and four of which are *not* spelled like they sound. If they were to be pronounced as they are spelled, how would they sound?

speakers can begin attaching social attributes to one form or the other. In some communities, the [w] form might have seemed wrong or something that younger folk used. In others, the [ʍ] form might have increasingly been associated with old-fashioned speech, or perhaps as pretentious: I know of a high school class which teased its teacher for her [ʍ] pronunciations. The variation between [ʍ] and [w] did not itself *cause* any of the social connections people made, but the variation allows for social attributes to be attached to fluctuating forms.

Social meaning is perhaps most easy to notice when it is attached to some sounds but not others. In those cases, the question comes up, why are some instances socially marked, but others are not? Take the first sound in the words *threat*, *three*, and *throw*. This sound is named *theta*, [θ]. It is one that does not necessarily get used in *all* varieties of English, but in most of them, it does. As sounds go, [θ] is an odd one. To produce it, you have to put your tongue between your teeth and blow air around your tongue. Like other not-so-smart ideas, sticking your tongue between your teeth while moving your teeth is not the safest thing. In part because of these unusual qualities, it is one of the consonants with less stability. For Modern English, [θ] in many words is undergoing some changes. Most often, it is being pronounced as [f], like in *birfday*. For speakers in Michigan, this pronunciation is associated with lower social class speakers from urban areas. In some rural areas of North Carolina, this pronunciation is used by all speakers from every social class group and every ethnicity. Perhaps not surprisingly, the [θ] to [f] variation is heavily stigmatized in the US North, but completely unnoticed in rural areas of North Carolina. It is the same alternative pronunciation, but the social meaning attached to it differs because the perception of the speakers using it differs.

Reference meaning results from sets of sounds being associated to concepts of objects, ideas, and actions in our minds. For many folk, the reference meaning of sounds is the dictionary meaning: If you want to know the meaning of a word, you look it up in a dictionary. There are hundreds of different dictionaries for English, and those meanings will shift depending on which ones you consult. The reference meaning could also be considered the denotation. The reference meaning of *shirt* most likely consists of at least *clothing used to cover part of the upper body*, but what *shirt* specifically means depends upon the context and the knowledge in the speakers' and listeners' head: The way you understand the phrase *Hand me that shirt* depends on how many shirts are around and which one is being pointed to.

Reference meaning results from certain sets of sounds being associated with certain meanings, as does social meaning. Yet, an important difference exists between these two types of meaning. All words must have a reference meaning, but not all words have a distinguishable social meaning. For example, these two words each have a reference meaning: *a* [e] or *eh* [e]. The first one has the reference meaning of *one*, whereas the second can work as a tag question at the end of a sentence (e.g. *You want to leave, eh?*). The first one does not have any social meaning, but the second is marked as 'Canadian,' at least in North America.

In Chapters 4 and 5, we delve further into reference and social meaning.

a sketch of sounds

The sounds of language are out in the air. They neither think nor feel nor show any signs of life. Yet, they move, and they vary, and they change. Like most things academics study, we divide them into categories. These categories are not absolute, and the boundaries between them leak, allowing at times a sound of one category to pick up qualities of a neighboring category. We go through the most major categories here.

Language scientists identify sounds by what they are not. An [s] is an [s] because it is not a [t]. A [b] is a [b] because it is not a [p] (or any of the other sounds). In more advanced courses, you learn how qualities of all the language sounds overlap and how they are not as separate as the symbols and spaces on this page imply. For this book, we stick with the story that sounds can be represented accurately by distinct phonetic symbols (e.g. *orthographic* [oɹθogɹæfɪk]).

Phonetics is the scientific study of sounds. There are several major categories of sounds. The categories discussed here are classified by how the sounds are produced in the mouth. This branch of phonetics is **articulatory phonetics**. The most basic category is the divide between consonants and vowels.

The consonants are placed into three categories: (1) where they get produced, the **place of articulation**; (2) how they get produced, the **manner of articulation**; and (3) whether the vocal folds are vibrating, the **voice of articulation**.

consonants and vowels

Vowels and **consonants** differ from each other in their *degree of constriction* in the **vocal tract**, which includes the mouth and the throat. Vowels have a less restricted passageway, and consonants have a more restricted passageway. The vowel in the word *knot* has an open pronunciation, but the [t] at the end has a completely closed pronunciation.

Try these words out loud:

pie [paɪ]

toe [to]

coy [kɔɪ]

Each one starts with the air in the mouth completely stopped. The mouth then opens up to let the air flow freely. In the following words, the airflow in the mouth goes from stopped, to fully open, to stopped. Try these words:

pipe [paɪp]

toke [tok]

cab [kæb]

Different consonants constrict the airflow in the mouth to different degrees. For the first sound in these words, the consonants have less constriction as you move down the list:

tea [ti]

sea [si]

Lee [li]

As you work through the following consonants, the degree of constriction will play a role in making each consonant sound.

Since the degree of constriction distinguishes vowels and consonants along a continuum, some sounds can be more consonant-like (with a greater degree of constriction) while other sounds can be more vowel-like (with a lesser degree of constriction).

The most consonant-like sounds are ones like these: [t], [d], [p], [b], [k], [g]. To produce them, you must stop the air completely and release it. When you stop the air, the airway in the mouth is 100% constricted. Accordingly, these sounds are called **stops**.

Sounds such as these are the most vowel-like: [a], [i], [u], as in the words <plot>, <bee>, and <boo>. At no point during these vowel sounds is the airway in the mouth closed, and this quality gets them categorized as vowels.

There are sounds where the degree of constriction is so low, sometimes consonants become vowels. In many US schools, to resolve the question of what is a vowel, one alphabet mantra is "A, E, I, O, U, and sometimes Y." In other schools, "sometimes W" is also included. How can a letter sometimes be a consonant and sometimes a vowel? It all depends on the context. Remember, spelled consonant letters and vowel letters do not *produce* sounds, they *represent* sounds. The <y> symbol represents the sounds in <boy> and <yes>, <buy>

and <young>. In the words <boy> and <buy>, the <y> represents a vowel sound. In <yes> and <young>, it represents a consonant. The last sound in <boy> is a vowel, represented by the phonetic symbols [ɔɪ]. The symbol [j] represents the first sound in <yes>.

Another major division in sounds is between **sonorants** and **obstruents**. One acoustic difference between them is that sonorants have more of a ringing quality. In the French song, "*Frère Jacques*," one line reads "*Sonnez les matines*," in other words, "Morning bells are ringing." The sonorant sounds ring (*sonnez*) just like those morning bells. Sounds such as [l], [n], [w], and [ɛ], all have more of a ringing sound. Please note that the sonorants include both vowels and consonants.

Obstruents are the nonsonorants of the language world. They do not ring. They include sounds such as the [t] in <tide>, the [tʃ] in <chide>, and the [s] in <side>. Sonorants and obstruents work together in many different ways: Many words in most languages are a mixture of obstruents and sonorants. For example, one pronunciation of the word <buttons> could be [bətn̩z] with two sonorants [ə n] sandwiched between three obstruents [b t z].

The next level of divisions requires that we discuss consonants and vowels separately. They are different enough that the same categories do not best describe their qualities. Both consonants and vowels can be categorized by where they are produced in the mouth, but vowels, because they are less constrained, move more freely and require different coordinates.

consonants

the place of articulation

With more constricted space in the mouth, the consonants have more definite places of articulation. For English, the consonants are given in Table 2.2.

Words to the Wise: The study of sounds

Phonetics is the scientific study of sound. The three main branches are articulatory, acoustic, and auditory. You should think of these as focusing on different parts of the speaking and hearing process. Articulatory phonetics studies how sounds are made in the mouth. Acoustic phonetics studies the qualities of the sounds in the air. Auditory phonetics studies what happens to sounds after they hit our ears.

This chapter sticks with articulatory phonetics, but the other branches have had many exciting discoveries and have grown over the last few decades. To play with acoustic phonetic tools, go to www.praat.org, download the free software, work with the tutorial, and investigate acoustic qualities of your sounds, such as the exact coordinates of your own vowels.

Table 2.2   Consonants in English

	bilabial		labiodental		interdental		alveolar		palatal		velar		glottal
stop	p	b					t	d			k	g	ʔ
affricate									tʃ	dʒ			
fricative			f	v	θ	ð	s	z	ʃ	ʒ	x		h
nasal		m						n				ŋ	
liquid									l	ɹ			
glide	ʍ	w							j				

Table 2.3   Glottal sounds

Glottal sounds		Possible glottal sounds	
\<hot\>	\<how\>	\<Batman\>	\<kitten\>
\<uh-oh\>	\<hope\>	\<hatrack\>	\<button\>

The places of articulation are in the top row of Table 2.2. Starting on the left, they run from the front of the mouth to the back of the mouth. We borrowed these terms from Latin, and they basically describe where in the mouth the sound gets produced. The **bilabial** sounds involve both lips, as in the first sounds of *pat* and *bat*. The **labiodental** sounds involve the top teeth and the bottom lip, as in *fee* and *vee*. To test out that place of articulation, try it with the bottom teeth and the upper lip and see how that works for you. The **interdental** sounds involve the somewhat odd move of sticking your tongue between your teeth while talking and blowing air over it, as in *thick* and *there*.

The **alveolar** area is where several sounds are produced, including the first sounds in *tea, dee, sea, zee, knee, Leigh,* and maybe *reef* (more on that later). As far as we are concerned in this book, the alveolar region is from the back of your upper teeth right up until the **palatal** region, the area where you would pronounce the first sounds in *she* and *chap*. The exact location is not terribly important, and it varies from person to person. More important is that you can distinguish between alveolar sounds and palatal sounds by noting that the alveolar sounds happen in front of their palatal counterparts.

The **velar** region is further back than the palatal region. Velar sounds include the first ones in *key* and *guy*. The last sound in *ring* is also velar, and perhaps for you the first sound in *red* is also a velar sound. In some Scottish dialects of English, the velar sound [x] can be heard in words such as *right* and *light*. The last area down the vocal tract for English is the **glottal region**. See Table 2.3 and the consonant keyword chart. In language variation and children's speech, similar sounds get switched up. What is similar about [k] and [t] in this *Natalie Dee* comic? http://www.nataliedee.com/082612

The <h> of *hot, how,* and *hope* represents the sound [h]. Try to pronounce those words and make that first sound last as long as possible. It is made by shoving air over the space between your vocal folds in your **larynx**. That space is called the **glottis**.

The word *uh-oh* is pronounced with a **glottal stop** in the middle. A glottal stop, [ʔ], is produced when the glottis snaps shut, stopping the air. For the last two columns of Table 2.3, these words are often pronounced with glottal stops where the <t>s are written. Note, however, that words like <truck> or <ton> or <toy> never have glottal stops pronounced where the <t>s are. Under what condition may glottal stops replace <t> sounds?

manner

Every consonant has a *manner* of articulation. The manner is *how* the sound gets produced: In other words, what do your tongue, jaw, and throat do when making consonants? The names for the different manners of articulation are fairly transparent. The manner of *stop* includes all the consonants where the air is stopped, such as [t], [b], and [k]. The manner of *glide* includes the consonants where the tongue glides from one point to another; English has two glides: [w] and [j]. The manners are listed in the first column of Table 2.2.

In the **stops** category, we can count seven sounds. The last of these sounds, the glottal stop, is really a stop in name only. As it is normally articulated, it most often resembles a short segment where your voice creaks. As discussed above, it is perhaps best represented in the middle of words like *uh-oh* or *Batman*. See the waveform in Figure 2.2 for pronunciations of *Batman* with first

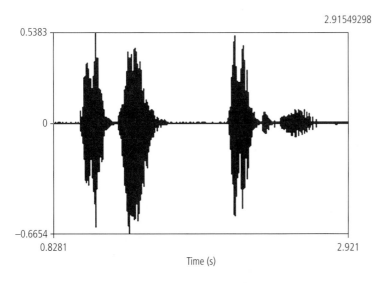

Figure 2.2   A representation of [bæʔmæn] and [bætmæn].

a glottal stop and then a full [t] represented as the little, sharp hump in the second instance. The others are sounds where the airflow stops fully, as in the first sound in the following words: *pea, bee, tea, dee, key, guy.*

The name of the **fricative** category requires further explanation. It comes from *friction*, when two things rub together. In this case, the friction is not between two solids, but involves flowing air. Air is like water in its movement, and water flows down hills and mountains in creeks and streams. From its source, the water flows smoothly, making little noise. As it flows, the water may hit rocks, branches, and the stream banks; when it does, more sound is made, and eddies and ripples appear. If it is a big enough mountain, and more massive rocks are in the stream, the sounds of white water appear as the water flow strikes the rocks and finds ways around them. The water beats itself about the rocks, causing friction and turbulence. In the mouth, fricative sounds are created just like that white water. The airflow crashes against the teeth, tongue, and lips to create turbulence.

In the world's languages, the fricative manner is the most common way to produce a sound, with a total of 22 sounds, two each for every place of articulation in the full International Phonetic Alphabet chart (http://www.langsci.ucl.ac .uk/ipa/fullchart.html). Most English varieties have nine fricatives, but a few might have 10. Fricatives can be found as the first sound in the following words: *face* [f], *vase* [v], *thigh* [θ], *thy* [ð], *sue* [s], *zoo* [z], *shoe* [ʃ], *genre* [ʒ], *who* [h]. Some English varieties will have a velar fricative as the second-to-last consonant in *right* [ɹaɪxt].

The **affricates** combine stops and fricatives. Accordingly, it takes two combined phonetic symbols to represent the voiceless [tʃ] and the voiced [dʒ]. These are the first and last sounds in *church* [tʃɹtʃ] and *judge* [dʒədʒ]. The best way to learn and remember this manner is by producing these sounds a few times slowly and stopping in the middle of the sounds themselves while making them. When producing the first one slowly, work from the [t] in <tea> to the [ʃ] in <shoe>. When producing the second one slowly, work from the [d] in <dog> to the [ʒ] in <genre>. The first sound releases into the second sound so quickly, the movement is felt and heard as one sound.

Identify the affricates in the following English words (and what letters represent which sounds?):

1. <joke>
2. <bungee jumping>
3. <gibberish>
4. <Gerry>
5. <juggle>
6. <gym>
7. <Jim>
8. <church>
9. <cheat>
10. <chattel>

11.   <butch>
12.   <budge>

How many different ways are there to spell [dʒ] and [tʃ] in English?

The next three manners are different in some ways: The sounds of nasals, liquids, and glides are all sonorants. All the manners before this point have been obstruents. Sonorants create more sound, and flow out of the mouth more freely. Technically speaking, sonorants are more resonant. Obstruents (stops, fricatives, and affricates) obstruct the air more than sonorants.

The next manner is **nasal**. The key quality for the nasal manner is that the air moves out of the nose rather than the mouth. In the mouth, the air is completely stopped (and these sounds can be thought of as oral stops). But during each of the three nasals consonants, the sound continues without interruption out of the nose. The difference between the three of them is where in the mouth they are produced, their place of articulation. The three nasals are the last sounds in *bomb*, *ton*, and *ring* (see Table 2.4).

Read each of the following words out loud and identify how the nasals differ:

Table 2.4   Nasals in English

Word-initial nasals	Word-medial nasals	Word-final nasals
<Moe>	<common>	<bomb>
<no>	<canon>	<ton>
	<ingot>	<ring>

You may want to try this exercise in private. Pronounce each word out loud, and then pronounce them a second time while pinching your nose shut. Each word will sound strange while your nose is pinched.

Then try pinching your nose while pronouncing these three words: <Poe>, <toe>, <go>.

These words should sound fairly normal. The reason the words in Table 2.4 are affected is because they contain nasal sounds. The sounds [m], [n], and [ŋ] (as in "ring") are produced by blowing air out of your nose.

In the first row, the [m] is produced by placing both lips together and stopping the air while letting the air out your nose. In the second row, your tongue touches the front part of the roof of your mouth, the alveolar region, while air flows out your nose. In the third row, your tongue touches the back part of the roof of your mouth while air flows out your nose. Can you think of an English word that begins with the sound [ŋ]?

The next manner is **liquid**. As the name indicates, both liquid sounds in English flow over the tongue and out of the mouth. The difference between them is how the air flows off the tongue.

Table 2.5   Liquids

Word-initial liquids		Word-final liquids	
<roe>	<low>	<bar>	<ball>
<rope>	<lope>	<par>	<pall>
<rip>	<lip>	<star>	<stall>
<rat>	<lat>	<gar>	<gall>

Table 2.6   Glides

Word-initial glide	Word-final glide
<well>	<tow>
<which> ~ <witch>	
<yo>	<toy>

Pronounce each of the words in Table 2.5 out loud while paying attention to the [ɹ] and [l] sounds.

The two sounds in English, [ɹ] and [l], are related to each other in both voice and manner, but the tongue does make different, subtle movements when producing them. For English speakers, the words in Table 2.5 contrast with each other, and these two sounds mark differences in meaning.

Since consonants differ in their degree of constriction, it is important to point out that liquids have a much lower degree of constriction than do obstruents. With that lower degree of constriction, the details of any one liquid pronunciation will have a wider range of variation. Consider these two words: *LOL* (as a word) and *Roar*. For most speakers, the liquid at the front of the word will be pronounced differently from the liquid at the end. This range of variation all fits under the two symbols [l] and [ɹ].

The last manner is the least constricted. For these two English sounds, the consonant *glides* from one place in the mouth to another. Pronounce the words in Table 2.6 out loud while paying attention to the <w> and <y> letters.

These two consonant sounds involve movement during pronunciation. Because of this movement, they are called **glides**. The sound [w] comes in two flavors in English: the voiced version [w] as in <wet> and the voiceless version [ʍ] as in some people's pronunciation of the <wh> in *Cool Whip*.[2] Many Americans have lost the distinction between the voiced and voiceless bilabial glide and produce [w] in all contexts. As discussed previously, this is a merger in that two distinct sounds are being merged into one sound.

The two sonorant consonant glides can be heard in the first sounds of *wet* and *yet*. In many lessons for young children learning to read English, the "vowels" are often described as "A, E, I, O, U, and sometimes Y (and sometimes W)." The "sometimes" comes from variation explored in Chapter 3, but as a hint, think about the different sounds in *bow* and *bowing*. In the first, the <w> letter represents more of a vowel sound; in the second, the <w> letter represents a consonant glide. The same distinction goes for *toy* and *toying*. Glides are extremely fluid and at times loose their constriction completely.

voice

The last distinction for consonants is also the simplest. It is a two-sided distinction based on the voice in your windpipe. If you feel the cartilage on the front of your throat, it will go up and down when you swallow. Go ahead, put your hand on your throat and swallow. That cartilage contains the larynx. Within the larynx, you control two flaps of tissue, the **vocal folds**. These are between half an inch to an inch long, depending on how big you are. In the simplest description, you direct your two vocal folds to do one of three actions:

1. loosen them so they can vibrate up and down to create sound
2. hold them stiff to whisper and make voiceless sounds
3. close them as in words like *uh-oh*

To understand the vocal folds, think of a stringed instrument such as a guitar or violin, or get a rubber band and stretch it between two fingers. The shape and size of the musical string influences the sound produced. To make a sound, the string must vibrate, whether it is plucked or bowed. When strings are tight, the vibrations are faster, and the sound has a higher pitch. When the strings are loose, the vibrations are slower, and the sound has a lower pitch. And here, size does matter. Thicker strings make deeper sounds. Thinner strings make higher pitched sounds. A stand-up bass has a much deeper pitch than a cello, which has a much deeper pitch than a violin.

Your vocal folds work the same way, except that you can adjust the tension on your vocal folds quickly, making them looser or tighter. Work with your vocal folds right now: Start with *ba* and hold it; then try *ba* in the lowest pitch you can find; next work *ba* up to the highest pitch you can manage without your voice shutting off. When you raise the pitch of your voice, you are adjusting your vocal folds to be tighter, vibrating faster, producing a higher pitch.

When you hold your vocal folds completely tight and stiff, the air passes over them and creates some high pitched white noise. This is the basic sound in [h]. It is also what you do when you whisper. Try to whisper the following sentence out loud: *Those bold quail ran over our blueberry muffins.* Your tongue and jaw move normally, but your vocal folds are stiff. Now try the sentence out loud without whispering. For many of the sounds, you do not whisper them, and the vocal-fold vibrations give you voice.

1. Say each word in the first column of Table 2.7 out loud, emphasizing the <th>. Does the larynx vibrate during the <th>?

Table 2.7 Interdental fricatives

[θ]	[ð]
bath	bathe
cloth	clothe
sheath	sheathing
think	that

2. Say each word in the second column out loud, emphasizing the <th>. Does the larynx vibrate during the <th>?

The <th> letters denote two different sounds in English. The first sound we call **voiceless** (e.g. bath) with the theta symbol [θ]. The second sound with the English spelling <th> is the **voiced** sound (e.g. bathe), which makes the vocal folds in the larynx vibrate; this sound is denoted with the eth symbol [ð].

For consonants, the range of vocal fold vibrations is divided into vibrating and nonvibrating. The voiced sounds have vocal fold vibrations. The voiceless sounds have no vocal fold vibrations: They are whispered. In Table 2.2, the voiced sounds are shaded, and the voiceless sounds are not shaded.

In the voiced consonants, if you take a sound like [d], [b], or [g], you can get a clear sense of the vibrations. Being stops, normally in these sounds you stop the air and then release it, as in *doh, bow*, and *go*. To experiment with these sounds, start them but do *not* release the stop or finish the word. Try to pronounce the [b] as loudly and slowly as you can. What you should feel are vibrations in your throat which run up your jaw and the sides of your head to your ears. Those vibrations are your voice.

McGurk effect[3]

What you hear is at times affected by what you see. Imagine how the scientists Harry McGurk and John MacDonald felt when they were trying to put together separately-recorded audio sounds and video images of a person talking. It seems simple enough. If you can get the audio to align in time with the lips moving, it will appear like the audio is from the lips even if it is not, like well-performed lip syncing. Their lab at the University of Surrey in England went through some confusion in the early 1970s when they tried to put together the audio recording of *ba* and the visual recording of *ga*. What they experienced as the audience was *da*. It must have been like seeing a ghost, but knowing that there was no ghost. The scientists were experiencing a sound illusion, much like a visual illusion. The human perceptual system (both auditory and visual) has no evolutionary experience with such mismatches, so it repairs the scene to the best of its ability.

There are several videos on the internet that illustrate this point, but not all the videos work for all audiences, especially if you know what is going on *before*

Stops	Affricates	Fricatives	Nasals	Liquids	Glides	Vowels
b	dʒ	v	m	l	w	i

Figure 2.3 The sonorancy continuum.

you watch the video. It might be best to get some unsuspecting friends to try it out and then report back the results. Search for *McGurk effect*.

To sum up this section, consonants are the more stable members of the phonetic world. They fall along a continuum where those with a higher degree of constriction are further away from being vowels and those with a lower degree of constriction are closer to being vowels, as in Figure 2.3. In other words, obstruents are more constricted than sonorant consonants, which are more constricted than vowels. Starting with consonants, try to say the symbols in Figure 2.3 out loud in one single breath without stopping between them, and then go backwards starting with vowels. The differences are small along the continuum, but small differences have big effects. Such small differences allow a range of variation which supports the 6,900 human languages. To study this wide range of variation, linguists divide the qualities of consonants into place, manner, and voice.

vowels

For most students, remembering the consonant symbols is easier than remembering the vowel symbols. There are most likely two reasons for this situation. First, English consonants (sounds) correspond fairly well to consonant letters: The [k] sound fits nicely with the <k> letter in <kit>, and the [w] sounds fits nicely with the <w> letter in <well>. Real trouble only comes up with the less familiar symbols such as [ð] [θ] [ʒ] [ŋ], which do not have any direct letter representation. Second, vowels have a less definite place of articulation and are therefore harder to pin down.

But, vowels do have ways in which they get made, and we can contrast them to each other by those different qualities. For vowels, linguists position them on a map called **vowel space**. Like a map of the world, there is longitude and latitude. With those coordinates, we can precisely pin down where each vowel is produced. In more advanced courses, you work with measuring those exact coordinates, but in this course, we will work with a simplified description which allows us to still describe each vowel that makes a difference in meaning for English.

Our simplified map relies on a side-view of the mouth. The vowels are produced in different places in the mouth, and this two-dimensional side-view allows us to talk about those differences. Figure 2.4 provides our map of the mouth and the English vowels inside. Table 2.8 provides keywords as reminder prompts for the vowel symbols. The keywords work for many, but not all,

Table 2.8   Keywords for vowels

Keyword	Vowel	Descriptor	Phonetic transcription
bee	i	high, front, tense	[bi]
bit	ɪ	high, front, lax	[bɪt]
boo	u	high, back, tense	[bu]
book	ʊ	high, back, lax	[bʊk]
bait	e	mid, front, tense	[bet]
bet	ɛ	mid, front, lax	[bɛt]
but	ə	mid, central, lax	[bət]
boat	o	mid, back, tense	[bot]
bought	ɔ	mid, back, lax	[bɔt]
bat	æ	low, front, tense or lax	[bæt]
(ro)bot	a	low, back, lax	[bat]
by	aɪ	low, back, lax rising to high, front, lax	[baɪ]
boy	ɔɪ	mid, back, tense rising to high, front, lax	[bɔɪ]
house	aʊ	low, back, lax rising to high, back, lax	[haʊs]

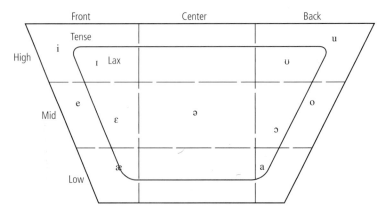

Figure 2.4   Vowel space.

English speakers; you will need to discover the keywords that fit best for your own dialect. The vowels in Figure 2.4 are called **monophthongs** because they are in one place (mono) in the mouth.

The next thing to learn about English vowels is how they are packaged in our minds: How we hear one vowel as different from another vowel. The rest of this section describes three qualities that English speakers use to divide vowels. In other languages, other qualities are used, but English primarily uses three (and sometimes a fourth). Unfortunately, the one quality most people use to talk about categories of vowels is not a quality of Modern English, and we have to tackle that issue before stepping any further into the discussion.

For a long time, primary school teachers have talked about long and short vowels, as do most popular dictionaries. In older varieties of English, roughly before 1500, English vowels did support differences in meaning based on the length of the vowel: A word like <bet> had a shorter vowel and a word like <beet> had a longer vowel. As you can see, the spelling reflected the vowel difference: one <e> for the short vowel and two <ee> for the long vowel. Many vowels were in pairs with a long and short partner. For example, the short <i> in <bit> used to have a partner in the Middle English long <i> in <bite>. During that time, the vowels in English went through a fundamental change (the Great Vowel Shift). The pairings were broken apart, and along with them went the distinction between long and short vowels. It is a safe bet that the length of vowels (in terms of time) has not made a difference in meaning between words in English since 1600.

We still have vowels that are longer in time than other vowels, but the number of milliseconds a vowel lasts does not affect a word's meaning. In the words *bid/bead* and *bit/beat*, two vowels, [ɪ] and [i], distinguish the pairs. The vowels in *bid/bead* are longer than the vowels in *bit/beat*, yet people hear the vowels in *bid* and *bit* as the same vowel and the vowels in *bead* and *beat* as the same vowel. So, physical length differences (in milliseconds) do occur in vowels, but Modern English does not rely on them to distinguish meanings. Pronounce the words in Table 2.9 out loud:

Table 2.9 High, front vowels

[ɪ]	[i]
<bid>	<bead>
<hid>	<heed>
<nit>	<neat>
<sit>	<seat>
<flit>	<fleet>
<it>	<eat>

In reading between columns, there should be a clear pattern of the vowels. The first column has the vowel [ɪ]. Many children are taught that this is short "i." The second column has the vowel [i]. Many students learn that this is long "e." In modern English, these vowels may both be longer or shorter, but there is no consistent time difference between them that has an effect on meaning. But if you say them out loud (and pay attention to your mouth while doing so), [ɪ] has a more lax mouth shape, and [i] has a more tense mouth shape. One of the better oral-practice exercises is to slide back and forth between vowels and notice what your mouth is doing: Start with [ɪ], hold it, slide to [i], and then back to [ɪ]. Also, note the spelling correspondences between the two vowels.

Some vowels are further front in the mouth, while others are further in the back. This quality is called vowel **advancement**. Start with the sound *boo,* and while holding the vowel for a few seconds, shift to *ee* of *bee.* You should be able to notice that your tongue shifted from the back to the front. The three distinctions we make are between *back vowels, central vowels,* and *front vowels.* In many dialects of North American English, the back vowels include [u], [ʊ], [o], and [ɔ]. The central vowels include [ə] and [a].[4] The front vowels include [i], [ɪ], [e], [ɛ], and [æ].

The second distinctive quality of vowels is **height**. We make three distinctions in height for North American English.[5] The *high* vowels include [i], [ɪ], [u], and [ʊ]. The mid vowels include [e], [ɛ], [ə], [o], and [ɔ]. The low vowels include [æ] and [a]. The important quality to practice and note for height is that the absolute highness or lowness of any particular vowel between speakers does not matter. What does matter is the relationships amongst the vowels: For example, your [e] will be lower than your [i].

The third distinction we make for vowels in North American English is between those closer towards the center of the vowel map and those more on the edge. This quality we name **peripherality**, with those vowels closer to the edge of the map being **tense** vowels and those closer to the center being **lax** vowels. The tense and lax distinction largely replaced the long and short system of Old and Middle English.

This system allows us to talk about the vowels in English as each having unique qualities. In *meat* there is a high, front, tense vowel, and in *mitt* there is a high, front, lax vowel. A high, back, tense vowel in *loose* can be described differently from a high, back, lax vowel as in *look.*

Pronounce the words in Table 2.10 out loud:

Table 2.10   Mid, front vowels

[ɛ]	[e]
<bed>	<bade>
<med>	<made>
<fled>	<flayed>
<shed>	<shade>
<sled>	<Slade>
<bet>	<bait>
<net>	<Nate>

For most speakers in the United States, the vowel in the first column is the mid, front, lax vowel [ɛ], and is traditionally called the short "e." The vowel in the second column is the mid, front, tense vowel [e], traditionally called the long "a." As with the vowels of <bit> and <beat>, the difference between these two is that [ɛ] is lax and [e] is tense. What is the pattern of the spelling for [ɛ] and [e]?

A few caveats are in order about vowels. First, do not be surprised if you have moments of confusion when learning the vowel symbols. Your years of extensive training with regular spelling will trip you up at first, but it gets easier with time. Second, these vowels do not accurately describe all English speakers. For example, many British English speakers have a vowel, [ɑ], which is further back than what American English speakers produce, as in the word *bath* (British English [bɑθ] vs. American English [bæθ]). As discussed earlier, many American speakers from the West have a merger between two of these vowels, [a] and [ɔ], as when the words *cot* and *caught* are pronounced the same. If you are one of those speakers with the *cot/caught* merger, you have one less vowel than in Figure 2.3. This merger is also called the low-back merger after its relevant region of vowel space.

Pronounce these words out loud, and identify with phonetic symbols the low, front vowel in English:

A	B
<hat>	<ham>
<bag>	<ban>
<slap>	<Sam>
<Alex>	<fan>

The vowel represented in list A and B is the front vowel [æ]. For some Americans, this vowel is tense, but it is lax for some others. For some Americans, this vowel is pronounced more in the front, mid-region of the mouth, while for others it is low. Pronounce column A and B out loud. Is there a difference in the [æ] produced between the two columns? When we look at dialect variation across dialects of English, we find different pronunciations of this vowel across these words. Try to figure out if anyone in your class has their [æ] vowels higher and possibly more peripheral than other people in your class.

Pronounce the following words out loud, and identify with phonetic symbols the high, back vowels in English:

A	B
<look>	<Luke>
<nook>	<nuke>
<put>	<boot>
<foot>	<shoot>
<stood>	<food>
<good>	<mood>

In these words, the vowels most likely alternate for you. The high, back, lax vowel [ʊ] is in column A. Its comrade, the high, back, tense vowel [u], is in column B.

What is strange about the spelling of the vowels in columns A and B for these two vowels? What is helpful about the phonetic alphabet in comparison with the standard orthographic alphabet in these examples?

There is another set of vowels which English speakers use. These are more complex vowels. They involve moving the tongue and mouth *while* producing the vowels. In the words *my*, *boy*, and *house*, the vowel glides from one place in the mouth to another. These vowels are called **diphthongs**, as they have two parts. Their symbols are combinations of two other vowel symbols, but these are still single vowels: *my* has the [aɪ] vowel; *boy* has the [ɔɪ] vowel; *house* has the [aʊ] vowel. Dialects of English vary greatly between the single-part vowels discussed above, called monophthongs, and the two-part vowels discussed here. For example, some English speakers have the vowel in *day* as the diphthong [eɪ] and the vowel of *boat* as the diphthong [oʊ].

To sum up this section, vowels have three distinctive qualities, and consonants have three distinctive qualities. Consonants are distinguished by voice, place, and manner. Vowels are distinguished by height, advancement, and tenseness. The vowels are further divided between those with stable articulation, the monophthongs, and those with moving articulation, the diphthongs. With those qualities, speakers of English make differences in meanings.

are all language sounds important to all languages?

Some of the sounds discussed for vowels and consonants are found in many of the world's languages. These basic sounds, such as [a] [t] [f], are found in thousands of languages.

Some are less common, such as [θ], [ð], and this one, which English does not have: the voiced pharyngeal fricative/approximant, [ʕ]. Not many languages have that sound. Chechen, spoken by about 1.5 million in Chechnya, has the word [ʕan] 'winter,' and Sioux, spoken by about 33,000 indigenous peoples in the United States and Canada, has the word [maʕazud] 'rain.' To make the [ʕ] sound, take the very back of your tongue and press it against the back of your throat (the pharynx) and release it while saying the [a] vowel. If that does not feel right at first, try to put together this sequence first [aŋa], and then work your tongue further and further back. In between the velar area of the mouth and the pharyngal area is the uvular area; the uvula is that little punching bag that hangs down at the back of your mouth (it often gets confused as tonsils, but those are on the sides).

Some sounds are rare. Clicks used as consonants are found in languages of Africa but rarely outside African languages. As with other consonants, clicks have different places of articulation. Two of them are similar to sounds English speakers make in other contexts, yet both clicks work the same way: Instead of pushing air *out* of the mouth, like a [b], the clicks are created by pulling air into the mouth. The pop-sound of the click is created by the difference in air pressure created before the tongue is released. One of these sounds is a click made with the side of the tongue and the teeth, as some people do to call a dog or a horse. In the Zulu language, spoken by 10 million people mostly in South Africa, the word for the verb *to chat/converse* is *xoxa* [‖ɔ:‖a]. You will need to try this one slowly a few times before trying it at full pace. It would be similar to [tɔ:ta], but replacing the lateral clicks for the [t]s.

The other click is with the front of the tongue and the back of the teeth, as some people do to disapprove of something (pulling the air *in*). These dental clicks appear in other African languages, including the Khoekhoe language spoken in Namibia, Botswana, and South Africa by about 270,000 speakers. Here, the word *rain* is !nanub [|nanup] with a dental click up front before the [n]. You may need to practice this as [tnanup] before you try pulling the air in for the click (see this video for a demonstration: http://www.youtube.com/watch?v=NKEiUHoSAtU).

making a difference: contrasting sounds with minimal pairs

Read through the following list, paying attention to which sounds are the same and which are different.

	A	B
1	<pad>	<bad>
2	<tad>	<dad>
3	<could>	<good>
4	<lobe>	<lope>
5	<mad>	<mat>
6	<buck>	<bug>

The differences between them are with the stops. Listen again to the first sound of A 1–3 and the last sound of A 4–6:

- What three sounds are contrasted in each pair?
- Now compare 1A and 1B? How do the first two sounds differ?
- Compare then the A-B pairs of words in 2–6. In each pair, how do the two different sounds differ?

In each pair of words, there are two different words. These two words differ by a single sound. As speakers of English you know this. *How* you know this is an important question. Two different words that differ by one sound are called a **minimal pair**. How many of these words in the table below are minimal pairs? Minimal pairs are important because they highlight the contrasts native speakers of a language use to distinguish one sound from another. By setting up minimal pairs, we can figure out what sounds make a difference in meaning and what sounds do not.

In the following list, the partial window frame [⌐] (the upper right corner of that window frame) means that the sound before it does not finish. With a sound like [t̚] in [bət̚], the tongue goes to the alveolar ridge but does not pop off to make the stop explosion as in [tʰi] *tea*. Now consider the following list of pronunciations.

A	B
[kɪtɪn]	[kɪʔɪn]
[bətɪn]	[bəʔɪn]
[bætmæn]	[bæʔmæn]
[sit]	[sit̚]
[bək]	[bək̚]
[sɪp]	[sɪp̚]

Read the words in the first three rows out loud. For each pair, there should be a difference of one sound. Does this difference of one sound allow each set to be a minimal pair? Next work through the last three rows: In column A, the sound is a voiceless stop, but in column B, the sound is an unreleased voiceless stop (whatever is stopping the air does immediately release). Are any of the words in 4–6 a minimal pair?

Minimal pairs require that two different pronunciations are connected to two different meanings. The forms [bəgɪŋ] and [bəkɪŋ] are two different words because English speakers have learned to recognize [g]/[k] as different sounds and store them in their mental dictionaries. The forms [kɪtɪn] and [kɪʔɪn] also differ by one sound, but they do not represent different words: The [t]/[ʔ] are different sounds, but English speakers have not learned to store them separately in our mental dictionaries and use them to mark different meanings.

playing with voicing

In this section, you will play with the quality of voice, specifically how to turn the first sounds of <pat> and <bat> into something in-between.

To play with this distinction between "different sounds" and "sounds that make a difference in meaning," think about [t]~[d]. One difference between them is voice: The [t] is voiceless, while the [d] is voiced. Read the following list and listen for any other difference between them:

A	B
[pʰæt]	[pʰæd]
[sit]	[sid]
[tʰun]	[dun]
[tʰim]	[dim]

In the first pair of words, the key sound quality which distinguishes the two alveolar sounds is whether or not the vocal folds are vibrating. In the last two rows, something different is going on for almost all English speakers. The voiceless alveolar stop [t] has some breath attached to it, as if the [h] of <hit> were stuck *in* the [t]. You can feel this if you say [tʰun] and [tʰim] out loud and hold your hand about six inches in front of your mouth. This breath is called **aspiration**. There is a much smaller burst of air when you say [dun] and [dim] out loud. For most people, aspiration is the key quality they listen for in order to distinguish <till> from <dill>. Try to pronounce [tun] and [tim] *without* the aspiration. To do that, you will need to close your glottis slightly or maybe pull back your tongue while making the [t]. The result may sound like a [d] to those around you. Next time you are out in public, try a few words in regular conversation without the aspiration, and see how people react. Aspiration also works with [k] and [p] sounds at the start of words, so you could fit in *It is really a* [kold] *day* and *It is about* [pɪlz] to see if anybody hears *gold* or *bills*.

variation through time: how many sounds did English start with?

Modern English speakers have a few more consonants in their arsenal than did Old English speakers (who lived between 450 and 1100 CE). Many of the same sounds were produced back then, but people did not use them all to mark differences in meaning. For example, the words *heofon* and *efen* were the Old English words for *heaven* and *even*. At the time, the consonant in the middle of each word probably was voiced, but no minimal pair was able to be made with them in Old English. Minimal pairs like *face/vase* did not exist because we had yet to borrow *vase* into the English from French. In Old English, it is safe to say that three fricatives did not make a difference in meaning – [z], [v], [ð] – but acted as partners to the voiceless fricatives – [s], [f], [θ].

Two other sounds were introduced independently. One, the [ŋ] at the end of <ring>, was homegrown while the other, the [ʒ] at the start of <genre>, was imported from France. As the least used nasal in English, [ŋ] was developed over hundreds of years when the alveolar [n] came before the velar stops [k] and [g] in words like *ring* and *sink* (originally pronounced [ɹɪng] and [sɪnk] rather than [ɹɪŋg] and [sɪŋk]). Over time, these nasals became less alveolar and more velar, similar to its following sound.

It is not often that sounds are imported from one language to another, and even after they arrive, they have a tough time holding on. The voiced alveopalatal fricative [ʒ] has never had a large following in English. It is found most often in words such as *genre*, *measure*, and *vision*, all three originating in varieties of French. The words *garage* and *beige* also have [ʒ] for some speakers, but others pronounce them with the affricate [dʒ]. It is doubtful that marketing companies will develop new product names with the [ʒ], unless they want to create a French allure to the product: *Check out the new zuom-zuom; it will zuom your place clean in no time.* In all, the [ʒ] is still an outsider in the inventory of English sounds.

Most Modern English speakers do not have all of the sounds which Old English speakers had. When consonants change, they change slowly, over hundreds of years, not decades. Old English speakers had the sound [x] in words like *right* and *night*. The <gh> letters, which are silent for most Modern English speakers, spoke fully for our linguistic ancestors. The fricative [x] sound is made in the velar [k]/[g] region; instead of an [s] at the alveolar ridge, you have a [x] at the velar portion of the roof of the mouth. This [x] has lasted more than 1,500 years and can still be found in some areas of Scotland. This consonant has been a survivor for native English speakers.

the story of R: part 1

In English writing, the <r> symbol represents several different sounds. Read the following sentence out loud and note where your tongue is highest in the mouth for each R sound: *The horse ran through the worst puddle.* For some students, their tongues during the R sound might be bunched up in the velar region, around the area where we pronounce the [k] of *kick*: a bunched R. For the other students, their tongues lie flatter except for the tip, which is curled back slightly in the front of the mouth: a curled R. One way to test if you have a curled R or a bunched R is by pronouncing the words *horse* and *worst*: If the <s> sounds more like a [ʃ], as in *harsh* or *marsh*, then you probably have curled Rs.

As you probably know, different varieties of English and different languages have different kinds of Rs. Although the trilled Scottish R is socially different from the curled British R, the different US Rs do not seem to have any social values attached to them. Students might even vary between bunched and curled Rs depending on the sound context of the R. Curled Rs are more likely in words like *rat*, *read*, *pry*, or *try* whereas bunched Rs are more likely in words like *bark*, *large*, *poor*, or *fair*. Many speakers of British English, Australian English, and New Zealand English have a vowel sound where the spelled <r> is in words like *soar*, *beer*, and *perk*. With all these different sounds being represented by the same letter, there is a lot of opportunity for confusion when learning to read. It is also a good demonstration for how our spelling system is a historical system, maintaining spellings which represent pronunciations of centuries past.

Some students will not vary between types of R. But, with this next sound variation, almost all English speakers produce different sounds. In human language, some sounds are related to each other, and just like siblings, they sometimes act the same way: The sounds of R and L are such siblings. Like the R sounds, the L sounds can be produced either more in the front of the mouth or more in the back of the mouth, depending on the sound context of the L. Say the words <leaves fall> out loud. For *leaves*, the L sound will probably be in the front of the mouth, called a light L, [l]. For *fall*, the L sound will probably be in the back of the mouth, called a dark L, phonetically [ɫ]. As you work through the following list of words, check where in your mouth the Ls fall. Which column has light [l] and which column has dark [ɫ]?

Different flavors of:
  1. Leak
  2. Laugh
  3. Probably
  4. Lift
  5. Left
  6. Bowl
  7. Cool
  8. Stall
  9. Pull
  10. Control

For most speakers of English, the light [l] will be in the first column, and the dark [ɫ] will be in the second. When the L is in a part of the word where it could be made dark, some dialects turn it not just dark, but completely into a vowel. Just like with the letter <r>, the spelled letter <l> can represent vowels. Across the English-speaking world, in areas of Appalachia as well as areas of Australia, speakers produce words like *doll* and *vowel* with a final vowel. In other words with <l>s, because language norms have changed over the centuries, English speakers vary widely on whether or not they produce L sounds (e.g. *palm, calm, balm, psalm, salmon, wolf, golf, chalk, stalk*).

In the geographical triangle formed by Philadelphia, PA, Columbus, OH, and Knoxville, TN, a lot of speakers have their L sounds made into vowels for words like *fold, bill, vowel*, and *school*. I once received an in-class test where a student from this area wrote that syllables contain "vows and consonants" rather than *vowels* and consonants. As a sonorant, [l] has a very ringing nature to it, wherever it may show up in a word. Part of the tongue makes contact with the roof of the mouth, but for most of the tongue there is no contact. For [l] to slip into a vowel, all that has to happen is for the tongue to lower and lose contact with the roof of the mouth. Remember, the difference between a consonant and a vowel is the degree of constriction. As sounds lose constriction they become more vowel-like. For most communities which have Ls as vowels, this variation is not socially noticed. Historically, it has happened to several words which originally started with an [l] sound, including *walk*, *psalm*, and *folk*.

chapter summary

This chapter detailed how vowels and consonants are produced for human language. These smallest parts are in themselves complex, each composed dynamically with several different articulatory properties. The articulatory phonetics of consonants involve the place, manner, and voice of articulation. The place of articulation for consonants is *where* the sound is made, such as the bilabial sounds [b p] being produced with both lips. The manner of articulation is *how* the sound is made, such as the stop sounds [d t] being produced by stopping the airflow. The voice of articulation is whether the vocal folds vibrate or not during the production of the sound, such as [k] being voiceless and [g] being voiced. The articulatory phonetics of vowels involves the height, advancement, and peripherality of articulation in vowel space, the area in the mouth where vowels are produced. In the mouth, some vowels such as [i] are higher than vowels like [a]. Some vowels like [ɛ] are more advanced toward the front of the mouth than vowels like [o]. Some vowels like [e] are more on the periphery of vowel space than a vowel like [ə] is. Both consonants and vowels vary from production to production, from person to person, and from region to region. We use some of this variation to mark social meanings, although some of the variation goes completely unnoticed.

key concepts

- Advancement
- Affricate
- Alveolar
- Articulatory phonetics
- Aspiration
- Bilabial
- Consonant
- Diphthong
- Fricative
- Glide
- Glottal
- Glottal region
- Glottal stop
- Glottis

- Height
- Homophone
- Insertion
- Interdental
- Labiodental
- Larynx
- Lax
- Liquid
- Manner of articulation
- Minimal pair
- Monophthong
- Nasal
- Obstruents
- Orthographic symbols
- Peripherality
- Phonetics
- Phonetic symbols
- Place of articulation
- Reference meaning
- Social meaning
- Sonorant
- Stop
- Tense
- Velar
- Vocal folds
- Vocal tract
- Voice of articulation
- Voiced
- Voiceless
- Vowel
- Vowel space

Notes

1 The [ʍ] symbol is the voiceless version of [w].
2 http://www.youtube.com/watch?v=lich59xsjik
3 http://www.haskins.yale.edu/featured/heads/mcgurk.html
4 The [a] vowel in the IPA scheme is listed as a front vowel. English speakers around the world fluctuate between front and back low vowels, ranging between the more front [a] and the back [ɑ]. In many Americans' attempted impersonations of British RP speakers, it is the back [ɑ] in <bath> which gets profiled.
5 The IPA scheme describes the vowels by jaw position: High vowels are produced with a closed jaw, and low vowels are produced with an open jaw.

references

An Inconvenient Truth (2009) was released to draw attention to climate change (www. climatecrisis.net/).

http://www.haskins.yale.edu/featured/heads/mcgurk.html

http://www.nataliedee.com/082612

http://www.youtube.com/watch?v=lich59xsjik

http://www.youtube.com/watch?v=NKEiUHoSAtU

www.praat.org

further reading

A Course in Phonetics. Peter Ladefoged and Keith Johnson. 6th edition. 2010. Wadsworth Publishing.

This book provides straightforward description of the scientific analysis of speech, including theories of sound waves, types of analysis, and acoustic phonetic qualities of sounds. A CD of sounds to analyze is included. As you can tell from it being the 6th edition, it is a classic book in phonetic studies.

Sounds of the World's Languages. Peter Ladefoged and Ian Maddieson. 1996. Blackwell.

This book's goal is simple yet extremely ambitious: to phonetically describe the range of sounds in human languages. Data from nearly 400 languages is used. The book works through places of articulation, stops, nasals, fricatives, laterals, rhotics, clicks, vowels, and multiple articulatory gestures. The extensive use of figures and tables makes the book extremely valuable as a reference book also.

Sociophonetics: An Introduction. Erik R. Thomas. 2011. Palgrave Macmillan.

Thomas's book is an approachable introduction to the field of sociophonetics. This field uses acoustic and perceptual analysis to answer sociolinguistic questions. It is one of the fastest growing fields in sociolinguistics because of its strong empirical base and its sophisticated methods. The book covers the different possible studies of production and perception, along with specific techniques for consonants, vowels, prosody, and voice quality. Thomas also takes up the topics of sound change and how to incorporate social analysis into sociophonetics.

exercises

individual work

1. <f>s and <v>s and things like these:

A	B
gift	give
life	live
calf	calves

half	halves
wolf	wolves
loaf	loaves
shift	shriven
press	present
posse	pose
house (N)	house (V)

a.   By checking your vocal folds in your larynx, identify how many of the <f>s are voiceless and how many of the <v>s are voiced.

b.   Next, identify which of the <s>s are voiceless and which of the <s>s are voiced.

c.   Transcribe the preceding words into phonetic script.

2.   The big <th>:

A	B
three	that
thought	there
throw	though
thigh	thy
bath	bathe
teeth	teethe
cloth	clothe
oath	loathe

a.   By checking your vocal folds in your larynx, identify how many of the <th>s are voiceless (i.e. [θ]) and how many of the <th>s are voiced (i.e. [ð]).

b.   Transcribe these words into phonetic script.

c.   Is it harder to figure out the difference between [θ] and [ð] than the difference between [f]/[v] or [s]/[z]. Why might it be harder?

3.   Fricating:

A	B
<fat>	<vat>
<sue>	<zoo>
<thistle>	<this>
<waif>	<wave>
<bus>	<buzz>
<teeth>	<teethe>
<ether>	<either>
<mesher>	<measure>
<shoe>	

(Mesher = One who meshes!)

a.   Say the first letter of A 1–3 out loud: What do these three sounds have in common?

b. Say the first letter of B 1–3 out loud: What do these three sounds have in common?

c. In looking at 4–6, A and B, what is the difference in each pair of words?

d. What is the pronunciation relationship between the first consonants in 7?

e. Numbers 8 and 9 contain two sounds which are not the most common in any variety of English. The sound in 8A and 9 is voiceless, and the sound in 8B is voiced. Can you think of a word in English that begins with a voiced sound like the one in 8B?

4. IPA to orthographic:

Transcribe the following words into orthographic script (regular spelling).

a.   [bo]
b.   [no]
c.   [go]
d.   [flo]
e.   [sto]
f.   [stɹo]
g.   [stɹob]
h.   [stɹobɪŋ]
i.   [tom]
j.   [mot]
k.   [pon]
l.   [nop]
m.   [slop]
n.   [stɹaɪp]
o.   [also]
p.   [flæpɪŋ]
q.   [əðɹ]
r.   [kɹk]
s.   [bɹd]
t.   [ɛləfænt]
u.   [tʃaɪm]
v.   [bɹtʃ]
w.   [kɹitʃɹ]
x.   [skwɪd]
y.   [skjud]
z.   [sədz]
aa. [haɪwe]
bb. [həwaɹi]
cc. [sakɛt]
dd. [bɪldɪŋ]

ee.   [batl]

ff.   [bætl]

gg.   [mɛʒɹ]

hh.   [fləfi]

ii.   [staɹtld]

jj.   [əndɹwətɹ]

kk.   [aɹɹet]

ll.   [pazətɪv]

mm.   [væskjulaɹ]

nn.   [iɹes]

oo.   [æktjuəli]

pp.   [plɛʒɹ]

qq.   [ɛkstɹim]

rr.   [nemz]

ss.   [dʒæklɪn]

tt.   [dʒosɛf]

uu.   [lɪli]

vv.   [mædəlɪn]

ww.   [ɛstɹ]

xx.   [istɹ]

yy.   [mæɹi]

zz.   [bijanse]

aaa.   [dʒelo]

bbb.   [dʒɛlo]

ccc.   [kanje]

ddd.   [ɛmɪnɛn]

eee.   [dænjɛl]

fff.   [ʃaɪlo]

ggg.   [naʊnz]

hhh.   [lɪŋgwɪstɪks]

iii.   [bolts]

jjj.   [pulteblz]

kkk.   [pʊlovɹ]

lll.   [θɔts]

mmm.   [ots]

nnn.   [fɹæktlz]

ooo.   [gɹes]

ppp.   [gɹis]

group work

5. Spoken to IPA:
   Read the following words, written in regular orthographic script, out loud and transcribe *someone else's pronunciation* into IPA:

   a.   prescribe
   b.   percolate
   c.   bribery
   d.   become
   e.   science
   f.   centrifuge
   g.   messenger
   h.   number
   i.   development
   j.   shoe
   k.   cycles
   l.   phone
   m.   glasses
   n.   bag
   o.   hallway
   p.   orangutan
   q.   organ
   r.   Oregon
   s.   NSF
   t.   NATO
   u.   DVD
   v.   MBA
   w.   NBA
   x.   FIFA
   y.   USC
   z.   UofM
   aa. refrigerator
   bb. exaggeration
   cc. university
   dd. desk
   ee. lava lamp
   ff. thermometer
   gg. bathroom
   hh. mother
   ii. moth
   jj. Halloween
   kk. Thanksgiving

ll.   Christmas
mm.   Fourth of July
nn.   kitty-cat
oo.   purr
pp.   bird
qq.   world
rr.   Zappos
ss.   zebras
tt.   wifi
uu.   tissue paper
vv.   leather
ww.   bushes
xx.   garages
yy.   mazes
zz.   confounded
aaa.   amazed
bbb.   tricked
ccc.   Paris
ddd.   Appalachia
eee.   share
fff.   suffer
ggg.   cheeses
hhh.   vacuumed
iii.   couch
jjj.   music
kkk.   roughest
lll.   clothes

6. The distribution of sounds:
   a. Which sounds can appear anywhere in a word (beginning, middle, end of a word)? Provide an example of each.
   b. Which sounds cannot appear everywhere in a word (beginning, middle, end of a word)?
   c. Which sounds do you think are most common?
   d. In English, which sounds are more rare?
   e. Which sounds are easier for making minimal pairs?
   f. Which sounds (and in what positions) are hardest for making minimal pairs?

7. Searching the internet for sounds:
   There are several good locations on the internet to hear recordings of different English voices, including these:

   Accents of English: http://accent.gmu.edu/
   IDEA: http://www.dialectsarchive.com/
   BBC Voices: http://www.bbc.co.uk/voices/

Using these sites, collect together five examples of English words from other dialects whose vowels are different from your own. Note for each one how the vowel is pronounced differently, describing it with phonetic symbols.

8. Vowel differences:

A	B
<bought>	<boat>
<fought>	<float>
<naught>	<note>
<sought>	<soak>
<caught>	<quote>
<hawk>	<hoax>

The vowels in column A are pronounced differently than those in column B for most Americans. The vowel that is traditionally pronounced for A is [ɔ], the mid, back, lax vowel. In column B is [o], the mid, back, tense vowel.

How many minimal pairs are in this dataset? Why aren't the others minimal pairs?

9. Merging:

A	B
<caught>	<cot>
<talk>	<tock>
<hawk>	<hock>
<Dawn>	<Don>
<Salk>	<sock>

Say columns A and B out loud. If you do not pronounce the vowels in columns A and B differently, please identify yourself to your instructor, and special seating will be arranged for you. With proper training, your instructor should be able to correct your horrible speech impediment by the end of the semester. Perhaps the morbid culture which fostered this kind of decaying language can also be eradicated from your system in the upcoming remedial language sessions.

Actually, you are just fine. If these words sound the same in your pronunciation, you have one of the most geographically widespread vowel mergers in the United States. This change is one of the many vowel mergers around the world. What is interesting about this merger is its lack of social stigmatization (which is why the previous satirical paragraph {might have} worked: no one has strong negative feelings about it). Few people are aware of this merger and relatively few have been picked on for it. Why might people with this vowel merger not be socially stigmatized?

10. Spelling vs. sounding:
    In the following table, read across these words, working left to right for each row. For many speakers in the United States, the first column has the vowel in <boot>, the second has either the vowel of the first column or the vowel in the third column. The third column has the vowel as in <nook>, and the fourth column has the vowel as in <bud>.
    Vowel differences in English for the <oo> spelling:

[u]	[u] ~ [ʊ]	[ʊ]	[ə]
groom, boom, gloom, loom, bloom	room, broom		
aloof, hoof, groove	hoof, roof, behoove		
shoot	soot		soot
moot, boot, loot	root		
food, brood, mood		stood, wood, good, hood	flood, blood
loon, boon, soon, spoon, noon			
loop, stoop	whoop, hoop		
spook		book, cook, look, hook, shook	

- Do your pronunciations match the columns in which they are categorized?
- As far as we can tell from the history of the English language, all of the double <oo> spellings started off as the Middle English long-o sound, the modern pronunciation [o]. Starting around 1500, because of a change we explore in Chapter 3 called the Great Vowel Shift, these vowels started to drift. In terms of vowel space, what path do you suspect these vowels have traveled over the years?

11. Consonant keyword chart:
    These are suggested keywords for each sound. Your ideal keywords may be different from the ones listed here:

<Keyword>	Consonant	Descriptor	Phonetic Transcription
pat	p	voiceless, bilabial, stop	[pæt]
bat	b	voiced, bilabial, stop	[bæt]
tight	t	voiceless, alveolar, stop	[taɪt]
dad	d	voiced, alveolar, stop	[dæd]
keep, cut	k	voiceless, velar, stop	[kip], [kət]

<Keyword>	Consonant	Descriptor	Phonetic Transcription
gate	g	voiced, velar, stop	[get]
uh-oh	ʔ	voiceless, glottal, stop	[əʔo]
church	tʃ	voiceless, palatal, affricate	[tʃɹtʃ]
joke	dʒ	voiced, palatal, affricate	[dʒok]
thigh	θ	voiceless, interdental, fricative	[θaɪ]
thy, father	ð	voiced, interdental, fricative	[ðaɪ], [faðɹ]
fee	f	voiceless, labiodental, fricative	[fi]
vote	v	voiced, labiodental, fricative	[vot]
sea, soft, pass	s	voiceless, alveolar, fricative	[si], [sɔft], [pæs]
zit	z	voiced, alveolar, fricative	[zɪt]
sheep, bush	ʃ	voiceless, palatal, fricative	[ʃip], [bʊʃ]
measure, vision	ʒ	voiced, palatal, fricative	[mɛʒɹ], [vɪʒɪn]
Bach, van Gogh,	x	voiceless, velar, fricative	[bax], [vɑŋgɔx]
house, hot	h	voiceless, glottal, fricative	[haʊs], [hat]
yum, mat	m	voiced, bilabial, nasal	[jəm], [mæt]
tan, name	n	voiced, alveolar, nasal	[tæn], [nem]
ring	ŋ	voiced, velar, nasal	[rɪŋ]
lake	l	voiced, alveolar~velar, liquid	[lek]
river	ɹ	voiced, alveolar~velar, liquid	[ɹɪvɹ]
whip	ʍ	voiceless, bilabial, glide	[ʍɪp]
wish	w	voiced, bilabial, glide	[wɪʃ]
yes, yuck	j	voiced, palatal, glide	[jɛs], [jək]

study questions

1. Which came first: language or writing?
2. Is writing a human invention?
3. What are orthographic symbols, and how are they represented?
4. How is our spelling system a historical system?
5. What are phonetic symbols, and how are they represented?
6. What is sound symbolism?
7. Are vowels or consonants more likely to change?
8. What is a vowel merger?
9. What is social meaning?
10. What is phonetics?
11. What is articulatory phonetics?
12. What is the difference between vowels and consonants?
13. What are the three qualities of consonants?
14. What is the difference between sonorants and obstruents?
15. What is the manner of articulation?
16. Which manners are the sonorants?
17. What do the vocal folds do?
18. What is the difference between voiced and voiceless sounds?
19. What does the vowel map represent?
20. What was the change that eliminated long and short vowel distinctions?
21. What qualities distinguish vowels from each other in English?
22. What is the low-back merger?
23. What are monophthongs?
24. Does every language have every human language sound?
25. What is a language sound that is absent from English?
26. What are minimal pairs, and how are they useful?
27. Do all sound differences trigger a difference in meaning?
28. What is aspiration?
29. What are the different pronunciations of <r>?
30. What is the difference between a light and dark <l>?

Visit the book's companion website for additional resources relating to this chapter at: http://www.wiley.com/go/hazen/introlanguage

3 Patterns of Sounds

An Introduction to Language, First Edition. Kirk Hazen.
© 2015 John Wiley & Sons, Inc. Published 2015 by John Wiley & Sons, Inc.

chapter overview

This chapter explores the patterns we weave with language sounds. Starting with simple pairs of words, the contrastive qualities of sounds illustrate how people use patterns with meanings, both reference meanings and social meanings. We engage the ideas of natural classes and syllables to find the hidden structure in our language. The chapter then turns to several different sound patterns of English that we use regularly, but ones which students have most likely not noticed were part of their daily speech. From familiar sounds, we move on to other languages where the sound patterns use the same machinery, but with different results. There is variation in these sound patterns, both between people now and over time. In looking at variation in sound patterns through time, we work through problems such as why *gift/give* divided the <f/v> between them. Sound patterns are still in variation today, and we take up dialect differences at the end of the chapter.

predictable differences

In the last chapter, the nature of sounds was introduced by looking at their differences and similarities. This chapter also deals with differences, but it will focus on predictable differences in sound patterns. A sound like [t] by itself does not make meaning. It does more work in *stick* [stɪk], because it distinguishes between *sick* [sɪk] and *stick* [stɪk]. For language, the contrast between sounds marks meanings. These patterns are organized and systematic.

meanings with minimal pairs

In the words *pick* [pɪk] and *pit* [pɪt], the only difference is in the contrast of [k] and [t]. For the child acquiring a language, or the second-language learner picking up the language, the [k] sound and the [t] sound are *not* predictable. There is no way to know that the last consonant in the word for 'choose' is going to be a voiceless, velar stop [k]. That is the nature of arbitrariness and works the same for all languages.

So, all those sound combinations that are unpredictable have to be memorized. It seems like a gargantuan task, especially considering that in a language like English, most people know at least 30,000 words. The sounds have to be stored as parts for all the words in the mental lexicon, but note that we do not have 30,000 distinct sounds, just combinations to represent that many words. In this book, we distinguish the *mental* symbols for sounds with forward slashes /k/ rather than in square brackets [k]. This allows us to easily (and visually) recognize a mental form as it is stored in the lexicon (e.g. /kɪn/) and the out-loud pronunciation (e.g. [kʰɪ̃n]), which is a normal pronunciation of *kin* in US English.

With words like /pɪk/ <pick> and /pɪt/ <pit> or /pɪl/ <pill> and /kɪl/ <kill>, the /k/ and the /p/ contrast to distinguish the meanings of the words. These nearly matching words are called minimal pairs. A minimal pair is a set of two separate words which differ in form by one contrasting sound.

In the exercise below, think up a minimal pair for each context with the following sets of sounds. Remember, to have a minimal pair, the two sounds in question must contrast with each other, and no other sounds in the word can contrast. The sounds themselves, such as their voice, place, or manner, do not make the contrast, but the psychological difference for native speakers does make the contrast.

Example:

[b, f]
Word initially   [bən]   [fən]
Word finally   [læb]   [læf]

[s, l]
Word initially   _____   _____
Word finally   _____   _____

[g, t]
Word initially   _____   _____
Word finally   _____   _____

[e, i]
Word initially   _____   _____
Word finally   _____   _____

The examples above (from American English) clearly contrast by one sound in phonetic script, but it is sometimes harder to figure out with letters: *bun, fun*; *lab, laugh*. The word *laugh* looks like it is different by three letters, but letters are not the focus. Minimal pairs tell us about the structure of a language's sound system. Because you are able to find minimal pairs with [g, t], we know that those two sounds must be stored in the lexicon for words like [bæg] and [bæt].

Some sounds in English are more difficult to make minimal pairs with the other sounds. Try to make a minimal pair with the interdental fricatives [θ, ð]. As another challenge, are there any minimal pairs in English which differ only by whether the vowel is nasalized or not?

Now consider the following forms: Are all three distinct words in English?

_____ [kɪtɪn] _____   _____ [kɪʔɪn] _____   _____ [kɪtʃɪn] _____

The first and last forms are a minimal pair (*kitten* and *kitchen*), but the middle one is just a different way to say *kitten*. Although [kɪtɪn] and [kɪʔɪn] are different forms, they are *not* a minimal pair because those two forms have the same meaning (and they would not be considered synonyms). What do [kɪtɪn] and [kɪʔɪn] tell us about how the sounds [t] and [ʔ] are stored in the lexicon? Those two sounds do not need to be separately distinguished in the lexicon because they do not trigger a difference in meaning. There is no minimal pair in English where [t] and [ʔ] contrast. How then would the word *kitten* be stored in our mental lexicon? The most distinctive way to store it would be as /kɪtɪn/. The mental grammar could then have a rule to change the /t/ to a [ʔ] when needed.

The mental representations of sounds in the lexicon are called **phonemes**. Phonemes are the smallest units of language that make a difference in meaning. The sounds [t] and [k] are distinctive sounds in English because they trigger differences in meaning for English speakers, and they can be represented therefore as separate phonemes: /t/ and /k/. The sounds [t] and [ʔ] are *not* distinctive sounds in English because they do not trigger differences in meaning for English speakers, and they can be represented in the lexicon by the phoneme /t/.

To work through the idea of phonemes and the mental grammar's transformation of sounds, consider what happens to the vowels in the following words (as pronounced in US English).

1. [bĩn]   \<bin\>   [bɪd]   \<bid\>
2. [ɹʌ̃ŋ]   \<rung\>   [ɹʌg]   \<rug\>
3. [kɹæ̃m]   \<cram\>   [kɹæb]   \<crab\>

Try these words as pairs. Listen (and feel) for the difference between the vowel in the first member of the pair and the second one. If you have trouble hearing a difference, pinch your nose while saying them. The first vowel in each pair is nasalized and should sound funny while your nose is pinched. The second vowel is not nasalized.

As you can probably tell, each vowel in the first column comes before a nasal consonant. On our consonant chart in Chapter 2, nasals fall towards the end of the consonant chart with other sonorants. As sonorants, nasals are closer to being vowels than sounds like [k] and [s], which are obstruents. Because of that quality, in these words, the nasal sound bleeds into the preceding vowel, affecting how it sounds. Note that it only works for preceding vowels: In the words [no] *no*, [nalɪdʒ] *knowledge*, and [nət] *nut*, the following vowels are not nasalized.

Given that we have both nasalized and non-nasalized vowels in English, how do they get represented as phonemes in the mental lexicon? Should a vowel like [ɪ] be separately represented in the lexicon from a vowel like [ĩ]? The standard answer can be found with minimal pairs. Are there any minimal pairs in English which differ only by whether the vowel is nasalized or not? No, to get a nasalized vowel in English, there has to be a following nasal consonant. The phonemes of *bin*, *rung*, and *cram* would be the following:

Lexicon	/bɪn/	/ɹəŋ/	/kɹæm/
Phonological Rule	N a s a l i z a t i o n		
Pronunciation	[bĩn]	[ɹə̃ŋ]	[kɹæ̃m]

The part of the mental grammar that handles the external expression of language is called **phonology**.[1] For a spoken language like English, a speaker's phonology produces sounds from the phonemes (the raw material), modifying them to fit the patterns of the language. The specific patterns applied to the phonemes can be considered rules. The phonemes are the input to the rule, and the sounds you hear are the output.

Words to the Wise: The physicality of nasals

Nasalization is not a mysterious process if you understand how nasals get made. In the mouth, the roof is labeled with different names. The area where you produce a [g] is called the velum or soft palate. If you feel it with your finger, you can note that it is softer than the bony structure at the front of your mouth where you produce a [dʒ] sound. The hard palate cannot move, but the velum can, and when swallowing, it covers up the passages to the nose (no one likes food up their nose). When speaking, the velum raises and lowers, covering over the nasal passages for some sounds but not others. For oral sounds (e.g. [b] [s] [ɹ] [j]) the velum covers the nasal passages, only allowing air to flow through the mouth. For nasal sounds (e.g. [m] [ŋ] [ẽ] [õ]), the velum is lowered and air escapes out the nose. For the nasal consonants [m] [n] [ŋ], the air *only* flows out the nose; for the nasal vowels (e.g. [ũ]) the air flows out the mouth and the nose.

some sound patterns linked with social meaning

The difference between nasalized and non-nasalized vowels does not trigger a meaning difference for speakers of English. In a language like French, however, nasalization does make a difference in meaning. The words *beau* [bo] and *bon* [bõ] only differ by that **nasalization**, and these two words form a minimal pair in French. An important point to note is that the quality of the sound (nasalized or not) does not trigger the difference in meaning. Instead, the contrast in the phonology is set up by having words in the lexicon stored with those sounds. We use the patterns of the sounds to distinguish words. Because of these differences, French phonology has different sound patterns from English. You can hear French accents in English and English accents in French because of these different phonologies. When listening to other languages, part of the lack of understanding is the difference in phonological patterns.

Some nondistinctive sound patterns in English do trigger *social meanings*. **Social meanings** are connections between language and social groups, and these connections are a regular part of what humans do. For example, at the word level, the word *rock n' roll* was originally associated with African Americans before it became mainstream. As noted in Chapter 2, at the sound level, certain patterns of sounds get associated with certain groups. In the US North, pronouncing *with* as [wɪf] or *birthday* as [bɹ̩fde] is associated with lower social classes. This kind of sound variation can be considered a **social minimal pair**. In the US North, the switch between [bɹ̩fde] and [bɹ̩θde] triggers a difference in social meaning in the same way that the switch between [fĩn] and [θĩn] triggers a switch in reference meaning. In some rural parts of the US South, switching [f] for [θ] goes completely unnoticed because it is not associated with any particular social group, and it would not make social minimal pairs in those areas. The ability to connect certain sound patterns to specific social meanings appears to be a natural human quality and is most likely part of our evolutionary history. The most widespread set of examples are regional affiliations associated with certain sound patterns. In the United States, the backed British [ɑ] in a word like *bath* is usually associated with higher social class standing and perhaps a pompous attitude, regardless of the actual attitude of the speaker. A tensed /ɪ/ in a word like [piˀt] <pit> is often seen as a Southern US feature.

The linguistic qualities of a sound are not naturally connected to any certain social meaning. It would be ludicrous to argue that people in the US North disliked [f]s in general, although the idea of a raucous, anti-voiceless-labiodental-fricatives group is funny ("Down with VLFs! VLFs are corrupting our children!"). For some sound patterns, one region may view it as lowly and another may view it as prestigious. The best example is R-dropping. This sound pattern involves making [ɹ]s into vowels when they come at the end of syllables, like in *soar* as [soɔ] or *hard* as [haːd]. With R-dropping, the vowel is longer because the [ɹ] has become part of it.[2] In the US South since World War II, R-dropping has been heard as "country," "redneck," or "poor." R-dropping could be used to make

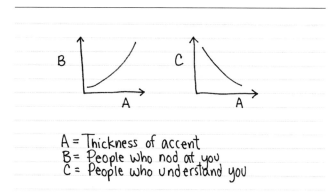

A = Thickness of accent
B = People who nod at you
C = People who understand you

Figure 3.1 The term accent usually refers to the phonological patterns of a dialect (and everyone has a dialect). What does thickness mean in this *Indexed* comic? http://thisisindexed.com/2013/08/and -they-speak-loudly-and-slowly-to-help-you-understand/. Rollover text: "fun with dialects." *Indexed,* by © Jessica Hagy.

social minimal pairs in that region. In England, Australia, and New Zealand, R-dropping is the prestige form. The sound pattern of R-dropping is linguistically the same in all these regions, but it is associated with different social groups, and its social meanings are therefore different.

structure

natural classes

The phonology in a person's mental grammar does not randomly decide on patterns. **Phonological rules** do not work like this: "The sounds [ŋ ɛ s] all change to [d]." Communication with language might not even work with such random rules. Instead, phonological rules operate with groups of sounds called **natural classes**. These are divided by the qualities of the sounds, and in Chapter 2 you learned about many of them. Divisions in the place of articulation, such as bilabial, alveolar, and velar, are all natural classes. In other words, we can talk about what happens to alveolars as a group of sounds. The same is true for the natural classes of manner, where we can describe sound patterns with groups like stops, fricatives, and glides. The division between voiced and voiceless sounds is also a natural class. This kind of description is important for understanding a common phonological process like nasalization, where the natural class of nasals affects the natural class of vowels.

Beyond the natural classes of place, manner, and voice for consonants, vowels also have natural classes. Vowels' natural classes fall along the dimensions we use to qualify them, namely height, advancement, and peripherality. Phonology sometimes works with front vowels or with tense vowels. Some of the sound changes discussed later in this book affect front lax vowels and front tense vowels in different ways.

After the major divisions of vowels and consonants, three other natural classes are the focus of phonological rules: **sibilants**, obstruents, and sonorants.

- Sibilants are hissing sounds. The language Parseltongue from the world of Harry Potter consists mostly of sibilants. There are six sibilants: [s] as in *Sue*, [z] as in *zoo*, [ʃ] as in *shoe*, [ʒ] as in *genre*, [tʃ] as in *chew*, and [dʒ] as in *Jew*. When you get these sounds together, which never happens during regular speech, you get a steady hissing: [s] [z] [ʃ] [ʒ] [tʃ] [dʒ].
- Obstruents are blocking sounds. People block the air in a wide variety of sounds. Obstruents include stops ([p] [b] [t] [d] [k] [g] [ʔ]), fricatives ([f] [v] [θ] [ð] [s] [z] [ʃ] [ʒ] [h]), and affricates ([tʃ] [dʒ]). These sounds do not let the air flow freely, either by stopping it or by causing a lot of turbulence.
- Sonorants are ringing sounds. These are the liquids ([l] [ɹ]), nasals ([n] [m] [ŋ]), glides ([w] [j]), and vowels ([i] [ɪ] [e] [ɛ] [æ] [a] [ə] [o] [ɔ] [u] [ʊ] [aɪ] [ɔɪ] [aʊ]). For these sounds, there is less constriction in the mouth, and they fall out more freely.

What natural classes do the following sets of sounds belong to?

[o ʊ ɔ] _____

[t s f] _____

[d z] _____

[k g] _____

[i e æ] _____

Obstruents are half of all language sounds; sonorants are the other half. Voiced sounds and voiceless sounds also divide up all sounds into two groups, yet these groupings are not the same as obstruents and sonorants. As a natural-class check, are there voiced obstruents? Can there be voiceless sonorants?

In the following sections, natural classes play a role in the phonological patterning of sounds.

syllables

Phonology uses lots of methods for putting sounds into patterns. One of these methods involves grouping sounds together into **syllables**. Syllables are templates for sounds. Like cookie cutters pressed into dough, syllable templates separate the material into different shapes. Different languages have different types of syllables, but all languages share some basic ones, such as a C(onsonant) V(owel) syllable (e.g. CV = [ma]). Although there are lots of different models for how syllables work, the one provided here is direct enough to illustrate how all the cookies of syllables get made from the dough of sound.

Syllables are the first step in a discussion of **hierarchy**. Hierarchy is the quality of having some units nested inside of other units, like mixing bowls stacked one in the other. When discussing hierarchy, instead of bowls holding other bowls, linguists talk of **nodes** dominating other nodes (see Figure 3.2). For syllables, the top level is the node which holds the entire syllable, represented by lower case sigma: σ. Connected to that node are two divisions, the **onset** and **rhyme**. In every syllable, the onset comes before the rhyme. The rhyme is divided into two subdivisions on the third level of a syllable diagram: the **nucleus** and the **coda**.

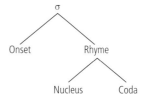

Figure 3.2   A blank syllable tree.

The three levels of the syllable allow us to see how sounds are organized by phonology in the mental grammar. In this template the onset and the coda are optional. Only the nucleus is required. So a syllable could be just a single vowel, as in the word *a* of *a book*:

The nucleus is the fulcrum on which the syllable balances. Like a teeter-totter (or perhaps see-saw in your dialect), the onset and coda are attached to that core through two connections. For all languages, there is a large bias for one side of that balance: Onsets are greatly favored and much more frequent than codas in human language.

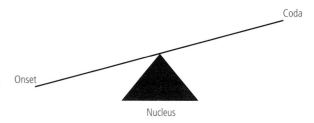

Figure 3.3   A teeter-totter of a syllable.

Syllables such as <bay>, <flay>, and <stray> represent the diversity of onsets in English. Up to three consonants in the onset are possible in English, but as discussed later, the possible choices are highly structured. Most languages do not allow for this range of onsets. See the three figures below for some sample onsets.

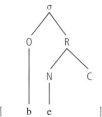
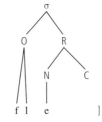
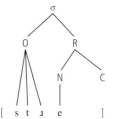

Codas in general are more limited. Some languages do not allow codas at all (e.g. Hua, spoken in Singapore, and Hawaiian). English, with its Germanic roots, is unusual in that it allows one, two, or three consonants in the coda, although most people reduce three-consonant codas to just two consonants. Consider the following one-syllable words with codas of three different complexities: <Len>, <lens>, <lengths>.

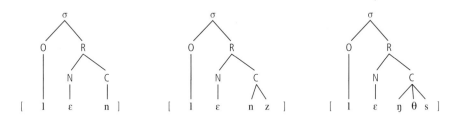

For multisyllabic words, the syllable nodes go one after the other, as in the word <biting>.

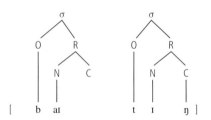

One question you should ask is why the [t] of [tɪŋ] is not in the coda of the first syllable. Although it could be for some speakers, some of the time, for most speakers the tendency is to have it in the onset. This tendency is called **onset maximization**. It is such a strong trend that we find its consequences in many places in language. First, when babies babble, they do so with CV syllables (e.g. mama, dada), and not VC syllables (e.g. am am; ad ad). Second, throughout all the world's languages, the most common syllable structure is CV. No language has a VC syllable template that does not have a CV structure, although many have CV syllables but do not allow VC syllables. Onset maximization is variable in languages which allow codas, but for drawing syllable trees, the simplest thing to do is draw them in this order: 1. Nucleus; 2. Onset; 3. Coda. Try it here:

σ

σ

O   R

O   R

N

C

N

C

[f   aɪ   t   ɪ   ŋ]

Consider the following words and render their phonetic forms into syllable templates.

Single syllable words:
a
ab
row
robe
tribe
strike
ant
strengths

Multiple syllable words:
straighten
bowling
Mississippi
shrapnel
buying
bilking

Words to the Wise: Syllable diversity in language

Syllables are a basic part of human language, but their structures vary widely. Some languages have only the most simple syllables possible. Blevins (1995:217) cites a language like Hua, spoken in Botswana, as having only one syllable type: every syllable has to be a CV combination. That does not restrict the size of their words, nor does it impede the ability of people to communicate in Hua. It just means that it is a different kind of language. In contrast, English has over ten syllable templates, although some, such as CCCVCCC support many fewer words than the basic CV shape.

Different languages also allow different kinds of sounds to be the nucleus of their syllables. A language like Estonian, the predominant language in Estonia and spoken by more than a million people worldwide, allows for up to three vowels worth of sound in the same nucleus, CVVVC. The language Shilha, a Berber language in Morocco, can have obstruents such as [s] and [f] as the nuclei of syllables, allowing for words such as "t-fk-t=stt" 'you gave it.'

possible and impossible combinations

Onsets in English can have up to three consonants, but that does not mean it is a free-for-all competition to see which sounds get which slots. Syllables are not mosh pits. There are restrictions. For the one-consonant onsets, the competition is more wide open, with only [ŋ] and [ʔ] disqualified as potential onsets. This disqualification is called a **phonotactic constraint**. It is not a biological impossibility to have [ŋ] and [ʔ] as single onsets, but the normal sound patterns that English children ingest do not contain such forms as [ŋa] or [ʔa]. Comparing across languages illustrates some different patterns. For example, the African language Wolof allows the velar nasal [ŋ] to start some words, such as *you*, the second person pronoun: *Degg nga* [ŋa] *Wolof?* 'Do you understand Wolof?' Looking at the pronunciation of borrowed words in different languages also illustrates different phonotactic constraints. The word *psychology*, originally from Greek, has become part of English and French. In English, the onset of the first syllable is [s], but in French, the onset is [ps], which is not a possible onset in English.

For the two-consonant onset, the choices are more limited by phonotactic constraints. Only most stops and fricative can combine with a following liquid (see Table 3.1). The exception is the prolific [s], which can combine with voiceless stops as well as [l]: [stap] or [slap]. As [s] and [ɹ] are very similar, they find the close confines of an onset too small to be wedged together; consequently, we have no [sɹ] onsets in English.

For the three-consonant onset, the choices are yet even more limited: only one possible first sound, the prolific [s]; only one narrow natural class in second position, voiceless stops [p t k]; and the liquid [ɹ] in third position. The sound [s] also gets special privileges for the three-consonant onset, as it is able to afford the [spl] combination in words like *splay* and *splice*. For the majority of three-consonant onsets in English, only four sounds work. Table 3.1 provides the breakdown for possible onset combinations in English.

Table 3.1 Possible onset combinations in English

Onset type	C	CC		CCC		
Natural classes	Consonants (except [ŋ] and [ʔ])	Stops (except [ʔ])				
		Fricatives (except [ʒ] and [h])	liquids [l ɹ]	[s]	Voiceless stops [p] [t] [k]	[ɹ]
Exceptions		[s] combines with voiceless stops like in *sky*		[spl] and a few [skl] words like *sklent* and *sclerosis*		
Examples	[bo] <bow>	[pɹo] <pro>		[stre] <stray>		
	[ðo] <though>	[blo] <blow>		[spɹe] <spray>		
	[no] <no>	[θɹu] <through>		[skɹep] <scrape>		
	[ʃo] <show>	[tɹu] <true>		[sple] <splay>		
	[jo] <yo>	[slo] <slow>		[splæʃ] <splash>		
	[ho] <hoe>	[ʃɹæpnəl] <shrapnel>				

Some combinations are more rare and come into English from other languages: Except for "vroom," the most <vr> combinations in English are from French (e.g. *vraisemblance*). The velar nasal is not possible in the onset position in English, except for names from languages which allow them. For example, Ngũgĩ wa Thiong'o is a novelist from Kenya whose Bantu language Gĩkũyũ allows for velar nasals in the onset. Glottal stops are not fully stops (but more like a short burst of creaky voice) and are not produced by native English speakers in the onset.

Some onsets are more rare than others. The [s] and [t] sounds are common in English, but the [ʒ] sound is more rare (e.g. *genre* entered from French at the end of the eighteenth century). In Old English, [h] combinations with [ɹ l n] sounds in the onset were possible, with words such as *hrōc* 'rook,' *hlūd* 'loud,' *hnutu* 'nut.' For quite a long time, [hw] combinations were the norm in English, with Old English *hwelp* 'whelp,' *hwīl* 'while,' and *hwǣr* 'where' as examples. For some dialects of English, words such as *which* [ʍɪtʃ] and *witch* [wɪtʃ] are still distinct.

In all languages, the syllable pattern follows a simple plan of sonority. **Sonority** is a quality which sonorants have more of and obstruents have less of. It is the amount of "ringyness" a sound has, or more technically, the amplitude of the sound waves (given the same amount of energy put into the sound). The manners of the consonants in Table 2.2 are arranged top to bottom from least to most sonorant. Stops are the least sonorant sounds, and glides are the most sonorant consonants. In a word like *Bob* [bab], the sonority rises from the onset to the nucleus and falls between the nucleus and the coda. This works for a syllable like *trench* [tɹɛntʃ]:

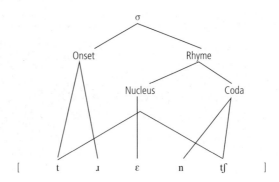

sound patterns

a sample consonant pattern

We are pattern matching machines. We find bunnies in clouds and religious figures on toast. Much of our early survival as a species was based on recognizing patterns: The ability to distinguish between leaves moving from the wind or a predator can keep you alive. Our language is also a large set of interwoven patterns. In this section, we work through several patterns of sounds, some of which trigger social meaning and some of which do not.

One pattern involves [l]. There are different flavors of [l] depending on the surrounding sound environment. Consider the following data.

List 1: Different flavors of <l>
1. a. Leak   b. Bowl
2. a. Laugh   b. Cool
3. a. Probably   b. Control
4. a. Lift   b. Stall
5. a. Left   b. Pull
6. a. Leaf   b. Fall

In column A, the [l] sound is produced further to the front of the tongue, closer to the high front region of the [i] sound. In column B, the [ɫ] sound is further back in the mouth, near the velar area of [g]. When it is pulled further back in the mouth, it is less of a consonant and more of a vowel. That is to say, there is less constriction with the front of the tongue. The L sound at the front of the mouth is a light [l], and the L sound at the velar area is called a dark [ɫ]. What is the environment where these sounds occur? The light [l] is in the onset of syllables and sometimes in the coda after high front vowels (e.g. [bɪl] *bill*, [bil] *Beale*). The dark [ɫ] sound appears in codas most prominently after back vowels (e.g. [bɔɫ] *ball,* [fɔɫ] *foal*). Welsh English, spoken in Wales, is known for its clear Ls, even in coda position (e.g. [skul] *school*).

a sample vowel pattern

Vowels have different kinds of patterns. Vowel mergers happen when the distinction between two separate phonemes is lost. As discussed in Chapter 2, for many speakers in the US and Canada, the two words *cot* and *caught* are pronounced the same. As you can see from their spelling, they were previously pronounced with different vowels by all English speakers and continue to be distinct in the US Northeast and parts of the US South. For the merged speakers, the different sounds of [a] and [ɔ] are no longer linked to separate words: For example, *caught* could be either [kʰat] or [kʰɔt], and no one in the merged communities will hear a difference.

This merger is called the **low-back merger** because it involves two vowels from the low-back region of vowel space. When speakers have this merger, they have one vowel phoneme instead of two. It is not a deficiency, but it is a different organization in their lexicon.

In the following list of words, many American English speakers have the low-back merger. In some parts of Ohio, speakers may have it only before /t/ or /n/.

The low-back merger:

1. don   dawn
2. hock   hawk
3. cot   caught
4. bot (robot)   bought
5. knot   naught

In the next list is another common merger, the **front-lax merger**. In this phonological process, the /ɪ/ and /ɛ/ vowels are sometimes pronounced the same. From the following list, can you discern under what conditions the two vowels are pronounced the same?

Pronounced the same
1. Jim   gem
2. tin   ten
3. bin   Ben
4. Tim's   Thames (with an /ɛ/ vowel)
5. ping   penguin

Pronounced differently
1. pit   pet
2. nick   neck
3. bid   bed

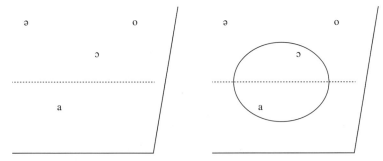

Figure 3.4 Representation of the low-back merger.

4. pig   peg
5. bliss   bless
6. crypt   crept

For many Southerners in the United States, the vowels in the first list are pronounced as [ɪ] before nasal sounds. Unlike the low-back merger discussed above, the front-lax merger is a **conditioned merger** in the United States. For this merger, the **conditioning environment** is before nasals. In other English-speaking areas, such as Australia, the /ɪ/ and /ɛ/ vowels are merged in more environments than just nasals. One former performer from the famous Australian children's music group, The Wiggles,[3] was named "Jeff" (the dude in the purple shirt, now retired). Plenty of kids outside of Australia heard him pronounce his name as "Jiff," leaving some children to wonder if his parents named him after a type of peanut butter.

Considering the conditioned front-lax merger is phonologically less extensive than the unconditioned low-back merger, it would make sense if the front-lax merger were less noticed. Yet, this is not the case in the United States. The front-lax merger is much more stigmatized outside of the US South, and its speakers receive many more comments about it. The low-back merger is not associated with any social group, whereas the front-lax merger is generally associated with African-Americans and most Southerners. Both of those social groups have received more than their fair share of stigma over the years, and the front-lax merger has been stigmatized accordingly.

schwa rule

The next phonological process can be considered the **schwa rule**. The vowel schwa is dead in the center of the mouth and is the most lax of lax vowels. In a lingual magic trick, this phonological process turns any vowel into a schwa under the right conditions. Consider the following list, and try to figure out when the schwas are produced:

1. *about* /əbaʊt/   → [əbaʊt]
2. *because* /bikəz/   → [bəkəz]
3. *the* /ði/   → [ðə]
4. *pencil* /pɛnsɪl/   → [pɛ̃nsəl]
5. *elocution* /ɛlokjuʃɪn/   → [ɛləkjuʃɔ̃n]

In these words, the schwa appears in unstressed syllables. Consider the word *elocution*. If you say each syllable with the same amount of stress, as if you are testing each sound, you can come out with /ɛlokjuʃɪn/ as a pronunciation. In normal conversation, the first and third syllables (/ɛl/ and /kju/, respectively) receive the main stress, but the second and fourth syllables do not. When a vowel is unstressed, it can be transformed into schwa. The word *the* can receive primary stress in a sentence, such as *I want THE drink,* and when it does, the vowel is [i]. Most of the time, however, *the* does not receive the main stress in a sentence and therefore has schwa as a vowel.[4] As one of the most common rules in English, the schwa rule transmogrifies a lot of vowels every day.

deletion and insertion

In casual conversation, it is normal to delete sounds which might otherwise have been used. **Deletion** is a phonological process where certain sounds in a word are not produced. Schwas, created by the previous phonological process, are often subject to deletion. Consider *about* and *because*. These two words are often rendered as [baʊt] and [kəz]. It is also normal to delete consonants at the ends of syllables. Say these words out loud: *west side*; *lived there*; *park grill*.

west side	[wɛs saɪd] or [wɛst saɪd] ?
lived there	[lɪv ðɛɹ] or [lɪvd ðɛɹ] ?
park grill	[paɹ gɹɪl] or [paɹk gɹɪl] ?

Do you pronounce the final consonant of the first word?

Next, try these words out loud: *west over*; *lived on*; *park out*.

west over	[wɛs ovɹ] or [wɛst ovɹ] ?
lived on	[lɪvɔ̃n] or [lɪvdɔ̃n] ?
park out	[paɹ aʊt] or [paɹk aʊt] ?

You are much more likely to delete the consonant in the first set than in the last set. In the first set, *west*, *lived*, and *park* come before consonants, and in the last set, they come before vowels. Deletion is more likely when consonants get together.

In contrast, **insertion** is more rare. In the tug-of-war between speakers and listeners, both sides want more. Speakers want the language they produce to be more simple. Listeners want the language they hear to be maximally distinct, so that words and meanings are easily identifiable. Since we are all listeners and speakers, we are all engaged in this tug-of-war. Deletion helps speakers produce simpler forms of words. Insertion does not always help listeners more easily identify words, and simply does not have the same level of psychological support.

Insertion can happen with consonants or vowels. With forms such as the following, we have insertion with the consonant [p].

Clemson   [kʰlẽmpsɪ̃n]
hamster   [hæ̃mpstɹ]
Chomsky   [tʃãmpski]

For these examples, between what sounds does the [p] occur? As you learned from Chapter 2, the [m] is voiced and the [s] is voiceless. In addition, despite the [m] being a nasal continuant, with air flowing freely out the nose, it is also a stop consonant in the mouth. When that bilabial stop is released into the voiceless [s], all the ingredients are there to create the [p] sound: a voiceless, bilabial stop.

assimilation

Through **assimilation**, speakers make some sounds more similar to other sounds. If you consider the words to be like a plate of food, assimilation is when the flavor of one food is absorbed by other nearby food on the plate. Pretend we have a plate of pork, potatoes, and cabbage with vinegar. The vinegar, being liquid and of strong taste, leeches into the pork and potatoes. Whether or not that is a good thing depends on if you like vinegar.

For sounds, the degree of similarity varies, so that the changed sound could be slightly more similar or completely identical. Consider the following words as (historical) examples of assimilation:

1. inevitable
   inoperable
   inexpensive

2. insufficient
   intolerant
   independence

3. impractical
   immature
   imbalance

4. illegal
    illicit
    illiterate

5. irresponsible
    Irregardless[5]
    irregular

The prefix "in-" with the meaning of "not" attaches to many different words in English. Over the history of the language, the [n] of this prefix has made its place of articulation more similar to consonants that follow it. In group 1, the [n] does not change because the following sound is a vowel. In group 2, the following sound is a consonant, but [s], [t], [d] are all part of the same natural class of alveolar sounds. Since the [n] sound is already alveolar, it has the same place of articulation as the following sounds. In group 3, the [p], [m], [b] are all part of the same natural class of bilabial sounds, and the alveolar [n] has changed to a bilabial [m]. In groups 4 and 5, the [n] sound has been completely assimilated in both place and manner of articulation. What special quality do the [ɹ] and [l] sounds share? They are both liquids, and since assimilation is a process of one sound flowing into another, these sounds are especially good at it.

Assimilation is one of the most common phonological processes for all languages. It happens with both consonants and vowels. Below are seven types of assimilation which are common enough as sound patterns to have earned their own name.

nasalization

Earlier, we worked through what makes a vowel nasalized in English. Unlike some other languages (e.g. French), English speakers need to have a following nasal consonant to create a nasalized vowel. In the examples of [bĩn] ~ [bɪd] and [ɹ̃ʌ̃ŋ] ~ [ɹəg], the environment for nasalization is clear. As with other kinds of assimilation, a phonological environment triggers the nasalization, called a conditioning environment.

flapping

The conditioning environment for **flapping** is more complex than the one for nasalization. The **flap** is a sound in the same natural class as the alveolar [t] and [d] sounds, except that when producing it, you do not fully stop the air, but you almost do. For most Americans, it can be heard in words like *butter* [bəɾɹ] and *rider* [ɹaɪɾɹ]. With a more formal pronunciation, American speakers may be able to produce *butter* [bətɹ] and *rider* [ɹaɪdɹ], but most of the time, their pronunciations are with the flap [ɾ].[6] It is a kind of assimilation because the alveolar stops become less constricted, like their surrounding sounds. The conditioning environment also includes the relative stress in the words: The syllable following the flap has to be unstressed.

devoicing

Devoicing is a fairly straight name for a process where a sound becomes transparent. In the words, *crypt*, *clean*, *trip*, and *tread*, many English speakers can produce the liquid [ɹ] and [l] sounds as voiceless. Sounds made voiceless are marked with a small circle subscript: [ɹ̥] and [l̥]. In terms of when this happens, devoicing can be a "sometimes" feature for people, so that the same person can produce *trip* [tʰɹɪp] sometimes and *trip* [tʰɹ̥ɪp] at other times. As far as we can tell, no social factors drive when devoicing happens and when it does not. (Perhaps you could start a new trend where all the cool people in your clique devoice liquids all the time.) In terms of when it happens, we have a better understanding of how two super sonorants like [ɹ] and [l] become voiceless. This devoicing happens when an aspirated consonant comes before the [ɹ] and [l] sounds. The aspiration, a voiceless sound unto itself, bleeds through the liquids, bleaching them of their voice (e.g. *creep* [kʰɹ̥ip]).

palatalization

In this kind of assimilation, speakers make alveolar sounds more palatal when they come before the palatal glide [j]. In the following combinations from US English, the alveolar stops [t] and [d] become the palatal affricates [tʃ] and [dʒ] by absorbing the [j].

It hit you.   [ɪthɪtju] → [ɪthɪtʃu]
Did you?   [dɪdju] → [dɪdʒu]

Palatalization can also happen within single words, but there is a lot of variation between speakers in these:

OSU   [oɛsju] → [oɛʃu]
Tuesday   [tʰjuzde] → [tʃuzde]

Both the place and manner of articulation are changed for the [t] and [d] sounds, but only place with the alveolar [s].

The next two kinds of assimilation are related linguistically, but socially, they are vastly different. Most English speakers have sharp social evaluations for R-vocalization (either positive or negative). For L-vocalization, hardly anyone notices it.

the story of R (and L): part 2 ─────────────

The terms *R-dropping* and *L-dropping* are the popular names for a process linguists call **vocalization**. For both R- and L-vocalization, the term *vocalization* means turning a consonant into a vowel (making it *vocalic*). Also for both R- and

L-vocalization, the consonant does *not* get deleted but is instead transformed into a vowel sound, as in *bar* [baː] and *ball* [bɔː].[7] Generally, the length in time of a word with a vocalized liquid is the same as unvocalized one (e.g. *bar* [baː] vs. [baɹ]).

Where do R-vocalization and L-vocalization happen in the linguistic environment? Consider the following data:

horse	[hɔːs]	*rose*	[ɹoz]
cord	[kɔːd]	*rod*	[ɹad]
beer	[bɪə]	*read*	[ɹid]
help	[hɛːp]	*leap*	[lip]
coal	[koː]	*lock*	[lak]
bail	[beə]	*lewd*	[lud]

For those in the left column, the [ɹ] and [l] become vowels (of different types depending on dialect-specific rules). For the words on the right, the [ɹ] and [l] remain as consonants. The ones on the left have the liquids word finally, while the ones on the right have the liquids word initially. Now consider the following data:

peel	[piə]	*peeling*	[pilɪŋ]
pare	[pɛː]	*paring*	[pɛɹɪŋ]
sole	[soː]	*soling*	[solɪŋ]
soar	[sɔː]	*soaring*	[sɔɹɪŋ]

Although these data have no [ɹ] or [l] sounds at the start of the words, the left side has R- and L-vocalization while the right side does not. What is the pattern? Think back to our earlier discussion of syllables and reassess the data. The words on the right side of the table have the [ɹ] and [l] in the onset of the syllable, while the words on the left have them in the coda. This kind of assimilation is coordinated with the syllable structure of the words.

R-vocalization is common in British English and most related varieties, including Australian English and New Zealand English. Some American speakers also have it, particularly in the US South, the New England area (e.g. Boston), and parts of New York City. Socially, the divide between the United States and British varieties could not be more stark. In the United States generally, R-vocalization is a stigmatized dialect feature (the exception might be the regional pride in the Boston area). In British English, R-vocalization is the prestige feature.

L-vocalization is mostly under the social radar for English speakers around the world. It is a common feature in large parts of England, Australia, New Zealand, and the Eastern United States, but socially it is invisible.

Englishes and other languages

aspiration

In Chapter 2 we worked through a quality of sounds called aspiration, where a bit of breathiness gets attached to some sounds. For English, aspiration is restricted to voiceless stops at the start of a stressed syllable. For the following English words, aspiration happens with the left column, but not with the right.

A	B
[tʰæn] *tan*	[dæn] *Dan*
[tʰək] *tuck*	[stək] *stuck*
[pʰõn] *pone*	[bõn] *bone*
[pʰɪt] *pit*	[spɪt] *spit*
[kʰot] *coat*	[got] *goat*
[kʰɪt] *kit*	[skɪt] *skit*

Aspiration in Sindhi, a language with 22 million speakers, has a different role than it does in English. For Sindhi speakers, the [p] and [pʰ] are used to mark a difference in meaning between words. Consider these two Sindhi words:

| /perʊ/ | 'the foot' or 'footprint' |
| /pʰerʊ/ | 'difference' |

Here the only difference is the aspiration. For children acquiring the Sindhi language, there is no way to predict that [p] or [pʰ] will show up in certain places. In the same way that children acquiring English have to memorize where the [b] and [p] show up, Sindhi children have to memorize the difference between [p] and [pʰ].

intonation

The pitch in your voice, whether your voice is lower or higher than normal, operates within complex parameters. English uses higher and lower pitch to make some differences in meaning, as all verbal languages do. Some of these languages use pitch for limited ranges of meaning. For English, these meanings include disbelief, question, and surprise. For example, by changing the pitch of your voice, how many different meanings can you squeeze from the phrase "you are going out tonight." At the very least, you can make it a statement or a question, or possibly imply disbelief also.

Some other languages, called tone languages, use pitch to mark differences between words. In Ethiopia, the Bench language of the Omotic branch of the Afroasiatic family has at least five different tones which work phonemically. That means different pitches on the same consonants and vowels will yield different words. The different varieties of Chinese are the most populated of tone languages, and for those speakers, both the relative highness-lowness of the pitch is important, as is whether the pitch is falling or rising across a syllable. In Mandarin Chinese, for example, the same consonant vowel combination can carry five different tones, yielding five different words. For example, the word *horse* /mǎ/ has a mid-level pitch rising to a high pitch (on the same vowel!), but the separate word *mother* /má/ has a high-level tone. Considering that Mandarin-speaking children do not like to get in trouble any more than children of other languages, distinguishing between *horse* and *mother* is important. This kind of tonal system is acquired as a regular part of phonology.

variation through time

In terms of sounds, language change results from the small variations speakers perform every day. Variation in a language at one time is called **synchronic variation**. The variation in language over time is called **diachronic variation**. The "chron" in both of those words is the same root in "chronograph" and "chronicle." The phonological processes discussed above have changed how words are pronounced from Old English (450–1100 CE) until today. For example, the Old English form for 'chicken' was *kiken*, probably pronounced [kikẽn]. Through palatalization, it developed the modern form [tʃɪkẽn]. This palatal assimilation also allowed for the creation of the word *church* as developed from *kirkja*, which separately gave us the word *kirk*. Notice that for these words, the velar sounds were pulled *forward* in the mouth toward the palatal region, which is different from our previous examples.

   Speakers' daily phonological variation can eventually add up to big changes in the system of sounds for a language. Regular assimilation resulted in a tremendous change for English during the beginning of Middle English (1100–1500 CE). Up until then, English had fewer fricatives that triggered a difference in meaning. There was a labiodental voiceless fricative [f] but no [v] (e.g. *yfel* 'evil'). There was a voiceless alveolar fricative [s] but no [z] (e.g. *risan* 'to rise'). There were no Old English words such as *vase* or *zoo* to contrast with words like *face* or *sue*. The assimilation of the [f] and [s] fricatives took place between two voiced sounds: The voice bled through the fricatives, turning them into [v] and [z]. Once French became an influential language in England (1066–1348), the English language began to gain words which did have contrasting voiced fricative sounds, such as *veal* (by 1386) and *zodiac* (by 1390). One echo of our Old English past is the smaller number of words which begin with [v] and [z] than those which begin with [f] and [s].

Old English pronunciations and modern glosses

[gɪft] 'gift'	[giovan] 'to give'
[wulf] 'wolf'	[wulvaz] 'wolves'
[half] 'half'	[halvəz] 'halves'
[baθ] 'bath'	[baðian] 'bathe'
[hus] 'house' (N)	[huzian] 'to house' (V)

The effect can also be heard in the following sets of modern words if you say them out loud:

1. gift   give
2. half   halves
3. wolf   wolves
4. leaf   leaves
5. loss   lose
6. house (N)   house (V)

In the words on the right, the final consonant was originally followed by a vowel (which was eventually dropped although the letter was kept). Note that even when the [f] is preceded by an [l] it is still a voiced sound and promotes assimilation. This same process also most likely happened with the two interdental fricatives, [θ] and [ð]. Consider the final consonants of *bath/bathe* and *teeth/teethe*.

variation today

spoonerisms

Sound patterns sometimes get sidetracked. Almost everyone at some point has sounds which are switched with other sounds. It may seem like a mess when you say, "lable teg" rather than "table leg," but there is a pattern to the mistake. This kind of sound switch is called a *spoonerism*. It is named for William Spooner (1844–1930), a reverend and warden at the New College, Oxford. Renowned as a lecturer and leader of the college, Spooner also had many slips of the tongue which entertained his listeners, including these attributed to him: "q̲ueer old d̲ean," "f̲ighting a l̲ire," "s̲hoving l̲eopard," "b̲lushing c̲row." What is switched in these words?

/laɪtɪŋ e faɪɹ/	[faɪtĩŋ ə laɪə]
/ləvɪŋ ʃepaɹd/	[ʃəvĩŋ lɛpaːd]
/diɹ old kwin/	[kwiə old dĩn]
/kɹəʃɪŋ blo/	[bləʃĩŋ kɹo]

In the first two, the consonants at the beginning of the two words are switched, but in the last two, there is something else going on. Can you tell what unit of sound organization is being used here? The onset of the syllable is switched in each case. Using the onset as the unit of switching works for all the examples.

at the word's end: consonant loss

With spoonerisms, the intended meaning of the words is obscured. For what-ever evolutionary, psychological reason, the beginnings of words are more important for language communication than the ending of words. Given that quality, the endings of syllables and words are often shortened in languages where there is a coda. The more complex the coda, the more likely the coda will be shortened.

Consider your normal pronunciation of the following phrases:

Consider your strength tonight
The front door fell down
A broken flask gasket
Went around a blind curve

In many English speakers' pronunciations, several consonant sounds will likely not be produced, including the [θ] in *strengths*, the [t] in *front*, the [k] in *flask*, and the [d] in *blind*. Now try the following phrases:

Strength on the floor
The front edge
Leave the flask open
A blind alley

With these words, fewer people will drop the consonants in *strength, front, flask,* or *blind.* Consider the following phonetic representations to figure out why.

Deletion more likely	Deletion less likely
[stɹɛ̃ŋθ tənaɪt]	[stɹɛ̃ŋθ ɔ̃n]
[fɹɔ̃nt doɹ]	[fɹɔ̃nt ɛdʒ]
[flæsk gæskət]	[flæsk opĩn]
[blaɪ̃nd kɹv]	[blaɪ̃nd æli]

The case of the [θ] in *strength* is a bit different from the others. It is a rare sound across languages in the first place, so it is less frequently used in English (than other consonants) and is more subject to change. The [t], [k], [d] do not have that same excuse. What is it about the phonological environments which prompt them to deletion? It appears that whether the following sound is a consonant or a vowel greatly influences deletion. The following vowels do not encroach upon the final sound nearly as much as following consonants do.[8]

Every variety of English deletes stops and fricatives before following conso-nants. It is socially unremarkable. However, some vernacular dialects have more consonant deletion before following vowels, including English in Appalachia and some varieties of African-American English.

yod variation

Some sound variations in English are new, while others happened and then disappeared. This next one has happened on and off for a long time. In the word *Tuesday*, variation between a pronunciation with [j] and a pronunciation without [j] has been ongoing since Middle English: [tjuzde] vs. [tuzde]. Originally, the word for the day after Monday was a compound of the Germanic sky god's name *Tiw* and the word for *day*. The pronunciation has certainly changed since then. The Oxford English Dictionary finds that British speakers have the [tjuzde] version, while US speakers variably have [tjuzde] or [tuzde]. This process is called *yod variation*. The [j] sound has the name *yod* (borrowed from the Hebrew name for the tenth letter of that alphabet). This process is often called *yod dropping*, although with words like *coupon*, it is actually *yod insertion*: [kupãn] (the original) vs. [kjupãn] (the innovation).

Throughout the English world, the following words have had yod variation: *suit, educate, dew, tune, assume, Houston*. As sounds go, these pronunciations fall in and out of fashion. The form of *suit* [sjut] without the yod [sut] was non-standard for some time in English, but has become standard in the United States. These variations rarely come up in spelling differences. The exception may be during NCAA basketball season when Duke University is playing, and their opponents hold up various "Dook" signs.

glottalization of /t/

Although flapping might be a regular part of English in the United States, many British dialects use a different phonological process on [t] sounds inside of words. Glottalization is when the glottal stop [ʔ] is substituted for [t] in words like *kitten*, *water*, and *bottle*. What phonological environment do all three of these words have? The [t] sound precedes an unstressed syllable in each case (if you doubt that, try to say each word with the main word stress on the last syllable and see how that sounds). North Americans also have glottalization, but it is less frequent and competes with flapping.

The following pronunciations illustrate the difference between flapping and glottalizing.

	Flapping	Glottalization
Kitten	[kʰɪɾĩn]	[kʰɪʔĩn]
bottle	[baɾl̩]	[baʔl̩]
water	[wəɾɹ̩]	[wəʔɹ̩]

chapter summary

This chapter explains the complex patterns people create with the sounds of human language. The sounds themselves are grouped into categories called natural classes. Our mental grammars use these natural classes to alter certain sounds but not others. Another structure used to organize sounds is the syllable. Syllables function as templates to order sounds by sonority, with the most sonorant sounds at the center of syllables and the least sonorant sounds at the edges. Another structural feature is the set of restrictions on impossible combinations of sounds, called phonotactic constraints. With these structures, the mental grammar produces patterns such as the schwa rule, deletion, and assimilation. Intonation is another feature of sound which English speakers use to form questions, but other languages use intonation to distinguish lexical items. All these sound patterns differ from language to language and from dialect to dialect within the same language. These patterns also change over time. This diachronic variation results from synchronic variation.

key concepts

- Assimilation
- Coda
- Conditioning environment
- Conditioned merger
- Deletion
- Devoicing
- Diachronic variation
- Flap
- Flapping
- Front-lax merger
- Hierarchy
- Low-back merger
- Minimal pair
- Nasalization
- Natural classes
- Nodes
- Nucleus
- Onset
- Onset maximization
- Palatalization
- Phoneme
- Phonological rule
- Phonology
- Phonotactic constraint
- Rhyme
- Schwa rule
- Sibilants
- Social meanings
- Social minimal pair
- Sonority
- Syllables
- Synchronic variation
- Vocalization
- Vowel space

Notes

1   Phonology also handles the input of the physical language, sounded or sighted, into the body. The same patterns people produce filter the sounds they hear. This chapter only explores the production of sounds.

2   Remember from Chapter 2 that [ɹ] is a liquid like [l], and both can become vowels at the ends of syllables.

3   http://en.wikipedia.org/wiki/The_Wiggles

4   I have heard of some dialects of English developing a system for *the* where unstressed [ðə] comes before vowels and equally unstressed [ði] comes before consonants.

5   A restaurant in Raleigh, NC; also a commonly used word that means "without regard."

6   Yes, it does look very much like an <r> symbol, and the flap is related to rhotic sounds.

7   The vowels may shift for some speakers, but these shifts are not represented here.

8   If the final consonants functioned as onsets in the following syllables, then the voiceless stops would be aspirated, but that does not seem to be the case.

references

Blevins, J. (1995) "The syllable in phonological theory." *The Handbook of Phonological Theory*, ed. J.A. Goldsmith. Blackwell.

http://en.wikipedia.org/wiki/The_Wiggles

further reading

English Phonetics and Phonology. Philip Carr. 1999. Blackwell.
This very readable book provides clear explanations of phonological processes for beginners. It pulls examples from a variety of English dialects and uses relatively straightforward phonological assumptions to analyse the data. The author works through phonemes, syllable structure, word stress, rhythm, intonation, and synchronic variation.

The Handbook of Phonological Theory. 2nd edition. John A. Goldsmith, Jason Riggle, Alan C.L. Yu. 2011. Wiley Blackwell.
This book is not for the faint of heart, but it is rewarding to read through the different systems phonologists have created to answer questions about how sound systems work, how they are learned by children, and how people use them variably. This handbook has 23 chapters and over 900 pages of information on the latest theories about a fascinating corner of the human mind: phonology.

A Handbook of Varieties of English: Phonology. Edgar W. Schneider, Kate Burridge, Bernd Kortmann, Rajend Mesthrie, and Clive Upton. 2004. Mouton de Gruyter.
This massive volume collects together the phonological characteristics of most major varieties of English in the world, including those in the British Isles, the Americas and the Caribbean, the Pacific and Australasia, Africa, and Asia. Despite the size, the editors have ensured that a uniform system of discussing the range of variation is used. The result is a manageable reference volume which allows comparison of many phonological qualities.

exercises

individual work

1. Which of the following sets of words are minimal pairs? For the ones that are not minimal pairs, why are they not? To answer these questions, you must read the phonetic symbols out loud and determine whether your mental grammar interprets them as two different words or different pronunciations of the same word.

1	[batl̩]	[baʔl̩]
2	[bəsɹ̩]	[bəzɹ̩]
3	[ɹɛ̃nĩŋ]	[ɹɛnɪŋ]
4	[bət̬ɹ]	[bəɾɹ]
5	[pap]	[pʰap]
6	[məŋk]	[mənθ]

2. For the following natural classes, give the sounds that belong to each class. You can answer either with the complete set of individually-bracketed sounds (e.g. nasal = [n], [m], [ŋ]) or with the subclasses of sounds (e.g. vowels = back vowels, front vowels, and central vowels). Either way, you must include in your answer all and only the sounds of the natural class in question.

Fricatives:

Sibilants:

Obstruents:

Front vowels:

3. Natural classes:
Identify which natural classes the following sounds come from. None of the rows contain an entire set from a natural class. Choose the smallest possible subclass (e.g. for [d b g] "obstruent" is accurate, but not as specific as "voiced stops").

Sounds	Natural class
[m p w]	
[h v θ]	
[n l j a]	
[i u e]	
[t l z]	

Sounds	Natural class
[d b k]	
[ŋ k]	
[a ɪ ʊ]	
[ð g ɹ]	

4. English has a history of stress patterns that change. As a result, different dialects of English today pronounce some words differently. In the Southeastern United States, the following words are often pronounced with the stress of the first vowel in the word, but other varieties of English pronounce these words with the stress on the second syllable. How do these two different stress patterns affect the vowels? Try pronouncing them out loud with the stress on either the first or second syllable to hear the difference. Phonetically transcribe the different pronunciations in the appropriate columns. What sound pattern operates between the two pronunciations of each word?

	Stress on 1st syllable	Stress on 2nd syllable
<police>		
<cement>		
<pecan>		
<about>		
<because>		

The first word, <police>, can be pronounced numerous ways around North America. It is difficult to say which pronunciation is more common, but some of the more frequent pronunciations are [pʰəlis] and [pʰl̩is]. In the Southern United States, you can also hear [pʰolis].

If we assume that in the lexicon, the memorized version is closest to the production [pʰolis], the question to ask is *by what rules do we get the other pronunciations*? Consider the following derivational chart, and identify which patterns emerge and what rules are required.

	Lexical listing and derivations		
Rules	/polis/	/polis/	/polis/
	pʰolis	pʰolis	pʰolis
		pʰəlis	pʰəlis
			pʰl̩is
			pʰl̥is
Pronunciation	[pʰolis]	[pʰəlis]	[pʰl̥is]

5. /aɪ/ ungliding:

The /aɪ/ vowel is complex, and its complexity allows people to stretch it and pull it into many different shapes according to their social needs. As it is written phonetically, the /aɪ/ vowel starts with a mid, low, lax vowel that rises to a high, front, lax ending. The first part is called the on-glide, and the second part is called the off-glide. Since vowels do not have stable places of articulation, this vowel can change both in its on-glide and off-glide. The next few exercises lead you through some data to assess the language patterns of the /aɪ/ vowel in different North American dialects.

5.1 /aɪ/ ungliding in the Southeastern United States:

Consider the following phonetically transcribed data (note that in these data other linguistic patterns are not transcribed). Remember, these pronunciations may be different from your own, but they are legitimate forms spoken by native speakers. We consider two forms of the /aɪ/ vowel: the full diphthong /aɪ/ and the unglided /aː/. It is called *unglided* because it is missing its off-glide. In regular speech, the unglided /aː/ might actually have a shorter transition to [ɪ], but speakers react to the extremely short off-glide as if it were fully absent. The first question to ask of this data is *when does the /aɪ/ appear and when does /aː/ appear?* Secondly, figure out *what phonetic environment triggers the /aɪ/ form.*

[baɪt] <bite>	[faːɹ] <fire>	[naːnθ] <ninth>
[taɪp] <type>	[taːm] <time>	[laɪf] <life>
[ɹaɪs] <rice>	[baː] <buy>	[faɪt] <fight>
[ɹaːz] <rise>	[ɹaːd] <ride>	[taː] <tie>
[faːl] <file>	[ɹaɪt] <right>	[baɪk] <bike>
[baːd] <bide>	[tɹaːb] <tribe>	[taːgɹ] <tiger>

One helpful step will be to sort all the data above into two columns and then search for a natural class in one of the columns. For example:

[aɪ]   [aː]
[baɪt]   [ɹaːd]
[taɪp]   [tɹaːb]
. . . .

5.2 Flapping:

As discussed earlier, one common rule in North American English is the flapping of alveolar stops [t, d] when they are an onset of unstressed syllables, rendering *butter* with a voiced flap as [bəɾɹ]. In words such as *writer* and *rider*, both the rule of /aɪ/ ungliding (as you figured out in 5.1) and flapping can occur for Southern US speakers. Work through the following data and figure out how both rules can operate in the same word. Which rule has to happen first? Please explain your answer.

[baɪɾɹ̩] <biter>	[taɪɾɹ̩] <tighter>
[ɹaɪɾɹ̩] <writer>	[ɹaːɾɹ̩] <rider>
[slaɪɾɹ̩] <slighter>	[ɹaɪɾɹ̩] <righter>
[faɪɾɹ̩] <fighter>	[slaːɾɹ̩] <slider>
[glaːɾɹ̩] <glider>	[kənfaːɾɹ̩] <confider>

For this question, try putting the rules in both orders and see which one produces the correct results:

First guess	<writer>	<rider>
Lexical listing	/ɹaɪtɹ̩/	/ɹaɪdɹ̩/
flapping		
/aɪ/ ungliding		
Pronunciation	[ ]	[ ]

Second guess	<writer>	<rider>
Lexical listing	/ɹaɪtɹ̩/	/ɹaɪdɹ̩/
/aɪ/ ungliding		
flapping		
Pronunciation	[ ]	[ ]

5.3 Parts of Appalachia and Texas:
The pattern in the following table is different because it is found only in parts of Appalachia and Texas. What is different in this pattern?

[baːt] <bite>	[faːɹ] <fire>	[naːnθ] <ninth>
[taːp] <type>	[taːm] <time>	[laːf] <life>
[ɹaːs] <rice>	[baː] <buy>	[faːt] <fight>
[ɹaːz] <rise>	[ɹaːd] <ride>	[taː] <tie>
[faːl] <file>	[ɹaːt] <right>	[baːk] <bike>

5.4 Canada and bordering US areas:
For the following set of phonetically transcribed Canadian English data, figure out the relationship between [aɪ] and [əɪ], as well as [aʊ] and [əʊ]. The different variants in this case have the on-glide of the vowel raised up to the mid-central lax region. Although there are

several competing ideas for why these vowels work this way, perhaps the most intriguing is that they have not fallen down in vowel space since the Great Vowel Shift. Despite this idea, this alternation is called *Canadian Raising*. Work through the following data and identify the sound environment for when the raised [əɪ] and [əʊ] vowels occur. Just like 5.1, sort the different forms into two columns to look for a trend in the natural classes.

[bəɪt] <bite>	[faɪɹ] <fire>	[əbəʊt] <about>	[naɪnθ] <ninth>
[təɪp] <type>	[taɪm] <time>	[əbaʊnd] <abound>	[ləɪf] <life>
[ɹəɪs] <rice>	[ʃaʊwɹ] <shower>	[həʊs] <house> (N)	[fəɪt] <fight>
[ɹaɪz] <rise>	[ɹaɪd] <ride>	[haʊz] <house> (V)	[taɪ] <tie>
[faɪl] <file>	[ɹəɪt] <right>	[ʃaʊt] <shout>	[bəɪk] <bike>

6. Dialect discovery exercise:
   With the spread of access to the internet, many different dialects are represented. Find internet clips demonstrating three sound patterns discussed in this chapter. At least one of the clips has to be from a nation which is not your own. For example, you could find examples of speakers flapping, aspirating voiceless stops, deleting yods, or vocalizing a liquid.

group work

7. Drawing syllables (and figuring out onset maximization):
   The goal here is to find regular patterns with syllable structure and to understand the effects of onset maximization. In regular speech, onset maximization varies, occurring the majority of the time but not all the time. In these exercises, treat onset maximization as categorical.

   For the following words, figure out the Consonant (C) and Vowel (V) structure. Each numbered row has words with the same CV structure. For example, the structure of <bee> [bi] is CV, but the structure of <bootstrap> [but.stræp] would be CVC.CCCVC.
   a. a, I
   b. bee, new
   c. bat, sag, tab, tack

    d.   flee, pray

    e.   stray, strew

    f.   trip, tripe

    g.   knight, rite

    h.   stripe, strip

    i.   bench, lunge, bunt

    j.   brunch, trucks, plucks

    k.   bunks, temps,

    l.   bricks, crux

    m. strengths

8. For the following words, draw syllable trees to represent their hierarchical sound structures. You must use phonetic script to draw these syllable trees. For this exercise, please use this chapter's template:

    a.   Bat

    b.   Batter

    c.   Bolting

    d.   Backing

    e.   Ballpark

    f.   String

    g.   Strikeforce

    h.   Mississippi

    i.   Psychology

    j.   Strengths

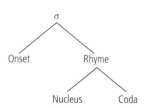

9. Syllabification differences:

Outside Morgantown, West Virginia, is a small community named <Dellslow>. The native pronunciation of this name is /dɛlzlo/. Given that many people from outside the area refer to it as /delslo/, what can you conclude about the natives' syllable structure for this name vs. outsiders' syllabic rendition? Please use syllable trees to explain your answer.

10. For the following words, please identify the sound patterns (i.e. what rules predict the alterations between the top level and the bottom level):

	<hamster>	<polite>	<impossible>
Lexical listing	/hæmstɛɹ/	/polaɪt/	/ɪnpasɪbl/
Rules			
Pronunciation	[hæ̃mpstɹ̩]	[pʰlḁːt]	[ĩmpasəbl̩]

	<tuneful>	<nature>	<writer's cavalry>	<Tuesday's prizes>
Lexical listing	/tunfʊl/	/netjuɹ/	/ɹaɪtɛɹ s kævalɹi/	/tjuzde s pɹaɪz s/
Rules				
Pronunciation	[tʰũnfl̩]	[netʃə]	[ɹaɪɾɚz kʰælvəɹi]	[tʃuzdezpʰɹaːzɪz]

11. Consider the prescriptive advice at http://grammar.yourdictionary
.com/style-and-usage/mispron.html. Find ten of these "mispronun-
ciations" that result from sound patterns discussed in this chapter.
Which sound patterns are the most productive for this list?

12. Survey 10 people before the next class on the following list of words.
Phonetically transcribe the initial consonant from each person's
response. The list is designed to elicit the potential merger between
[w] and [ʍ].

Word	Pronunciation	Word	Pronunciation
<witch>		<which>	
<weather>		<whether>	
<wear>		<where>	
<wail>		<whale>	
<wipe>		<whip>	
<wile>		<while>	

study questions

1. What is a minimal pair?
2. How are mental symbols for sounds represented?
3. What is phonology's job in the mental grammar?
4. What are social meanings?

5.   What are natural classes?
6.   What natural classes can divide all sounds into two groups?
7.   What are syllables?
8.   Do all languages have the same syllable structures?
9.   What is hierarchy?
10.   What is the structure of syllables?
11.   What is onset maximization?
12.   What are phonotactic constraints?
13.   What is sonority?
14.   What are the names of the two L sounds?
15.   What is the low-back merger?
16.   What is the pattern for the front-lax merger?
17.   What is deletion?
18.   What is assimilation?
19.   What is the conditioning environment for nasalization?
20.   What happens in devoicing?
21.   What is palatalization?
22.   What is the social difference between R-vocalization in the United States and England?
23.   What is aspiration?
24.   How is aspiration used in languages other than English?
25.   Does English use pitch to mark a difference in meaning?
26.   What is synchronic variation?
27.   What is diachronic variation?
28.   What is a spoonerism?
29.   What kinds of things can happen to yod?
30.   What is glottalization, and who uses it?

 Visit the book's companion website for additional resources relating to this chapter at: http://www.wiley.com/go/hazen/introlanguage

4 Simple Words in the Lexicon

An Introduction to Language, First Edition. Kirk Hazen.
© 2015 John Wiley & Sons, Inc. Published 2015 by John Wiley & Sons, Inc.

chapter overview

The lexicon is an important place in our tour of language in the human mind. In it, we hold our raw material for constructing conversation, which is shelved in the lexicon like books in a library. This chapter focuses on how we organize the shelves, specifically with one-part words. We start by exploring the relationships between form and meaning, the foundation for words. We move next to the kind of work words do. Most simple words can be divided into content and function categories, with content words acting as the bricks, and function words acting as the mortar used to bind them together. Content words have lexical categories such as adjectives, nouns, and verbs. Function words have lexical categories such as determiners, pronouns, and prepositions. Each lexical category has specific qualities, and we build phrases according to those qualities: Prepositions can connect nouns (e.g. *in the house*), but not adjectives (e.g. *in smart). Verbs have the most specific qualities and are a special point of focus in this chapter.

lexical ambiguity and arbitrariness

The human ability that allows for meanings to be assigned to certain sets of sounds is probably one of the most basic language traits in our species. It is certainly one of the most overlooked by the average language user. Words themselves are complex, but the fundamentals of a word are easy. The relation between form and meaning is inherently arbitrary, but conventionally determined by a society. For sounded languages, the form is the sound: the physical quality of sound waves. For signed languages, it is the form of the sign: the physical quality of gestures. The meaning is whatever each individual has connected to that form (and the meanings can differ between individuals). The relationship between the two, which eventually forms a word, is created and applied by people in a society. For any word, the relationship between form and meaning is set by convention.

Word Play: Homophones in lame jokes

Identify the homophone in the following joke:

A mushroom walks into a bar and the bartender says, "We don't serve your kind here." Then, the mushroom says – "Why not? I'm a *fun guy*."

All humor is built off of contrast between the expected and the unexpected. In this joke, several unexpected things happen, including a walking and talking mushroom, but the humor is not in the mushroom's human qualities.

What kind of contrast is the punchline of this joke? Is it a contrast in sound, in spelling, in meaning, or in some other function?

One of the observable facts of all living languages is that they change over time. But how is that possible? Even with the most basic of changes, how does it happen that a set of sounds can mean one thing one day and something different the next year? As with sounds discussed in the previous two chapters, the small daily variations in the conventional connections between meaning and form result in slight changes. For example, the word *bead* today usually refers to small pieces of jewelry, but it used to mean *prayer*. Earlier in England, prayers were supposed to be counted using a rosary. The difference between an 885 usage like "Ðæt he sceolde <u>ða bedu</u> anescian" (that he should weaken <u>the prayers</u>) by the Venerable Bede and a 1589 usage like "About their neckes great beades of glasse of diverse colours" can be called diachronic variation.[1] How do we get to the two different meanings? Little by little the synchronic variation builds up, with individuals slightly shifting the relationship between meaning and form, so that *bead* first refers to prayers, and then to the items used to count prayers, and eventually to those small objects themselves.

Is the lexicon just a free-for-all? Probably not. The lexicon does restrict synonyms, but its design does not seem to restrict **homonyms**. These pairings of words illustrate the arbitrary foundation of words in human language.

Homophones are different words which have the same phonological form. In other words, they sound the same. At times, they can be spelled the same, such as *bat* (flying mammal) and *bat* (stick to hit things), or they can be spelled differently, as in *air* and *heir*. The ones that are spelled the same could also be considered **homographs**, since they have the same orthographic form. Not all homographs are also homophones, since *bass* [bes] (instrument) and *bass* [bæs] (fish) are not pronounced the same. Words that are homographs and homophones, such as *bat/bat*, are considered *homonyms*. From Natalie Dee, the consternation of homographs: http://www.nataliedee.com/index.php?date =071713

Identify the homophones, homographs, and homonyms:

bore ('drill')	*bore* ('cause boredom')	
read (present)	*read* (past)	
cache	*cash*	
bye	*buy*	
cannon	*canon*	
tire (noun)	*tire* (verb)	
desert (dry area)	*desert* (abandon)	*dessert* (sweet part of meal)
to	*too*	*two*
claws	*clause*	
pair	*pare*	
house (noun)	*house* (verb)	

Since we find such an abundance of homophones and such a lack of synonyms, a description of the lexicon should take this pattern into account. It appears that reference meaning slots can partially match, but not fully, and that lexical items are primarily stored by their meanings. The phonological forms do not compete with each other and can fully match.

Word Play: Crossing homonyms

How many forms do you know which have sets of homonyms in different lexical categories? For example, the form *bat* can be a noun (*the black bat*) or a verb (*I batted in three runs*).

Are most homonyms in the same lexical category or in different ones?

In a regular dictionary, the meanings are listed under the spellings, so that the spelling for *bat* has both a description of a flying mammal and a stick to hit things. In the language lexicon, these would be separately stored, and they are considered to be separate words. Ponder that for a minute: *Bass* (music term) and *bass* (fish) are separate words and so are *table* (noun) and *table* (verb). Spelling is not the ruler of all.

Humans have widely diverse collections of memorized chunks of language in their lexicons. In Chapters 5 and 6, we will explore further what types of language are stored in the lexicon, but here we will stick with full and simple words, like *gecko*, *love*, *grant*, *squid*, and *Mississippi*. It is difficult to accurately estimate how many words a person might know for a given language.[2] A decent guess is that high school graduates have around 40,000 words (see Pinker, *The Language Instinct*, 2007). The more you work with language and the more diverse it is, the more words you probably know. Does that mean that people can actually list the words they know? No. Language knowledge is accessible, but the nature of that knowledge (How many words do I know? Do nouns feel different from verbs in my head?) is not directly accessible to us. *Knowing* a word consists of having a paired form and meaning stored in your lexicon and being able to access that information through recognition or production.

our mental dictionaries: unlike paper dictionaries in several ways

For paper dictionaries, a set standard has evolved over the last few centuries. Samuel Johnson (1709–1784) developed many of the conventions of modern dictionaries, including the use of quotations to aid in defining words. Noah Webster (1758–1843) published his dictionary in 1828, although his impact on American spelling came about through his speller, which sold more than 60 million copies between 1783 and 1890. Today, in standard dictionaries like *The American Heritage Dictionary of the English Language* and *Merriam-Webster's Collegiate Dictionary*, the words are arranged in alphabetical order. The order is based on the orthographic spelling of the word: The word *coma* comes before *comb* in paper-based dictionaries because *a* comes before *b* in the alphabet.[3] *Coma* is not next to *trance* or *unconscious*, and *comb* is not next to *brush* or *hair*, although those words would be more connected to their meanings. Note that standard dictionaries also opt for the more conservative spelling rather than shifting pronunciations. A word like *physical* is not listed next to *fiscal*, and *psychology* is not found near *science*.

In our heads, we also store words, and we store them differently than they are stored in paper dictionaries. Regular spelling is not a concern. Remember that for most of human history and for the majority of languages, there has been no written form. Writing is a useful technology, but writing is not language. Words in the mental lexicon are connected by two different threads. One thread that connects words in the lexicon is related meaning. Collections of words such as *car*, *automobile*, *wheels*, *ride* are sometimes synonyms (with different social meanings). A *thesaurus* is a book organized by headwords and their related meanings. The other thread is the similarity of sound. Consider the following tongue-twister.

Read the following ten words *out loud*, all in a row. Then answer the next question out loud quickly afterwards.

10 Words:

coast, coast, coast, coast, coast, coast, coast, coast, coast, coast.

Question: What do you put into a toaster?

Answer: _____

By having you repeat those words out loud, your sound system in the mental grammar (your phonology), is set up to be reminded of similar words. You have primed your phonology to think of words that rhyme. So when most people are asked the subsequent question, the answer they provide is usually "toast," which is of course what comes *out* of a toaster. Most people actually put bread *into* the toaster.

Words are connected by their sounds, and in the above example, they are connected not by their initial sounds but by their final sounds.

the lexicon and synonyms

The *syn-* of *synonym* means "together," "similar," "alike." It is the same prefix as in *syllable* (to take together), but with that word, the *n* turned into an *l*. The *nym* means "name," which is why we have *antonyms* and *homonyms* also. Often, synonyms are not treated the same by the lexicon.

The lexicon is restrictive in some ways, actually guiding what are possible words and what are not possible words. Synonyms illustrate the lexicon's restrictions. Words can have similar meanings, so that adjectives like *skinny* and *scrawny* both refer to someone who weighs less than expected. Yet, *scrawny* has an extra nudge of negative. With *scrawny*, images of weak and powerless come to mind, whereas *skinny* leaves that semantic area unspecified. Sometimes words with similar reference meanings have different social meanings, especially taboo names for body parts. Take a term like *penis* (a Latin term first cited in English in 1578). This male genital organ is also referred to with terms such as *cock* and *pee-pee*. But just because the references are the same, does that mean that the three words are interchangeable? Certainly, any one person can use all three in a single day, but what contexts would be more appropriate for one vs. the others?

In the following exercise, try to find true synonyms where the meanings match in every way. If sets of words are close in either reference meaning or social meaning to each other, describe how they differ.

For the topics below, try to pull together sets of words with similar reference meanings:

1. Visual light
2. Clothing for the top half of the body
3. Kinds of people
4. Life at the beach
5. Kinds of writing
6. Objects in the kitchen

Even when words start as exact synonyms, they end up shifting their meaning over time. If we look back in the history of English, the words *skirt* and *shirt* appear to have come from the same Old English term *scyrte*, but their meanings diverged. The words *skiff* and *ship* followed a similar split. The earlier Latin term *candle* and the later French term *chandelier* both came from the same source, with the Latin *candle* being borrowed into English centuries earlier. The first part of *chaise-lounge* is a phonetic variation of *chair*. These started as similar forms, but their meanings diverged. For a large divide, consider the difference between the two columns below.

Column A	Column B
cow	*beef*
pig	*pork*
calf	*veal*
sheep	*mutton*
chicken	*poultry*

In Column A, the words are all of Anglo-Saxon origin. In Column B, the words are all of French origin (particularly Anglo-French origin after 1066). When the words in Column B were introduced into English, they had the same meanings as the words in Column A (they *were* synonyms). How are the words in the two columns different now? Except for *poultry*, the words in Column B are used for food on the plate, whereas the terms in Column A are the animals. After the Anglo-Norman invasion of 1066, the French-speaking rulers of England brought their French terms to refer to the food they wanted on their plates. The

English-speaking servants, who were still slopping the pigs and tending the sheep in the pasture, raised and provided the food. Their words started with a social distinction.

In more recent times, consider the past tense forms for *hang*. In many communities and across many dialects, there are now two forms: *hanged* and *hung*. In the history of the word *hang*, different regions in England had different forms. The north of England supported *hanged*, and the south of England preferred *hung*. Eventually, *hung* took over for the past tense. Yet, since these two forms were true synonyms, their meanings diverged. The term *hanged* came to be used as a transitive past tense for execution by hanging. Charles Dickens writes in *Oliver Twist* (1838): "To be hanged by the neck till he was dead – that was the end." This special usage persists today in many English-speaking communities, and it allows for *hanged* and *hung* to both exist as related but non-synonymous terms.

structure

So, words are pairs of form and meaning linked together, but as we explore in the next few chapters, the arrangement of words makes a difference for how they work. We need another quality by which we can define how words work in certain contexts. What would be the difference between the form *duck* in the following two sentences?

1. The ducks landed on the dock.
2. The swimmer ducked under the dock.

In the first sentence, the word *duck* comes after a *the* and has an *-s* attached to it, which marks it as plural. In the second sentence, the word *duck* comes after *the swimmer* and has an *-ed* on it, which marks it as past tense. The form *duck* is part of two separate words in these sentences, with the first *duck* meaning a certain kind of 'waterfowl' and the second having a meaning something like 'to lower ones head and torso to miss an object at head level.' Words that can be made plural and can come after *the* are considered **nouns**. Words that are connected to subjects and can be made past tense are considered **verbs**. How do such types fit into the lexicon? These are called **lexical categories**. Every language user who picks up a new word labels it as a lexical category. Now consider the following sentence.

I saw her duck.

What is going on here? Without further context, it is difficult to tell. In a normal conversation, the context is supplied by either the social/physical scene (e.g. there is a girl holding a pet duck) or by the previous language scene (e.g. we just talked about going under a low volleyball net). Linguistically, you are presented with two choices for the sentence, *I saw her duck*. In the first, *her duck* could refer to waterfowl owned by a female; in the second, *saw her duck* could refer to viewing a female bending down to avoid hitting her head. This kind of uncertainty is similar to *The bat hit me in the face*. In that sentence, the noun *bat* works as the subject, but given only that information, we do not know what kind of bat it is mammal or piece of wood (and which one would be scarier?). When different words with the same form could be in a phrase, there is **lexical ambiguity**. Importantly, note that lexical ambiguity is between two (or more) words. In Chapter 8, we introduce structural ambiguity, which is where the organization of words triggers different meanings. Lexical and structural variations are not the only reasons why ambiguity happens. How does it get created in this *xkcd* comic: http://xkcd.com/1160/?

how to identify lexical categories

In traditional terms, words like *noun* and *verb* are called parts of speech. There is nothing inherently evil about the term *parts of speech*, but the term *lexical category* keeps us grounded in the idea that our language is created in our heads by a highly regulated process. An important component of that regulation is the role a word plays as a lexical category. In this book, no grand argument is made to determine the exact number of lexical categories or even substantiate their indivisibility (in other words, whether each one is made up of smaller units, like molecules made of atoms). Our lexical categories are tools we use to better understand how our language works.

How do we determine a lexical category? Is there an Ultimate List of Lexical Categories? Do they come in different colors, or perhaps even different tastes and smells, so that adjectives taste like lemon drops and verbs smell like cinnamon? Apparently the process of evolution found no motivation for attaching sensory activation to our evaluation of lexical categories. We have no natural means of easily determining which words work as certain lexical categories. As with so much of our language's workings, the evaluation of lexical categories is part of what our brains process very rapidly, but we do not have conscious knowledge of that evaluation.

So, as students of language, we must work to figure out what is what. Fortunately, we do have mental grammars to create as much data as we would like. We have no shortage of material to analyze. Here is how to work it out: First, you must take a word and play with it in different contexts; second, find similarities in the patterns of how the words fit together. For example, ponder the word *yellow* (the color). How can we assign a lexical category to the word *yellow*? First, make some phrases with this usage of *yellow*:

The <u>yellow</u> car
A very <u>yellow</u> light
That bird is really <u>yellow</u>

Next, we compare what other words fit in those phrases to replace *yellow*. The meanings do not need to match. Figuring lexical categories is not about the meanings of words. It is about how the words are used according to the descriptive grammar of the language.

The <u>old</u> car; The <u>small</u> car; The <u>cheap</u> car; The <u>imaginary</u> car; The <u>alien</u> car

A very <u>soft</u> light; A very <u>bright</u> light; A very <u>sharp</u> light; A very <u>glaring</u> light

That bird is really <u>rare</u>; That bird is really <u>smart</u>; That bird is really <u>beautiful</u>;

All of these underlined words fill the same slots as *yellow*. At this point, we can figure that they are all part of the same lexical category. As you have most likely guessed, they are all used as adjectives in these phrases.

The important point to take in here is that the essence of the category *adjective* is not defined by the meaning of the word in question; rather, the lexical category is determined by the relation of the word to the other parts of the phrase. We develop this concept further in Chapters 7 and 8, when we work on the construction of phrases by syntax.

In the next few sections, we progress through bare-bones description of six lexical categories, including adjectives.

These lexical categories are divided into two larger groups. These two groups do not work the same way when we weave words into phrases. The one group, **content** lexical categories, carries most of the reference meaning for our language. The other group, **function** lexical categories, establishes relationships between words so we can figure out how the different parts hook together. The content categories are presented first.

content lexical categories

adjectives

The first content lexical category is **adjective**. These words modify nouns or verbs. Yes, or verbs. Those that modify verbs are traditionally called *adverbs*, but it is a lot more coherent to think of adjectives as the larger category and that some of them modify verbs and some modify nouns.

In both *the quick sniper* and *the sniper is quick*, the word *quick* works as an adjective. With the suffix *-ly* attached, the adjective *quick* can modify a verb: *She ran quickly*. Now how about *fast* as in *the fast sniper* and *the sniper is fast*. In those phrases, *fast* is an adjective, modifying the noun. Now, how about *she ran fast*. Here, the suffix *-ly* would not be the norm for most speakers. The majority of folk would not produce *she ran fastly*. Yet, the adjective *fast* is an adjective modifying the verb *ran*.

Does every word with an *-ly* modify only verbs? The answer today is that some do, but certainly not all of them. In earlier periods of English, such as

Early Modern English (1500–1700), there were even more words working as adjectives with -*ly*. The -*ly* was added to both adjectives modifying nouns and those modifying verbs. Now consider the word *friendly*. In the frames we have used so far, it seems to work fine: *the friendly sniper*; *the sniper is friendly*. So this -*ly* word is an adjective, and it does not modify verbs in a grammatical fashion, as can be seen in **she spoke friendly*. The formula for concocting words like *friendly* is Noun + -*ly* = Adjective. So we have words like *man-ly, coward-ly, king-ly, scholar-ly, dai-ly, year-ly, week-ly*. For some other words, the -*ly* form is composed of adjectives, and the result can work as an adjective or adverb: for example, *kindly* (*The council hopes he will <u>kindly</u> accept the position*; *She was a <u>kindly</u> queen*).

Some adjectives in English can also modify other adjectives. Consider a word like *deadly*. In a phrase like *the deadly disease*, the word *deadly* modifies a noun. In *a deadly serious proposition*, the word *deadly* modifies another adjective, *serious*. Traditionally, such adjective use has been called *adverbial*, but this arrangement has nothing to do with verbs.

In traditional classification, here is the breakdown of what category modifies what other category:

Adjectives	Adverbs
Nouns	Verbs
	Adjectives
	Sentences

Sentence adverbs

Another kind of adjective modifier is the **sentence adverb**. While it does not modify a verb, it does modify the meaning of the entire sentence where it is attached. In *Ideally, this rope will save us before the waterfall*, the word *ideally* does not describe how the rope will save us, but instead it provides the best case scenario. Again, the -*ly* suffix does not always mean it modifies a verb. One sentence adverb has received a lot of grief over the years, but, hopefully, things will get better for it in the future. The sentence adverb *hopefully* has been maligned, spit on, stomped, and left for dead through the last century. It is an odd fate for a single word which does the same kind of work as *ideally, ironically, thankfully*, and *clearly*. In a sentence like *Hopefully, we can put out the fire*, there is no intent to extinguish the flames with hope; instead, the purpose is to get the desired results.

Positioning

In English, adjectives often come in front of the words they modify. The exception is the adjective in a verb phrase modifying a noun in the subject. For example, in the sentence *The elephant is thirsty*, the adjective *thirsty* modifies *elephant* through the verb *is*. In the sentence *This beer seems flat*, the adjective

Figure 4.1   A grader works well on dirt but not on adjectives. Naypong/Shutterstock.

flat modifies *beer* through the verb *seems*. This position for adjectives is called **predicative**, since the adjective is in the **predicate**, an older term for the verb phrase. When the adjective comes before the word it modifies, we call it **attributive**, as in *a wicked smile*. In many other languages, the adjective follows the noun it modifies. In Spanish, the adjective follows the noun: *el chico alto* 'the tall boy' and *la chica alta* 'the tall girl.'

Grading

Adjectives in English are usually gradable, meaning they can be separated on different levels and have three forms to help describe whatever they are modifying. In *the black dog*, the adjective is in its plain state. In *the blacker dog*, the adjective is in its **comparative** state. In *the blackest dog*, the adjective is in its **superlative** state (it is super!). The *-er* and *-est* endings are Germanic suffixes from Anglo-Saxon, and they foster comparison between the modified noun and something else, even if it is not named. The superlative *-est* not only makes that comparison but also claims that the noun being modified is the most supreme in the quality of its adjective.

Not all English adjectives are gradable. For example, adjectives such as *phonetic* and *federal* are generally not packaged along a scale: The *phonetic symbol* could be not rendered as *the more phonetic symbol* and *the most phonetic symbol*, as if there was a continuum of phoneticiness. If in your experience, an adjective has a range of qualities (e.g. *red, redder, reddest*), then it is a gradable adjective for you.

English adjectives have taken different paths for making comparative and superlative forms. Many of the Anglo-Saxon adjectives take *-er* and *-est*. Adjectives from Latin, French, and Greek usually take the separate *more* and *most*. Those adjectives often have several syllables already, and the added suffixes would be unwieldy for most people.

Anglo-Saxon	Latin or French
pretty, prettier, prettiest	*beautiful, more beautiful, most beautiful* (Old French)
hard, harder, hardest	*resilient, more resilient, most resilient* (Latin)
narrow, narrower, narrowest	*tangential, more tangential, most tangential* (Latin)
round, rounder, roundest	*spherical, more spherical, most spherical* (Latin & Greek)

Some words have flipped back and forth as to which way they take up the comparative and superlative forms. *Fun*, for example, seems to be a British English word, but its etymology is not clear: The noun *fun* seems to have come from a verb *fun*, meaning to cheat or trick someone. In terms of its adjective status, in phrases like *fun times*, it seems gradable to most people, but in what form? Do we go with *more fun* and *most fun*, or since it is a shorter word, do we use suffixes to make *funner* and *funnest*. There is some general upset out there in the blogosphere about *funner* and *funnest*, so it is safe to say that this issue is not settled yet. You will need to check with locals about the customs for *fun* before engaging in a comparison of it.

Other adjective forms

For portable phones, there is a wide variety of skins and cases to dress up your device for different occasions. In earlier varieties of English, adjectives used to wear different cases depending on the type of noun they modified. Languages like Spanish, French, Italian, and German have adjectives which change with their nouns. For these languages, nouns come in different kinds, such as feminine, masculine, and neuter, as well as singular and plural:

German	French	Italian
Das gebrauchte Auto	la petite étoile	I divani rossi
'the used car'	'the little star'	'the red couches'

During the Old English period (450–1100), the adjectives in English worked more like these modern languages. In a phrase like 'to the good king,' suffixes would be added to the adjective *gōd* 'good,' producing *gōdum cyninge*. The *-um* is there to represent the 'to the' part of Modern English and and the masculine grammatical gender of *cyninge* in Old English. We have since dropped our gender suffixes in English. In Old English, a neuter noun like *sweord* would get the adjective *gōdes* with a different suffix in a possessive construction like *the good sword's strike*. Over the years, these different suffixes became increasingly difficult to tell apart, and people began to use them less. Consequently, the categories of feminine, masculine, and neuter nouns faded away through Middle English (1100–1500).

nouns

Most students feel comfortable with the next lexical category: **Nouns**. How tricky could they be? The answer is "not that tricky," but the path we take to that answer may not be the one you anticipate.

Nouns are normally defined by their meanings, so that the regular saying in many schools is "A noun is a person, place, or thing." An internet search for the string "person, place, or thing" brings up over five million hits. For some people, this phrase is the most they can remember of their school-trained knowledge about grammar, and it has to be the most successful grammar phrase (in terms of popularity) ever created. Unfortunately, it is not extensive enough as a definition to be accurate. Consider the nouns *fork* and *game*. A fork falls in the category of thing, but a game is a set of relationships amongst the players. To play a football game, the athletes must play with a set of similar purposes in a (somewhat) coordinated pattern of relationships: Who is on offense? Who is on defense? Who has possession of the ball? *Game* is a common noun. It regularly turns up several hundred million hits in internet searches. Yet, it is not a person, place, or thing.[4]

Instead, to understand what nouns are in language, we have to examine how they are used with the words around them. Look at the underlined words in the following sentences:

> <u>The game</u> fell flat today.
> <u>A game of poker</u> would be nice.
> We lost <u>the game</u>.
> Could you drive us <u>to the game</u>?

In each of these sentences, the word *game* is part of either a subject or an object. This context is where nouns go. The meaning of *game* is not the crucial information we need to figure out its lexical category. What we need to know is where it falls in phrases.

Regular noun plurals

Another distinguishing quality of nouns is that they can be plural or singular. Everyone reading this book will easily be able to produce many singular and plural noun forms, but here we need to distinguish between different types. Several ways of making plurals have existed since the beginning of English. These different methods from previous centuries have been carried forward as irregular forms today.

The most typical kind of plural form is the plural *-s*, as in *wombat, wombats*. This suffix is a holdover from Anglo-Saxon and is directly attached to **count nouns**. As you may have guessed, these are nouns you can count: *trenches, rockets, continents, stars*. Some variation exists between the *-s* and *-es* plural, but it has nothing to do with the lexical category of noun, so we save that discussion for Chapter 6.

In contrast to count nouns are **mass nouns**. These nouns have meanings which are more easily quantified by the volume of a container than by countable objects. Nouns like *water, air, rice, gasoline* are all mass nouns. However, these nouns are mass nouns not because of their meaning, but because of how they are made plural in their context. In the sentence *I bought three crickets for my crested gecko*, the noun *cricket* gets made plural with an *-s* and follows directly after the numeral *three*. Now try the mass noun *water* in the same sentence: **I bought three waters for my crested gecko*. This is not a possible construction for most English speakers and certainly ungrammatical unless you have the term *waters* for "bottles of water" or (oddly here) "bodies of water." Mass nouns require some unit of measurement before they can be pluralized: *three pints of water*, *two cups of rice*, *five gallons of gasoline*. The mass noun *beer* usually has a unit of measure, such as *cases of beer*, *kegs of beer*, *pints of beer*. Yet, in plenty of social situations, telling the bartender *two beers* (or *two waters*) will get you served just fine. How come? It is well understood that everyone wants their beer or water in a container, not just loose in their hands, so glasses and bottles are understood to be part of the deal.

Irregular noun plurals

Beyond count nouns and mass nouns is the realm of irregulars. It is an unfortunate name because this realm used to be more than an amorphous category of odd plurals. Instead, irregular plurals were themselves another normal way to make a noun plural. As time passed, the plural -*s* took over more and more forms, swallowing them like the monster in *The Blob*, a 1958 horror movie.

The first irregular noun plurals are the **zero forms**. These usually include collections of nonhuman animals: *deer, deer*; *sheep, sheep*. This category contained the Anglo-Saxon word for 'people,' *folc*, and the word *folk* still has the unmarked plural. This type of pluralization has taken in a few other words, including *fish, elk*, and even *moose* (originally a word from Algonquian, a Native American language). The word *word* used to be part of this pack of plurals, but it has since fallen in with the -*s* plurals as a regular count noun.

For some nouns, their plural suffix was -*en*.[5] Few words today end in -*en*, although this used to be the regular way to make *name* and *eye* plural. Various spellings of the plural *eyen* held on into the sixteenth century, but the plural -*s* suffix caught up with it and took *eye* over. We have three -*en* plural forms today, two of which are *oxen* and *brethren*, neither one being all that common. Both seem fairly stable as plural forms, although *brethren* is restricted to formal register and, usually, religious contexts.

The most common -*en* plural is truly bizarre: *children*. It is not that children themselves are strange, but the history of its plurals is. (Yes, that is "plurals.") The singular form *child* is from the Old English period, and its original plural was simply *child* (spelled <cild> in both forms). It got pulled into another class of nouns which took an -*ru* plural suffix, so the plural subject would be *Cildru singaþ* 'The children sing.' This plural form *childru* lasted into Middle English, especially in the north of England. For some of these areas, the normal local form for the plural of *child* is still *childru*, an impressive run of a thousand years for the lone survivor suffix of a small noun class. For the south of England in the Middle English period, people either grew dissatisfied with the -*ru* plural, or perhaps the idea that it was a plural faded from their lexicons. In either case, they began to add another plural suffix onto the word, -*en*. This double-marked plural *children*, which still contains vestiges of the -ru plural, has become the normal form for standard Englishes around the world.

Other irregular plurals baffle modern speakers. One fairly common set of plural nouns contains those that shift vowels to show their plural status.

Singular	Plural
foot	feet
goose	geese
louse	lice
mouse	mice
tooth	teeth
man	men
woman	women

These plurals seem to have some pattern, but it is not the same one in all of them, and note that not all similar words work the same way. We do not have *spouse*, *spice* or *moose*, *meese*. These vowel-changing plurals come from a very old pattern of adding a vowel suffix on the end of the word. So, for example, *foot* would have earned an *-i* suffix to make a plural, resulting in *footi*. This suffix affected the preceding vowel. If you remember back to Chapter 3, assimilation is the process where one sound becomes more similar to another sound. In this case, the long [o] vowel of *foot* was shifted to the front of the mouth to be more like the front vowel [i]. This assimilation gave us the long mid-vowel [e], [fet] (which was then raised to its modern position of [fit] in the Great Vowel Shift). Eventually, the suffix, like so many word-final vowels, dropped off, and only the vowel distinction was left to indicate the difference between singular and plural. This small group of words is the product of a regular linguistic process which people eventually dropped. The result is a seemingly irregular pattern.

A different set of irregular plurals comes from languages which had different regular processes for making plural nouns. In adopting the nouns, we adopted their patterns for plurals.

alumna	alumni
basis	bases (homographic, but not homophonic with the plural of base)
hypothesis	hypotheses
stratum	strata
datum	data
focus	foci (geometry term, also *focuses* now}
fungus	fungi (also *funguses* now)

Some of these are changing in different ways. A word like *fungus* can be pluralized using the original Latin pattern, *fungi*, or it can be pluralized with the Anglo-Saxon pattern on the English word, yielding *funguses*. A word like *data* is now used variably as a singular noun (e.g. *the data shows* …) and as a plural noun (e.g. *the data show* …).

The other situation where an unexpected plural comes up is when a count noun is used as an adjective before the noun, as in *We went for a three-mile walk*. Most speakers would also say *We walked three miles*. Why is there no plural suffix when it is a modifier before another noun? The answer has to do with the history of that construction. In Old English, there was a suffix to denote its plural status, an -a suffix. With English phonology, some sounds get treated better than others, and perhaps the most tossed aside sounds are vowels at the ends of words (consider all the "silent -e" words out there). As with many other word-final vowels, this suffix got dropped, and its function took on a zero form to mark the plural. In a way, it is now a ghost suffix.

Gender and case for all

Modern German, Dutch, French, Italian, and Spanish all have a few different systems of noting classes of nouns. English used to have such systems, but they have mostly faded away, except for one tiny corner of the grammar, the corner of gender and case. Unfortunately, in that corner are some terms muddled with confusion, namely, *female, male, neuter.*[6] Old English had **grammatical gender** for nouns, meaning that each noun was either feminine, masculine, or neuter. The Old English speakers themselves did not label their nouns in this way; they just had three different types of nouns. The word for 'woman' *wif* was neuter, and the word for 'valuable gem' *sincgim* was masculine. That grammatical system has faded from use, so when people now think of the gender of nouns, it is associated with cultural ideas of gender. The Old English word *scip* 'ship' was neuter (in grammatical gender), but today most ships are considered to be feminine (in natural gender).

The other noun marking system used in Old English was **case**. To mark case in a language requires that speakers have some kind of marker, like an affix, and an unconscious understanding of how a noun is used in a sentence, whether it is a subject or object. In Old English, case was marked with suffixes on every noun. If the word 'boat' *bāt* was used as a subject, it would just be *bāt*. If it were plural and the object of a preposition, as in *to the boats*, it would be *bātum*. If it were singular and marked for possession, as in *the boat's mast*, it would be *bātes mæst*. This last suffix on *bāt* is where Modern English gets its possessive *'s* for *boat's* or *ship's* or *eye's* or *earth's*.

Since suffixes do not receive the most prominent stress in a word, most eventually got lost through the centuries. With them, English speakers were able to show which word was a subject and which word was an object. Without them, English speakers had to find other ways to point out what is what in a sentence (more on those solutions in Chapter 8).

The only corner of Modern English grammar where case marking still survives is with personal pronouns. Consider the following sentences:

I shot him.	*He shot me.*
I shot her.	*She shot me.*
We shot you.	*You shot us.*
I shot them	*They shot me.*

The subjects have one form, and the objects have a different form (except for *you*). These different forms indicate case marking. We can figure from the form of the word that *her* is the object, and *she* is the subject. A sentence like *The officer shot the suspect* does not mark the object and subject in such identifiable ways.

Possession is also shown on the personal pronouns in Modern English. Consider what the pronoun *our* indicates in this sentence: *Julia read our cookbook.* Here *our* is not the object of the verb *read*. It is a modifier for the noun *cookbook*. If we switched out *our* for something like *my*, *your*, *her*, or *their*, we would be switching who owns the cookbook. That information is wrapped in each word marked with case.

verbs

One ring to rule them all: The verb. In Tolkien's *Lord of the Rings*, a magical ring controls other rings and those who wear them.

> *…One for the Dark Lord on his dark throne*
> *In the Land of Mordor where the Shadows lie.*
> *One Ring to rule them all, One Ring to find them,*
> *One Ring to bring them all and in the darkness bind them*
> *In the Land of Mordor where the Shadows lie.*

Verbs are probably not evil (probably). But they certainly do control those other lexical categories around them. For this reason, Steven Pinker in *The Language Instinct* writes: "Within a phrase, the verb is a little despot…". Within this section, the details of how it controls other parts are revealed.

Like the lexical category of nouns, verbs are not definable by meaning: Action is not the key. In the two sentences *She runs fast* and *She seems fast*, the first one has action, but the second does not. Both *seem* and *run* are verbs in these sentences, but *seem* describes a state of being and *run* describes an action. So what does make a verb a verb?

As with nouns, how the word operates in a sentence provides the clue as to its lexical category. Nouns work as subjects and objects for verbs. In English, verbs require a subject, even if it is a place filler. In the sentences *The book hit the table* and *It is raining*, the subjects *book* and *it* are connected to the verbs *hit* and *is*, respectively. The word *it* is itself just a placeholder so there can be a subject and does not actually refer to anything. The arrangement of parts around verbs is introduced in this subsection.

Consider the following forms: *dog*, *collar*, *rope*, *table*. Are they nouns or verbs? Without context, both are possible in Modern English.

> *That sales rep will <u>dog</u> me all day.*
> *They eventually should <u>collar</u> the stray.*
> *The cowboy could <u>rope</u> the horse in the pasture.*
> *The representative should <u>table</u> the proposal.*

In each of these sentences, the underlined word is a verb. No special suffix tells us this information, but its position with other words does. As a usage note, some people do not like verbing nouns. They consider it bad taste to take a noun like *verb*, and make a verb out of it. A sentence like *She verbed the word 'book'* upsets some people's aesthetic sensibilities.

Verbing nouns; nouning verbs

In Modern English, we do not have many suffixes which do grammar work. We actually have *no* prefixes which do grammar work. Given this situation, we have no clear way to mark a verb as a verb or a noun as a noun (more about this in Chapters 7 and 8). In other languages, each word gets a little flag to wave, proudly proclaiming its solidarity with the nation of nouns or the tribe of verbs. In French, verbs have certain suffixes: Verbs ending in *-er* form a group, and verbs ending in *-ir* form a different group. In English, our nouns and verbs are comparatively bare.

So, our verb forms can be made into nouns. Probably the most common usage of the forms *talk, run, hit* are as verbs, and it is certainly the first guess most people make about their lexical category. Yet, context is needed to figure out how the form is being used and, thereby, which lexical category it fits into: The lexical categories for *run* in the phrases *a run* and *to run* are different. In these sentences, the underlined words are nouns.

She gave a really good <u>talk</u> today.
He went on his longest <u>run</u> last night.
Bruce has had many <u>hits</u>.

Transitivity

The transitivity of verbs is a tricky subject, and scholars do not agree on how many there should be. In this book, we keep the situation simple in two ways. First, we only talk about three categories of transitivity: **intransitive**, **transitive**, and **ditransitive**. Second, we stipulate that each verb is lexically specified for transitivity. In other words, when you memorize a verb, such as *kiss*, you memorize its form, meaning, lexical category, and (since it is a verb) that it requires both a subject and object (that it is transitive). In the sentences *She <u>kisses</u> him all the time* and *She <u>kisses</u> all the time*, the verb is transitive in both cases. The object in the second sentence is simply not expressed.

Intransitive:	Subject → Verb|
Transitive:	Subject → Verb → Object
Ditransitive:	Subject → Verb → Object → Object

For transitivity, what is *trans-ing?* What does it mean to *trans?* For verbs, we are talking about whether the subject goes *across* the verb or not.

Intransitive verbs are the simplest. They do not logically require an object: *I fell*. Even if there are words following the verb, they are not objects for the intransitive verb. In the sentence *I fell down the steps*, the prepositional phrase *down the steps* is where the falling took place, not the object. Note the difference for a sentence like *I felled the tree*, where the weight of the verb *fell* is bearing down on the noun phrase *the tree*. Consider the following division:

Intransitive	Transitive
She <u>runs</u> three days a week.	She <u>runs</u> her dog three days a week.
We <u>sleep</u> all night.	We <u>sleep</u> the computer each night.
He <u>walks</u> downtown every afternoon.	He <u>walks</u> the dog every morning.

How could *walk, run*, or *sleep* be both intransitive and transitive? Well, consider that there are two verbs for each line and not one: *Walk* as the intransitive verb means simply 'to ambulate,' but *walk* as a transitive verb means 'to cause something to walk.' With a different meaning, it gets a different lexical slot. Remember, words are pairings of form and meaning.

The following sentences also contain intransitive verbs:

The clock <u>is</u> ticking in the kitchen.
I <u>laughed</u>; he <u>cried</u>.

Now consider these transitive verbs:

The big fish <u>ate</u> the little fish.
The cat <u>chased</u> the squirrel out of the yard.
The teacher <u>threw</u> the book.

With the transitive verbs, an object is on the receiving end from the verb. The verb ties together the subject and object in each sentence.

Ditransitive verbs go one step further. Instead of just one object, <u>di</u>transitive verbs have two. Really, transitive verbs could be called "monotransitive" verbs, but even linguists have a limit on silly names. Here are some verbs regularly considered to be ditransitive in their logical structure:

The child <u>gave</u> the chicken to the cat.
They <u>exchanged</u> the vacuum for a blender.
You should <u>put</u> the pen on my desk.
I <u>passed</u> the ball to her.
She <u>read</u> him a book.

In these sentences, the subjects reach across the verbs to two objects (hence the name *ditransitive*).

Subject → Verb → Object → Object
child   → gave → chicken → cat

For all verbs, their quality of transitivity is stored with the verb in the lexicon. So an intransitive verb like *jump* has with it the lexical category of *Verb* and a structure like "_____ *jump.*" A transitive verb like *kiss* would have a structure of "_____ *kiss* _____" for the subject and the object.

Tense

For verbs, tense is a function of the verb's form, and in Modern English, we only have two tenses: past and non-past. These do not strictly refer to placement along a time-space continuum, and somehow it is disappointing to students (and many current teachers) that we do not have a future tense. English *can* indicate future time, but we use the non-past tense to do it.

> Non-past verb form: *The squid <u>slaps</u> me in the face every morning.*
> Past verb form: *The squid <u>slapped</u> me in the face every morning.*

Non-past includes every construction that is not past tense. Since we mean "verb form," every time we use the technical terms *past* and *non-past*, you need to keep in mind that past tense forms can be used to refer to events that have not already been completed. Consider the following two sentences:

> Future time reference: *I thought the school year <u>began</u> next month.*
> Hypothetical situation: *I would make him dinner if the squid <u>slapped</u> me.*

In the first sentence, the past tense form is used to indicate the hypothetical nature of the statement. The same potential is shown in the second sentence. Now consider referring to a future time frame, as in these three sentences:

> *They <u>should</u> eat at 7:00 tonight.*
> *They <u>will</u> eat at 7:00 tonight.*
> *They <u>are</u> going to eat at 7:00 tonight.*

In the sentences above, all three conjugated verbs are in the non-past, but all three sentences refer to a future time. The conjugation of the verb can be separate from the time frame of the utterance. In a sentence like *We play cards every evening during the summer*, the time reference is to both the past and the future, but the verb is conjugated in the non-past.

In English, past conjugations usually take on a special form. Like plural nouns, speakers originally produced a wide variety of past tense patterns. The modern irregular patterns still have fossils from previous ages of English. These fossils used to be regular patterns themselves, but their numbers got so few that they became memorized chunks in the lexicon.

Regular past tense forms receive an *-ed* suffix. Like plural *-s* for nouns, the *-ed* form was not always the "regular" form. Previously, it was one of many ways to mark the past tense, but over time, bit by bit, the *-ed* forms began to expand, taking in new members.

Infinitive	Past	Participle
bake	baked	baked
stone	stoned	stoned
trip	tripped	tripped
bat	batted	batted

The participle category contains verb forms used in various functions discussed below and in Chapter 8. For example, the participle forms could fit in a frame such as "She has _____" and perhaps some object where needed.

Irregular verbs form an unruly group of previously distinct patterns. For many of them, you can most likely discern the patterns.

Infinitive	Past	Participle
swim	swam	swum
ring	rang	rung
sing	sang	sung

In this set, the vowels switched from a non-past form <i> to a past form <a>. There were different classes of verbs that formed their past tense with vowels, and their distribution in Modern English is explored further in Chapter 6.

Aspect

Aspect, like transitivity, is a topic over which scholars have spilled much ink – bottles and gallons and vats of ink. A basic definition of aspect is that it specifies the semantic quality of the verb on a time scale. In *I am walking* and *I was walking*, the action continues over time. In both *I have walked* and *I had walked*, the action is complete, regardless of the tense. In *I walk*, the completedness of the action is not specified. The distinction between *I walked* vs. *I have walked* concerns the speaker's at-the-moment consequences of past events.

Aspect for human language overall can be quite complex, with perhaps ten different aspect categories. In terms of the forms of verbs for English, we work with three in this book. These are **progressive**, **perfect**, and **neutral** (the catch-all category for everything that is not progressive and perfect).

Progressive

The progressive aspect indicates an ongoing event, whether it was in the past or is described by the non-past (e.g. the future or the present time). In English, the progressive (sometimes known as the imperfect) is created through the use of the auxiliary verb *be* and a non-auxiliary verb with an *-ing*.[7]

Progressive Aspect

We <u>are</u> gett<u>ing</u> out of the pool.
We <u>were</u> fall<u>ing</u> off the raft.
We could <u>be</u> jump<u>ing</u> off the boat.

Neutral Aspect

We get out of the pool.
We fell off the raft.
We could jump off the boat.

The first example is in the non-past tense (conjugated verb = *are*). The second example is in the past tense (conjugated verb = *were*), and the third is again in the non-past but with the modal *could*. These examples illustrate that the form of the verb *be* does not matter, but the combination of *be* + Verb*ing* does.

Perfect

Perfect aspect has nothing to do with how well the verb worked, whether the topic be construction or love. For most verbs, perfect aspect indicates that the action is completed. In English, the perfect aspect is developed through the auxiliary verb *have* and the participle of a main verb.

Perfect Aspect

We <u>have</u> eat<u>en</u> the ice cream.
We <u>have</u> fall<u>en</u> off the noodles.
We <u>had</u> jump<u>ed</u> off the boat...
If he <u>had</u> <u>had</u> the binoculars...

Neutral Aspect

We eat the ice cream.
We fell off the noodles.
We jumped off the boat.
If he owned the binoculars...

The first sentence has the perfect aspect in the non-past tense and portrays the meaning of the ice-cream eating being a completed action: It is done. The same sense comes out of the next sentence: It is a completed action. In the third sentence, the conjugated verb *have* is in the past tense. Here, the action is also complete, but it gives the meaning of the verb completed before some other past time verb (e.g. *We had jumped off the boat before it exploded*). This combination of tense and aspect is accordingly called the past perfect. In the fourth phrase, *If he had had the binoculars*, the lexical verb *have*, denoting possession, is rendered in the perfect aspect with the participle form. As a matter of happenstance, the participle form of *have* is the same as the past tense of *have*, so we have the relatively rare situation where two of the exact same forms appear adjacent to each other. In the first two phrases, the verb's past participle is created with an -*en* suffix, whereas in the third, it is an -*ed* suffix, and in the fourth, it is a form particular to the verb.

What the past participle form of any verb happens to be is specific to the verb itself, and participle forms have undergone many changes. A verb like *work* used to have the forms *work, wrought, wrought*, but in its modern form, we have *work, worked, worked*. Other verbs have retained their previous forms, now deemed irregular: *swim, swam, swum; eat, ate, eaten; drink, drank, drunk*. Since these change over time, some English speakers may have one form and other people will have a different form. We have previously discussed *hanged* and *hung* as split forms, and some communities have *sank* instead of the past participle *sunk*. Other dialects have *growed* instead of *grew*. There is a survey of such forms in Chapter 6.

Neutral

The progressive and perfect aspects use specific auxiliary verbs and specific auxiliary forms to carry their meaning: <u>be Verb*ing*</u> for progressive and <u>*have* Partici-ple</u> for perfect. All other forms in English we lump together as **neutral**. It is a large category, and it could be divided down to smaller subcategories, but the dissection is messy, and we need to avoid it. The neutral examples used for comparison in the above sections indicate the contrast between the other two aspects.

Mood

Mood is the relation of the speaker to the audience as represented through the verb. The mood of a sentence is independent of its tense or aspect. We stick with four moods: **declarative**, **imperative**, **interrogative**, and **conditional**.

Declarative (Indicative)

Declarative is the most basic mood and the most commonly used. For most declarative sentences in English, the subject comes before the verb. In declarative constructions, the speaker is giving the audience a statement. The declarative mood is something like the category of neutral aspect in that it is defined in part by not containing any of the other moods. A declarative sentence is not imperative, interrogative, or conditional.

> *The bear fell off the table.*
> *The girl in pigtails walked through the puddles.*
> *I still believe in the US Constitution.*

Imperative

Imperative mood is a special construction in English. Not any sentence which directs an audience to do something can be an imperative sentence. Other conditions must be met: The verb must be in the non-past, and the subject must be implied to be the second person *you* (plural or singular).

Imperative	Not Imperative
Please, go home.	*We should go home.*
Run!	*Why don't we run?*
Dance like a fiend.	*I'm going to dance like a fiend.*

With these special details, the imperative is fairly easy to identify.

Interrogative

Interrogative verb constructions ask questions. The interrogative has two main forms in English, and both serve to turn a declarative statement into a question. In the following two sentences, the first is declarative, and the second is interrogative.

Declarative: *We are leaving*
Interrogative: *Are we leaving?*

For verbs which do not function as auxiliaries – such as *run*, *sleep*, and *counterfeit* – to create an interrogative takes an extra step. These verbs require the help of the auxiliary *do* to make their interrogative state.

Declarative	Interrogative
We run today.	*Do we run today?*
We sleep late every Saturday.	*Do we sleep late every Saturday?*
They forged those signatures.	*Did they forge those signatures?*

Note that the verb *do* takes on the tense of the sentence since it is the actively conjugated verb. Earlier in the history of English, up until the beginning of the 1600s, the auxiliary *do* did not help out in making interrogatives. The main verb itself was switched with the subject: *Run we this afternoon?* For everyone who has taken a Shakespeare course, this difference may explain some of the syntax you encountered in his works: "What say you of this gentlewoman?" (*All's Well that Ends Well*, Act 1, Scene 3).

Even the verbs *have* and *do* require this *do*-support when in an inverted interrogative mood:

Did you do it earlier?
Did you have it earlier?

In this typical form, the subject and verb are inverted from their normal, declarative order. As auxiliary verbs, *have*, *be*, and the modal verbs do switch with the subject. They are the ones that carry the tense and therefore do not need *do*-support:

<u>*Have*</u> *we left yet?*
<u>*Are*</u> *we leaving?*
<u>*Were*</u> *we leaving?*
<u>*Will*</u> *we leave?*
<u>*May*</u> *we leave?*
<u>*Can*</u> *we leave?*

> # Words to the Wise: Shall vs. will
>
> There is a tangled history between *shall* and *will*. For some prescriptivists, *shall* is to be used to mark intent with first-person subjects: *I shall do it, we shall go.* Accordingly, *will* would be used only with the other possible subjects.
>
> *Shall* has other uses in Modern English. Consider the sentence *You shall not pass!* The meaning here is not of simple future time reference. With *shall*, the speaker (here Gandalf) is imposing his will on the audience. The sentence *You will not pass* has a different sense.
>
> Additionally, *shall* can be seen as more emotionally forceful than *will*. To the question *Will you eat this chocolate cake?*, the answer of *I shall not* comes off as stronger than *I will not*.

Questions in English can also be asked by providing a declarative construction with a rising intonation at the end: *We are leaving?* For our purposes, the label interrogative will be used only to refer to the inverted structure.

Conditional

The last mood is **conditional**. For the speaker and the audience, the conditional foregrounds possibility. Consider some of these following modal verbs.

can	*They can yell*
could	*They could yell*
will	*They will yell*
would	*They would yell*
shall	*I shall yell*
should	*They should yell*
may	*They may yell*
might	*They might yell*

Modal verbs are a special subclass of verbs which function as auxiliaries and have a different pattern of conjugation: They do not take verbal *-s* for third-person singular and do not have a past tense form: *She can_ sing* vs. *she sings*.

Earlier in English, modal verbs did have past tense forms. *Can* had *could* as a past tense form, *will* had *would*, and *shall* had *should*. Over time, these previous past-tense forms lost that job. All modal verbs mark conditional mood, independent of tense: The mood of the sentence *They will yell* is different from the declarative *They yell*, despite both of those being in the non-past tense.

Conditional mood can also be created in English with a subordinate *if*, as in the sentence *If we take the left path, we will get there sooner.* The *if* creates the same state of conditionality for the phrase *we take the left path* as a modal verb would.

More discussion of verbs will take place in Chapter 6 when we turn to how past tense forms are built.

function words: the mortar for the bricks

The lexical categories of nouns, adjectives, and verbs contain only content words. Their main job is to trigger meanings in the minds of the audience. Function words help those content words do their work: <u>The</u> noun <u>with the</u> adjective noun verb <u>off the</u> noun (e.g. *The chair <u>with the</u> broken seat fell <u>off the</u> porch*). The words *the*, *with*, and *off* are function words. We touch on some of their qualities here, and we further explore in Chapters 7 and 8 how we use them to build phrases.

One metaphor that works fairly well for content and function categories is that of bricks and mortar. Sure, a brick building is made of bricks, but the bricks are held together with mortar. Just like mortar in a brick building, most people do not notice the function words in a phrase, yet they are essential.

For several years, a popular email circulated highlighting the camouflaged nature of function words. In the email was a paragraph where readers were asked to count how many times the letter <f> appeared. Take a stab at it here. Working through the sentence only once, how many <f>s do you count?

Finished files are the result of years of scientific study combined with the experience of years of work.

Most people find fewer <f>s than are actually there. The <f>s of *finished* and *files* are easiest to pick out, and the <f> of *scientific* is fairly findable, for a total of three <f>s. Yet, there are actually seven of them. Few people, at least on the first read, notice the <f>s protruding from the word *of*. *Of* is a function word, gluing together the words around it. It is not flashy, but it is necessary for English.

We take a brief tour here of four lexical categories of function words. Some of these may seem simple for you, while others are nebulous and mystifying. If you work through producing them in different grammatical contexts, you should note that you already have command over them. Now you just need to formally recognize what it is that they do.

coordinators

Coordinators are perhaps the simplest kind of function item. A coordinator such as *and* joins two similar phrases together.

I petted both the tiger and the lion.
I photographed the giraffe, and I videoed the zebra.
The bat flew at Julia and me.

Words like *me* and *the lion* work as phrases themselves, as we will discuss in Chapters 7 and 8. Both *or* and *but* are also coordinators, as in *He is old but not wise* and *She either dropped it or threw it down.*

determinatives working as determiners[8]

Determinatives are a class of words, but **determiner** is a function of determining a noun. Determinatives are parts of noun phrases which modify the entirety of the noun phrase, including any adjectives or prepositions inside of it. The most common determinatives are *the* and *a/an*.

The pasta	*The dry pasta*	*The dry pasta in the box*
A box	*A flattened box*	*A flattened box in the bin*

Other words that work as definite determiners are the demonstrative pronouns *this, that, these,* and *those.*

This pasta   That box   These sharks   Those alligators

Indefinite determiners include words like *each, every,* and *some*:

Get me some boxes out of the attic.

The *some* in the example sentence does not specify any certain box. It limits the number of boxes.

Not all varieties of English use even the most common determinatives in the same way. Phrases such as *He is going to _____ college this fall* may or may not be filled by a determinative, depending on the variety. In US English, *college* does not take a determiner. For some British varieties, *university* does not take a determinative nor does *hospital*: *She is going to _____ university; We went to _____ hospital after the accident.* A good deal of determiner variation exists in English; for most of Old English, the language functioned just fine without the word *the.*

pronouns

Pronouns come in many shapes and sizes, but they all have the quality of standing in for some other item. A personal pronoun like *I* does not always mean Prince William or William Shatner, but it does stand in for the person speaking. A demonstrative pronoun like *these* in *These are the ones I shot* stands in for something plural which is shootable. An interrogative pronoun like *what* in *What topping do you like?* stands in for a phrase like *hot fudge.*

Standing in for other words requires **deixis**. Note that the meaning of the pronoun is restrained: The personal pronoun *I* refers to the speaker, and the demonstrative pronoun *these* refers to several things at some distance. Deixis allows for the specific reference of the pronoun to change depending on the context of the word's usage.

Personal pronouns

Personal pronouns include a subject, object, and genitive form for each. The distinction between these forms is part of the discussion in Chapter 6.

Subjects	Singular	Plural
1st Person	*I*	*we*
2nd Person	*you*	*you*
3rd Person	*she, he, it*	*they*

Objects	Singular	Plural
1st Person	*me*	*us*
2nd Person	*you*	*you*
3rd Person	*her, him, it*	*them*

Figure 4.2 Singular *they* has been part of English for a while, and several alternatives have been proposed, as discussed in this *Dinosaur Comic*. http://www.qwantz.com/index.php?comic=2080. Rollover text: "There! now each person who wrote me an email about 'they' being singular should be happy. i … hope this is exactly what bitches was looking for?" *Dinosaur Comics* by Ryan North. www.dinosaurcomics.com

Genitive	Singular	Plural
1st Person	*my (mine)*	*our*
2nd Person	*your*	*your*
3rd Person	*her, his, its*	*their*

Demonstrative pronouns

Demonstrative pronouns fall into the following pattern for most speakers:

	Singular	Plural
Near	*this*	*these*
Far	*that*[9]	*those*

The distinction between *this parrot* and *that parrot* is supposedly one of proximity, with *this* being the closer one and *that* being the one farther away. In real conversations, the near/far difference is sometimes turned into a like/dislike distinction. For example, <u>*these*</u> *tax cuts will really help* vs. <u>*those*</u> *tax hikes will ruin the economy*. At other times, the near/far distinction marks how recently the topic was discussed: If two people are talking about wolverines and then launch into a discussion of hippopotamuses, at the end one person might say "those wolverines are dangerous, but these hippos are more dangerous," with the full realization that neither wolverines nor hippos are present.

This demonstrative pronoun system has been unstable in the history of English, and its flux continues today. Since the sixteenth century, *them* has been used as a demonstrative pronoun, usually in place of *those* but also *these* (e.g. *Them puppies are for sale*). In the United States, this form was marked as vernacular in the twentieth century, and its use has faded. In areas of England, such as London, demonstrative *them* is the most widely used form with teenagers.

Interrogative pronouns

The last set of pronouns is **interrogative pronouns**. These pronouns are primarily used to ask questions. Each of these has its quality of deixis, but each one takes a slightly different type of reference.

Interrogative	Declarative with rising intonation	Interrogative pronoun
What do you want?	*You want what?*	*What* = e.g. an egg, a chair, a win
Whose do you want?	*You want whose?*	*Whose* = e.g. hers, his, mine
To whom would you like to speak?	*You would like to speak to whom?*	*Whom* = e.g. your mom, him, them
Who wants it?	*You want whom?*	*Who* = e.g. he/him; she/her

In the non-inverted interrogatives, note that *what* substitutes for the object of *want*, but the other interrogative pronouns modify other parts of the sentence. Like most pronouns, these interrogatives have a history stretching back to Old English.

prepositions

Pronouns are relatively easy for people to understand, since they have some meaning along with all of their grammatical function. Prepositions also have some meaning, but at times, they seem to serve purely a grammatical function. For meaning, **prepositions** indicate relations of space and time. For their background, many of them developed out of Old English and Middle English as the language became more dependent on them to do the work of building sentences. A preposition like *on* can be used in a sentence focused on space, *Put the book on the desk*, or a sentence focused on time, *Get yourself home on time*. The nature of *on* does not change between the two functions.

Prepositions can take one of three complements: either a noun phrase, a clause, or nothing.

Preposition complements

Noun Phrase: *Throw the cat <u>out</u> the door.*

Clause: *I will flip the steaks <u>after</u> you open the wine.*

Bare: *Let me know when you come <u>in</u>?*

For all three of these functions, the prepositions deal with space and time, but they also connect other words together, serving as the mortar for the bricks of the nouns and verbs. In this grammatical role, as function words, the prepositions connect together other lexical categories into larger phrases.

chapter summary

This chapter presents you with the vocabulary needed to analyze words. The words are stored in the lexicon, our own personal mental dictionaries. The lexicon is different from paper-based dictionaries in its organization because it connects words with similar meaning and sounds while generally prohibiting true synonyms. Two types of lexical categories can group all words. The first type is the set of content lexical categories: adjectives, nouns, verbs. The second type is the set of function lexical categories: coordinators, determiners, pronouns, prepositions. The content lexical categories are the bricks for building language, and the function lexical categories are the mortar people use to hold the bricks together. Each of these lexical categories has special properties to distinguish them. For example, nouns function as objects and subjects, but verbs control objects and subjects, and are marked by tense, aspect, and mood. In each lexical category, special properties guide the use of words. For verbs, the mood could be declarative, interrogative, imperative, or conditional, and these control how we build phrases.

key concepts

- Aspect
- Attributive
- Case
- Comparative
- Conditional
- Content
- Count nouns
- Declarative
- Deixis
- Demonstrative pronouns
- Determinatives
- Determiner
- Ditransitive
- Function
- Grammatical gender
- Imperative
- Interrogative
- Interrogative pronouns
- Intransitive
- Lexical ambiguity
- Lexical categories
- Mass nouns
- Modal verbs
- Mood
- Neutral
- Nouns
- Perfect
- Personal pronouns
- Predicate
- Predicative
- Prepositions
- Progressive
- Pronouns
- Sentence adverbs
- Superlative

- Transitive
- Verbs
- Zero forms

---

notes

1   All word histories come from the *Oxford English Dictionary*: www.oed.com/
2   See the Language Log discussion here: http://languagelog.ldc.upenn.edu/nll/?p=2363.
3   The Greek etymology of *alphabet* is related to the first two letters of the Greek character system: the letter *Alpha* and the letter *Beta*.
4   When "idea" is thrown into the definition, the wheels really fall off the bus. Adding "idea" to the "person, place, or thing" definition of noun expands possible candidates to most verbs also.
5   The vowel varied in this suffix depending on the phonetic qualities of its companion noun.
6   For linguists like me, there is a wish we would like from our fairy godmother: We wish the purveyors of grammar who came up with the terms would have picked another category for labels other than gender. How about brown, green, and red instead? Or perhaps rocks, like granite, sandstone, and marble, or even igneous, sedimentary, and metamorphic. Those grammarians were just looking for names for different kinds – did the names need to be culturally loaded and cause such confusion?
7   Prior to the printing press, this suffix was *-ende*, and even today, many people still have a [n] as the final consonant for the progressive. Since about 1500, this progressive suffix has been spelled <-ing>.
8   This term and discussion follow from Huddleston and Pullum's work (2002:368).
9   The form *that* has several different jobs. Figuring out which job is which is a matter of understanding its linguistic context. *That* as a demonstrative pronoun is a different word from *that* in *the cookie that I like*.

---

references

Huddleston, R. and Pullum, G.K. (2002) *The Cambridge Grammar of the English Language*. Cambridge: Cambridge University Press.
Pinker, S. (2010) *The Language Instinct: How the Mind Creates Language*. HarperCollins.

---

further reading

English Words. Heidi Harley. 2006. Oxford: Blackwell.
   This book is an accessible introduction to the study of English words. The author works through a broad-based linguistic approach to help students gain skills in analysis. The book covers the structure of English vocabulary, including its phonology, morphology, syntax, semantics.
Words in the Mind: An Introduction to the Mental Lexicon. 3rd edition. Jean Aitchison. 2003. Oxford: Blackwell.

This book takes the reader through the linguistic modeling of the lexicon without drowning the reader in overly technical jargon and scholarly debates. As a very readable book, it is an excellent introduction to the workings of the mental lexicon. The author covers the meaning of words, prototype theories, semantic primitives, parts of speech, the role of verbs, the architecture of words, new words, word acquisition, and the overall organization of the mental lexicon.

Theories of Lexical Semantics. Dirk Geeraerts. 2010. Oxford: Oxford University Press.
This book offers a tour of the major traditions for researching word meaning. The lexicon has become a much more major part in building a theory of language over the last few decades, and this book covers that development as well as the roots of lexical semantics from the nineteenth century forward.

exercises

individual work

1. Identify the content lexical categories in the following sentences (taken from internet postings and recycled emails).
   a. The bandage was wound around the wound.
   b. The farm was used to produce produce.
   c. The dump was so full that it had to refuse more refuse.
   d. We must polish the Polish furniture.
   e. He could lead if he would get the lead out.
   f. The soldier decided to desert his dessert in the desert.
   g. As there is no time like the present, he thought it was time to present the present.
   h. A bass was painted on the head of the bass drum.
   i. When shot at, the dove dove into the bushes.
   j. I did not object to the object.
   k. The insurance was invalid for the invalid.
   l. There was a row among the oarsmen about how to row.
   m. They were too close to the door to close it.
   n. The buck does funny things when the does are present.
   o. A seamstress and a sewer fell down into a sewer line.
   p. To help with planting, the farmer taught his sow to sow.
   q. The wind was too strong to wind the sail.
   r. After a number of injections, my jaw got number.
   s. Upon seeing the tear in the painting, I shed a tear.
   t. I had to subject the subject to a series of tests.
   u. How can I intimate this to my most intimate friend?
2. For the preceding sentences, identify the potentially ambiguous words (e.g. *intimate* (verb); *intimate* (adjective)). Which ones are only homographs, which are only homophones, and which are **homonyms**?

group work

3. Tense? Try to Relax …
   For the following sentences, label the tense, aspect, and mood of each one.
   a. In the bow of the boat, the elf stood tall with bow in hand.
   b. Was the swan really skating on thin ice?
   c. The ogre has gorged on the goat.
   d. Were the Tigers a winning team this year?
   e. After the party, the manager had left the house in a huff.
   f. Won't thirty days be enough to recover the gold idol?
   g. Syntax trees are running through my head even now.
4. For the following tense, aspect, and mood sets, provide a sentence that accurately portrays each one.
   a. past, progressive, interrogative
   b. past, perfect, indicative
   c. non-past, perfect, conditional
   d. non-past, neutral, imperative
   e. past, neutral, indicative
   f. past, perfect, interrogative
   g. non-past, perfect, progressive, conditional, interrogative
5. Label the lexical category of the following words and label them as content or function:
   a. This gecko can catch that cricket.
   b. What did they lose?
   c. The asteroid created a tremendous hit on those economies.
   d. Who wants to wear which pair of socks?
6. Adjectives: An important step in figuring out how words work is creating phrases to frame the words. Using the creative powers of your group, concoct phrases to hold the following adjectives, and then answer the questions below.

   alone
   tired
   past
   previous
   navy
   responsible
   afraid
   smart
   pretty
   asleep

   Which adjectives are attributive only? Which are predicative only? How many of these adjectives are both? Of the ones which have both, do some have a greater likelihood of being one or the other?

7. Identify the lexical category of the following underlined words. If a function word, what job is each one doing?

   a. <u>The</u> thirteen small <u>boats</u> sailed <u>around</u> the pond in the park while the sun <u>rose</u> over the trees.
   b. I really <u>like</u> <u>that</u> book.
   c. It was small <u>like</u> a grain <u>of</u> sand.
   d. The eagle <u>had</u> landed before <u>I</u> saw <u>this</u> sign.
   e. Despite <u>her</u> <u>determined</u> <u>gait</u>, she never <u>looked</u> at <u>these</u> cabinets again.
   f. <u>That</u> pug <u>leapt</u> <u>into</u> the chair.

8. How many ambiguous nouns, verbs, or adjectives can you list? Are all those categories equal in their number of ambiguous words, or do some content categories have more ambiguous pairs?

9. When does a form~meaning combination become a word? Here is a group exercise for developing new words in English. Pull together a list of ten forms that could become words for you. These might be a new name for a spot on campus or a new word for cleaning up after a party. What would need to happen for those new creations to become words?

10. Ray Jackendoff in his *Architecture of Language* argues that *yes* and *no* have meaning and form, but no lexical category. Develop ten sentences that include *yes* or *no*, and assess their lexical status. Do they have a lexical category?

11. This is an exercise in finding true synonyms. Develop 20 pairs of words. In each pair, the meanings must be as close as possible. The other groups get to vote on whether the meanings are close enough to be considered synonyms or not. The group with the most pairs of true synonyms wins.

12. The comedian Brian Regan on the album *Brian Regan Live* talks about being "Stupid in School." Read through the following transcript (and listen to the audio clips if you have internet access: It is hilarious {although getting endorsed by an academic in a textbook might be a death knell for any comedian}). The skit is about young Brian living through a spelling bee. Figure out what pluralization patterns young Brian was following to form his plural nouns.

Monologue: Plurals were hard too.
Teacher Voice: "Brian, how do you make a word a plural?"
Young Brian: "You put a 's' … put a 's' at the end of it."
Teacher Voice: "When?"
Young Brian: (sigh) "On weekends and holidays!!!"
Teacher Voice: "No, Brian. Let me show you." So she asked this kid who knew everything, Irwin. "Irwin, what's the plural for ox?"
Irwin: "Oxen. The farmer used his oxen."

Teacher Voice: "Brian?"

Young Brian: (chuckling) "What?"

Teacher Voice: "Brian, what's the plural for box?"

Young Brian: "Boxen. I bought 2 boxen of doughnuts."

Teacher Voice: "No, Brian, no. Let's try another one. Irwin, what's the plural for goose?"

Irwin: "Geese. I saw a flock … of geese."

Teacher Voice: "Brian!"

Young Brian: (chuckling) "Wha-at?"

Teacher Voice: "Brian, what's the plural for moose?"

Young Brian: "MOOSEN!! I saw a flock of moosen! There were many of 'em. Many much moosen. Out in the woods – in the woodes – in the woodsen. The meese want the food. The food is to eatenesen. The meese want the food in the woodyesen! In the, food in the woodenesen!"

Teacher Voice: "Brian! Brian. You're an imbecile."

Young Brian: "Imbecilen."

study questions

1. What is the natural relationship between form and meaning?
2. Does the lexicon limit synonyms or homonyms?
3. What are the differences between homophones, homographs, and homonyms?
4. How is the lexicon organized differently from traditional dictionaries?
5. In what ways can the meaning of a word shift over time?
6. What is lexical ambiguity?
7. How are content lexical categories different from function lexical categories?
8. What are nouns?
9. What is an adjective's job?
10. How are count nouns different from mass nouns?
11. What does it mean to mark case, and where does case marking still exist in Modern English?
12. What is it that makes a verb a verb?
13. What are the three categories of transitivity?
14. What are Modern English's two tenses?
15. What do perfect and progressive aspects represent?
16. What is *do*-support, and how long has English had it?
17. What are modal verbs, and how are they different?

18. Why are coordinators a function category?
19. How are determinatives and determiners different?
20. What are the demonstrative pronouns?
21. What do pronouns do?
22. What is deixis?
23. What is the job of a preposition?

Visit the book's companion website for additional resources relating to this chapter at: http://www.wiley.com/go/hazen/introlanguage

5

Idioms, Slang, and the English Lexicon

Chapter outline

chapter overview

In this chapter, we explore more qualities of the mental lexicon and the types of language we store there. The lexicon does hold individual words, but it also contains idioms like *pain in the neck* and slang words like *weed*. Throughout our lives, we are able to learn new words, and this chapter provides examples of how people create new words – including the slang that teenagers use to separate themselves from their parents, like *cray-cray* and *sick*. We explore how idioms and slang change over time, as when the word *literally* comes to mean an intense 'figuratively.' Slang itself is partially defined by its highly fluid nature, showing its changes with words for 'excellent' such as *cool*, *bitching*, *wicked*, *legit*, and hundreds of others. In examining how lexical items change, we reconsider synchronic and diachronic variation: the variation of language at one time and through time. We also take a turn through the worlds of jargon to better understand the many different collections of words we work through in our daily lives.

meanings change

Words change over time. Literally. It is part of who we are. We also create new meanings for idioms and slang in the same ways we create new words. How people react to these changes is a different story. Take the reactions to the evolution of *literally*. In 2013, Ed Payne and Dorine Mendoza wrote an article for CNN.com with this introduction: "This is going to give grammarians a headache, literalists a migraine and language nerds a nervous breakdown. The definition of literally is no longer the literal definition of literally." The concern here is that the form *literally* has increasingly been given a different meaning than the *-ly* suffixed form of *literal*. Most likely, the majority of people with this shifted definition have *literally* as a single, memorized chunk in the lexicon. This change in meaning is similar to *breakfast* now meaning the first meal of the day rather than the meal that breaks your fasting. The CNN article was published because some people dislike language change and take it as a sign of decay of society. That decay includes topics like slang. Linguists, who are grammarians, find it to be perfectly normal and not headache-inducing. This chapter explores these kinds of changes to the English lexicon, including the nature of idioms and slang, two realms that show us how meaning and change work.

the English lexicon

To talk about the English lexicon is a bit bizarre. The noun phrase *English lexicon* seems like a single entity, as if we could walk into a library, find it, and flip through its pages. That situation would be convenient, but unfortunately, it is not true. When talking about the English lexicon, we set up an abstract idea for all the words and other memorized chunks that are in every English speaker's head. And when we talk about the history of the English lexicon, we mean the collection of words for every speaker of English who has ever lived. That is a lot of people (well over a billion) and a lot of words (at least over 500,000, depending how you count 'a word'). The words you read about in this chapter are illustrations of influence from different periods of history, and they are designed to paint a picture of how our modern English lexicon developed its current texture.

The English lexicon comes from Germanic stock. Its foundational roots are from Germanic tribes living in Northern Europe, and they eventually (starting around 450 CE) came to the island of Great Britain. The tribes were Angles, Saxons, Jutes, and Frisians who invaded Britain, and these were the founders of the English language. So, if you are ever asked what kind of language English is, one of the basic answers is *Germanic*. The most common words used by English speakers are Germanic in origin: *man, woman, folk, I, we, water, land, and, was, what, when*, and many others.

On this Germanic lexicon, several other languages made their mark, some more deeply than others. One long-term influence comes from Latin, which influenced many Germanic dialects with words like *belt, cheese*, and *pole*. The tribes who invaded Britain had previously taken up Latin words such as *beer, cheap, mile, stop*, and *wine*. Words that are brought into one language from another are said to be **borrowed**. It is an odd term, since permission is never "given" and the words are never "returned." Since then, Latin words have continued to be borrowed by English speakers in every century. Some are discipline specific: Starting in 597 CE, the Catholic Church sent missionaries to convert the Anglo-Saxon tribes and with the conversion came Latin terms for religious matters such as *altar, mass, verse*, and *candle*. However, Germanic paganism held sway on the influence of some words. For example, the days

Words to the Wise: Lexicon transformed

In linguistics, the lexicon used to be conceived of very differently than it is today. From the time Noam Chomsky published *Syntactic Structures* in 1957 to the middle of the 1970s, the lexicon was a barren set of storage racks where meaningful parts were stored. The lexicon did not do anything itself. It just held language parts which other systems in the mental grammar then built into actual language. The key goal for linguistics at the time was maximum economy, following Occam's Razor, so that the system they built would be the simplest possible.

Since that time, researchers have realized that biological systems (including language) often have layers of redundancy and that the lexicon is a much more active and richly textured area of the mental grammar. Scholars like Joan Bybee, Jean Aitchison, and Dirk Geeraerts have developed theories of the lexicon that make it an active part of the mental grammar's production of language.

Tuesday, Wednesday, Thursday, and *Friday* are all named for Germanic gods: Tiw, Woden, Thor, and Frig. Even the holiday *Easter* takes its name from a Germanic goddess of dawn. Yet, the Latin influence has continued through our modern era, with Latin supplying many medical and legal terms (e.g. *laceration, legal*).

The Norse language was also a Germanic language, but it was different from the Germanic dialects of the Angles, Saxons, Jutes, and Frisians. Old Norse had important influences on English starting in the 800s. Some whole words were borrowed into English, such as *sky* and *egg,* as well as some suffixes, such as the *-s* on the verb in phrases like *he walks.* Perhaps the most important set of words borrowed from Old Norse was *they, them, their.* Borrowing pronouns is a rare event, but apparently Old English speakers collectively dropped their old pronouns – *hīe, hīe, hīera* – and adopted instead the new pronouns – *they, them, their* – because of contact with Old Norse speakers.

A later invasion brought a different set of vocabulary to English: the French language starting in 1066. The French influence on the English lexicon is huge and ranges through topics such as the military, the arts, food, entertainment, and fashion. Today, most of these borrowed words are never considered "foreign" but instead are a regular part of the English lexicon. From government regulations to culinary delights, historically French words have become normal English words, including the following: *tax, government, rent, poor, flower, chef, dinner, supper, art, judge, faith, battle,* and *uncle.*

 Consider these lines of the English writer Chaucer (1343–1400). They come from his Prologue for the *Canterbury Tales* (from www.canterburytales.org):

35	But nathelees, whil I have tyme and space,	'But nonetheless, while I have time and space'
36	Er that I ferther in this tale pace,	'Before I further in this story walk'
37	Me thynketh it acordaunt to resoun	'It seems to me reasonable'
38	To telle yow al the condicioun	'To tell you all the conditions'
39	Of ech of hem, so as it semed me,	'Of each of them, so as it seemed to me'
40	And whiche they weren, and of what degree,	'And which they were, and to what degree'

Words such as *while* and *I* are Anglo-Saxon in origin, but *space* and *pace* are Norman French in origin. Using an etymological dictionary (which contains word histories) what other words in these lines are from French and which are Anglo-Saxon?

Later, English speakers borrowed words from even more languages. Spanish has contributed words such as *anchovy, armadillo, barbecue, bonanza, canoe, hurricane,* and *plaza.* Modern German has given its cousin English plenty of words also, including *Lager, hamburger, Rottweiler,* and *kitsch.* English speakers

Figure 5.1 Etymologies are fun, although perhaps not always believable, as in this *Wondermark* comic: http://wondermark.com/829/. Rollover text: "How often does somebody actually WONDER ABOUT ETYMOLOGY in MY PRESENCE?? You GOTTA give me this!!" © David Malki! http://wonder mark.com/829/

have borrowed from languages indigenous to North America, such as Algonquian languages. Borrowed Algonquian words include terms for animals such as *chipmunk*, *moose*, and *caribou*, as well as names for food such as *pecan* and *persimmon*. In all, the English lexicon is a multi-colored quilt with swatches of fabric taken from a wide diversity of languages.

lexical semantic change and the arbitrariness of language

With all human words, the relationship between the form of the word and its reference or social meaning is determined by conventions in society. This quality of arbitrariness allows for dialects to have different forms for the same thing. In the United States, *hero*, *hoagie*, and *sub* can all be terms used to describe the same sandwich: The same reference meaning has three different names in different regions of the country. Plus with arbitrariness, we can apply the same form to different meanings. *Hero* can refer to a sandwich or a person of great valor, and a *sub* can refer to a sandwich or an underwater ship.

Since the relationship between form and meaning is set by convention in each society, that relationship can be reset again and again and again. However, this resetting of the form and meaning relationship is not always quick. Imagine how difficult it would be if every day you woke up, 100 different things in your life had received new names overnight. Some days your pet might be a *dog* or a *milkshake* or a *cactus* or a *proton*, all while being the same animal. It might be true for Juliet that a rose smells the same no matter what we call it:

Juliet:

"What's in a name? That which we call a rose
By any other name would smell as sweet."

Romeo and Juliet (II, ii, 1–2)

But, it would be terribly confusing to relearn words everyday. Thankfully, the pace of change for words is slow enough that we can learn them as they develop. There are a lot of reasons for developing new words over time, and the resourceful qualities of our language skills, such as arbitrariness, allows us to adapt our words to suit our needs. In this section, we work through a few ways that words can change.

Word Play: The most

People get excited by whatever is 'the *most*' of something: oldest, biggest, strongest, and any other most extreme category possible. Words are no exception, and in these kinds of competitions, defining what is meant by *most* can be taxing. Consider the category of longest word: Should you accept medical terms or words newly created to be longer than other words?

For many language scholars, the longest, nontechnical, non-coined word in English is *antidisestablishmentarianism*, 'opposition to the disestablishment of the Church of England,' although rarely is the word used. It is most often used as an example of a long word. One of the longest words in a major dictionary is a technical term coined for the purpose of being long: *Pneumonoultramicroscopicsilicovolcanoconiosis* 'a lung disease' and a collection of Greek wordparts.

The real question for you is: What is the longest word you use on a regular basis? Once you gather together a few candidates, describe how you are figuring *length*. Do you mean length in terms of number of letters, number of sounds, or number of syllables?

Some lexical questions seem silly at first because you are asked to examine a word that is so plain and common that you have never needed to examine it before. Part of the goal in this chapter is to help you learn how to examine supposedly simple words and find all the working parts. The hope is that you will not only learn about the words presented in this chapter but also develop the skills needed to accurately examine words for the rest of your life.

Take the word *weed* for example. What is a *weed*? For many people, a dandelion is a weed. Other people grow dandelions for salads; some use dandelions in wine; some make medicine out of dandelions; its roasted roots can even be used as a substitute for coffee beans. Apparently the negative meaning of *weed* is not a natural part of the dandelion plant. For another flavor, consider *mint* (the plant). People have a fairly clear idea of whether or not they like mint flavored ice cream, gum, or candy. Mint chocolate chip ice cream is a popular combination. Some people like mint in their tea. For all its uses in food, could mint be considered a weed? If you ever plant a garden and include mint, unchecked, as part of the garden, you will find out what *invasive* looks like. Mint will spread wherever it can reach, and when it is pushing past the squash and the tomatoes and through the flowers, you will need to *weed* the garden and clear the mint out where it is not wanted. This meaning of *weed*, an unwanted plant, is the modern meaning. So, whether or not any certain plant is a weed depends on whether anyone wants it to be where it is growing: Weediness is in the eye of the beholder.

This modern definition of unwanted plant did not hold true in Old English. During that time (450–1100), the word *weed* was more generally used for 'grass' or 'herb.' Consider the following line:

> Is awriten   ðæt hē sewe   ðæt <u>wēod</u> on ða   gōdan æceras.
> is a-written that he sewed that <u>weed</u> on that good acres
> 'It is written that he sewed the <u>grass</u> on the good acres.'
>
> (from the Anglo-Saxon version of Gregory's Pastoral;
> Bosworth and Toller, 1190)

This more general sense of 'plants' in the Old English *weeds* can be seen in compounds like *seaweed* and *ragweed*. In order to gain the negative effect, the Old English word *wēod* was modified by words such as *evil*. In more modern times, the form *weed* has been used to reference tobacco and marijuana. Tobacco first became the reference for *weed* at least by 1606. The word was first applied to marijuana by 1929. With these usages, some speakers might say the word has gone to pot, but the changing meaning of such words is normal for human language.

Semantics is an academic area of study where scholars examine meaning in language. For lexical semantics, the meaning of words, people can alter the reference or social meaning in different ways. No committee regulates these changes and no one person makes the changes in their entirety, but over decades and centuries, the meanings of many words do change. The major changes illustrated below are *combining, narrowing, widening, amelioration, pejoration, weakening,* and *denotation shift.*

how to create new words

Since words are the combinations of form and meaning, when one of those parts is changed, we have a new word. Remember, every word has several parts. In most standard, paper-based dictionaries, "a word" is simply a collection of letters, and the meanings are stacked underneath that collection of letters. As discussed in Chapter 4, our lexicon associates words in several ways, including by sounds, by meanings, and for written languages, by orthographic representation. In human evolution, the lexical associations that attend to sounds and

Figure 5.2   Few people consider the future jokes when creating new words. From *Buttersafe*: http://buttersafe.com/2011/10/13/pablo-padilla-time-chef/. © *Buttersafe*, by Alex Culang and Raynato Castro. www.buttersafe.com

meanings have had a much greater time to develop, and these associations are the strongest.

With this profile of the lexicon, where memorized chunks are stored, we can examine how those chunks are created. The most frequent type of creation is to combine parts already available in the language, and the least frequent type is to make up a word out of thin air (a new form and a new meaning). Creation through combination offers many more examples to examine.

There are two common ways to combine English forms together, through compounds or affixes. To **compound** English words means to stick two separate words together into a larger word. Like in other Germanic languages, compounding is a productive process in English.

Consider the following words:

1. *football*
2. *breakwater*
3. *undercut*
4. *wallpaper*
5. *mother-in-law*
6. *distance learning*

The first four compounds are closed together without spaces or hyphens. The fifth one has hyphens, and the sixth one has a space. They all function as compounds because their unique forms are tied to specific meanings. In the sentence *The distance learning classes end a week earlier than other classes*, the combined form of *distance learning* is related to a meaning which distinguishes one type of class from all others. The spelling tradition allows some compounds to be smushed together while requiring hyphens or spaces for others. Yet, these orthographic conventions do not make *mother-in-law* or *distance learning* any less of compounds.

For the following underlined words, try to figure out which are compounds and which are not. What is your rationale for including some forms as compounds?

1. *The demon of the <u>underworld</u> rose up against the dwarfs.*
2. *After the party, the intern threw up on the <u>office manager</u>.*
3. *The memo from the <u>White House</u> left us baffled.*
4. *The bird flew over the <u>white house</u>.*
5. *The <u>broken piano</u> was the last thing to get repaired.*
6. *The <u>player piano</u> earned a big price at the auction.*

Compounds have been part of English since English was simply a collection of German dialects at the start of Old English. Since then, words such as the following have become new words in English: *afternoon, backbone, chestnut, downfall, eggshell, fingernail, grasshopper, hardcore, infield, jailbird, knockout, ladybug, mailbox, nutcracker, oatmeal, pancake, quicksand, rainbow, scarecrow, toothache, underground, vineyard, waterfall, X-rays, yardstick, zebrafish*. There are thousands of English compounds, as can be seen on the Wiktionary page for English compounds (http://en.wiktionary.org/wiki/Category:English_compound_words).

The other main method of combining to make new words is through the addition of affixes. With a prefix like *anti-*, we can make words such as *antigravity* and *antibiotic*. With a suffix like *-ness*, we can make words such as *uniqueness*, and with agentive *-er* we can make *scrobbler* (one who posts information about music listening habits to a website). How these suffixes and prefixes are attached is explored in Chapter 6, but here it is important to realize how affixes are used to produce so many new forms.

Consider the following prefixes and suffixes. Come up with five words with each affix:

Prefixes	Suffixes
un-	*-ish*
non-	*-hood*
dis-	*-ful*
mid-	*-ly*
pre-	*-able*
ultra-	*-less*

For an extra challenge, try to work your way across to include the prefix/suffix combination in each row. Some of them will be highly unlikely, or possibly ungrammatical combinations for you. Others might be more permissible, such as *ultrashameless*.

Words to the Wise: Imitation is the sincerest form of flattery

Because of sound changes over time, sometimes two words end up sounding alike although they function differently. Think about the words underlined in these two sentences:

> I really <u>like</u> him.
> You are <u>like</u> your mother.

Most people would argue that *like* in the first sentence and *like* in the second are the same word, but sounding the same and being spelled the same do not make them the same word. They have two different meanings and even two different parts of speech. They are not the same word.

In the first sentence, *like* is a transitive verb, much as it was used in the 1200s. The transitive verb started off as an intransitive verb (*lician*) in Old English (meaning 'to be pleasing') and switched over to transitive in Middle English. In the second sentence, *like* works more as an adjective and preposition (*similar to*). The adjective developed as Middle English *liche* 'have the same characteristics.' The different forms started to resemble each other by the end of the Middle English period.

Like compounding, adding an affix to create a new word has been part of English since the beginning, and this creation process shows no sign of slowing down. Slang, discussed below, continues to use both ways of making new words.

The other ways of making new words are not as frequent as compounding and affixing: All together, it is estimated that combining words makes up more than half of all new English words in the last half of the twentieth century. The other ways of creating new words do get a lot of attention, in part because they are less common.

In general, there are two ways existing words can change, and both can be considered a kind of shifting – one for shifting meaning and one for shifting lexical categories. A shifted meaning would include something like *net*, which now refers to the internet much more often than it does to a fishing net. A shifted lexical category includes forms like *table*, which began as a noun, but can be used as a verb meaning 'to place a proposal in limbo, essentially killing it' as in *She tabled the bill*. This second kind of change is called a **functional shift**.

Over time, the meaning of words can shift in several ways, only a few of which are explored here. The first two are **narrowing** and **widening**. Each one involves a change in the meaning associated with the form. Narrowing involves a change from a broader range of reference to a more narrow range of reference. In Old English, *deer* referred to any hunted animal, but in Modern English, the word *deer* specifically refers to one kind of ruminant mammal. The range of things the term *deer* covers has decreased, and we can call that kind of meaning change *narrowing*. Since its earlier usage, the word *weed* has been narrowed down from a wider semantic range (all plants) to a more restricted semantic range (unwanted plants).

Widening is the same type of change but in the opposite direction. With widening, the semantic range to which the word refers gets bigger over time. The word *barn* used to be a storage building on a farm used only for *barley*: It was bere-ern, 'barley place.' From the Lindisfarne Gospel (Luke xii.24):

Ðæm ne is hordern   ne <u>ber-ern</u>
It   not is hord-place nor barley-place
'It it is neither hoard-place nor barley-place.'

Now, lots of different types of grains can be stored in a barn, along with tools and animals (but not usually deer).

With words, the reference meaning can often have two parts, a **denotation** and a **connotation**. Consider a word like *April*. Its denotation is 'the fourth month of the year in the Western Gregorian calendar,' but most likely some of the first thoughts to come to mind are rain showers, plants blooming and the start of spring, or instead perhaps pollen and allergies and regular discomfort. Those side thoughts are the connotations. The denotation is the most direct reference the word *April* makes in the mind. The connotations are the related side references connected to the word *April*, which might be positive or not, depending on each individual's associations with the word. Not every word will have strong connotations, but every word has the potential for personal or community-wide connotations.

With two of the semantic changes, the connotations change in opposite directions. **Amelioration** and **pejoration** are like narrowing and widening in that they are different directions along the same scale. For amelioration and pejoration, the scale is a general sense of whether the word's meaning is good or bad: more of a compliment or more of an insult. An example of pejoration would be the semantic changes to the word *silly*. If someone in the days of Old English called you *silly*, you would be pleased, because the word meant 'happy and prosperous.' Consider the following line from King Alfred's translation of Boethius:

> To hwon sceoldan la mine friend seggan ic ge*sælig* mon wære?

> To hwon sceoldan la mine friend seggan ic ge*sælig* mon wære?
> To when should   oh my   friend say   I silly   man were?
> 'For what did my friend tell me I was a happy man?'

In the more modern meaning, *silly* has meant 'feeble minded' or more recently 'ridiculous.' In Modern English, to hear *You are silly to take that loan* means that someone thinks you are foolish. To switch from 'happy' to 'foolish' is a shift in meaning towards the negative. It is not that *silly* is itself a less useful word, but its content is more negative.

Amelioration is a change to a more favorable meaning. For example, with amelioration, the denotation of the Old English word *prættig* was 'tricky, sly, wily' as in the following line from *Aelfric's Colloquy* (as cited in the *OED*):

> wille ge   beon <u>prættige</u> oþþe þusenthiwe on leasungum, lytige on spræcum?
> will you be <u>pretty</u>   or   shifty   in lying,   crafty in speaking?
> 'Will you be <u>sly</u> or shifty in lying, crafty in speaking?'

To be called *pretty* during Old English times would have caused concern since the term referred to crafty or tricky actions. The term shifted from this negative denotation to a more positive one, more in the sense of 'cunning' and then to one of physical beauty with the modern sense of the adjective *pretty*. With a different denotation, the modern modifier *pretty* came later, so that the phrase *a pretty hardy fellow* shows up in 1565 (OED). In both cases, the negative realm of 'sly' and 'tricky' are avoided in the modern meanings. In Modern English, people use *pretty* to refer to a well-crafted piece of jewelry or a pleasant sunset, but without the meaning of deceit. In this change, the word *pretty* has been through amelioration.

Two other changes are **weakening** and **denotation shift**. Weakening is when the impact of the word, its rhetorical force, is diminished over time. Consider the modern word *quell*. Its Old English ancestor is the word *cwellan*. Take this example from the Old English long poem *Beowulf* (lines 1333–4):

Hēo Þā fǣhðe wræc   Þē Þū   gystran niht Grendel <u>cwealdest</u>
She that feud   wrecked that thou yester   night Grendel <u>quelled</u>
'She has taken up the feud because of last night when you <u>killed</u> Grendel'

The seeds of modern *quell* are in Old English *cwellan*, but it was a more energetic word in the old days since it involved squelching through murder. In the modern sense, the word *quell* is closer to 'subdue' or 'suppress,' as in *The police quelled the riot before major vandalism took place.* Weakening is a shift in meaning, but it moves toward diluting the force of the meaning.

In contrast, denotation shift is a complete replacement of the basic referent for a word. One unexplained case is the Old English word *clūd* meaning 'rock, hill.' It seems like a stable enough of a word, with rocks and hills being available in England and many new lands beyond. Plus, the sounds of the word are not unorthodox.

<u>Cludas</u> feollon of muntum
<u>Clouds</u> fell   of mountain
'<u>Rocks</u> fell off a mountain'

(From Orosius' *History* (vi.ii) from the *OED*)

Yet, this Old English word has yielded two modern English words: a *clod* of dirt and a *cloud* in the sky. The clod of dirt is a somewhat similar meaning, although certainly different from a rock or hill. The modern form *cloud* has a completely different reference and is deemed a denotation shift. Perhaps the clumpiness of clouds reminded Middle English speakers of rocks and hills (in the distance), and the term transferred over as an original metaphorical extension. Although we do not know the particulars of how it changed, we can classify the type of semantic change and distinguish it from other types.

nonce words

There is yet one other way to make a new word. As mentioned before, the meaning of words is not relevant for discerning their lexical category, but how words fit into a larger phrase is. You should even be able to figure out lexical categories for newly minted words. These **nonce words** are invented with form but no conventional meaning.

Read through these sentences:

The <u>kepbleeg</u> fell off the back of the truck.
We dropped three of the <u>kepbleegs</u> off the bridge.
Considering what we paid, this <u>kepbleeg</u> is wicked fun.

In these sentences, *kepbleeg* works as a noun. It is the subject in two sentences and the object in one. It can be made plural with the suffix -*s*. Do we have a sharp understanding of what a *kepbleeg* is in English? Not exactly. We can discern that it is an object that can fall and that is apparently fun, but beyond that we are in the dark as to its meaning. Yet, given the context of the word, we can be sure about its lexical category: Noun.

idioms

Imagine this scene: You have bought yourself a set of bar stools with backs at your local mega-do-it-yourself hardware store. At your place, you have all the parts laid out on the floor, with the little pieces of Styrofoam debris clinging to everything in sight. You have put together the stool's legs and seat, and you ask your assembly partner for the back to the stool. Your partner says, "I've got your back," while handing you the part.

What is the difference between *I've got your back* in reference to a chair part and *I've got your back* to mean 'I'll support you'? The meaning of the chair-part sentence is something like 'the speaker is in possession of a vertically-attached piece of the chair.' The meaning of the other phrase is 'if you need help, I'll be there for you.' How do the same words in the same order work in different ways? The chair-part collection of words is a regular sentence; the help-in-need collection of words is an **idiom**.

Up until now, we have explored individual words, each with its form and sometimes changing meaning. All of these words have their different lexical categories, be they nouns or verbs or adjectives. Some lexical items are larger than single words but still count as single lexical items. These larger lexical items are called idioms. An idiom is an expression in a language that does not obey normal rules of adding up meaning from word to word.

Take the verb *kick*. It is a transitive verb, with both a subject and an object. It is a nice verb which has been used in sports for years and underwent a functional shift in science-fiction adventure movies like *Inception* (where the characters set up a *kick* to awaken them from one dream state to another). With a subject and an object, we have *She kicked the ball*. The meaning of the entire sentence is composed from the verb cradling the subject and the object. Those two complements to the verb are replaceable with many others: For example, *The elephant kicked the termite mound*. Now consider the idiom *kick the bucket* in the following phrases.

> Which celebrity is going to <u>kick the bucket</u> next year?
> Your first car will probably <u>kick the bucket</u> when you are 20.
> Fred <u>kicked the bucket</u> last Tuesday.
> As a phoenix, she <u>kicks the bucket</u> every once in a while, but always comes back strong.

The idiom *kick the bucket* has the reference meaning of 'to die,' as in become dead. As discussed in the slang section below, people from many different societies find other words to substitute for emotionally charged words. For each of the example sentences, the verb *die* could be substituted in for the entire idiom: For example, *Which celebrity is going to die next year?* In the third example, the verb *kick* has a suffix marking it as past tense. In the fourth sentence, the verb *kick* has a suffix marking it as the nonpast tense. From these examples we can tell that *kick* is still a verb, but the nature of an idiom blocks how the meaning of phrases is normally constructed. For speakers with this idiom, *kick the bucket* has nothing to do with actual bucket kicking. The entire chunk of *kick the bucket* 'to die' is stored in the lexicon, with the word *kick* still recognized as a verb.

There is also a children's game called *kick the can*. If you only knew the idiom *kick the bucket*, having a children's game named *kick the can* might seem a bit morbid. In the game, where one team of players tries to capture another team, there is no actual can kicking involved. Yet, the name of the game is still the three-word idiom, *kick the can*.

Idioms are more common than people might at first assume. As Ray Jackendoff has noted, the TV game show *The Wheel of Fortune* works much of its existence off of idioms. Its contestants must guess phrases based on partial completion of their spelled forms.

Here, we examine several idioms with a wide range of meanings: *dead as a doornail, don't give a damn, willy-nilly, eat my shorts, lipstick on a pig.*

Dead as a doornail 'really dead' has persisted since 1362. Most likely, its alliteration of the [d] sound allowed this idiom to live well beyond even its original exemplar of full deadness, the bent doornail. Rarely are modern doors built with nails. When they *were* constructed with nails, the wooden boards were held together by crossing boards (vertically across or diagonally). There were no bolts with nuts or other ways to fasten the boards. To secure the hand-forged nails through both layers of boards, the point of the nail would be driven through them and then bent over, making the nail *dead* (unusable again).

Don't give a damn famously made an appearance in the 1939 movie, *Gone with the Wind*. The character Rhett Butler caused quite a social stir when he said, "Frankly, my dear, I don't give a damn" to Scarlet O'Hara's plaintive questions of "Where shall I go? What shall I do?" Where does such an expression come from? There were plenty of poor, homeless men in the 1800s, and some of them traveled and did odd jobs as they were able. Some of them were called *tinkers*, and they were not known for their polite manners and ranked low on the social scale. To be *not worth a tinker's curse*, or *a tinker's straw*, or *a tinker's damn* meant to be not worth much. This last expression became common for many and became shortened to the form Rhett used.

Willy-nilly is a rhyming phrase with a long history. The idiom either means 'haphazardly' or 'without choice' in its modern form, but it is one of the few instances in Modern English which still holds a fossil of Old English negation before the verb. In Old English, negation came *before* the verb rather than after it (e.g. *It not is* vs. *It is not*). This idiom started as the verb *will* (not the modal) as in *I willed the door shut*. The negative was *ne wille*, contracted to *n'wille*. Its compounded form was something like "be it so, or be it not so." It now has a new meaning and an idiomatic form.

Not all idioms have a champion, a speaker who propels them to greatness (or at least worldwide recognition). But, the idiom *eat my shorts* has the unlikely promoter of Bart Simpson of *The Simpsons*. In an early episode of the TV show, where Bart is just meeting his future friends on the school playground, he entertains them in ways no teacher would approve. Principal Skinner challenges him to think about his future and the choices he is making. Bart's response is *eat my shorts*. In terms of attempted rhetorical impact, it falls in line with *go fly a kite*, *go jump off a bridge, take a long walk off a short pier* and many other more inflammatory idioms. Bart's creators did not create this idiom from scratch (it appears to have come from the 1970s), but they certainly did make it a catch phrase for many fans.

Expressions like *dead as a doornail* or *willy-nilly* are helped along because of catchy sounds. Other expressions persist because of the vividness of their meaning, and *lipstick on a pig* is one of them. It is a humorous image because of the contrast. The meaning is that a bad situation is a bad situation regardless of how someone tries to make it look better. It is usually leveled at a politician or leader who has tried to put rhetorical spin on a situation to improve how it is received. The phrase itself is new, one of the earliest uses is in 1985, but pigs have been the negative part of idioms for a long time. The expression *You can't make a silk purse from a sow's ear* was used in the 1500s.

Some idioms are not frozen phrases but have empty slots. Those slots are specified for certain lexical categories, such as nouns. In the idiom *flying by the seat of _____ pants*, the pronoun for the owner of the pants gets an empty slot so that it could be either *her* or *his*, *my* or *our*, and *your* or *their pants*. Another slot-idiom is *pull a(n) _____* where the empty slot is for someone's name or a more regular noun. To *pull a Jo(h)n* would be to do something (smart or dumb) in the manner of John (perhaps Jon Stewart or John Travolta). Other idioms include multiple slots. The idiom *to slap _____ with a _____* includes two slots for nouns, as in *The judge slapped her with a fine* or *The officer slapped Kayode with a citation*. With this idiom, there is no physical slapping involved, just an institutional punishment of some kind.

Some idioms vary not by nouns but by prepositions. In a phrase like *I feel sick _____ my stomach*, consider that *at*, *to*, and *on* all work in that frame for different dialects of English. The main job of function words is to hook other words together, and at times any content meaning they might have gets suppressed. Different dialects use different prepositions to get the job done. That they are a place holder and an arranger of phrases is important. None of them are *wrong* for *I feel sick _____ my stomach*, but some dialects of English greatly prefer one over another. The same preference is true for matters of time – *It's quarter (of, to, till) five* – and lines – *standing (in, on) line*.

jargon

Although the term **jargon** can be used in several different ways, it is meant here to be a set of words used in a profession with meanings particular to that profession. For medical professionals, there is medical jargon like *a.c.* (taking medication before meals), *FX* (fracture), and thousands of non-abbreviations from Greek and Latin such as *dyspnea* (shortness of breath). For legal professionals, there is legal jargon like *damages* (money won in a civil case), *mistrial* (an invalid trial), and *remittitur* (where a judge reduces damages awarded by a jury). Academic jargon is a wide collection of different sets of jargon, since academia holds hundreds of professions, and the professions of biology are different from the professions of engineering or linguistics. Folk who use the same jargon are united in having a shared purpose.

Many professions have acronyms as jargon. An **acronym** is a word made of the tips of other words (*acro* being Greek for tip). For literate societies which require extra mounds of words for technical definitions, acronyms come in handy as a process for word creation. Most governments are better at creating acronyms than they are at solving problems. There is no shortage, with acronyms such as NATO (North Atlantic Treaty Organization), DOD (US Department of Defense), and DHS (US Department of Homeland Security) established to create other acronyms. The last two are different from the first one in that they are **alphabetisms** for most people. Alphabetisms are acronyms pronounced letter by letter (with the name of the letter and not the sounds the letter represents). Try as one might, it would be difficult to consistently say DHS as [dhs] with no sonorants to ease the syllable along (note that the previous bracketed pronunciation is *not* at all like Dee-eyH-eS, which happens to be the following bracketed pronunciation). Because of that unpronounceability, we opt for pronouncing the acronym letter by letter, making it an alphabetism [dietʃɛs]. Acronyms include sports organizations, like NBA, MLS, and NFL, music groups like REM and U2, and entertainer roles like DJ and MC.

Some former acronyms have transitioned fully over to regular words since so few people actually realize what tips of words the letters stood for in the first place. Consider this sentence: *The laser shot past our Navy SEAL scuba tanks, letting us know that their radar had found our boat.* Which of those words began as acronyms? The clearest choice is SEAL, since it is still in the orthographic-acronym default mode of ALL CAPS. SEAL stands for the SEa, Air, and Land special operations of the US Military. The other words are more tricky because they have become a regular part of the English lexicon. Consider *laser*, which started off in 1959 as *light amplification by stimulated emission of radiation*. Even physicists and science fiction fans do not convert that phrase to *laser* every time they use the word. The other two are *scuba* and *radar*, with *scuba* originally standing for *self-contained underwater breathing apparatus* and *radar* in 1940 standing for *radio detection and ranging*.

Word Play: Jargontown

Sports and games have many different jargon and slang terms, allowing players to quickly identify what is going on and socially identify with each other. Becoming a regular at any sport or game involves learning the jargon, but outside of the context, it is difficult to guess at what the meanings of many terms are. Consider the following terms and try to guess what they mean (if you do not already know).

Football (soccer) Jargon: booked, set piece, selling a dummy, touchline, through-ball, juggle, onion bag, tackle.

Climbing Jargon: barn-dooring, whipper, wired, vapor lock, smearing, heel hooking, Elvis, cheese grater.

Cycling Jargon: bonk, bunny hop, bring home a Christmas tree, corndog, dab, endo, hardtail, wang chung, stoned, LBS, Granny Gear.

Poker Jargon: angle, wheel, wake up, to go, stand pat, snow, river, rainbow, purse, rock, cow, action.

Chess Jargon: en passant, rank, file, fork, Greek gift, pin, zugzwang, fish, check.

Ambiguities of form do occur even with acronyms. Most acronyms are created within specific professions as jargon. When more than one profession creates acronyms with the same set of letters, it can be confusing when those acronyms collide. Consider business's NP (net profit) vs. linguistic's NP (noun phrase). From the world of institutional technology, we have SLA (service level agreement) vs. linguistic's SLA (second language acquisition). Or, how about a four-way smash-up between publishing's HO (handover) vs. the Catholic Church's HO (Holy Orders) vs. business's HO (head office) vs. chemistry's Ho (Holmium)? With all of these acronyms, the specific relationship between form and meaning is created for each profession's need, but the basic ability to connect form and meaning is something all humans share.

slang

Much has been written about what the word *slang* should mean. If you are interested in slang, there are several good books on the topic, and these go to great lengths to fully flesh out a definition for slang. We keep the description simple here.

First, *slang* is not a name for a lexical category. Linguists have no indication that there is a type of word slot in the lexicon in which only slang fits. It is not like *noun*. For nouns, we can test where they happen. We can assess their context: In *The squid snipped at the cow* and *The cow snipped at the squid* we can tell that *cow* and *squid* are nouns because of determiners like *the* and their function as subjects and objects. The (somewhat older) slang term *fox*, meaning 'sexually attractive woman,' is a noun, but some slang terms are verbs (e.g. *hang tough* 'stay, remain') and others are adjectives (e.g. *plastered* 'intoxicated').

Second, slang is not a semantic category like 'cooking terms' (*spatula, frying pan, soufflé*) or 'banking jargon' (*annual percentage yield, variable-rate loan, stop order*). There can be categories of slang, such as restaurant slang (e.g. *blender tender, in the weeds, amateur diner*), but not all slang comes from the same semantic category. Slang terms do not require any certain content of meaning. Consider *poop* in these five sentences:

1. *He was <u>pooped</u> after the race.*   'tired' Adjective
2. *He <u>pooped out</u> before the work was done.*   'quit' Verb
3. *After his tenth shot of tequila, he was so <u>pooped</u>.*   'intoxicated' Adjective
4. *Do you know the <u>poop</u> on how my bumper got*   'detailed knowledge'
       dented?   Noun
5. *Your Shih Tzu just <u>pooped</u> on my Karastan® rug!*   'defecate' Verb

Apart from the sailing jargon *poop deck* 'the aftermost part of a ship,' there are five different meanings related to *poop* above. Six meanings, three lexical categories, one form. As the range of meanings illustrate, people do not restrict slang terms to only one area of meaning. However, be forewarned if you go looking for slang terms, a lot of slang terms *do* have to do with taboo topics, like sex and drugs: Searching for slang terms will get you discussions of just those things, although not necessarily the things themselves.

Slang *is* related to audience. For the different slang meanings of the form <poop> above, it is doubtful that many people have used all of them, and several of them might not be considered slang by most people. For some, only one or two of the meanings will be known. People often use slang to distinguish their in-group from others' out-groups. With this function, the slang is not only oriented to the audience but divides the audience: Whether or not you know what *Mary Jane will be at the party* means pretty much determines whether you should be at that party (considering that *Mary Jane* is an old-school term for marijuana).

Slang words are synonyms with an attitude designed for particular audiences. Slang terms have both social meaning and reference meaning, but with slang, the event of using the slang term is often the most important part. Slang refers to near synonyms used by a specific social group in order to mark themselves as separate from larger society. Usually, slang is used by younger speakers to mark themselves as different from older speakers. So, if older people feel that slang is off-putting in some way (e.g. offensive, bizarre, ridiculous, confusing), then it is doing its job.

In the witty book *Slang: The People's Poetry*, Michael Adams takes readers on a wide-ranging tour of English slang terms. He celebrates slang and the continuous employment of human creativity used to develop it. During this tour, he elucidates the defining elements of slang. For Adams (2009:6), slang is most fresh in its spoken form, and slang is "…a linguistic practice rooted in social needs and behaviors, mostly the complementary needs to fit in and to stand out. In addition, slang asserts our everyday poetic prowess as we manipulate the sounds, shapes, and effects of words; the pleasure we take in the slang we speak and hear is, at least sometimes, an aesthetic pleasure."

The foundation of arbitrariness is emphasized with slang: Near synonyms with foregrounded social meaning baked daily in our everyday speech. This lack of stability could drive the pedantic among us a bit crazy, but arbitrariness allows for continuously new creations. Consider two slang terms that have been mainstreamed in recent decades: *cool* and *rock n' roll*.

The definition for *cool* should include a positive evaluation by nonauthorities. If those in power say something is good, it is rarely cool. The term *cool* was in its grandest splendor in the 1950s when the US youth subculture was trying to assert itself against the prospering post-WWII adults. Unlike almost all other slang, it held on with easy-going tenacity through the 1960s and 1970s. Every decade's youth also added its own terms for *cool*. The 1980s had *rad* (from *radical*), *tubular*, and *gnarly* as intense substitutes, but none of them fully supplanted *cool*. To some extent, *cool* may be seen less as a slang term and more as a regular word in some communities. The youth who used it so extensively in the 1950s are now senior citizens.

Rock 'N' Roll is a term with a fairly short history, in comparison with *bones* for 'dice' which dates back to the 1300s, but one which started as slang and became mainstream. In other words, *rock 'n' roll* just became a regular word in the end (for a genre of music and all related events). According to the OED, its first citation is in 1938 as a term in a song about strong rhythm and rhyme, and it was carried forward in the late 1930s as a dance term. Its move to world domination came in the 1950s when rock 'n' roll became a vigorously promoted music sensation for post-WWII teenagers with cash to burn. Although most of the rock 'n' roll singers of the time would now be considered rhythm and blues, the music developed from that strong base. The term was related to sex early on, and may have originally been a slang term for sexual intercourse (which is exactly how it has been used thousands of times in lyrics for the last 60 years). By 1958, the *NY Times* was willing to put it in headlines (e.g. "Rock 'n' roll musical shows in public auditoriums were banned" (May 6, 21/4)). Today, the term has hundreds of millions of hits in any internet search and is a relatively mainstream genre of music.

Nifty was another term used with special enthusiasm in the 1950s, but one which has gone through ups and downs to reach the current day. It was always a term used by those youth searching for **overt prestige**, where the institutional authorities praise people for doing good by the system, whether it is in organized sports or social clubs like Girl Scouts or the debate team. **Covert prestige** does not come from adults but from peers, and it usually runs counter to institutional authority. People create slang to seek covert prestige, and they abandon slang when it no longer earns covert prestige.

Figure 5.3   Slang is often about taboo topics and requires creativity, as in this *Dumbing of Age* comic: http://www.dumbingofage.com/2013/comic/book-3/01-if-the-shoes-split/boffing/. © *Dumbing of Age*, by David Willis and dumbingofage.com

Connie Eble, an expert on slang, wrote in *Slang & Sociability* that slang is ephemeral, popping in and out of existence. It does occasionally happen that a few words hang on as slang for a long time: She notes that "*[b]ones* as slang for 'dice'...was used by Chaucer in the fourteenth century and is still slang." With *nifty*, it went from barely being on the margins of slang, to being ridiculed and dropped from usage, to being pseudo-slang for self-identified geeks who marked the awareness of their geekiness by using *nifty*.

There are thousands of slang terms in English, and many more in the other 6,900 plus languages on Earth. Here is a small sample of slang terms drawn from a study of US college slang. One of the many lexical treasures to be found in Eble's book is a list of top 40 college slang terms (from the local experience of UNC-Chapel Hill, 1972–1993). Here are five selections from that list:

1.   *sweet* 'excellent, superb'; *clueless* 'unaware'
20. *cool* 'completely acceptable'
30. *flag* 'fail'; *Sorority Sue* 'sorority member'

To what extent are these slang terms used on your college campus?

Some realms of meaning are served by more slang terms than others. What semantic areas get several slang synonyms on college campuses? Using Eble's book as a guide, it seems that the meaning of 'excellent' has a considerable following with *awesome, killer, bad, solid, bitchin', sweet, cool, tough, fresh, wicked,* and *key*. One topic with fewer groupies is the inverse: Words meaning 'worst situation' include *bummer*, and *(the) pits*.

From the previous turn of the century (1900) come several older terms (Eble 1996: 150–3). For most students today, it may be hard to conceive of them as slang because they are so common, but they were slang of the day.

cram 'to attempt to store a great number of facts in the mind hastily, particularly before an examination'
crush 'to have an infatuation for someone'
exam 'examination'
flunk 'to fail in academic work; a failure'
frat 'a fraternity'; 'a member of a fraternity'
gym 'gymnasium'
josh 'to make fun of by teasing'
swipe 'to steal'

Are any of these terms slang today? Importantly, why are the others *not* slang today?

The following words however did not make it through the century in the same shape and have mostly been lost (the exception might be *fiend* for some). Just to be clear, the form and meaning combinations noted here are now disassociated from each other for these *words*, although we do still have the forms such as *whale*.

yap 'a contemptible person'
whale 'a phenomenal scholar'
tumble 'to understand'
souped 'unsuccessful in a recitation or examination'
plunker 'a dollar'
hen-medic 'a woman studying medicine'
fiend 'one who excels in something'
bum 'a pleasurable excursion'

As we can sense from these former slang words, the slanginess of a word is an ephemeral quality. As Michael Adams writes, "Slang isn't 'in' words; it is an extrinsic feature of their use adapted by speakers to very precise human social and aesthetic needs and aspirations." It might be playful, extravagant, racy, vivid. Slang is definitely casual language with an attitude. Creating slang is showing off a skill of linguistic ingenuity. An important point here on the topic of arbitrariness is that *what* the slang specifically *is* does not matter. That it serves its social role of marking in-group vs. out-group distinctions does matter.

As an illustration, let us work through how the same slang term can unify and divide. Since most slang has considerably different connotations for different groups, we will use a completely fabricated, yet plausible, slang term: *to sleek* 'hanging out and showing off in public, generally to attract a significant other.' Now imagine two different scenes where the hypothetical slang term *to sleek* comes up.

Scene 1: Three high-school males in the school hallway between classes.

Dude 1: We playing Gears of War later?
Dude 2: Too much fake destruction sets us up for eternal geekdom.
Dude 3: We ought to grab our boards and sleek around the front of the mall.
Dude 1: Yeah, I need a better audience than you two.

In this scene, *sleek* does not stand out for these three because it is part of their culture. They can produce it and understand it as something *they* would do, but *authority figures* would not do. The slang term *sleek* makes the word a tool for reinforcing group cohesion. In Scene 2, it works the same way, but not for every audience who hears it.

Scene 2: Same three males walking by another friend in the mall; two senior citizens sitting on a bench

Friend: What are you three gamers doing out in the light?
Dude 1: Out to sleek.
Senior 1: What are they doing?
Senior 2: I have no idea. I can't understand half what these kids say today.

With *sleek* as a term that some people know and other people do not, it triggers meaning for some listeners and not for others. For the senior citizens in Scene 2, the social meaning of this term associates it with young people. This simultaneous inclusion and exclusion is why slang is a language process and a cultural artifact that endures. Slang carries social meaning to an extent that other words usually do not, and humans are evolutionarily crafted to attend to social meanings.

chapter summary

In this chapter we worked through the lexicon, and the larger parts it stores. The mental lexicon stores pairings of form and meaning, and as this chapter illustrates, the forms can be larger than traditional words. Idioms can be entire phrases yet still be associated with only one meaning. Lexical items themselves are not innate for humans, although the ability to pick them up and store them is. People create new lexical items by changing the forms of words (as discussed in Chapter 3) or by changing the meaning of words (as discussed in this chapter). People can create new words through combining older parts together in new ways, including compounding and acronyms. From the many ways people can create new words, certain types of words are used for special purposes. Jargon is used in specialized environments where people work together, be it in professional settings, like accounting jargon or mechanic jargon, or in nonprofessional settings, like model-train jargon. Slang, as a group's set of synonyms with an attitude, is used for social meaning to identify with certain groups. The many ways lexical items are regularly reborn allows for language to remain fresh and responsive to its users.

key concepts

- Acronym
- Alphabetism
- Amelioration
- Borrowed
- Compound
- Connotation
- Covert prestige
- Denotation
- Denotation shift
- Functional shift
- Idiom
- Jargon
- Narrowing
- Overt prestige
- Pejoration
- Semantics
- Slang
- Weakening
- Widening

references

Adams, M. (2009) *Slang, the People's Poetry*. New York: Oxford University Press.

Bosworth, J. (1964) *An Anglo-Saxon Dictionary*, ed. Thomas Northcote Toller. Oxford University Press.

Eble, C. (1996) *Slang & Sociability: In-Group Language among College Students*. University of North Carolina Press.

New York Times (1958) "Rock 'n' roll musical shows in public auditoriums were banned" (May 6, 21/4).

Payne, E. and Mendoza, D. (2013) "Dictionaries change: this is literally the end of the English language." An article for CNN.com: http://www.cnn.com/2013/08/15/living/literally-definition/

further reading

Slang, the People's Poetry. Michael Adams. 2009. Oxford University Press.

Adams takes readers on a tour of slang in English in order to flesh out its utility and show its beauty. He argues for an expanded appreciation of slang, including Raunch and the Hip types. On this tour, he works through the social dynamics of slang, the aesthetic dimensions of slang, and the cognitive aspects of slang.

Spoken Soul. John Rickford and Russell Rickford. 2000. John Wiley & Sons.

Spoken Soul is an entertaining book on the story of Black English in the United States. Rickford and Rickford describe the language of writers, preachers, comedians, actors, and rappers. They also explain for a public audience the vocabulary, pronunciation, grammar, and history of Black English. This book is an excellent resource for students of English.

The Dictionary of American Regional English. Volumes 1–5. Frederic G. Cassidy and Joan Houston Hall (eds.).

This five-volume dictionary is one of the greatest achievements for the American lexicon. Unlike a standard collegiate dictionary, it represents nonstandard words used in some regions but not others. Including both maps and copious quotes, readers discover the immense diversity of American English and its cultural history.

exercises

individual work

1. Rating slang (to discover what makes slang slangy):

   For the following 15 words, rate each one for how much it seems like slang to you. The rating is on a five point scale, with 1 being 'not at all slangy' and 5 being 'totally slangy'. After rating all 15 words, sort them by their ratings in the column to the right. What are the qualities that make a word definitely a slang term for you? Why are other words not slang?

Words	Rating	Re-sorted words	Sorted rating
Take care of _____ 'kill'			
sick 'really good'			
make the fur fly 'start an argument'			
down with that 'in agreement with'			
24/7 'always available'			
Ace (verb) 'perform well'			
knuckle sandwich 'a fist to hit with'			

Words	Rating	Re-sorted words	Sorted rating
uptight 'anxious'			
dope 'awesome'			
wicked 'really good'			
jock 'athlete'			
chiptease 'a bag of chips that faked you out because you thought they were full before you opened them'			
man cave 'space for man designed by a man for a man'			
time vampire 'someone who sucks away your time like a vampire would suck away your blood'			
clueless 'unaware'			
burned 'caught, in trouble'			

2. Consider the inverted-imperative idiom:

"Hang that up"	→	"I'll hang you up"
"Take out the trash"	→	"I'll take you out"
"Could you write up the report"	→	"I'll write you up"
"Please turn in your homework"	→	"I'll turn you in"
"Flip the burgers"	→	"I'll flip you"
"Would you finish your essay please?"	→	"I'll finish you!"

    a. What lexical categories are being transformed from the left side to the right side?

    b. What would be stored for this idiom in the lexicon?

    c. What meaning comes across with the new form?

3. Idioms, usage and association:
    For the following idioms, decide whether you use them, and if you do
    not use them, what kind of people do. Are they older or younger than
    you? Any other attributes for those people (bossy, popular, shy …)?

Idiom	Do you use it?	Who does use it?
A little hard work never hurt anyone 'one should expect and want to work hard'		
Get a rise out of _____ 'draw a reaction from someone'		
run off at the mouth 'talk excessively'		
take a whack at _____ 'try something'		
to beat the band 'very much or very fast'		
Make a killing 'have great financial success'		
Make a face 'wrenching up one's face to show dislike'		
Catch _____ red-handed 'apprehend someone in the act of wrong doing'		

4. Check out the invented terms at http://sportsillustrated.cnn.com/
    2011/writers/steve_rushin/11/16/sports.words/ (or search for "special
    language just for sports"). Which of these invented sports terms have
    the most potential to hold on and become widely used?

group work

5. Gathering slang:
   Obviously the words in exercise 1 are dated and not nearly as cool as the slang you use on a regular basis. This group work exercise is your chance to show off your slang expertise (or pick up some from others in your group). As a group, gather together a slang list and sort your list from least slangy to most slangy. Designate the ten most slangy as your group's top-ten list. As your group suggests words, keep a count on which words fall into which categories, even if they do not make the top-ten list (ask your instructor which topics are OK and which are NSFW). Use the table below to keep count of your terms' categories. Be prepared to share the top-ten list with the class.

	How many slang terms?	How many in top ten?
Sex		
Alcohol		
Drugs		
Education		
Food		
Music		
Evaluation (good~bad)		
Other		

6. In five minutes how many acronyms can your group remember (without the aid of the internet)? Of those, which are more prevalent, alphabetisms or regular acronyms? What kinds of things are most frequent in your list of acronyms: governmental topics? sports? technical terms? music groups?

7. Developing idioms:
   As a group, create some new idioms of your own. This task is harder than it first appears. What qualities do a group of words need to have before they can collectively be considered an idiom? Divide your list into those more likely to catch on and those less likely to catch on than others. Consider the previous list in exercise 3 for fodder.

8. For something like *This isn't my first rodeo* to mean 'I've done this plenty of times; it's under control' the reference is to an American event which carries a lot of social weight. What other idioms play off widely known events such as *rodeos*?

9. How many idioms are in the following paragraph? Which ones are on the border between an idiom and just a regular collection of words?

In a Nutshell
by Delhi Lucas & Courey DeGeorge

In a nutshell, she caught him running around, even robbing the cradle (the whole nine yards!), and he thought for sure he'd be in the doghouse. "Oh, well, there's plenty of fish in the sea," he thought to himself. Fortunately, she was head over heels, and she let him off the hook. He finally got all his ducks in a row, and they started back at square one. It wasn't long before they were on the road again when he popped the question and they made plans to get hitched. At the last minute, he got cold feet, and thought, "Why buy the cow, when I can get the milk for free?" But she told him to just hold his horses and he'd get his two cents worth. He thought to himself, "All right, let's take a shot in the dark. I guess I need to get my feet wet." Eventually they tied the knot, and not much later they had a bun in the oven. At first they were up the creek and without a paddle, but soon they learned the ropes. They got cooking with gas, and she just seemed to be popping them out. It was one special delivery after another, and most people said they had lost their marbles. They took the criticism with a grain of salt and turned a blind eye to the teasing. Like sand in an hourglass, they were soon over the hill and even farther out in left field. "Let's cut to the chase," she'd say to him, "you're off your rocker!" He smiled, knowing he'd gone off the deep end, but it was a good ride. He had crossed all his T's and dotted his I's. "How about them apples?" he thought to himself. Eventually, he was ready to kick the bucket, and he finally croaked.

study questions

1. What does the term *English lexicon* mean?
2. What are the roots of the English lexicon?
3. From what languages has English borrowed words?
4. What is an etymological dictionary?
5. Why can different dialects have different words for the same thing?
6. What is semantics?
7. What is compounding?
8. How is semantic widening different from semantic narrowing?
9. What is a denotation?

10. What is a connotation?
11. What is semantic weakening?
12. How is an idiom different from a sentence?
13. What are some types of jargon?
14. What makes an acronym an acronym?
15. How is an alphabetism different from an acronym?
16. What is slang?
17. Who uses slang for what purposes?
18. What is the difference between overt and covert prestige?
19. How is covert prestige related to slang?

 Visit the book's companion website for additional resources relating to this chapter at: http://www.wiley.com/go/hazen/introlanguage

6

Words Made of Many Parts

An Introduction to Language, First Edition. Kirk Hazen.
© 2015 John Wiley & Sons, Inc. Published 2015 by John Wiley & Sons, Inc.

chapter overview

Chapter 4 dealt with single-part words, and Chapter 5 dealt with unusual lexical items such as idioms. This chapter completes our tour of the lexicon by focusing on how we construct complex words from the most basic lexical unit: the morpheme. The morphemes introduced in this chapter include prefixes and suffixes, along with the less familiar infixes. With all these parts, the mental grammar combines them to produce more complex words, such as *dehumidifiers* and *deinstitutionalization*, within organized structures. Later in the chapter, like scalpels on frogs, we use word trees to dissect how such words work. The need to build words of many morphemes differs from language to language. Some languages restrict words to be only one or two morphemes. Other languages have words with 10 or more morphemes (e.g. Greenlandic has *Aliikusersuillam-massuaanerartassagaluarpaalli* with 12 morphemes). These extreme differences affect how larger phrases are constructed. Lastly, our dissection of words reveals the history of English in the language variation you produce daily.

putting parts together

How is a word like *snugly* different from a word like *ugly*? In a sentence like *I put the gun snugly in the ugly holster*, the two words differ in more than just their meaning and sound. They do rhyme, and from Chapter 3, we know they actually have the exact same syllable rhymes. We also know that *snugly* has an onset [sn] and that the reference meaning of each is different. It is simple to decide that *ugly* is stored separately in the lexicon: We could replace it with words like *pretty*, *smart*, *shiny*, or *black* and figure out that its lexical category is adjective. But what about *snugly*? Is *snugly* a single lexical item? If it is not a single item in the lexicon, what is it?

There are two ways we can figure out this answer. One way would be to argue that every *word* we produce is stored as a single chunk in the lexicon. In that case, *snugly* would get its own slot. The other approach is to check whether the word has any meaningful parts in it. With *snugly*, we have *snug* and the suffix *-ly*. In this second approach, the lexicon stores both parts separately. Scholars have written many articles about these different approaches, and the current consensus is that they are both true to some extent. In other words, we might keep frequent words like *direction* in our lexicons while still holding separate slots for *direct* and *-tion*.

This chapter focuses on how we put together word parts to make larger words. To illustrate the workings of this corner of the mental grammar, we will assume in this chapter that the second approach is true. In other words, when someone says the word *government*, we assume that the person's mental grammar snagged *govern* and *-ment* from the lexicon and combined them to form *government*. Anybody hearing *government* will do the reverse process where *government* is broken down, and the meanings of *govern* and *-ment* are individually checked in the lexicon. If you continue to take classes in language study, you should realize that the process is more complex than these assumptions. Yet for this chapter, we keep this **assumption of composition** in order to explain how the different parts fit together.

---

morphemes

These different word parts need a name to identify them as stored units in the lexicon. The term we use is **morpheme**. A morpheme is the smallest unit of language that has a meaning or grammatical function. This definition is simple enough to read, but to analyze language with it takes practice.

Consider these words:

snugly	ugly
Mississippi	Miss
behave	have
system	stem
Saturn	sat

In each of the words on the right, there are sets of letters also found on the left. The letters <u-g-l-y> are part of <snugly>. In some pairs, the sounds are the same on the right as they are on the left, whereas in others they are not. The letters <h-a-v-e> in *behave* do not represent the same sounds as the <h-a-v-e> in *I have a gun*. What is most important is the match between meaning and form. The morpheme *sat* is not a part of *Saturn* because the meaning of *sat* is not part of the word *Saturn*. In fact, the word *Saturn* has only one meaningful part. The word *snugly* has two parts, but *ugly* is not one of those parts. Why? The meaning of *snugly* is not composed of the meanings of *sn* + *ugly*; it is built out of the meanings of *snug* + *ly*. Note that *ugly* itself is a single morpheme. Nobody makes *ugly* from the stem *ug* and the suffix *-ly*.

Some morphemes are long. *Mississippi* has probably four syllables and eight sounds for most folk: [mɪsəsɪpi]. Yet, how many morphemes are inside of all those sounds? Just one. Some morphemes are short. Consider the indefinite determinative *a* in *A chipmunk landed on me*. It is a single syllable and a single sound, yet it has as many morphemes as *Mississippi*. The overall length of the morpheme is not regulated by syllables. For this chapter, it is important to keep the form/meaning combination in mind. A morpheme is the smallest bit of language with meaning or grammatical function, and that definition sets up units different from syllables.

Sometimes word boundaries and morpheme boundaries overlap. Free morphemes such as *squid*, *pipe*, *wave*, and *Massachusetts* are words that can stand on their own in a sentence. A **free morpheme** does not need to be attached to another morpheme to be part of a larger phrase.

Bound morphemes are not free. They cannot stand on their own in a phrase. Bound morphemes like *pre-*, *un-*, *-ness*, and *-y* need a free morpheme to lean on. With the sentence *The pregame left me unfazed despite its geeky happiness*, each of those bound morphemes found a free morpheme to hook up with. Most lexical items in English are free morphemes, but some bound morphemes have played important roles in the history of English, as illustrated below.

Chapter 4 introduced content and function words. We also label morphemes as content and function. Content morphemes carry most of the meaning for language. In contrast, function morphemes establish relationships between words so we can understand how everything hooks together. In the phrase *the ladies of the lakes*, the words *lady* and *lake* are free content morphemes. The words *of* and *the* are both free function morphemes. The bound plural suffix, *-s*, is also a function morpheme.

affixes

In dividing up words, there are three main units we need to contemplate: roots, stems, and affixes. Consider the phrase *the governmental policy*. You can tell that *governmental* is long and has several morphemes to it: *govern* + *-ment* + *-al*. The original piece at the bottom of this pile is called the **root**. Here the root is *govern*, and it is the foundation on which the rest of the word is built. The *-ment* is an **affix**. Affixes are bound morphemes, and the full set contains prefixes, suffixes, and infixes. **Stems** are the root plus an affix. In this example, *government* is the stem for *-al*. Stems could be much longer and include multiple morphemes: For *governmentally*, the stem for *-ly* is *governmental*. Two types of affixes are quite famous, as grammar terms go: prefixes and suffixes.

prefixes

Prefixes are bound morphemes placed on the front of a free morpheme. In English, they range from *a-* in *agnostic* 'not knowing' to *zoo-* in *zootoxin* 'a toxin derived from animals.' Also, prefixes in English rarely change the part of speech. See Table 6.1 for the most commonly used prefixes.

Table 6.1   Most commonly used prefixes

re-	in-	un-	dis-
inter-	mis-	de-	non-
anti-	super-	sub-	under-

Source: *Teaching Reading Sourcebook: For Kindergarten Through Eighth Grade*, Bill Honig, Linda Diamond, and Linda Gutlohn. © 2000 by CORE.

According to Honig, Diamond, and Gutlohn (2000), the four most common prefixes are in the first row: *dis-*, *in-*, *un-*, and *re-*. These four make up 97% of prefixed words in "printed school English." Considering that three of the four most common prefixes are for negating their root words, apparently printed school English is a fairly negative realm. There is variation even for those top four: The *in-* prefix actually comes in a few different forms, such as *im-* and *il-*, as discussed below.

suffixes

Suffixes are bound morphemes that attach to the end of their roots. There are more suffixes in English than prefixes, but their greater number does not matter much. Only a few suffixes are used most of the time. These most common suffixes include the following:

Table 6.2   Most commonly used suffxes

-ed (past tense)	-ing (progressive)	-s (plural)	-ly
-able	-er (comparative)	-est (superlative)	-tion
-less	-ness	-y	-ful

In English, suffixes are a more diverse group than are prefixes, and their ranks are divided into content and function morphemes in the next section. You might wonder why a suffix like *-able* is a suffix at all and not just the free morpheme *able* as in *The beaver was able to slow the unstoppable truck.* Couldn't they just be the same lexical item? Both of their meanings are related, with *able* having a host of meanings from 'having capacity' to 'strong enough' to 'decent wealth' and *-able* meaning 'having capacity to do whatever verb it is attached to.' Both were borrowed into English from Norman French around 1300 and have been in English ever since. The difference is how they work. Consider phrases like *the able nurse* or *The miner was able to work.* The free morpheme *able* functions as an adjective independent of other words. On the other hand, in phrases like *the breakable vase* or *a winnable game*, the bound suffix *-able* is attached to verbs and makes them into adjectives. These different jobs require different lexical listings. Additionally, the histories of these two forms are different from each other. Although they were borrowed into English from Norman-French in Middle English, they have been separate morphemes ever since.

infixes in English and other languages

An **infix** goes inside of another morpheme rather than on its front or backside. English does not have many infixes, but other languages do have some. Arabic uses an infix *-t-* in words like *iktataba* 'copy (something), be recorded' from the verb *kataba* 'write.' In the Austronesian language Tagalog (pronounced [təgalɔg]), spoken by 21.5 million people in the Philippines, the active verb form is produced with an infix *-um-*. The verb for 'write' in Tagalog is *sulat*, and with the *-um-* infix, Tagalog speakers can have sentences like *Sumulat ako* 'I wrote.'

English speakers have tried to develop infixes, although they appear to be mostly for rhetorical effect. The three most famous are *-bloody-*, *-fucking-*, and *-iz-*. The adjective form of *bloody* dates back to 1000, but its use as an intensifier seems to have picked up in England from 1660 onward. Some authorities claim it is a low-class marker, but it is still open for public consumption. The adjective form of *fucking* dates back to 1528, so if you are young and believe your generation invented this term, you are wrong by almost 500 years. Its use as purely an intensifier began in the middle of the 1800s. Both of these intensifier forms can be used to split up multisyllabic words such as these:

Absolutely	Abso-bloody-lutely	Abso-fucking-lutely
Irresponsible	Irre-bloody-sponsible	Irre-fucking-sponsible
Saskatchewan	Sas-bloody-katchewan	Sas-fucking-katchewan

The infix -iz- had short bursts of fame, first in the early 1980s and then again in the 1990s. In 1981, Frankie Smith released the single "Double Dutch Bus" with the fun slang infix -iz- in phrases like *Hizey gizirls* 'Hey girls' and *Yizall bizetter mizove* 'Y'all better move.' Snoop Dogg repopularized the infix in his 1993 album *Doggystyle*. Although it was usable after the onset of any word, it never seemed to have a reference meaning. Its social meaning was its key point, with its users demonstrating their authentic credibility. As with many slang forms, this infix faded rapidly as it became so well known and imitated that its original social meaning was lost in the mouths of not-so-authentic users.

content and function morphemes

Now that we have the basic concepts firmly in place, we explore how morphemes can be divided into content and function. Content and function morphemes do different jobs when we weave words into phrases. Content morphemes carry most of the reference meaning. In a word like *unshakable*, there are three content morphemes, each supplying their own meaning:

un- 'not'
shake 'vibrate irregularly'
-able 'ability to do _____'

Thankfully, we do not have to figure out what is content or function on a case-by-case basis. Lexical categories all fall in one basket or the other. *Shake* is a verb, and all verbs are content morphemes. The lexical categories of nouns and adjectives are also both content morphemes.

Function morphemes perform a different task. They establish relationships between words to show how the different parts hook together. In this next phrase, there are six function morphemes.

Sentence	*The*	*wombats*	*of*	*Australia*	*mated*	*successfully*			*for*	*years*
Content		wombat		Australia	mate	success	-ful	-ly		year
Function	**The**	**-s**	**of**		**-ed**				**for**	**-s**

Some of those function morphemes are free morphemes, and others are bound morphemes. There are also seven content morphemes in this phrase, and even without the function morphemes in the sentence to direct traffic, we could figure out what is intended. The collection *wombat Australia mate successfully year* sounds like a headline except that there might be (humorous?) confusion with the pairing of *wombat* and *Australia*. The headline solution for any reasonable editor would be to work another content morpheme into the phrase and change the order of the words: *Australian wombats mate successfully*. There the *-ian* suffix brings the content of 'one who is from _____,' and it changes the word from a noun to an adjective. The function morphemes show how the content morphemes are to be interpreted. We detail below the work these function morphemes do.

To make clear the boundaries in the world of morphemes, consider the division of bound/free cross-cut with the division of content/function. For English, the results turn out with these divisions:

	Free	**Bound**
Content	Nouns Verbs Adjectives	All prefixes Derivational Suffixes
Function	Prepositions Pronouns Coordinators Determinatives	Inflectional Suffixes

For other languages, the divisions are different. Many languages have nouns as free morphemes, but a Native American language like Cherokee has pronouns as bound prefixes: *ge:ga* 'I am going' with the prefix for *I* being *g-*. Languages like Latin would have suffixes to show who was receiving something rather than using a preposition: *Mercator feminae stolam tradit* 'The merchant hands over the dress <u>to</u> the woman.'

The free function morphemes were discussed in Chapter 4. Like their content cousins in the land of the free morpheme, the role the word plays is the key element in determining whether it is content or function. As we see in the discussion of structural ambiguity in Chapter 8, a form like *up* would be part of a verb in *He might throw up the biscuit* but a preposition in *He might walk up the ramp.*

The trickier area is within the realm of bound morphemes. Prefixes in English are easy because 100% of them are content morphemes. Every prefix in Table 6.1 carries a meaning with it. The prefix *sub-* means 'under' as in *subcutaneous* or *submarine*, and *inter-* means 'between' as in *interstate* and *intertextual*. No prefix in English does work arranging relationships in a sentence.

Suffixes in English are a different story. Some suffixes bring meaning to their attached stems while others establish relationships. The bound suffixes with content are **derivational** suffixes. The bound suffixes with functional powers are **inflectional**. Work through these following phrases to figure out what is what:

> *The quick<u>est</u> run<u>ner</u>*
> *A gang<u>ster</u> lif<u>ted</u> the lid*
> *Canad<u>ian</u> tourist<u>s</u>*

Each underlined suffix is a bound morpheme. Which ones are content, and which are function?

content

> The *-er* of *runner* means 'one who _____.'
> The *-ster* of *gangster* means 'one who belongs to the group _____.'
> The *-ian* of *Canadian* means 'one who is from _____.'

Note that sometimes the suffix happens to change the part of speech of the word it makes. The *-er* of *runner* makes the verb *run* into a noun, but the *-ster* of *gangster* does not transform the noun *gang* into anything different. The name *derivational* comes from this category's ability to sometimes change the part of speech of the entire word.

function

> The *-est* marks its adjective as 'the most _____.'
> The *-ed* marks the sentence as 'past tense.'
> The *-s* marks its noun as 'plural.'

These inflectional suffixes set up relationships and affect the grammar. The -*est* is a superlative and makes the adjective *quick* compare this runner to all others under consideration and evaluates that runner as the most quick. Like its partner, the comparative -*er*, the superlative -*est* relates its adjective and accompanying noun to others of the same set. The -*ed* marks the verb as past tense, a relationship that holds for the entire phrase. The -*s* of *tourists* marks the word as plural, but it does not add any meaning to the concept of tourist. All bound, function suffixes are inflectional suffixes, and in Modern English, there are nine of them.

The first three have the same sound, all hissing [s]. The plural -*s* attaches to nouns. The verbal -*s* attaches to verbs; the possessive -*'s* attaches to nouns. The next two, -*er* and -*est*, are the comparative and superlative; they only work on adjectives. Progressive -*ing*, past tense -*ed*, and the two perfect participle forms (-*ed* and -*en*) only attach to verbs. The last suffix, -*n't*, does not get a lot of press. It is probably the least well known inflectional suffix in English,[1] but its job is important. The -*n't* suffix negates the verb and therefore the verb phrase. Consider the following two sentences.

The principal was unhappy vs. *The principal wasn't happy.*

What morpheme does the work of negation in each sentence? For the first sentence, it is the prefix *un*-. For the second sentence, it is the suffix -*n't*. As a bound, content morpheme, the prefix *un*- only negates its attached word. As a bound, function morpheme, -*n't* negates the entire sentence. Does -*n't* attach to all verbs equally?

Forms	Function	Example
-s	plural	birds
-s	third person singular	She walks
-s <'s>	possessive	The bird's stick
-er	comparative	The taller tower
-est	superlative	The highest rope
-ing	progressive participle	She is walking
-ed	past	She walked
-en, -ed	perfect participle	She has walked She has eaten
-n't	verb phrase negation	They haven't walked

Keep in mind that each morpheme is a combination of form and function. These are the only nine bound, function affixes in English. All of them are suffixes. All the other suffixes in English are derivational and content.

suffixal homophony

As you can tell from the table of inflectional suffixes, several have the same spellings. Between inflectional and derivational morphemes, there are even more overlaps of form, where different morphemes are spelled the same. Thankfully, you know that to be separate morphemes, the form and the function combinations must be considered. Similar to the discussion in Chapter 4, some bound morphemes are homophones with others. By historical happenstance, English has homophony only with suffixes.

Word Play: New word fun

The Washington Post newspaper runs regular language contests as part of its style section. One particular contest in 1998 has been reported and re-reported on the internet for years. In this contest, the contestants had to switch one letter, rendering a new form, and supply a humorous definition. The resulting words are new combinations of morphemes which hint suggestively at their intended meaning (especially when the original form is taken into consideration).

For these new words, try to figure out what meanings are brought in from the old words, and what morphemes are suggested in the new ones.

Here are some of the better results:

Sarchasm: the gulf between the author of sarcastic wit and the recipient who doesn't get it
Giraffiti: vandalism spray-painted very, very high
Doltergeist: a spirit that decides to haunt someplace stupid
Tatyr: a lecherous Mr. Potato Head (for this one, you have to know what a satyr is and how 'tater' relates to Mr. Potato Head)
Foreploy: any misrepresentation about yourself for the purpose of obtaining sex
Cashtration: the act of buying a house, which renders the subject financially impotent for an indefinite period of time

Original post: http://www.washingtonpost.com/wp-srv/style/invitational/invit980802.htm

---

Consider the following sentence and figure out how many different suffixes are in it:

The teacher went for a run after all the chatter from the smarter students.

The first task is to figure out what is and what is not a suffix. Working only visually across the orthographic scene is not all that instructive. There are four *-er* sequences. Could they all be morphemes? It depends on what they do. For the

-er in *teacher*, it makes the verb *teach* into a noun, and it has the meaning of 'one who _____.' For the -er in *after*, does it do anything? Is the word *after* decomposable into the separate parts *aft* and -er? Despite having the word *aft* in English, it is not the stem for *after*, which was an original Anglo-Saxon word complete with the -er. The -er on *chatter* is different from the previous two -ers. We do have a verb *chat* in English, which means to engage in a small conversation, so if it were the same -er as *teacher*, then the resulting noun would mean 'one who engages in small conversation.' But, that is not what *chatter* means. Instead, it means small, repetitive, annoying talk. To get at the meaning of the -er of *chatter*, consider *patter* and *shimmer*. With both of those nouns, an action (making a patting noise and shining) is repeated. The -er of *chatter* is the repetitive -er. Three of the four -er forms are accounted for, but how does the -er of *smarter* work? This -er makes a relationship between the students in the sentence and others, yet the -er does not change the meaning of the word *smart*, just the degree of smartness. Because of this relationship, the -er of *smarter* is an inflectional morpheme. In all, the four -ers in the sentence had three different morphemes and one which was not a separate morpheme at all.

The same kind of suffixal homophony works with <ing>. What are the jobs represented by <ing> in the following sentence, and how many separate morphemes are there?

The San Francisco fire department is racing through traffic to the building.

Here, we have the words *racing* and *building*, and we have -ing with each one. Does the -ing do the same job for each word? With the word *racing*, the -ing is conceptually connected to the verb *be* and renders the progressive aspect: Consider *I raced* with *I was racing*. In contrast, the word *building* is built out of the verb *build* and is transformed into a noun with the derivational -ing suffix. The same thing can happen with most other verbs like *walk*, *eat out*, and *think*.

*Walk**ing** is still healthy.*
*Eat**ing** out is my favorite.*
*Think**ing** is not a privilege.*

All of these -ing forms work as nouns because this -ing suffix has transformed the verbs. The -ing of *building* is a derivational suffix, but the progressive -ing of *racing* is an inflectional suffix.

word trees

hierarchy

There are several different ways life gets organized in nature. One of the more productive ways to understand how parts are arranged is through the structure of a hierarchy. A hierarchy involves making connections between parts on different levels of organization. Consider a simple hierarchy in a company.

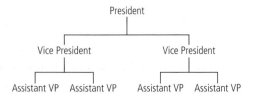

At the top level is the president, and this position is connected to vice presidents at the next level. The assistant vice presidents are connected to the president only through the vice presidents. Each position in the hierarchy is called a node, and the nodes on different levels are connected with lines. Such a hierarchy provides a schematic representation of organization. In Chapter 3, we worked with syllable hierarchies.

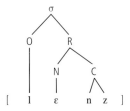

With hierarchy trees, the syllable node is in the top level, and it dominates the onset and the rhyme directly. The rhyme in turn dominates the nucleus and the coda.

In words with multiple morphemes, we can find a similar organization. By examining multimorphemic words with a hierarchical tree structure, we can better understand how they are constructed.

With the word *glassy*, first figure out its morphemes and its part of speech. Here are a few phrases to help you out:

He had a glassy stare.
Her grin was glassy.

In these phrases, *glassy* is an adjective. It also has two morphemes; *glass* (noun) and the suffix *-y* (noun to adjective). Here, the suffix *-y* itself does not have a lexical category such as verb or adjective, but it does contain in its lexical listing the information that it transforms some nouns into adjectives. Other *-y* combinations include *velvety*, *grassy*, and *watery*. How would such bimorphemic words be represented in a hierarchy?

With this drawing, the adjective node is on top because it represents the whole word's part of speech.[2]

Plenty of words have more than two morphemes. Consider the word *widen-ings*. How many morphemes are in that word? It is not even that long of a word, but consider that the root is the adjective *wide*. It is then made into a verb with the suffix *-en* (*widen*) and then back into a noun with the derivational suffix *-ing* (*widening*). Its last morpheme is the inflectional plural suffix *-s*. Four morphemes are all packed into three syllables. Its word-tree hierarchy would be like this:

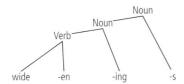

The hierarchy for *widenings* is not that tricky because it starts with the root *wide* and then just leans right to the end.

For words with more morphemes, sometimes choices have to be made. Consider the word *redivision*. The free morpheme *divide* is the root and a verb. The bound prefix *re-* attaches to the root, but like most prefixes (in English) it does not change the overall word's part of speech: *divide* and *redivide* are both verbs (e.g. *You have to divide and redivide until you get the right answer*). The suffix *-ion* is sometimes spelled as *-tion* and sometimes as *-sion*. Plenty of words get a small spelling change, and with the word *division*, the final *-d* is dropped when the morphemes are combined.

In order to understand the word tree, a choice must be made about the first connection: to the right or to the left. Why do we have to make this choice? In an attempt to make our model as much like the human mind as possible, we start with the assumption that branches on word trees (and phrase trees in later chapters) can only have one or two branches, no more. These are **binary branching trees**. With only two branches, we cannot have a single node to connect three or more morphemes.

So, which way to go? Which one do we attach to *divide* first? We must consider the nature of the morphemes to decide. Here is the information that has to be listed in the lexicon for each morpheme:

re-: bound, derivational prefix, attaches to verbs, makes them verbs (V → V)

divide: free morpheme, verb

-sion: bound, derivational suffix, attaches to verbs, makes them nouns (V → N)

To figure out this kind of lexical information for any multimorphemic word, take the affixes and determine their roles by putting them in other contexts. A prefix like *re-* can attach to stems such as *make, do, heat* to form *remake, redo, reheat.* The prefix *re-* seems to attach to verbs and leaves their lexical category alone: e.g. *They remade* Godzilla *yet again* (the noun *a remake* is derived through functional shift from the verb *remake*). A suffix like *-sion* can attach to verbs such as *correct, inflate,* and *institutionalize.* This suffix changes the part of speech, so that after *-sion* is attached, the total word is a noun: e.g. *Institutionalization would be the best choice.* Note that this suffix reacts the same to a root like *inflate* (*inflation*) and a multimorphemic stem like *institutionalize.* The word's status as a verb is all the suffix *-sion* cares about when getting hitched.

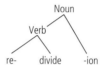

With that information, the choice of which way to connect the first word-tree node is solved. If we attach *-sion* first, the word *division* becomes a noun, and the prefix *re-* does not attach to nouns. It attaches to verbs. The only path to take is to attach the prefix *re-* first, yielding *redivide* (a verb), and then attach *-sion*, rendering the final word: *redivision.* This process allows us to illustrate the hierarchy of morpheme connections, the nature of morphemes in the lexicon, and the combinatorial complexity of human language. It is a win-win kind of analysis.

structure

As syllable trees and word trees illustrate, structure is important to language. Parts cannot be randomly assembled in the mental grammar. They must be arranged according to the patterns of the language, and children learn those patterns to build their own mental grammars, based on the blueprints of the Universal Grammar. As with the pairings of meaning and form for lexical items, at times the surface form of language allows for ambiguity. The possibility of multiple interpretations is resolved in the structure, but the structure itself is not physically represented when language is produced. We do not see syllable trees or hear word trees. We consciously experience sounds for spoken languages, gestures for signed-languages, and meanings for both. Most of the work goes unnoticed by our consciousness.

structural ambiguity in words

In Chapter 4, we discussed lexical ambiguity with words. In English, structural ambiguity with words is also possible. As review, lexical ambiguity is when the same form is associated with different meanings: *round* as a set of drinks or a game of golf or a single piece of ammunition. With words, structural ambiguity involves possible different hierarchies in a word tree.

Consider the word *unwrappable*. What does it mean? The stem *wrap* means to cover something completely: *We wrapped the present*. The prefix *un-* inverts the meaning, so that *unwrap* means to reverse the process of wrapping: *The pug unwrapped the present*. Note that adding the prefix *un-* leaves the word as positive; to *unwrap* a present is different from <u>not</u> wrapping a present: *The pug did not wrap the present*. There is nothing structurally ambiguous about *unwrap*.

At the other end, the suffix *-able* attaches to verbs and transforms them into adjectives. With *wrappable*, the resulting adjective means 'having the capacity to be wrapped': *The chocolates are wrappable*. There is no structural ambiguity with *wrappable*.

Yet, when the three morphemes come together, the mental grammar has to make a choice. Which two morphemes get hooked together first, and which one gets added last? Depending on which choice gets made, you end up with different meanings. If the *un-* and *wrap* are attached together first, the meaning of 'taking the wrapping off' is made into an adjective by adding the *–able*, as shown in the figure below. The meaning can be seen in this sentence: *All of the crates in this zone are unwrappable and should be fully unpacked by 11:00.*

It is able to be unwrapped. [Adj [Verb un- [Verb wrap]] -able]

Alternatively, if the suffix *-able* is first attached to *wrap*, then the word *wrappable* means 'able to be wrapped.' The prefix *un-* negates that meaning. When *un-* attaches to adjectives, it adds the meaning of *not* (e.g. *uncontrollable*, *unfriendly*), but when it attaches to verbs, it adds the meaning of inverting the process (e.g. *uncork*, *unpack*). The *un-* then renders the word to mean 'not able to be wrapped': *With all those jagged edges sticking out, this broken-glass sculpture is unwrappable.* This meaning is shown with the word tree in the figure below.

It is not wrappable. [Adj un- [Adj [Verb wrap] [-able]]]

A few more structurally ambiguous words are presented in the exercises, but overall in English, there are many more lexically ambiguous words than there are structurally ambiguous words. Lexical ambiguity plays off one of the most basic qualities of human language: The arbitrary connection between form and meaning. The structural ambiguity results from the hierarchy of parts, in this case morphemes. Different hierarchies yield different results. Hierarchies are useful for organizing information, but the hierarchy of the word structure is not hearable in the sounds of a normal conversation. It is possible to put in the appropriate boundaries if needed (e.g. *I said un…wrappable*), but there is no sound which means ONE NODE DOWN in language. Word trees allow us to investigate and clearly illustrate our knowledge of the workings of multimorphemic words.

morphemes and other systems

Morphemes get put together to form words, but these combined morphemes must interact with other systems. In this section, several examples of how morphology works with phonology and the lexicon are given to show the complexity of our language.

adding morphemes and making the sounds fit

We have treated morphemes up till now as if they were individually packaged cookies, each in their own wrapping. Morphemes, when combined, are no longer separate but form larger parts. These larger words need to be externally realized, and that is the job of phonology. In this subsection, we discuss an example of how English works out the mash-up of morphology and phonology.

Word Play: Magic morphemes

Humans have been searching for different ways to control their environments for more than 100,000 years, and one of the most natural yet least effective ways is through language. It only works on other humans. It does not work on rocks or wind or waves. Mice and fish and birds might notice our sounds, but they cannot understand our words. Their communication systems are not our communication systems.

Yet, that has not stopped us from using magic words to try to control the world. In modern times, these magic words have morpheme combinations which give hints about the desired results.

In the 1964 Disney film, *Mary Poppins*, one of the longest words associated with magic was morphologically crafted from some English parts: *Supercalifragilisticexpialidocious*. Although its meaning can be loosely translated as 'making up for an educated mind through delicate beauty,' the characters in the film relate it to having a word to say when you have no other comments.

In the Harry Potter books, Latin morphemes are used to generate magical words. A word like *accio* is related to summoning in Latin, and it is the incantation for summoning objects. The word *incantation* itself is from the Latin meaning to sing (chant) upon some topic. The levitation charm has perhaps several parts to it: *wingardium leviosa*. How many morphemes can you find in that one or *serpensortia*?

The regular past tense form of English verbs does not get much attention in most school systems, beyond teachers arguing that the suffix needs to be there. Having been through the early sections of this chapter, you now know that this -*ed* suffix is a bound, inflectional morpheme. What few people have ever stopped to ponder is what happens to this suffix *after* it gets attached to the verb. In English, like in many other languages, the sound patterns of the language get applied to whole words, and forms like *walked* get treated as single units.

The past tense markers you attach to words come in three different forms: [t], [d], or [ɪd]. Here, the focus is on the sound of the -*ed*, not its orthography. It will be spelled <ed> for all regular verbs. Yet, this <ed> spelling represents three different pronunciations, all of which you mastered probably by the time you were five. Like most patterns your mental grammar produces, you have no conscious knowledge of your abilities with this pattern. If you are like most educated English speakers, no one has ever told you this before now. Nor was there any reason for a school system or a teacher to spend time on this topic. The distribution of which form of the morpheme goes on which verb is some-thing your mental grammar (specifically, your phonology) takes care of just fine all on its own. Work through the following 12 words, saying each one out loud in its past tense form. Consider the following words to all be regular verbs (yes, these spellings are associated with other words in other lexical categories, but this exercise is about verbs).

1. slap
2. knit
3. kick
4. score
5. stretch
6. bag
7. bat
8. explain
9. need
10. cry
11. side
12. flex

Notice the sound of the past tense marker for each of them. If you need to, use each one in a sentence so that you can say the word naturally (if not a bit slower than normal). It is not always easy to observe your own voice, so you may want to listen to a partner's pronunciation and vice versa. Now sort the verbs into one of the following three columns according to which past tense marker attaches to them.

[t]	[d]	[ɪd]
_____	_____	_____
_____	_____	_____
_____	_____	_____
_____	_____	_____

Now that the verbs are sorted, the question you face is this: How did your mental grammar know which ending to put on which verb?

The three columns of sorted verbs will help us figure that out, since the verbs in each column have some quality in common. What kind of criteria should we look for? Since we are dealing with different sounds, the semantics or transitivity of the verb would not help us out. Instead, we need to examine the sounds of the verb. For the first column, find out what quality the final *sounds* of the verbs all share (before the -*ed* is attached). Then, do the same for the second column. Be sure to focus on the sounds: You might want to transcribe each word phonetically to help you think about the sounds (e.g. [flɛks]) and not the orthography. Lastly, what articulatory qualities do the sounds of the third column have in common?

The patterns you find can be described with two rules, and we discuss the rule which covers the broadest range of cases first. For the first column, the sounds on the ends of the verbs are [p], [k], [tʃ], and [s]. What quality do those sounds have in common? It is certainly not place of articulation, since we have a range from bilabial to alveolar to palatal to velar. Neither is the unifying quality manner, as we have both stops and fricatives. As these are all consonants, that leaves us with simply the voice of articulation, and all of these sounds are voiceless. Now examine the second column's last sounds: [ɹ], [g], [n], and [aɪ]. What do those sounds have in common? Here, the breadth of sound is wider, as we have both consonants and vowels. For the three consonants, we do not have a single place of articulation, and manner of articulation is certainly not an option (vowel is an even more sonorant manner of articulation than glide). What about voice of articulation? These consonants and vowels are all voiced, and that is the quality they have in common.

So our first column is voiceless, and our second column is voiced. How do these two qualities relate to the [t] and [d] pronunciations of the -*ed* inflectional morpheme? The [t] is the sound produced for the verbs with the voiceless final sounds, and [d] is the sound produced for the verbs with the voiced final sounds. We have not mentioned the possible lexical representation of this past tense morpheme, but at this point we could consider it to be either unmarked for voicing or either voiced or voiceless. Either way, the phonological process here is assimilation, with the final morpheme assimilating to the voice of the preceding sound.

Does assimilation work for the third column? We need to find out the final sounds of the verbs to see if it works. These are [t] and [d]. We seem to have a problem with our first rule because these two sounds differ in their voicing. What do they have in common? Actually, they have more in common than any other column. Beyond their voicing, both of the other main consonant qualities are the same. Both are alveolar stops. To handle this situation, the lexicon and phonology have conspired to devise a form of the past tense inflectional morpheme with a vowel-consonant combination, [ɪd]. The final consonant of the suffix is necessarily voiced, since the vowel is voiced. The result is a much more phonotactic-constraint friendly CVC pattern. Otherwise, it would be really hard to say [tt] and [dd] at the end of verbs like *bat* and *need*.

Just like the past tense morpheme in English, so it is with every morpheme in a spoken language. They not only have to be added to their stems, but their sounds have to combine in some way with those around them. Figuring out how they combine is phonology's job. Morphemes also interact with other systems in the mental grammar, most obviously the semantic system, which determines meaning. For bound, derivational morphemes, their meanings are added together with that of the stem, and our semantic system builds the total meaning. A word like *unteacherliness* may be new to you, but given that you know what *un-*, *teach*, *-er*, *-ly*, and *-ness* all mean, then the semantic part of our mental grammar can figure out that *unteacherliness* means 'qualities not belonging to someone who teaches.'

The system of morphemes in any language is also tightly related to the system of syntax. Remember, morphology builds words, and **syntax** builds phrases. Both systems of the mental grammar put parts together in hierarchical patterns. Think of them as both playing on the same see-saw. As one goes up, the other goes down. As one becomes more important in a language, the other one becomes less important. This next section introduces how morphology and syntax work together, and the following section explains how English speakers have shifted the balance of that see-saw.

how many morphemes in a word: a question for every language

Dialects of different languages are more different from each other than dialects of the same language. With dialects of the same language, it is often the sounds and some of the words that carry the difference. In some of the dialects of Northern England and Scotland, the Great Vowel Shift never much affected the back vowels, so the distinct pronunciations of words like [dun] for *down* can still be heard. Dialects of different languages differ in many words but also in other more striking ways. These differences are sometimes abstract and not easy to classify at first glance. One of the most subtle, yet most important, is the

Figure 6.1 Slicing up words into morphemes should not rely on just sound patterns, as shown in this *Buttersafe* comic: http://buttersafe.com/2012/07/03/merman/. © *Buttersafe*, by Alex Culang and Raynato Castro. www.buttersafe.com

balancing act between putting together morphemes to form words and putting together words to build phrases.

Some languages have many morphemes in a single word. A language like Spanish marks its verbs so distinctively with suffixes that from the form of the verb alone, we can tell what the subject would be: *comemos* 'We eat' vs. *como* 'I eat.' These languages are more **synthetic**. They synthesize the morphemes into larger words. Synthetic languages depend on morphology to do their grammatical work. The most extreme forms of synthetic languages are those with many morphemes per word, aptly named polysynthetic languages. For example, Athabaskan languages, spoken by indigenous peoples in northwestern Canada and Alaska, can have numerous morphemes in a single word: The Upper Kuskokwim in Alaska can have *hodił* to mean 'they are walking along.' Consider how different that is from English: A sentence's worth of meaning in a single word.

Some languages have very few morphemes per word. A language like Mandarin Chinese has no affixes in any words. These languages are more **analytic** because they analyze the meanings into fewer morphemes per word. For nouns in Mandarin, there are no inflections: Considering some romanized Mandarin, whether it is 'one boat' *Yītiáo chuán* or 'three boats' *Sān zhī chuán*, the noun does not have a plural inflection. The notion of plural is carried in the number, which makes the arrangement of that number more important.

In a more synthetic language like Russian (here romanized), the suffix changes with pluralization on the noun.

Odna lodk<u>a</u> zatonula   'One boat sank'
Dve lodk<u>i</u> zatonuli   'Two boats sank'

Also note that the conjugation on the verb *zatonul* changes in the past tense between the singular *-a* and the plural *-i*. In English, our past tense verbs do not agree in number with the subject, again showing how Russian is a more synthetic language than English.

With more than 6,900 languages, there is a wide range between the most synthetic languages and the most analytic. It is best to see these extremes as poles on a continuum and our many languages ranging between those poles. Most languages have both analytic and synthetic qualities. English's journey along the syntheic-analytic continuum is explored in Chapter 7.

Regardless of where a language falls in this continuum, the result of the morphological difference can be seen in how phrases get arranged. Languages with fewer morphemes per word rely on syntax to do the work of telling who did what to whom. If the morphemes are not doing the grammatical work of marking relationships among words, the syntax has to pick up the slack.

When there are more morphemes per word, morphology does the work arranging parts and meanings. With languages like Spanish and Italian, which clearly mark their verbs, speakers are not required to always have a pronoun subject, since that information is already marked on the verb itself. For polysynthetic languages like the Athabaskan family, the meaning of entire sentences can be contained in a single word.

variation through time

from rules to exceptions

Up until this point, we have worked with morphemes whose meanings and grammatical functions were neatly paired for each unit. The word *unhappiness* has three morphemes in it, and each one has its own job. In these next two subsections, we discuss a regular feature of many languages: forms which contain more than one morpheme. The first handles special forms molded together out of previously separate morphemes. The second handles irregular verbs in English and their variation over time. The goal is to help you understand how the relationship of form and meaning can be complex in human language. With both sections, the variation we have in Modern English results from historical changes. Our modern lexicon and morphology are echoes of previous Englishes.

One of the old grammar-school slogans of the twentieth century was "Good, Better, Best, never let it rest, till your Good is Better, and your Better Best." Although it sounds like an overly enthusiastic motivational poster, the intent was to remind students that the adjective *good* does not take the normal comparative and superlative inflectional suffixes (e.g. *gooder, goodest*). Such advice is social etiquette and part of what formal education is supposed to provide. It also highlights the oddity of *better* and *best*. If we have *smart, smarter,* and *smartest*, why do we have *good, better,* and *best*?

On the flip side, why do we have the series *bad, worse, worst*? If we have *mad, madder, maddest*, it certainly cannot be a restriction about the possible sounds, and even if it were a sound issue, what phonological rule changes *all* the sounds in a word? The solution rests in a language event called **suppletion**. With the term *suppletion*, think of a supplement, something that is added in: A vitamin supplement is something you add to your diet. With suppletion in language, a separate word like *bad* is melded into being a different form of the same lexical entry as *worse*.

Suppletion is a historical process, not something that happens exclusively in one speaker's mental grammar. Over time, different free morphemes get smooshed together in speakers' lexicons. With *good* and *better*, these were originally different words. Over time, speakers began to see them as different versions of the same word. Suppletion is a statistically rare process. It happens to very few words. It is also a slow process. It takes at least a century or longer to fully smoosh different words together. Yet, several common words we have today result from suppletion.

Consider these:

Adjectives:
good   better   best
bad   worse   worst

Verbs:

be   *is, am*   *was*
go   *went*

The form *go* comes from the Old English verb *gan*. The form *went* comes from the Old English verb *wendan* 'to follow a trail'. As a separate verb, *wend* eventually fell out of general use with the meaning of 'to go off' at the end of the 1800s (e.g. from the OED: *thou mayst wend to the ship joyful in spirit*, 1879). Yet, its form *went* had been in place as a past tense of *go* since the late 1400s. The same stories work for the comparative and superlative forms of *good* and *bad*, although for *better*, it had combined with *good* long before Old English. The forms *badder* and *baddest* were in use in Old English, but *worse/worst* began to replace them in the late Middle English period.

irregular? tense? try to relax

Suppletion happened more in English with verbs than with nouns. One of the reasons is probably that verbs lead more complex lives than do nouns. Despite the orderly presentation of word trees and the divided nature of derivational and inflectional morphemes, the shapes of multi-part words go through a lot of variations. We work through alternative ways of marking tense in English to show the history of how our modern past tense forms developed and how complex morphemes are in the lexicon.

In the following survey, fill in the blanks with the past tense form of the verb. These are paired in ways to highlight the diversity of English past tense forms. If you are doing this exercise in a group, you might find that not everybody has the same answers. Like all living languages, English speakers produce variation, and this variation pushes some dialects in one direction and other dialects in different directions.

COUCH-POTATO VERBS AND VERBS ON STEROIDS:

A. *Find*: I don't know where he lost it, but he *found* it by the sofa.
   Mind: I don't *mind* if it makes noise, but last night I certainly _____ all the noise it made.

B. *Teach*: A teacher who _____.
   Preach: A preacher who _____.

C. *Sink*: The boat was about to *sink* when she fell off; it eventually _____.
   Think: The professor had a lot to *think* about. Eventually, he _____ about all of it.
   Wink: She thought about *winking* at him, and eventually, he _____ at her.

D.   *Speak*: Yesterday, she _____ to me.
        Leak: Yesterday, the pipe _____.
        Seek: For years, I _____ the desires of my heart.

The patterns you find for verbs like *teach* used to be part of Old English, where verbs changed their tense through changes in their vowels: *speak* > *spoke*. This process is called **ablaut**. With these words, a past tense form like *taught* is actually bimorphemic. These kinds of verbs are called **strong verbs**. Each one contains two morphemes: both the verb *teach* and the past tense morpheme (except it is not a separate suffix).

The English verb system is a hodgepodge. We sometimes attach the inflectional suffix *-ed* to verbs to make the past tense. We sometimes show tense through a change internal to the verb like ablaut. Some irregular verbs, like *be*, have forms that come from suppletion. We have accumulated these different patterns over the history of English.

We must have the irregular forms memorized. The past tense of *teach* has to be stored in the lexicon as *taught*, or else speakers would produce *teached*. As children acquire the language, they go through a stage after they have learned the *-ed* rule where <u>all</u> verbs get marked with *-ed*s, so that they have *speaked*, *teached*, and *thinked*. Only after this point do children (re)learn the exceptions to the *-ed* rule.

A verb like *teach* is a strong verb because it has ablaut to mark its past form, *taught*. A verb like *walk* is a **weak verb** because it just takes an *-ed*. (I did not pick these names, and I do not like them because they are oddly suggestive about the psychology of the verb. I would have picked *brown* verbs and *blue* verbs.)

Here are some other fluctuations from the past:

    E.   *Steal*: Last week, I _____ second base.
        Kneel: In the garden yesterday, I _____ for hours.
        Feel: This is the best I have ever _____.

But what about a verb like *feel*? It gets a slightly different vowel but also a *-t* at the end. The same goes for *sweep* (*swept*) and *deal* (*dealt*). These are **semi-weak** verbs (another not so great name) because they contain both some weak-verb qualities and some strong-verb qualities. (I think they would have felt much better about themselves if they would have been called semi-strong, but it is difficult to change such long traditions.) Verbs that start as semi-weak verbs, such as *kneel*, sometimes become regular verbs, gaining past tense forms such as *kneeled*.

Consider some of these weak and strong variations:

    F.   *Catch*: Yesterday, I _____ the ball.

    G.   *Drag*: Yesterday, I _____ the body to the grave.

    H.   *Sneak*: Yesterday, I _____ into the game.

I.   *Strive*: By the end of the game, she _____ to score a goal.

J.   *Hang*: Last month, Texas _____ three men.

K.   *Dive*: At the pool, she _____ five times in a minute.

The six verbs in F through K have all been variably produced by speakers in the last few centuries. The verb *catch* was originally borrowed from Old French by 1300, but its modern meaning of 'capturing' was transferred from another English verb (*lacchen*, like 'he will latch on to you'). Both the strong form of *caught* and the weak form of *catched* were used through the 1800s, when the *caught* form won out in the popular imagination. Certainly *catched* was still used later, but increasingly it became associated with speakers who had less education. The verb *drag* (originally from *draw*) has the form *drug* for the past tense and participle forms, but the form *dragged* is widespread in parts of the United States. *Sneak* has two past tense forms with *sneaked* and *snuck*. Strive has both *strived* and *strove*. Hang has both *hanged* and *hung*. Dive has both *dived* and *dove*. As you may note, all six are weak-verb/strong-verb pairings.

How do you decide which one to use? If you are working by rhetoric, basing your decision on what your local audience expects to hear, then you should hold off on using it until you check with your local audience because the answers vary widely.

Do you decide by which one was the original? Most of these have changed over the years, and for some verbs, it is tough to tell what people have preferred. *Strove* appears as the past form of *strive* a little earlier than *strived* in Middle English, so it seems to have dibs on being the "original" form. Still, the form *strived* shows up all the way from the 1300s to the 2000s. It is such an uncommon word that many people do not know the original past tense form. Considering how many strong verbs have become weak verbs over the last 1,000 years, it is normal for modern speakers to produce *strived*.

Fossils:
L.   *Work*: Last week, I ____ hard to learn to be a blacksmith; I made a *wrought* iron gate.

M.   *Melt*: The ice _____ in the spring, and then the volcano threw *molten* lava everywhere.

Work and *melt* are similar to a lot of regular verbs today. They take the *-ed* form, and life is simple. Yet, they have slightly different histories from many regular verbs because their older forms have supplied new words in other lexical categories. Both *work* and *melt* were previously conjugated as strong verbs with ablaut. Both *wrought* and *molten* are previous versions of *work* and *melt*, respectively. The Old English form of *wrought* was the past tense of *work*, but the Old English form *molten* was the perfect participle of *melt*. For *melt*, it would be as if *broken* had survived as an adjective (e.g. *the broken chair*) but not as a verb (e.g. *I have broken the chair*). As with a large number of Old English strong verbs, they became weak verbs. They now seem normal as weak verbs with *-ed*. There was of course a transition period, where both the older strong forms of *wrought* and *molt* and the weaker forms of *worked* and *melted* were used.

Consider these potential future changes:

N.   *Know*: Before I took the test, I thought I _____ the answer.

O.   *Grow:* With all the sunshine last spring, the lettuce really _____.

Most varieties of English have *know* and *grow* as strong, but some speakers and some varieties have moved these two verbs over to the weak verb category. This move switches them to be conjugated like *work* and *melt*: knowed and growed. There is nothing remarkable about strong verbs being switched over to the weak-verb category. As we just saw with *work* and *melt*, the linguistic process of adding an *-ed* has no problem with new verbs. The sticking point for these two is the social judgments about the users of *knowed* and *growed*. Socially, *knowed* is usually stigmatized. However, there are areas of southern Michigan where *growed* is the standard form. Whether or not the weak verb form is accepted depends on which group of speakers is using which form. If stigmatized social groups innovate the new *-ed* forms of *knowed* and *growed*, then the forms are stigmatized. That *knowed* and *worked* follow the same linguistic rule is irrelevant to anyone making such a judgment.

variation today

English is not a morphologically rich language in its modern state, but English speakers over the ages have made some innovations and continue to do so today. The patterns of morphemes sometimes take on social meaning, and when this happens, the social patterns can become the most important ones. The two cases discussed below show how we use language variation patterns for our daily social work.

the story of g-dropping

In English, one bit of morphological variation receives a lot of comments. The alternation between the alveolar nasal [n] and the velar nasal [ŋ] in words like *walking* has caught many people's attention over the last few centuries. This alternation has a complex path of diachronic variation, but its modern pattern is quite clear. Synchronically, *-ing* variation marks social variation in two ways. First, communities with lower social status usually use the [n] form more often than the [ŋ] form. Second, in almost every English-speaking community in the world, the [n] form is used more often in informal situations, and the [ŋ] form is used more often in formal situations. We might guess that the surrounding sounds push the nasal one way or another, but that is rarely true. In almost every community studied, the sounds around the *-ing* do not affect whether it is alveolar or velar. What does? The morphological category of the word to which *-ing* is attached. Think about these sentences:

1. Chuck Norris was <u>cussing</u> a fan.
2. You were <u>swimming</u> in that pond?
3. Why are you <u>looking</u> out there?
4. <u>Cussing</u> is totally different down South.
5. <u>Running</u> is still my favorite exercise.
6. <u>Watching</u> sports is not a sport itself.

What is the part of speech of each underlined word? From Chapter 4, we know that the aspects of the first three sentences are progressive. In sentences 4–6, the first word is a gerund, a verb transformed into a noun. What are the jobs of the *-ing* in each word? For the first three sentences, they mark the progressive aspect along with the verb *be*. For the last three sentences, the *-ing* marks the previous verb as a noun. As discussed earlier under the topic of suffixal homophony, the *-ing* of *cussing* in the fourth sentence is a derivational suffix, but the progressive *-ing* of *cussing* in the first sentence is an inflectional suffix.

Now here is the important question: What seems more natural to you in terms of the *-ing* form? Say each sentence out loud at a normal pace. Make some of the *-ing*s the [n] form and others the [ŋ] form. Which form fits with the inflectional progressive in sentences 1–3, and which form fits with the derivational gerunds in sentences 4–6?

If you are like most people, the historical echoes of centuries past still resonant in your language. The Old English present participle suffix was *-ende* (e.g. *wrīt-ende)*, and the verbal-noun suffix was *-inge* (e.g. *wrīt-ing)*. The alternation between *-ing* and *-ind* led to the modern use of the velar and alveolar nasals in these two different suffixes. Most people today still have [n] more often with the progressive marker and [ŋ] more often with the gerund marker. The two forms had variable spellings up until the introduction of the printing press in England, and the *-inge* form was becoming more widely used in England by the 1400s, especially in the south. During that time, the spelling system was essentially standardized and frozen, usually based on the London norms where the printing houses were established. Both the progressive suffix and the gerund suffix were spelled the same at that point. Yet, from the patterning in earlier varieties of English, people have adapted the grammatical difference to do social work, marking formal and informal speech and distinguishing vernacular from less vernacular varieties.

So the next time someone talks about "g-dropping," feel free to fill them in on the history of *-ing* variation. Rarely in English are Gs actually dropped, but the two forms of *-ing* do a lot of social work for speakers.

slang with affixes

Affixes like *non-* and *-ed* serve in upstanding roles in society, attaching to stems and going unnoticed. Some affixes may be considered to live a slightly wilder life by getting noticed when they attach to stems. They are almost slangy in their social status, and the *-y* suffix is one of the most prolific. If you consider a word like *sleep* and then its suffixed form *sleepy*, nothing remarkable happens. But when a word like *linguistic* is transformed to *linguisticy* [lɪŋɡwɪstɪki], the process of affixation is highlighted for everyone to notice.

Michael Adams in *Slang: The People's Poetry* and in *Slayer Slang* discusses the rise of the *-y* suffix in the *Buffy the Vampire Slayer* series. Stephen Colbert made the word *truthy* hugely popular starting in 2005, along with its further derived *truthiness*. To convince yourself how popular this suffix has been, try searching online for words you might never expect to take *-y*, such as *kitchen*, *baseball*, or *Google*.[3]

chapter summary

A morpheme is the smallest unit of language with a meaning or grammatical function. Some morphemes are whole words. Some are affixes. All morphemes are discrete units. When people use language, their mental grammars pull out morphemes to put them in combinations to produce language, or they break down incoming words into morphemes to help understand language (e.g. *thickeners* → *thick|en|er|s*). Some morphemes are bound to others, unable to stand on their own, while others are free and can move about a sentence without aid. All morphemes help out, but their jobs are split into two categories: Content morphemes carry the meaning (e.g. *reader perspective*) while function morphemes set them up in relationships (e.g. *the perspective of the reader, the reader's perspective*). Suffixal homophony is an instance where different morphemes sound the same and can only be distinguished by their meaning or function (e.g. *The building was exploding*). All of these morpheme combinations are not arranged in random fashion (e.g. *nesshappyun*) but instead are in a hierarchical organization (e.g. *unhappiness*). We worked with word trees to figure out the kinds of connections prefixes, stems, and suffixes have in a word. Not all languages combine morphemes to build larger words. The more analytic languages have few morphemes per word, and the more synthetic languages have more morphemes per word. Modern English fits in the middle of that continuum, but Old English was closer to the synthetic end.

key concepts

- Ablaut
- Affix
- Analytic language
- Assumption of composition

- Binary branching trees
- Bound morpheme
- Content morpheme
- Derivational
- Free morpheme
- Function morpheme
- Infix
- Inflectional
- Morpheme
- Prefix
- Root
- Semi-weak verbs
- Stem
- Strong verbs
- Suffix
- Suppletion
- Syntax
- Synthetic language
- Weak verbs

notes

1   See Zwicky and Pullum (1983): babel.ucsc.edu/~hank/mrg.readings/ZPCliticsInfl.pdf.
2   http://ironcreek.net/phpsyntaxtree/ is a nifty site to draw the trees you need, and the practice will help you better understand hierarchies.
3   Michael Adams discusses this process on Language Log: http://languagelog.ldc .upenn.edu/nll/?p=1538.
4   These exercises were inspired by Walt Wolfram's work.

references

Adams, M. (2004) *Slayer Slang: A Buffy the Vampire Slayer Lexicon*. New York: Oxford University Press.

Adams, M. (2009) *Slang, the People's Poetry*. New York: Oxford University Press.

Honig, B., Diamond, L., and Gutlohn, L. (2000) *Teaching Reading Sourcebook: For Kindergarten through Eighth Grade*, CORE.

http://ironcreek.net/phpsyntaxtree/

http://languagelog.ldc.upenn.edu/nll/?p=1538

http://languagelog.ldc.upenn.edu/ nll/?p=3290

http://www.washingtonpost.com/wp-srv/style/invitational/invit980802.htm

Zwicky, A.M., and Pullum, G.K. (1983) "Cliticization vs. inflection: English n't." *Language* 59, no. 3): 502–513.

further reading

Stories of English. David Crystal. 2005. Overlook TP.
  David Crystal leads readers through some of the most entertaining stories about the English language. Along with this lexical adventure, Crystal helps readers understand how

English has developed from a collection of German dialects into a wide diversity of varieties scattered around the world.

What is Morphology? 2nd edition. Mark Aronoff and Kirsten Fudeman. 2010. Wiley Blackwell.

This book is a concise introduction to linguistic field of morphology. It includes information on productivity and the mental lexicon, along with experimental and computational methods. Basic concepts are well explained, but the authors also offer a look at what researchers do with morphology. The data analyzed in the book come from a wide diversity of languages.

The Handbook of Morphology (Blackwell Handbooks in Linguistics). Andrew Spencer and Arnold M. Zwicky (eds.). 2001. Blackwell.

If you are considering taking up linguistics as a major or a future profession, take a look at this book to see the range of research to be done in morphology. The book has 32 chapters by a strong collection of authors. Those chapters discuss morphology as an area of linguistics (e.g. inflection, derivation, compounding, productivity) and morphology as it connects to other areas of language (e.g. phonology, syntax, and semantics). The authors also describe morphological variation in many languages and handle morphological questions coming from the fields of language change, psycholinguistics, and language acquisition.

exercises

individual work

1. Creativity in advertising always helps one's cause. One painting company uses this logo: "We paint interiors, exteriors, any terior." What is their hook in this advertisement?
    In the same vein, what is the morphological twist in the following joke?

    Q: Did you hear about the kidnapping?
    A: It's ok, they woke him up.

2. Slashing affixes and identifying morphemes:[4]
    In order to work with morphemes, you must be able to identify what morphemes are. In this first exercise, we take the most basic step. Separate the following words with slashes into productive morphemes. Assume that a productive morpheme is one which can be used to produce more than one word. Some words may only have one morpheme.
    a.   unbelievable
    b.   crystallization
    c.   forgetfulness
    d.   restaurant

e.   runners
f.   satisfied
g.   sleepiness
h.   truthiness
i.   biannually
j.   antidefamation
k.   trimmings
l.   deformity
m.   friendlier
n.   designations
o.   malignancies
p.   bimonthly
q.   strengthener
r.   unsinkable
s.   scapegoat's
t.   teaspoonful
u.   reconciliation
v.   blackened
w.   nonreality
x.   reexaminations
y.   deinstitutionalization
z.   counterrevolutionaries
aa.   anticreationisms
bb.   kindness
cc.   misplaced
dd.   disabilities
ee.   disagreement

3. In this next exercise, label the morphemes you divided in the previous list as either free or bound. Next, label each morpheme as content or function. To make it easier to complete the exercise, feel free to use abbreviations: F = free, B = Bound; f = function; c = content. For example, a word like *unhappiness* would be labeled as *un*-Bc *happy*-Fc *ness*-Bc.

4. With suffixal homophony, isolated words provide no hints about the status of suffixes: If you only have the word *swimming*, there is no way to know if the *-ing* is derivational or inflectional. To expand your morpheme analysis skills, it is important to observe morphemes in their natural habitats, specifically phrases. For the following sentences, identify each morpheme with the same abbreviated labels used in exercise 3. Remember, free morphemes (F) can be content (c) or function (f).

    a. Thirteen fish jumped out of the boat before we shut the lid to the cooler.
    b. Under the bridge, a small snail is slithering over a leaf.

c.   Bacteria never throw wild parties, nor does the fallen tree host a gathering.

d.   The quickest of the three country stars tripped into the vat of maggots on the really stupid TV show.

e.   The Venus flytrap snapped shut on the unsuspecting moth which had flown from the prefabricated cabinets. Strangely enough, the running joke between the mothers was that when they were leaving the cabinets, the slower mother, who was also a writer, would not be able to shoo them towards the unobservant carnivorous plants.

f.   Those quicker speakers worked out a deal with the CEO of North American operations. They arranged for recordings of their speeches to be stored on the company's web servers. Whether a speaker wanted to talk about antifungal medicine or the niceties of suburban compost piles, she or he would be able to preorder as much space as needed.

g.   The environmentally friendly composting compound was constructed on the outskirts of the unurbanized town. It was running efficiently when the machinery was blown up by the atomic breath of the Space Godzilla, which had quickened its pace since the faster runner began to chase it. Thankfully, the youngster with the guns helped ease its concerns.

5.   English past tense revisited:
Earlier in the chapter, we developed rules to determine the forms for the past tense suffix in English. These rules cover new verbs as well as many current verbs. In each of the following nonce verbs, identify which past tense -ed form ([d], [t], [ɪd]) should occur, and explain why a certain form appears with a certain verb. Feel free to use your mental grammar for help.
a.   blib
b.   kleesh
c.   zleet
d.   tlog
e.   stoval
f.   kratch
g.   noolod
h.   shreelm
i.   huiteelut

6.   Negative prefixes:
Identify the negative prefix (ir, il, im, in) used with each of the following words. Explain how the natural class of the first sound in the word influences the form of the negative prefix.
a.   relevant
b.   logical
c.   modest
d.   equitable

   e.   adequate
   f.   movable
   g.   legal
   h.   regular
   i.   possible
   j.   admissible
   k.   reversible
   l.   literate

7.   Adjective formation through suffixing:
     With adjectives like *thirsty*, *rainy*, *hairy*, and *sunny*, we can tell that a
     noun is at the root of each one and that the suffix -*y* is added on to
     each noun. With an adjective like *falling* in *the falling leaf landed on
     my head*, we can work backwards to remove the -*ing* and get the verb
     fall. But what do we do with a word like *wicked*? In the phrase *I am
     wicked*, the word *wicked* has the scent of a verb, but we cannot get
     *I wicked or *I wick. Wicked* certainly seems to be an adjective, as in
     the wicked iguana. Plus, it also acts like an adjective when we convert
     it to an adverb to modify verbs: *They acted wickedly*. Work through
     the following examples to determine what kind of -*ed* is on each one.
     Which of the following have a verb as a root, and which do not? You
     might need to look up words like *dogged*, *wretched*, and *peaked* to see
     how they were regularly used in earlier times. Also note the pronun-
     ciation difference when you look up these words in a dictionary: For
     example, the word *beloved* is pronounced [biləvɪd].

     -ed forms
     accursed
     aged
     beloved
     bended (knee)
     blessed
     crooked
     cussed
     dogged
     jagged
     learned
     naked
     ragged
     wicked
     wretched
     peaked

     After working on these -*ed* forms, check out some of the debates about
     -*ed* and its history on Language Log: http://languagelog.ldc.upenn.edu/
     nll/?p=3290.

8. Word trees:
   Draw a morphological tree (a word tree) for each word below, and label the root and all higher nodes.
   a. *antiindustrializations*
   b. *unconstitutionality*
   c. *untruthfulness*
   d. *reatomizations*
   e. *noncompositionality*
   f. *renationalizations*

9. Ambiguous word trees:
   Draw a morphological tree (a word tree) for each meaning (two meanings per word) of the words below. Label the root and all higher nodes. In addition, label the meaning of each tree.
   a. *unlockable*
   b. *uncoverable*
   c. *unwrappable*

group work

10. Creating the most morphologically burdened sentence:
    As a group, develop a sentence that has the highest morpheme per word average you can imagine. Then develop an equally long sentence with the lowest morpheme per word average.

11. Putting the plural under the microscope:
    The following words are all regular nouns, but for many people the plural marker attached to them comes in three different forms: [s], [z], or [ɪz].
    a. cap
    b. bus
    c. stick
    d. pole
    e. bet
    f. bag
    g. bench
    h. cow
    i. bush
    j. fly
    k. maze
    l. judge
    m. garage
    n. shoe
    o. bowl

p.   cuff

q.   behemoth

r.   buck

Say each of these verbs out loud as a regular plural noun. Notice the sound of the plural marker for each one. Sort the verbs into one of the following three columns according to which past tense marker attaches to them.

[s]	[z]	[ɪz]
_____	_____	_____
_____	_____	_____
_____	_____	_____
_____	_____	_____
_____	_____	_____
_____	_____	_____

From the first two columns of this sorted list, determine whether the last *sound* of the verb itself is voiced or voiceless. What do the last sounds of the third column have in common?

If the preceding exercise did not help, try saying the following nouns out loud.

a.   runs, bums, rungs

b.   kettles, shutters, girls

c.   bows, boys

d.   bees, bays, canoes, crows, laws

e.   taps, bats, backs

f.   tabs, lads, bags

g.   laughs, waves

h.   baths, lathes

i.   bushes, garages (try it with the voiced palatal fricative sound [ʒ])

j.   busses, mazes

k.   churches, judges

12. Special cases:

In language as in life, there are exceptions. Some of the nouns below are exceptions to the regular pluralization rule in English. How do each of the nouns change when a plural is added? Are there regular patterns to the pluralization? Is this change a phonological or mor-phological rule?

a.   life

b.   chief

c.   loaf

d.   thief

e.   hoof

f.   shelf

     g.   leaf

     h.   elf

     i.   wolf

     j.   knife

     k.   riff

     l.   dwarf

     m.   scarf

     n.   brief

     o.   belief

     p.   half

     q.   chief

13. The suffix -er demonstrates a case of "suffixal homophony" in English. There are three different uses: (1) comparative suffix (e.g. bigger, fatter), (2) agentive suffix (e.g. singer, teacher), and (3) repetitive suffix (e.g. patter, chatter). How is the -er used in each of the following sentences?

     a.   This is heavier than I thought.

     b.   The jabber of the students' voices was reassuring.

     c.   The fighter is a jerk.

     d.   The chatter of the people was irritating.

     e.   The runners collapsed after the endurance test.

     f.   The shimmer of the evening light was romantic.

The -ing suffix may function as a nominalizer (e.g. *The trimmings are nice*), adjectivizer (e.g. *The trimming master was at it again*), and progressive (e.g. *He was trimming the tree*). In the following sentences, identify the function of the -ing suffixes.

     a.   The machine was not functioning properly.

     b.   Running is great for cardiovascular fitness.

     c.   It was an appropriate ending for class.

     d.   The working man was too exhausted.

     e.   The bird was flying an airplane.

     f.   Do you like working with sentences?

     g.   The fascinating thing about grammar is its intricacy.

     h.   Grammar is fascinating.

14. Reading Old English, suffixes unbound: Cædmon's In The House. Using the following Old English poem, its gloss, and translation, try to identify the suffixes in Old English and their jobs.

1.	Nū wē sculon herigean	heofonrīces Weard,
2.	Meotodes meahte	ond his mōdgeþanc,
3.	weorc Wuldorfæder,	swā hē wundra gehwæs,
4.	ēce Drihten,	ōr onstealde.
5.	Hē ǣrest sceōp	eorðan bearnum
6.	heofon tō hrōfe,	hālig Scyppend.

7. Þā middangeard   monncynnes Weard,
8. ēce Drihten,   æfter tēode
9. firum foldan,   Freā ælmihtig.

Gloss

1. Now we must praise   heaven-kingdom's Guardian (Ward)
2. The Measurer's might   and his mind-plans
3. the work of the Glory-Father, so he wonders for each,
4. eternal Lord,   a beginning established.
5. He first created   for men's sons
6. heaven as a roof,   holy Creator.
7. Then middle-earth   mankind's Guardian,
8. eternal Lord,   afterwards made–
9. for men earth,   Master Almighty

Translation with case and number marking

1. Now we shall praise heaven's kingdom Protector (subject, singular),
2. creator's power and his purpose (conception),
3. work of the Father of Glory, as he wonder (genitive, plural) for each,
4. eternal Lord, established a beginning.
5. He firstly created earth (genitive, singular) son (dative, plural)
6. heaven as a roof, holy Creator.
7. the world (middle-earth)(direct object, singular) mankind's Protector,
8. eternal Lord, after adorned
9. people (indirect object, plural) earth (object, singular) Lord (subject,
    singular) almighty.

Flowing translation

Now we shall praise the Protector of heaven's kingdom,
The creator's power and his purpose,
The work of the Father of Glory, as he for each of the wonders,
Eternal Lord, established a beginning.
First, he created the earth's sons with
heaven as a roof, holy Creator.
The world, mankind's Protector,
Eternal Lord, the Lord almighty after adorned
The earth with people.

15. Below is a list of verbs in their bare form, their past tense form, and
    their perfect participle form. Survey your group to see if any of the

verbs show variation for the perfect participle form (this category is often the most common one to change) or the past tense form. Additionally, your instructor might ask that you search for variations on the internet and report back in what context you found which variations.

Bare	Past	Participle
drink	drank	drunk
sink	sank	sunk
stink	stank	stunk
ring	rang	rung
spring	sprang	sprung
shrink	shrank	shrunk
swim	swam	swum
blow	blew	blown
know	knew	known
grow	grew	grown
throw	threw	thrown
fly	flew	flown
slay	slew	slain (slayed)
break	broke	broken
catch	caught	caught
teach	taught	taught
sneak	snuck (sneaked)	snuck (sneaked)
stick	stuck	stuck
dig	dug	dug
drag	dragged (drug)	dragged (drug)
tell	told	told
eat	ate	eaten
make	made	made
sit	sat	sat
hit	hit	hit
hide	hid	hidden
slide	slid	slid

study questions

1. What kind of information is stored with each morpheme in the lexicon?
2. What are some categories of free morphemes?
3. What are bound morphemes?
4. What kind of morpheme is an affix?
5. Which lexical categories are content morphemes?
6. What do function morphemes do?
7. Are prefixes content or function in English?
8. What is suffixal homophony?
9. How is lexical ambiguity different from structural ambiguity?
10. How are morphology and syntax different?
11. In what ways is Spanish a more synthetic language than English?
12. In what ways is Mandarin Chinese a more analytic language than English?
13. What kinds of languages rely more on syntax than morphology?
14. How does suppletion happen?
15. How are strong verbs different from weak verbs?
16. What is the difference between weak and semi-weak verbs?
17. What are the social qualities associated with *-ing* variation?
18. What do word trees represent?

Visit the book's companion website for additional resources relating to this chapter at: http://www.wiley.com/go/hazen/introlanguage

7 Putting Pieces Together

An Introduction to Language, First Edition. Kirk Hazen.
© 2015 John Wiley & Sons, Inc. Published 2015 by John Wiley & Sons, Inc.

chapter overview

In this chapter, we step beyond individual lexical items and beyond combinations of morphemes. We move to the factory production line where all the parts get welded together in specific orders. In this chapter, we explore how words get built into larger units, like how a handle, panel, wiring, and glass get built into a car door. To start at a reasonable pace, we limit our focus to three kinds of phrases: Noun Phrases, Adjective Phrases, and Prepositional Phrases. We first ask how it is that the factory of our mental grammar can build such large phrases, and second, we ask how do they fit so cleanly inside of each other. The vast number of language parts we move in our mental factories could get messy, like a cluttered computer desktop. Yet, the same idea of hierarchy that was important for syllables and morphemes again plays a major role in the structure of phrases. The trees in this chapter are based on simple templates that press words into shapes, and we find the same shapes everywhere we look in phrases. The organization of phrases from different languages is explored to illustrate some of these basic patterns. With this expanded understanding of the organization of phrases, students will be ready to move further into the organization of sentences in the next chapter.

meaning and ambiguity

In examining sounds in Chapter 2, we did not find a meaning for every sound. We only found meaning for those sounds which were also lexical items, such as [e] in *a book*. Single-part words have meaning because their combination of sounds is associated with one or more meanings, and those pairings are memorized in the mental lexicon. Multi-part words come about when we take attachable parts out of the lexicon and stick them together. In those cases, the combinations of morphemes results in a word where the total meaning is the combination of the smaller parts: The meaning of *unstoppable* is the result of *un + stop + able*. The way around this assumption of composition is the lexicon's amazing ability to learn new meanings for many combinations: *Collateral damage* has come to mean 'dead civilians in a military struggle,' but not because there is anything in combining *co + lateral + damage* that means *civilian* or *dead*. Such phrases are the idioms of Chapter 5.

With small phrases, combining meanings still works. The Noun Phrase *a smart squid* usually triggers meaning in a listener's mind because of the specific combination of those words. No matter if there are multi-part words, the resulting meaning will still derive from the combination of the individual word meanings: *unhelpful presidential policies*. The same is true for Adjective Phrases like *very brown* or *lightly fluffed*: In *The very brown gecko stepped on my lightly fluffed pancakes*, the meanings of the two Adjective Phrases are the sum of their parts, and they, in turn, form part of the meaning of their corresponding Noun Phrases.

Even for Prepositional Phrases, the third focal point of our chapter, we gain meaning from combinations of smaller parts: words. For the Prepositional Phrases *in the castle* and *at the winter solstice*, the locations are connected each to a Noun Phrase (here, space and time are treated the same by prepositions): In the sentence *The ogre in the castle decided to open an omelet stand at the winter solstice*, the two Prepositional Phrases convey the meanings of space and time, both locations of a sort.

With these three kinds of phrases, their meanings are obvious combinations of their parts. Yet, their structure is invisible. Words are connected to make phrases, but these connecting points have no audible sound. In this chapter, we will reveal how these three phrases are organized. As with syllables and morphemes, the concept of hierarchy plays a major role for this realm of human language. Hierarchy allowed humans to get past just two word phrases, making possible as many combinations of words as desired, for as long as we have breath and time.

How long can these phrases be? In terms of a regular conversation, all three types of phrases are held back only by the intent of the speaker and the attention of the audience. Normal folk begin to lose focus if a political candidate has Noun Phrases with more than five words each: *my extremely successful tenure as governor*; *the dimwitted and mean-spirited policies of my opponent*. With writing, the readers' memory is better (since writing can be reviewed), so writing often has longer phrases. Even if rhetoric restricts the length of phrases, does grammar? The answer is no. Take a look at what can happen to a Noun Phrase: *tree*. It can gain a determiner, as in *a tree* or *the tree*. It can gain an Adjective Phrase (*the artificial tree*) and a Prepositional Phrase (*the artificial tree beside the piano*). Both of those can expand (*the grossly artificial tree right beside the piano*). There is no structural reason to stop adding phrases, including phrases that could pass for entire sentences in other contexts: *The grossly artificial tree beside the piano in the old house which sold last week*. We will call this remarkable quality **expansion**. One question to answer in this chapter is what allows expansion to happen?

In Russia, there are matryoshka dolls, painted wooden dolls that are uniquely arranged. The largest doll contains the second largest doll. This second doll opens up in turn and contains the third doll. This nesting of one doll inside the other continues until the final tiny doll. These matryoshka dolls share a quality with phrases: They can contain each other. Phrases are able to fit one inside the other. Adjective Phrases and Prepositional Phrases can fit in a Noun Phrase: *The <u>old</u> murderer <u>in the greenhouse</u>*. Noun Phrases are of course part of Prepositional Phrases, *in <u>the greenhouse</u>*, and Adjective Phrases can be part of those Noun Phrases, *in the <u>drafty</u> greenhouse*. Adjective Phrases are a little more restricted in English, but they can have modifiers which expand them. Adjective Phrases like *bright blue* or *deep blue* both have modifiers for *blue*. This skill of **nesting** one phrase inside another is what allowed humans to expand beyond simple expressions and construct larger, structured phrases. But, how does nesting take place? As with expansion, we need to introduce some scaffolding to erect the hierarchy of these phrases.

Figure 7.1 Nested Matryoshka dolls. http://en.wikipedia.org/wiki/File:Russian-Matroshka2.jpg. Creative Commons Attribution-Share Alike 3.0 Unported license.

The other quality of interest for our syntactic small phrases is ambiguity. In earlier chapters, we dealt with lexical ambiguity, where one phonetic form (e.g. [bæt]) is associated with two or more meanings, forming two or more words. In Chapters 6, 7, and 8, the ambiguity is different. It is called **structural ambiguity**. With this kind of ambiguity, the meaning connected to the phonetic form of a word does not have to change. Instead, the syntactic structure of the phrases can be arranged differently. Consider the ambiguity of *the deep blue pool*. Do you see the two meanings? I realize that with a hyphen to connect *deep-blue*, we get the color, and with a comma to separate them, we get a blue pool of a good depth. Yet, in spoken language you get neither hyphens nor commas. What kinds of structures can we produce with such possibilities? On one hand, we can have *the [deep] [blue] pool*, meaning both *deep* and *blue* are separate modifiers of *pool*. On the other, we get *the [deep blue] pool* where *deep* modifies the color *blue*, which in turn modifies *pool*. As syntactic parsing machines, we figure this kind of ambiguity out (unless of course, we cannot pull meaning from other contexts). To **parse** means to disassemble to better understand. As ambiguity is a part of all human languages, it appears to be part of who we are. How do we set up the structures to choose? Again we need some specialized terms to figure out how ambiguity arises.

In this chapter, we dismantle and reassemble Noun Phrases, Adjective Phrases, and Prepositional Phrases to more thoroughly explain these three syntactic qualities: expansion, nesting, and ambiguity. The structure of human language is best understood as a discrete combinatorial system, and this approach certainly works well with phrases (see Pinker 2007). By discrete, we do not mean that they are polite or discerning, but instead that language has separable chunks which get combined as if they were being assembled in a factory production line: a discrete combinatorial system. When we bring language into ourselves, hearing a sounded language or seeing a signed language, our mental grammars decipher the discrete combinations, checking the parts against those stored in our lexicons and assembling meaning. The work on syntactic phrases is more abstract than organizing sounds in Chapter 3 or categorizing words in Chapter 5.

From expansion and nesting also comes the ability to create both really large phrases and new phrases. We can understand and produce a potentially infinite number of new phrases. At the time of this writing, the phrase *those pesky dragons on her roof* did not match any hits in search engines on the internet. It is not an exotic phrase, but because of the ability to combine words together, the entire unit, as a single phrase, is new to most people. It is a specific quality of human language that we are able to understand phrases which we have never heard before.

The structures in this chapter cannot be heard, and no one will shout, "Look, there's a syntactic tree on the corner!" But, remember from Chapter 1 where we are looking for these trees. We want to make a model of how language works in the human mind. To build that model for syllables, complex words, and phrases, we must talk about how the different parts are connected. Those connections are abstract because they organize mechanisms in the mind. The mind is simply a model for what actually happens in the brain, and since we actually do language every day, a model of what we do is our goal.

structure and hierarchy

With syllables, we had a specific template to fill out, one where we hooked together phonetic segments. Each node was labeled, and there were different levels:

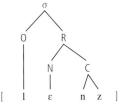

With the word trees, we connected morphemes to each other through higher points in the hierarchy, labeling the different levels with lexical categories as their parts of speech changed:

Word Play: Crash blossom ambiguities

We have chased down several types of ambiguity in this book, including lexical and structural ambiguity. For professional writers, you might think ambiguity would be avoided with appropriate rephrasing and contextualization, but there is one area of professional writing whose conventions almost seem to encourage ambiguity of all types (both lexically and structurally). This area is headlines for news stories. The writing tradition for headlines has a convention where the copula verb *be* is dropped, often creating a pile of nouns, adjectives, and prepositions crying out to the reader for interpretation. *Language Log* (at languagelog.ldc.upenn.edu/nll/) has termed this particular kind of jumble of words a **crash blossom**.

These are humorous to most people because they present unreal situations and obvious confusion. All humor is based on contrast between what people expect and what they experience. This contrast is why slapstick physical humor works as well as stand-up comedy: Both forms present situations where something unordinary happens, and the contrast makes us laugh. In the following headlines, all drawn from *Language Log*'s amazing powers of observation, a pile up of words can be interpreted as a Noun Phrase, but they can also be interpreted as other phrases. Can you pick out which potential phrase combinations go with which meanings? The URL for each story is given below the headline, or you can search for key words from each headline:

- "Mansell guilty of missing businessman's murder"
  http://languagelog.ldc.upenn.edu/nll/?p=3548

- "Sex quiz cricket ace in hotel suicide leap"
  http://languagelog.ldc.upenn.edu/nll/?p=3559

- "Virginia Beach man accused of decapitating son to stay in hospital"
  http://languagelog.ldc.upenn.edu/nll/?p=3454

- "Transgenic grass skirts regulators"
  http://languagelog.ldc.upenn.edu/nll/?p=3304

- "Police chase driver in hospital"
  http://languagelog.ldc.upenn.edu/nll/?p=2769

The trees for phrases will show hierarchy in syntax through different levels, just like syllable trees and word trees. However, one difference with syntactic trees is that each node in a phrase tree can have one or two branches, but not three or more. This restriction is called binary branching, and it is an assumption about how information gets processed in the brain. You can think of it as binary code, with computers reading instructions as sets of 1s and 0s. It is a restrictive life with phrases: no three-way hookups allowed.

Yes:

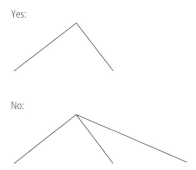

No:

The other difference is that phrase trees will have a basic set of templates, and this basic set will be used again and again. There will also be some special parts that allow for variation. Before we work through the special parts, let us take a trip down memory lane, back to younger school days: algebra. It might not have been everyone's favorite class, yet I suspect we all remember some of it. In algebra, we were faced with formulas like this one: x + 2 = y. We were then asked to figure out what x would be if y = 6 (and then 8 and 140 and −3). If y = 6, then x = 4. If instead, y = 8, then we substitute 8 in the formula and get x + 2 = 8, and x = 6. OK … but why would you need to remember this kind of formula with x and y in a book about language? Do you remember the name for the kind of things x and y are? Right, they are *variables*. They are place holders for other numbers in the formula. Their value varies depending on their context (and then we solve for a variable). For the phrase trees you will be using in this chapter, the basic template has variables with possible values of Noun, Adjective, and Preposition. Luckily, you do not have to solve for any numbers with phrase trees.

The top of the phrase tree starts with a node, just like the syllable trees. This first node is labeled XP (the P is for Phrase), and it branches into two other nodes, a determiner slot and an intermediate node ($\overline{X}$, pronounced X-bar).

This intermediate node, the $\overline{X}$, is useful because it can be copied as much as you need it to be. Here, we have it copied once. The YPs branching off are other kinds of phrases:

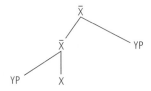

At the bottom is the head of the phrase (X), its most basic root:

When assembled, the basic phrase tree (with variables X and Y) looks like this:

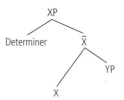

What do these Xs mean? The X at the bottom of the phrase tree is the **head of the phrase** and gives the particular phrase its flavor. The X (or Y) is a variable to be replaced with either a Noun (N), an Adjective (A), or a Preposition (P). (In the next chapter we add a few more items to substitute for the X.) The top level is the XP, and the P stands for Phrase (as in Noun Phrase, Adjective Phrase, and Prepositional Phrase). A single-line rule for this tree would be the following: XP → Determiner; $\overline{\text{X}}$. The semicolon between "Determiner; $\overline{\text{X}}$" means that those two are on the same level and adjacent to each other. As discussed later, they could come in either order depending on what is preferred in the language: either Determiner; $\overline{\text{X}}$ or $\overline{\text{X}}$; Determiner.

What would connect to the determiner node in this phrase tree? The answer depends on the head of the phrase, but think of what a word like *very* does for an adjective like *awkward*. The Adjective Phrase *very awkward* specifies a kind of awkward. For a noun like *aardvark*, the determiner *the* picks out specific aardvarks, whereas a determiner like *an* points at a single, unspecified aardvark. In English, prepositions are more restricted in their determiner flamboyance, but think of an expression like *I spilled the ice cream by the fridge* as compared to *I spilled the ice cream only by the fridge, not on the rug*. The *only* restricts the place where the ice cream was spilled.

The X with the line over the top is the X-bar, a node in the tree that falls between the top level and the bottom level. This intermediate $\overline{\text{X}}$ node provides places to make connections to other trees. It is like having a closet with as much room as you need to hang up clothes because you have an ever-expanding choice of extra hooks and racks (or perhaps hangers in your dialect). With this template, a phrase tree is infinitely expandable. If you need 10 extra nodes to hang more phrases, you can make them (and I will show you how in a few paragraphs).

Within any particular tree, regardless of the type of head used, every X between the XP and the head needs to be the same kind of unit. So if it is an N, then the intermediate node will be an $\overline{\text{N}}$, and the top-level node will be an NP, like this:

This kind of template would fit an NP like *the dog* in the following way:

An Adjective Phrase would look like the following with an A (for adjective) as its head, an Ā as its intermediate node, and an AP as its top-level node:

An AP like *really young* would fit into the phrase tree like this:

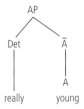

With Prepositional Phrases, we see the special quality of intermediate X̄ nodes: their ability to connect to other phrases. To mark a difference with XPs, we use the variable Y to go along with YPs. YPs take the same heads of phrases as XPs: Nouns, Adjectives, and Prepositions. The reason for the different variable is to show that the YP has its own head of phrase separate from its XP. Take a look at the PP here:

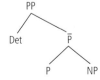

With a PP like *under the mountain*, the tree structure, with its YP branch, would look like this:

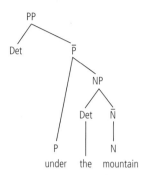

Note that the Noun Phrase inside of this Prepositional Phrase expands just like all other Noun Phrases. There is no need for additional syntactic machinery to handle this Noun Phrase differently from others. The Noun Phrase under the P̄ node will be its own phrase. The single-line rule for this template would be X̄ → X; YP, where X is the head of the phrase (in this case a P) and YP is some other kind of phrase (in this case, an NP).

There is one more condition we need to illustrate. For this illustration, we need a slightly expanded phrase. Consider what is going on in this phrase: *a sharp bayonet in the basket*. How many phrases are inside this one Noun Phrase? Since every head of a phrase demands an XP, we can figure out which words are heads, and we will then know how many XPs are needed.

A   sharp   bayonet   in   the   basket

There is the N of *basket*, so we have an NP.
There is the adjective *sharp*, so we have an AP.
There is the preposition *in*, so we have a PP.
Finally there is the noun *bayonet*, which gives us another NP.

With all those phrases, what kind of hierarchical order do they have? Think back to our work with single-part words in Chapter 4. If we were to substitute a pronoun for the entire unit of *a sharp bayonet in the basket*, what would it be? Perhaps this sentence might help: *A sharp bayonet in the basket frightened the Chihuahua* would be transformed to *It frightened the Chihuahua*. The entire unit in question is an NP because it can be replaced with *it*. What is the anchor for this Noun Phrase? The head of the top-level Noun Phrase is *bayonet*. But how do the other parts fit?

Consider splaying out the words into a few bracketed groups before you represent the entire collection with a phrase tree: a [sharp] bayonet [in the basket]. Here, the Adjective Phrase and the Prepositional Phrase are part of the Noun Phrase headed by *bayonet*. There are three parts to be connected with the head of the top-level Noun Phrase. How should these phrases be arranged, given that we can only have up to two branches per node? We need one more type of phrase tree to create this representation:

This X-bar diagram may be a bit confusing at first, but it is quite useful for making space to hang extra phrases. What it means is that an intermediate node in a phrase can be copied on one branch (the $\bar{X}$), and we can take care of another phrase on the other (YP). Remember that a YP is just like the XPs we have dealt with earlier. They are simply headed by a different lexical category than the XP. The single-line rule for this phrase structure is the following: $^{*}\bar{X} \rightarrow \bar{X};YP$. The star at the start of this rule has a special name, **infinite recursion**. This quality means that the rule can be repeated as many times as needed to allow for expansion of a phrase. For our particular Noun Phrase, it allows us to take care of its Prepositional Phrase, its head (*bayonet*), and its Adjective Phrase:

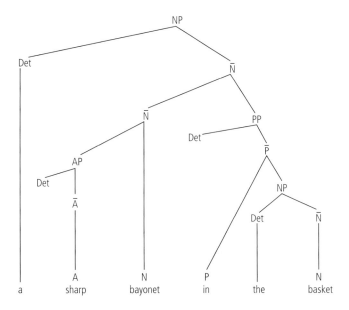

Here, the $\bar{N}$ is repeated to allow the first branch to connect to the Prepositional Phrase and the second $\bar{N}$ to connect to the AP, as well as the head of the overall phrase. Note that our heads of phrases are the lexical categories originally discussed in Chapter 4 and that these categories cover many, many words. The same tree's structure above would cover *the dark cloud under the bridge* and *those broken bricks on the roof*.

What do we do with a phrase like *a glass of water*, where the second NP does not have a determiner?

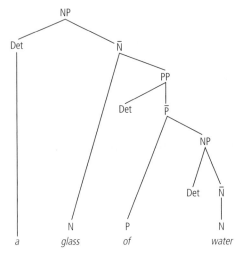

The tree structure remains intact, but not all slots are filled by lexical items. In this phrase tree, neither the determiner of the Prepositional Phrase nor the determiner of the second Noun Phrase have a lexical item in them. In more advanced syntactic analysis, you would be required to erase the unfilled nodes at some later point, but for our purposes, empty slots are just fine if it makes you more comfortable to include them.

Our three rules are worth repeating because these are the only three syntactic rules we use to build phrases in this chapter and the next. They are ordered from the top of the phrase tree to the bottom and displayed with the variables in place.

$$XP \rightarrow Det; \bar{X}$$
$$^*\bar{X} \rightarrow \bar{X}; YP$$
$$\bar{X} \rightarrow X; YP$$

Several of these rules have optional elements, meaning that they can be used or not.

For example, in the Noun Phrase *my squid* the word *my* fills the determiner slot, but in the Noun Phrase *I*, there is no word in the determiner slot; as a result, it does not have to be drawn in the phrase tree. If all the optional elements were marked with parentheses, the rules would look like this:

$$XP \rightarrow (Det); \bar{X}$$
$$(^*\bar{X} \rightarrow \bar{X}; YP)$$
$$\bar{X} \rightarrow X; (YP)$$

There are several different methods for organizing phrases, but these three rules demonstrate the important qualities of human language. Together, they can describe many of the structures we use every day. With them, you can demonstrate both how our phrases are able to expand as they do and how they are able to nest one inside the other. The lines within the trees also tell of the relationships in the phrases. For example, in the tree above for *a glass of water*, the determiner node is connected to the rest of the phrase through the top node and modifies the entire unit contained under that intermediate node, namely *glass of water*. In the earlier Prepositional Phrase *under the mountain*, the node for *under* dominates the entire Noun Phrase *the mountain*. Even if that Noun Phrase were expanded to include adjectives, like *the ancient, foreboding mountain*, the preposition *under* would dominate the entire Noun Phrase in that hierarchy. This relationship is a meaning relationship carried through the structure of the connections. With the methods we use in this book, the phrase trees allow for that structure. If we drew the relationships between the words non-hierarchically, so that you would get

under—the—ancient—foreboding—mountain

the Preposition *under* would only modify the determiner *the* instead of the entire Noun Phrase. This flat structure does not work well for our species's language. A regular feature of human language is that we can substitute similar phrases for each other. We can substitute this particular Noun Phrase for others and still have descriptively grammatical phrases, such as *under my thumb, under the ground, under her desk*, and *under the bush*. Each of those Noun Phrases is expandable, and *under* dominates each one in the hierarchy of the phrase.

Words to the Wise: From prepositions to prefixes

By the end of the Roman Empire, Latin was a language in transition. It had prepositions, but traditionally had a Subject-Object-Verb order. This kind of word order is usually found with languages that have postpositions. The later forms of Romance languages, such as French, Spanish, and Italian, would develop the word order more typically found with prepositions, Subject-Verb-Object.

A number of the prepositions from Latin have been inherited in English, although in roles different from their original ones. Consider the following English words: *adjunct, advance, antecedent, antebellum, circumnavigate, circumlocution, contraceptive, contralateral, international, interact, postpone, postposition, transport, transponder*. All of these English words start with prefixes that used to be free prepositions in Latin. *Ad* involved motion to a destination. *Ante* involved a position before something. *Circum* and *Contra* were both prepositions for *around*. *Inter* was a preposition meaning *between*. *Post* was a preposition meaning *after* {shame it was not a postposition}. *Trans* involved motion across something. English had the opportunity to borrow these Latin prepositions as English prepositions, but function words are closed lexical categories: New members are rarely admitted.

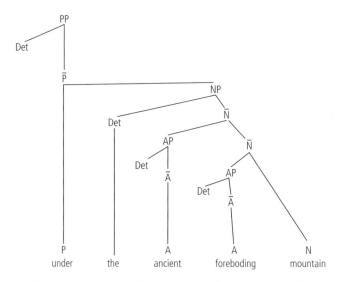

In the tree for the Prepositional Phrase *under the ancient foreboding mountain*, the determiner slots for each Adjective Phrase is empty, but they could have been filled with words like *very* and *really*. Those Adjective Phrases are expandable just like the other phrases, and they still would have fit inside and underneath the Noun Phrase's top node. That is the nature of expansion and nesting. The determiner slot for the Prepositional Phrase is also empty but could have been filled with a word like *only* or *deep*. Our X-bar trees illustrate the semantic relationship of these words through hierarchy and constituency. The Noun Phrase *the ancient foreboding mountain* is a constituent of the preposition *under*. The Adjective Phrases of *ancient* and *foreboding* are both constituents of the Noun Phrase *the mountain*. These semantic relationships will be used to differentiate meanings more in the next section on ambiguity. Working with the relationships between words and phrases will help you understand the nature of syntax in human language.

Yet, before you continue reading in the next section on ambiguity, first take a moment to draw out your own phrase structure trees for the following phrases. Much like learning the phonetic symbols in Chapter 2, you learn how phrases are hierarchically organized by drawing the trees yourself and wrestling with choices of hierarchical organization, expansion, and nesting on your own.

The phrases below should be represented by X-bar rules in phrase trees. Words like *those* and possessive pronouns like *my* can be best handled in the determiner slot, since **the those dunes* or **the my shoes* both come off as ungrammatical. As a first step to splaying out these phrases, figure out how many heads of phrases are in each one: For example, the first phrase has two. Once you know how many heads of phrases you have, you will know how many XPs you need to draw:

the large circles
a sunset on the horizon

those worn Western dunes
my gecko in the terrarium on the dresser
a scintillating musical at our local theater

For those who need extra challenge with a longer Noun Phrases, attempt the following:

the very young, really cute puppy only on the old newspaper in the new kitchen

If you work through these, you will find that the tree structures used in one part are repeated again and again in other parts. This repeatability is an extremely useful quality of human language and other biological systems. Think of DNA and some of its basic building pairs of nucleotides (A&T; C&G). From these simple combinations of pairs, all life flourishes. With human syntax, a few simple combinations give rise to an infinite number of phrases.

Everyone who is new to the analysis of syntax is struck by its abstract nature and how far removed it appears to be from actually saying and hearing phrases. Some people scoff and say, "But we have no trees in our heads with these branches and X̄s sticking out everywhere." Linguists agree that we do not have drawings of lines and variables in our heads, but in our brains, the material representing words **is** hierarchically organized. The lines and variables we use in this book model the organization in the brain.

To explain syntax, how words fit together in such regular patterns, we must explain the qualities of expansion and nesting. How do phrases keep growing and remain the same kind of phrase? How do phrases get put one inside the other, keeping their identity but becoming part of a larger phrase? The answer is that we carry around an organizational plan in our mental grammars where multiple phrases are ordered in a hierarchy. The X-bar templates presented in this chapter allow for the description of these qualities.

ambiguity and constituency

Now that you have worked through some phrase trees yourself, developing hierarchies to show off the qualities of expansion and nesting, it is time to confront the concept of structural ambiguity. This quality is a basic one for human language, and our phrase trees should be able to handle the organization of the different meanings. We touch upon the solutions here, and we explore structural ambiguity more fully in Chapter 8.

Consider the ambiguity in the Noun Phrase of this sentence: *The deep blue pool was cold.* For the sake of sanity, at this point let us only consider the Noun Phrase, which is where the ambiguity resides. As mentioned earlier, the meanings coming from this sentence are that either the pool was blue and of considerable depth, or it was the color deep blue. To tackle this problem with a sense of confidence, we need to consider the constituency of the Noun Phrase.

Words to the Wise: The Cognitive Revolution: From blank slates to genetically prepackaged programs

The study of the human mind underwent a transition in the late 1950s and 1960s, and the changes are traditionally referred to as the "cognitive revolution." Previously psychologists and linguists only studied what people did in an attempt to be as objective and scientific as possible. Scholars such as George Miller, Noam Chomsky, Jerome Bruner, and Roger Brown began to examine models of information and language in the brain. None of them were investigating a spiritual world beyond science. They were studying mental models with physical instantiation in the brain.

From the 1960s forward, the cognitive sciences have grown to include branches of neuroscience (connecting models of the mind to patterns in the brain) and computer science. With computer science, human computer language interaction has grown greatly in the 2000s. Bank machines, call centers, and even public toilets talk to customers. A listening program, Siri, comes standard on iPhones and translates a speaker's voice into text to execute commands. The programs needed for such computer magic took decades to develop and grew out of models of the human mind.

Steven Pinker, in his book *The Blank Slate*, argues that some of the hallmarks of cognitive science include the assumption that mental models can be grounded in the physical world, that an infinite range of human behavior can be produced from mental programs, and that the mind is a complex system of many interacting parts. Pinker's main argument is that humans are born with some knowledge, such as language knowledge, that is already genetically coded. In other words, humans are not born as blank slates, a belief previously held by many western scholars.

Constituency is the organizational quality of one unit being represented by another unit higher up the hierarchy. Just like a member of a legislative branch represents constituents in political realms, an XP represents constituents in syntactic realms. To consider the two different meanings of *deep blue pool* is to consider a change of constituency of the adjectives. Before you go further in this text, try to sketch out the two different phrase trees and label each one with a different meaning. (Cue Jeopardy theme music.) If you want, you can use brackets to divide out the parts: [The subject] [is divided from the predicate].

In the first tree, the adjective *blue* is modified by *deep*. The constituency of *deep* puts it under *blue*'s Adjective Phrase, and that entire phrase modifies the noun *pool*. {If you really would like to stretch your hand further, feel free to make *deep* an adjective modifying *blue*, rather than a determiner. The point of constituency would be the same: *Deep* would be inside the Adjective Phrase of *blue*.}

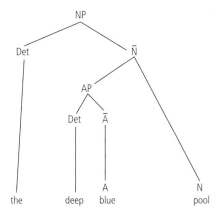

In the second tree, the adjective *deep* modifies *pool* in one Adjective Phrase, and the adjective *blue* modifies *pool* in a separate Adjective Phrase. Both adjectives are constituents of the Noun Phrase, but they are not constituents of each other. Constituency matters. To think of the second tree another way, the order of the adjectives could be reversed (*the blue deep pool*), and the tree's structure would be the same.

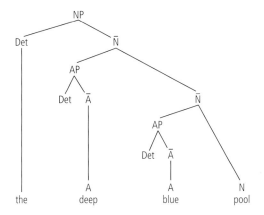

We will use this template scheme for the remainder of Chapter 7 and all of Chapter 8, where we expand our repertoire of phrases to Verb Phrases and Inflectional Phrases (sentences). The same three rules of X-bar are used again and again and again to explore how phrases are constructed. As with the study of sounds in Chapters 2 and 3, the best way to understand the complex relationships of all the language you construct is to practice using the parts and to practice making the analysis. After 15 phrase trees (give or take), it will get much easier for you to be able to discuss and illustrate qualities of human language, especially hierarchy, constituency, expansion, nesting, and ambiguity.

Englishes and other languages

In English, we call words like *in, on, at, under,* and *between* prepositions. Consider the breakdown of that word: *pre-position*. The word *position* is about something's location, and one of the other technical terms for prepositions is **locatives** because they locate nouns in time or space. English is one of many languages which have such locatives. Some languages, such as Latin, had prepositions, but also had some words where the location was marked with suffixes: For example, *ad senatum ambulare* would be to 'walk (ambulate) to the Senate,' but *domus* 'home' (domestic, domicile) would become *domi* 'at home.' Since this suffix would be on a noun to mark its grammatical relationships with other words, it would be considered a case marking (Chapter 4). Languages today such as Turkish can also have suffixes to mark the locative: For example, *okul* 'school' would take *-da* to form *okulda* 'in the school.' Yet, Turkish and many other languages have their locatives as free words which come <u>after</u> their noun complements. Look at this subsection in Hindi from the United Nations' Universal Declaration of Human Rights:[1]

गौरव और अधिकारों के मामले में
gaurav aur adhikārom̥ ke māmle <u>mem̥</u>
<u>in</u> *dignity and rights*

These locatives are not called *pre-positions*. Instead, they are called *post-positions*. This may seem odd to most English speakers, but everyone should understand that languages with postpositions are in the majority. Prepositions do not work any better than postpositions or locative suffixes.

How could such postpositional phrases be organized within the phrase tree structure we have been using? The apparent problem is that the head of the Postposition Phrase needs to be on the other side of the Noun Phrase. Note that PP can cover both *pre*-positional phrases and *post*-positional phrases. The answer is actually quite easy. In the X-bar scheme, despite the lines and spaces being two-dimensional, think of it as a mobile, which can swing freely back and forth.

The tree with the preposition is not remarkably different from the tree with the postposition, except for where the head of the phrase falls. Note that the determiner in the postpositional phrase also swung around to the back side of the PP. Consider the Japanese phrase *yuka ni* 'on the floor.' Japanese is a postpositional language, but its tree is similar to the English one:

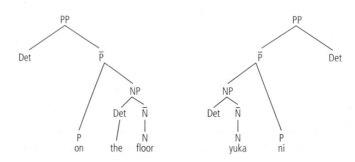

This variation between languages brings up some important points of comparison. When we look across all human languages, there are patterns which could not arise simply by chance. Some of these will be explored in Chapter 8, but a few are discussed here. The basic idea is that there seem to be constrained patterns for human languages. These patterns are not randomly organized. They appear to follow some set of blueprints. With the locatives, the postpositional languages do not have postpositions simply because they have all had contact with each other. Neither have prepositional languages borrowed the pattern from each other, like so many fashion choices. Mark Baker in *The Atoms of Language* describes a Nigerian language, Edo, that has its ordering of words organized like English. If this similarity resulted from contact with English and Edo, a language with a million speakers, no one would be surprised. But Edo and English's patterns of word order were in place for a considerable time, and contact between these languages happened only recently. What could be driving languages to have the same sets of word orders? Our best answer is that humans start off with a species-specific set of blueprints for constructing languages. These basic plans constrain the ways language can develop.

What could the blueprints be? Mark Baker describes these biological plans as the Universal Grammar. Remember from Chapter 1 that the Universal Grammar is the biological endowment for building a mental grammar. This approach is one of several ways a mental grammar could be built. Another approach is called emergence, where other in-born qualities develop together to build a mental grammar. Think of qualities such as our desire to recognize patterns, like finding shapes in clouds or religious figures on toast, as well as our ability to classify everything around us. As William O'Grady (2010) describes it, the similarities and differences we can find in human language result from the way the brain works and the lexicons we ingest as children.

Either way around, human languages have patterns in them, and it is important to recognize these patterns in order to understand the nature of phrases. How humans acquire these patterns or how they produce them in their day-to-day lives cannot be adequately explored in this book, but it is a fascinating set of questions. This version of the story will follow a simplified model of the Universal Grammar in order to introduce patterns of phrases.

As this story goes, the mental grammar of a language is the mechanism in the mind/brain that takes the language in and puts the language out. The Universal Grammar in itself is not a mental grammar of any particular language, just as blueprints are not useful as a shelter. The Universal Grammar is the set of genetic instructions we use as infants to acquire languages. It most likely contains instructions for building a lexicon with arbitrariness as a basic tenet, along with a module to learn phonological patterns and one to pay attention to the ordering of morphemes into words and phrases. Along with such a set of requirements, traditionally called **principles**, the Universal Grammar probably contains design choices for the child acquiring a language.

With those design choices, consider this metaphor: In many new subdivisions across the United States, homebuyers are given some set design plans (three-story, three bathroom house) and some choices (marble or Formica counter tops; wood floors or tile). The choices are constrained choices: You do not get to choose any kind of flooring material, just wood or tile. One way to imagine language acquisition proceeding is to consider the acquiring child as having a constrained choice of options for certain language structures. The constrained choices for locatives would be head first or head final. Either the locative comes before its Noun Phrase or it comes after it. This particular choice is called the **headedness parameter**. Parameters like the headedness parameter are hypothesized to be part of the Universal Grammar. In the positional phrases, the head of the phrase, the locative, can either come first or last. This either/or quality is called a **parameter** because it seems to operate like a toggle switch. For the acquiring child, the switch can be in one of two positions.

The headedness parameter is not an absolute law, like gravity is, but instead is a strongly directed constraint. Mark Baker, in *Atoms of Language*, works through the motivation for the parameter hypothesis in human language. That these patterns line up the way they do defies the odds (especially when matched with the patterns of Verb Phrases and sentences from Chapter 8). The biological endowment of the Universal Grammar also helps to explain why such disconnected languages have such similar grammatical patterns. Japanese and Hindi both have postpositions but have historically not had any extensive language contact. It is clear that after comparing these languages, their grammatical patterns did not pop up because of contact and do not require a social connection. In other words, postpositions did not spread like the flu where one person infected another.

The same quality of head directionality is true for languages with determiners and nouns. Here, I have to admit a bit of sleight of hand with our Noun Phrases. If you notice, the headedness parameter has the head either first or last, and the P swings around in the PP. In the NP, the determiner is in front with a language like English and in back with a language Machame, a Bantu language of 300,000 in Tanzania (e.g. *bhandu bhalyá bhákwa* 'people those mine' or 'those people of mine').[2] The Noun Phrases seem backwards to the headedness principle. How could this issue be resolved? It is common in syntactic study to represent combinations like *the octopus* not as Noun Phrases, but instead to represent them as Determiner Phrases (DPs). With that configuration, the head of the phrase, the determiner D, is first for languages like English (which also have *prepositions*) and last for languages like Lakota, spoken by Sioux Indians (which also have *post*positions). In the Lakota sentence below, the noun for 'blanket' has a determiner and the demonstrative indicating nearness:

Šiná   kiŋ lé   mitȟáwa.[3]
blanket the this (is) mine.
This blanket is mine.

This difference in order is true for Lakota adjectives also:

mní   šmá
water   deep

As well as adjective determiner combinations:

Šúŋka   ská   kiŋ
dog   white   the

And even postposition compositions:

Šúŋka   ská   kiŋ   ohlate
dog   white   the   under

Lakota and Japanese did not develop their modern structure through contact with each other. Neither did Edo and English. Speakers of these languages followed constrained choices of where to place the heads of phrases. Once the choice of head first or head last got made, all the other options for locatives, determiner phrases, and adjectives fell into place.

variation through time: a shift from more synthetic to more analytic

Adjectives, nouns, and verbs are different creatures in modern varieties of English than they were in Old English (450–1100). These kinds of words wore a great deal more adornment in those days. The work they did required them to wear suffixes more often than they do in Modern English. For example, consider the following concocted sentences in Modern and Old English.

The good kings slew the wolf with their swords when he had bitten them.

Þa gode cyningas þone wulf slogon mid heorra sweordum, þa he heom biten hafde.

The underlined –as was reduced down to modern plural –s, and the double-underlined –um, which marked its noun as a plural object, was lost completely. One of the biggest changes in the English language is the shifting importance between morphology and syntax. Speakers of English over the last 1,500 years have increasingly made morphemes less important for building meanings in sentences, relying more on syntax. This change was neither committee-planned nor voted upon. The daily variation people created prompted one change after another, leading to our modern language. All together, these variations and changes have shifted English from a more synthetic language to a more analytic language. This subsection hits the highlights of those changes.

the first step: losing our inflections

The first step towards becoming a more analytic language affected neither how words nor phrases got put together. The first step was a change in the sound system of English. Before English was English, back before 450 CE when it was a collection of German dialects, the main stress on a word would come on the last syllable, so that in a CVCV combination, the stress would be on the last vowel. In these German dialects, the inflectional, grammatical morphemes were mostly suffixes, and that stress helped keep those suffixes in place. For example, the words like *bātas* 'boats' and *bātum* 'to the boats' are distinguished by their suffixes: The first is the plural subject/object, and the second is the indirect object. Yet, before the invading Angles, Saxons, and Jutes were fully settled, the tides of stress had begun to change. The first syllables became the place that received primary stress, so that in *axes*, the *ax* would be more stressed than the *es*. Suffixes became less important, but their fate would get worse over the following centuries. Some suffixes became buried in their words: For example, *ugly* was a stem + suffix in 1325 as in "an ugly snake" borrowed from Old Norse *ugglig-r* 'to be feared or dreaded,' but today *ugly* is monomorphemic. Most other suffixes faded away.

As we discussed in Chapter 3, one of the most frequent rules in English is the schwa rule. This rule changes unstressed vowels into schwa. As all the suffixes became unstressed, their previously distinctive vowels became indistinguishable. The three modern inflectional suffixes for possessive (-'s), plural (-s), and third-singular verbs (-s) originally all had different forms, but these forms were distinguished by their vowels. For example, the Old English form for *boat's* was *bātes*, but the Old English form of *boats* was *bātas*. Only the final vowel distinguished those two words. When all the vowels became schwa, these suffixes became indistinguishable.

Many of the suffixes were themselves *only* vowels, and after their unstressed selves became schwas, many of them were deleted. As this variable deleting of schwas continued for centuries, their orthographic form eventually fell into the category of *silent E*. Almost all of the silent Es today come from this process of deleting schwas. Consider these word pairs:

<u>Noun</u>	<u>Verb</u> (with a previously pronounced verbal suffix)
teeth	*teethe*
breath	*breathe*
gift	*give*
cloth	*clothe*

The vowels at the end of the verb forms used to not be silent. For example, *give* would have sounded something like [gɪvə] before losing the final schwa. They have been silenced over time, although they were mostly quiet by 1500.

the impact on phrases

As the inflectional suffixes slowly started to drop away from nouns, adjectives, and verbs, people had to adjust. It is one thing to not know whether a noun is feminine or masculine. It is completely different to not know if it is the subject or object. The loss of suffixes meant English speakers had to (unconsciously) find some other part of the language system to pick up the slack. Syntax became the answer. As a result, in Modern English, the two sentences *The diver slapped the squid* and *The squid slapped the diver* mean two different things because the arrangement of words helps determine the meaning.

One way that syntax picked up the slack was through prepositions. Prepositions were around even in the earliest stages of Old English, but they have become more important over time. Consider what morpheme is marking possession in each these following phrases:

The reader's perspective

The perspective of the reader

In the first phrase, the inflectional suffix is marking possession. In the second, the free morpheme *of* is marking possession. The grammatical work of English used to be carried out more often by bound morphemes. With the suffixes case marking the nouns in Old English, there was less of a need of prepositions to show relationships. As the suffixes faded, the need for prepositions became more pressing. Check out how these phrases are represented in the following phrase trees:

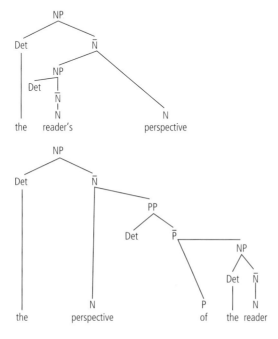

The meaning between *perspective* and *reader* is the same in each NP. The tree diagram for the second one is more complicated however. It contains a prepositional phrase which relates the ownership of the perspective to the reader. A single suffix takes care of it in the first phrase. The first one is a modern example which is reminiscent of Old English constructions, using a suffix born from the Old English time period. The second one with the *of* preposition is a more modern construction and has been on the rise since Middle English.

As we look across the modern morpheme landscape, English only has nine inflectional morphemes, but hundreds of derivational morphemes. Those nine are all that is left of grammatical marking with morphemes. All the rest of the work gets done with free morphemes arranged by syntax.

variation today

Syntax is the area of least variation for dialects of the same language. This lack of variation most likely results from our evolutionary history. The foundational pieces of language are the phonological form and the meaning, both referential and social. Our best guess is that our early ancestors made noises that meant things. The ordering of the form and meaning parts into larger units appears to be a secondary development in human evolution. This development gave our species a distinct advantage in communicating complex strings of information.

One area where syntax does vary is also a topic which draws a great deal of prescriptive attention: prepositions left to swing free at the ends of sentences. The prescriptive angst over free prepositions comes from Latin envy of earlier centuries. Starting around the 1600s, authors became increasingly concerned about the 'social' status of the English language's relation to other languages. In this comparison, one language had higher prestige than any other: Latin. This classical language had no native speakers and could be considered a dead language, but students and teachers at colleges used it daily. The direct descendants of Latin, such as Spanish, Italian, and French, were spoken by many people, and those languages had powerful academies that set out formal regulations for their languages.

More importantly, Latin was learned as a second or third language by all people in academia. All important work in science and other fields was done in Latin. The basic thought was that good work could not be done if it were in any other language. Latin did not dangle its prepositions at the ends of phrases. Those who were concerned about the status of English wanted to improve its lot in the world, and they figured that making it more like Latin would help its status. English writers began to follow the lead of Latin, prescribing the remedy that future authors should avoid phrase-final prepositions in favor of a more Latin-like pattern.

Prepositions go through variation in several ways. Do you remember what kind of morphemes prepositions are? They are free morphemes, of course, but are they function or content? As their job is mostly to tie other parts together, they are function morphemes. In the example in Chapter 4 that asked readers to count the number of Fs, it was the prepositions (e.g. *of*) which almost everyone skipped, not the content words like *feed* or *beef*. In some varieties of English, the prepositions switch around from others: Do you feel sick *to*, *at*, or *on* your stomach? The meaning is all the same regardless of which preposition people use. The job of the preposition is to connect *stomach* with *sick*. With phrases like this, especially in idioms that function as single units, which preposition is used matters little.

In the Upper Peninsula of Michigan (and areas around the UP), there is another kind of preposition variation. Kathryn Remlinger and Wil Rankinen both found that prepositions in certain phrases are completely optional. People from the UP are called Yoopers, and Yoopers' prepositions are optional in sentences like "Let's go mall" or "I'm going casino tonight." This pattern might come from Finnish, which has postpositions and does not require them in these constructions. Finnish was an influential language in the settlement of the Upper Peninsula. Second-language acquisition is a topsy-turvy and complicated process, but at times, the language patterns from one variety of language transfer to another language.

This is part of a wider range of variation between varieties of American English and British English, as was discussed in Chapter 4. Think about the American phrases "She went to college" vs. "She went to the university." In England, the constructions are different: "She went to the college" vs. "She went to university." Similar variation exists for other phrases like *going to town* and *going to the town*. In areas of the United States with sizable German migrant influence, such as Philadelphia, the phrase-final use of *with* has been common. Speakers can say *Do you want to go with?* or *Do you want to come with?*

chapter summary

In this chapter, we focused on the structural organization of phrases. The structure of human language is best understood as hierarchical arrangements created by discrete combinatorial systems. The phrases in this chapter are normally small, although one of the properties we explored has the potential for infinite expansion of phrases. For Noun Phrases (NPs), Adjective Phrases (APs), and Prepositional Phrases (PPs), each contains a head of the phrase along with one or more adjuncts to that head. The scheme for hierarchically organizing the head and its adjuncts derives from the X-bar template, used by linguists to help figure out and compare syntactic structures of the world's languages. For NPs, APs, and PPs, each has a head (an N, an A, or a P) which connects to the phrase node through an intermediate node(s) (an $\bar{N}$, an $\bar{A}$, a $\bar{P}$). We first asked how is it that phrases can grow so large, a quality we labelled *expansion*. The answer is that the use of intermediate nodes allows for potentially infinite expansion by way of the rule of infinite recursion. Second, we asked how phrases fit inside of each other so neatly, a quality we labelled *nesting*. The answer is that intermediate nodes provide connections inside phrases from which other phrases can grow, like budding branches from a tree. The phrase trees are constrained by having a maximum of two branches. The ordering of these branches and the arrangement of the head and adjuncts was illustrated in several languages to show the organizational parameters of the Universal Grammar.

key concepts

- Adjective Phrase
- Ambiguity
- Binary branching
- Constituency
- Crash blossom
- Expansion
- Head of the phrase
- Headedness parameter
- Infinite recursion
- Locatives
- Nesting
- Noun Phrase
- Parse
- Prepositional Phrase
- Principles
- Structural ambiguity
- Verb Phrase

notes

1   http://www.ohchr.org/EN/UDHR/Pages/Language.aspx?LangID=hnd and http://en.wikipedia.org/wiki/Hindi_language#Sample_text

2   SOAS Working Papers in Linguistics Vol.15 (2007): 135–148. "The Structure of the Bantu Noun Phrase" Josephat M. Rugemalira.

3   http://lakotadictionary.org/phpBB3/index.php

references

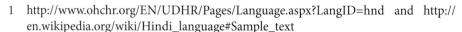
Baker, Mark C. (2001) *Atoms of Language*. London: Basic Books.

http://en.wikipedia.org/wiki/Hindi_language#Sample_text

http://lakotadictionary.org/phpBB3/index.php

http://www.ohchr.org/EN/UDHR/Pages/Language.aspx?LangID=hnd

O'Grady, W. and MacWhinney, B. (forthcoming) *Handbook of Language Emergence*. Boston: Wiley.

Pinker, S. (2003) *The Blank Slate: The Modern Denial of Human Nature*. Penguin Books; reprint edition.

Rugemalira, J.M. (2007) "The structure of the Bantu Noun Phrase." *SOAS Working Papers in Linguistics 15*: 135–148.

further reading

Atoms of Language. Mark C. Baker. 2001. Basic Books.

Baker explores the nature of human language through the variation of languages. To do this he works through the ideas of Noam Chomsky, especially the ideas of principles and parameters. While noting differences, Baker demonstrates how languages such as Navajo and Japanese have the same syntactic parts ordered by the same blue prints. In working through some of the basic structures and rules of human language, Baker details how our languages share the same qualities.

Syntax: A Generative Introduction. Andrew Carnie. 2012. Wiley Blackwell.

Carnie presents a thorough introduction to syntactic analysis in straightforward language. Most students find discussions of syntax to be overly abstract, but Carnie develops direct analysis with numerous examples and exercises. This third edition keeps most of the high-quality material of the first two editions and presents new material on different kinds of grammatical analysis. There is also a workbook that accompanies this text.

Emergentism. *The Cambridge Encyclopedia of the Language Sciences*, edited by Patrick Hogan (pp. 274–76). 2010. Cambridge, UK: Cambridge University Press.

This short essay is an excellent first step into ideas about how language might develop from more general (and necessary) cognitive processes. This chapter works as a gateway to an expansive literature about how human language works. It is an alternative to Chomsky's approach of the Universal Grammar.

Foundations of Language: Brain, Meaning, Grammar, Evolution. Ray Jackendoff. 2002. Oxford University Press.

This book provides a wonderful perspective on the linguistic study of the mental grammar. It is approachable by new explorers in grammar studies and offers insights to the human mind. By working through an interdisciplinary approach, Jackendoff establishes a theory of how both syntax and semantics work in the human mind.

exercises

individual work

Use the three X-bar rules for tree drawing in these exercises:

Rule 1 $XP \rightarrow Det; \overline{X}$
Rule 2 $^*\overline{X} \rightarrow \overline{X}; YP$
Rule 3 $\overline{X} \rightarrow X; YP$

Remember that some elements of these three rules are optional. The optional elements are marked with parentheses ( ).

Rule 1 $XP \rightarrow (Det); \overline{X}$
Rule 2 $(^*\overline{X} \rightarrow \overline{X}; YP)$
Rule 3 $\overline{X} \rightarrow X; (YP)$

Note that all of Rule 2 is optional. You might have a phrase, like *a squid*, where it is not required because Rule 1 and 3 account for all the relationships between the words. However, in a phrase like *a brown squid in the water*, Rule 2 will be required because binary branching requires you to choose about the constituency of *brown*, *squid*, and *in the water*. You cannot connect up all three at once, binary branching does not allow it, so one of them must be connected first and the other two second. The way to do that is through Rule 2.

Draw a tree for each of the following phrases. In doing so, you will show the hierarchy of the phrases and the constituency of each node, including the terminal nodes above the words. As an example, let us take up the phrase *those pesky dragons on her roof*.

To draw a tree, there are several steps to make, and it will help you if you follow these steps in order. Slapping at it randomly will not make your life easier. Also, do not rush: Pause with each step.

- First, turn your piece of paper landscape to give yourself as much room as possible; working in an overly confined space makes it hard to see all the connections.

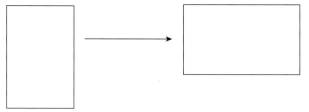

- Second, put the words flat across the bottom. Making the words carousel up and down will confuse you while trying to figure out the constituency relationships.

those	pesky	dragons	on	her	roof

- Third, identify the heads of phrases: In *those pesky dragons on her roof* there are the adjective *pesky*, the noun *dragons*, the preposition *on*, and the noun *roof*. Note that the word *her* in this phrase functions as a determiner and not as a noun. It just so happens that because of the history of English, the possessive form is *her* and the object form is also *her*.

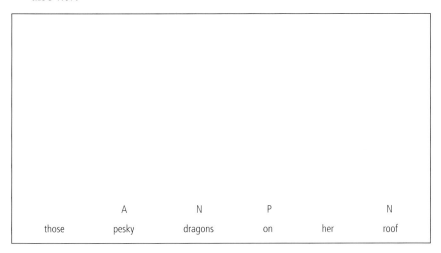

- Fourth, draw the top level node and follow Rule 1 for that node.

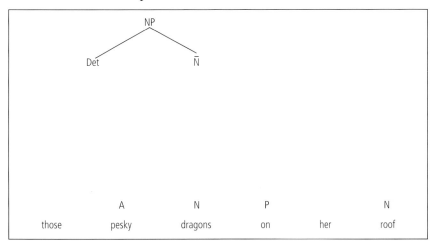

- Fifth, from this point on, consider each node to be a hill you just climbed. You could not see beyond the hill until you got to the top of it, but now that you are there, you have to decide what constituents to take care of next. How many nodes can you see from the one you are standing on? If there are more than two, you have to invoke Rule 2 and make a copy of the intermediate node to have enough space. With *those pesky dragons on her roof*, the first node after the NP is an $\bar{N}$, and from that node, an Adjective Phrase, a Prepositional Phrase, and the head of the phrase are all visible. Accordingly, you must make a copy of the N̄ to take care of the Prepositional Phrase.

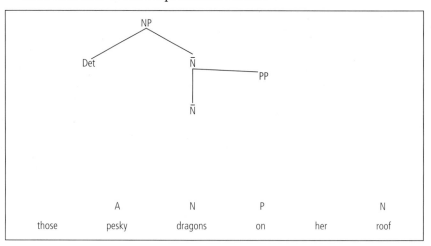

- Sixth, continue following Rules 1, maybe 2, and 3 until you reach the head of each phrase and connect every word to a slot in the tree.

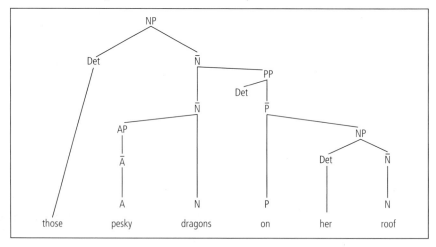

- Be sure to label all the nodes.

   Now draw a tree for these phrases:

1.   a squid
2.   a brown squid
3.   the water
4.   in the water
5.   a brown squid in the water

What parts are repeated for each numbered tree? How is #5 different from the first four?

Now draw a tree for each of the following phrases and pay attention to which of the three rules are most frequently used:

6. a camouflaged squid in the body of water
7. the thirteen bodies
8. the thirteen bodies of water
9. a reckless young man
10. a ridiculously reckless, really young man
11. on the frozen hill
12. in the well on the very frozen hill
13. the buzz of mosquitoes in our ears
14. the broken clock on the mantle
15. the tortured look on her face

group work

As a group, figure out the divisions of the following phrases:

1. For these sentences, divide the subject from the predicate:
   a. The house collapsed.
   b. I want the house to collapse.
   c. I would have wanted the house to collapse.
   d. That flame wavered under the moth's wings.
   e. Their car was engulfed by the flames.
   f. The old car I bought last Tuesday was driven off the cliff by the valet.
2. Next, for a–h, identify and label all the Noun Phrases, Prepositional Phrases, and Adjective Phrases:
   a. a chair
   b. on the porch
   c. his bike on the edge of the trail
   d. really dirty
   e. his very dirty jeans
   f. their really dirty jeans in the basket
   g. in the pot on the porch
   h. in the chipped pot under the antique bed
3. For the phrases in exercise 2, put brackets around each phrase and label each bracket: the dog → [NP[Det the][N̄[N dog]]] level, and one set of brackets each inside of that for the [Det] and the [intermediate node], and one set of brackets inside the intermediate node for the [head of phrase]. The thing to remember is that when you put down a left bracket [you will need to put down a right bracket]

somewhere further to the right. You should be able to count an even number of brackets in each analysis. If you are typing this up, you might want to use N' as a substitute for $\overline{N}$.

4. For each of the phrases in exercise 2, as a group, draw an X-bar tree representing the hierarchy and constituency. Label all nodes.

study questions

1. What is a Noun Phrase?
2. How is a Noun Phrase different from an Adjective Phrase or a Prepositional Phrase?
3. How long can a phrase be? What is the term for infinitely adding to a phrase?
4. What in the grammatical arrangement of phrases allows expansion to happen?
5. What is binary branching, and how does it affect phrase trees?
6. What does the X-bar model represent?
7. What are variables?
8. What is constituency?
9. What is a locative?
10. What is the difference between prepositions and postpositions?
11. What is Universal Grammar?
12. What is mental grammar?
13. Why were prepositions less needed in Old English, and why are they more important now?
14. What type of morphemes are prepositions?
15. Is Modern English more analytic or synthetic than Old English?
16. Where do many of the silent Es come from in Modern English?

 Visit the book's companion website for additional resources relating to this chapter at: http://www.wiley.com/go/hazen/introlanguage

8 Building Bigger Phrases

Chapter outline

An Introduction to Language, First Edition. Kirk Hazen.
© 2015 John Wiley & Sons, Inc. Published 2015 by John Wiley & Sons, Inc.

chapter overview

English is a language in which syntax, the part of the mental grammar that arranges words, works harder than morphology, the part that arranges morphemes. In our daily conversations, we rely on syntax to get meanings across by pushing words into phrases. Other languages rely more on morphology. In the last chapter, we worked on building Noun Phrases, Adjective Phrases, and Prepositional Phrases with hierarchical templates. Yet as you know, we do not go around speaking only with phrases. We put phrases in sentences, and these sentences build on each other to create conversations, instructions, scripts, and literature. In this chapter, we explore the sentence, along with its kernel, the Verb Phrase. We examine larger phrases controlled by verbs and sentence inflections. In order to understand these constructions, the qualities of verbs, including transitivity, are reviewed in this chapter. The arrangement of parts within sentences allows us to consider similar patterns across all human languages, as well as the role of Universal Grammar in guiding language structure.

meaning and ambiguity: part 1

What kinds of meaning are present in the simple sentences in 1–3? The words do not move from place to place, but each sentence has at least two meanings, with the last one having at least four. Can you figure out what the different meanings are?

Ambiguity in phrases

1. *One morning, I shot an elephant in my pajamas.*
        (How he got in my pajamas, I don't know).
2. *We need more intelligent leaders.*
3. *Nature bats last.*
4. *Umberto turned on the TV* {a four-way fun fest!}.

The first sentence is a quote from the movie *Animal Crackers* spoken by Groucho Marx, a famous comedian in the twentieth century. The beauty of it is that the first part starts off under normal expectations: People can shoot things, and (unfortunately) elephants are shootable. With the second part of 1, the reader is forced to go back and reinterpret the first part in an unexpected way. Our first thought is that the shooter is in the pajamas, but with the second line, we have to shift our interpretation so that it is the elephant wearing the pajamas. In 2, either we need a greater quantity of leaders with some level of intelligence, or we need leaders with a higher level of intelligence. The question for 2 is "what job does the modifier *more* have?"

The third sentence comes from a bumper sticker I saw in Morgantown, WV. This sentence is beautiful. In the first interpretation, Mother Nature is up to bat last in the rotation (think baseball). The meaning implied is something like: 'No matter how humans mess up the planet, Mother Nature will bat last, and the day of environmental reckoning is coming.' In the other interpretation for the third sentence, a certain kind of bat, a nature bat, lasts and lasts and lasts. The nifty subterfuge with that interpretation is that the word *bat* is lexically ambiguous, so it could be a noun (flying mammal or baseball equipment) or a verb.

Sentence 4, like *Nature bats last*, is multiply ambiguous. It is both lexically ambiguous and structurally ambiguous. Remember that with all lexical ambiguity, the form of the word remains the same, yet there are two lexical items with the same form: *The bank collapsed* can mean a financial institution failed or the side of a river eroded quickly, but the syntactic structure of the phrase is the same regardless of the meaning. Both *bank* (financial institution) and *bank* (side of a river) are nouns. In contrast, the phrases that are structurally ambiguous do have different phrase trees, by the definition of structural ambiguity. They have different hierarchical organizations, and therefore the units have different constituencies.

Word Play: Crash blossoms II

As with Chapter 7, newspaper headlines provide wonderful examples of structural ambiguity. The convention of these headlines is to arrange phrases resembling a beaver dam, with parts piled one on the other. These crash blossoms, so dubbed by the intrepid scholars at *Language Log*, are the kind of language phenomenon achievable only under the high pressure of genre conventions. The humor derives from the unreal situations and fluctuation of meanings. Humor is based on contrast between expectations and actual experience. When we fall upon a snare like "Squad helps dog bite victim," we have a small pause. In that small pause, your syntax is working hard to parse whether *bite* is a verb or part of a compound adjective with *dog*. On the first pass, most readers are led to interpret *bite* as a verb, but that interpretation forces an unexpected meaning. The contrast creates (potential) humor.

In the following headlines, collections of words can be interpreted as certain kinds of phrases, but they can also be interpreted with other hierarchical arrangements. Which

arrangements go with which meanings? The URL for each *Language Log* interpretation (which includes links to original stories) is given below the headline.

"Dog helps lightning strike Redruth mayor"
http://languagelog.ldc.upenn.edu/nll/?p=3531

"Flood damage dwarfs repair budget"
http://languagelog.ldc.upenn.edu/nll/?p=3433

"Qaddafi Forces Bear Down on Historic Town as Rebels Flee"
http://languagelog.ldc.upenn.edu/nll/?p=3022

"Hooker Overcomes Illness, Slaps Beaver"
http://languagelog.ldc.upenn.edu/nll/?p=2935

"Ghost fishing lobster traps target of study"
http://languagelog.ldc.upenn.edu/nll/?p=2509

"May axes Labour police beat pledge"
http://languagelog.ldc.upenn.edu/nll/?p=2416

"Missing women police find remains"
http://languagelog.ldc.upenn.edu/nll/?p=2359

In the sentence *Umberto turned on the TV*, both lexical and structural ambiguity show up. With this particular sentence, the lexical ambiguity depends on the structural ambiguity: Certain meanings are possible with only certain tree structures. What different meanings can you pull out? Perhaps the most mundane and common interpretation is that *Umberto* activates the television by making it illuminate, bringing up a channel and a show. Another meaning involves Umberto spinning while standing atop the TV. Certainly, it is an unlikely meaning, but it is possible to get that from "turn on the TV." The other meanings are connected to the lexical ambiguity of the verb *turn on*. It can, of course, mean 'sexually excite.' How one sexually excites a TV is beyond my range of knowledge, but many people are more technically adept than I am. The meaning of 'to betray' is also one of the possible interpretations of *turn on*, and perhaps Umberto was able to betray the TV, selling it to a parts store or giving it to Goodwill. The last possible meaning of the verb *turn on* is 'to attack in retaliation.' After all those years of bad comedy and shoddy infomercials, Umberto may have had enough and decided to beat the TV to death. Certainly, many TVs have deserved it. As the chapter progresses, and we move through the syntactic structure of Verb Phrases and finally sentences, we will return to the structurally ambiguous differences of these four sentences to plot out their hierarchical arrangements and to illustrate their differences.

Verb Phrases and traditional parts

The traditional parts for sentences are subjects and predicates. A regular indicative sentence like *The giant ate the kielbasa* has two parts: the subject and the predicate. The subject is [*the giant*], and the predicate is [*ate the kielbasa*]. The subject could be extremely short: In *I dance every weekend* the subject is the single word *I* (with only a single morpheme and only a single vowel). The predicate could be maximally short also: *The defending champs flopped*, with only a single verb and the past-tense inflection.

The subject and predicate can of course be longer. What is the subject in the following sentence? *Last year's defending champs who I bet would win the Super Bowl flopped*. In that sentence, everything up until *flopped* is part of the subject. Not everything in that subject is just one kind of phrase. There are adjectives and nouns and even a conjugated verb connected in that large Noun Phrase, but all those parts are in the subject. We will use both the terms *subject* and *predicate*, but we do not sketch out subject trees or predicate trees. Those terms were never created with the idea of representing hierarchical

Figure 8.1 Order is important in language, as in this *Bizzaro* comic. © Dan Piraro. bizarrocomics.com/

organization or constituency, but they often prove useful for identifying units in the larger sentence.

Verb Phrases are units to be described with X-bar templates, just like Noun Phrases, Prepositional Phrases, and Adjective Phrases. The head of a Verb Phrase is a verb. The units branching off the verb's tree are more diverse, but the verb itself controls how those units are arranged. With a ditransitive verb like *put*, a slot for the thing being put and a slot for where it is being put is needed: *The cook puts the pot on the rack*. For an intransitive verb like *snore*, there is no object available, although words after an intransitive verb are certainly allowed: *The tired clown was still able to snore after he was put on the edge of the ship*. In this sentence, there is a prepositional phrase detailing where and when the snoring took place. Yet, the verb does not require such information to complete its meaning.

structure of Verb Phrases (VPs)

To assess the structure of a Verb Phrase, let us first assess the simplest possible construction, the Verb Phrase in the sentence *I yawn*.

There is not a lot of complexity here, so let us add an adverb: *I quietly yawn.*

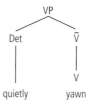

Even if there is extra material after this kind of intransitive verb, as we saw with the sentence *The tired clown was still able to snore after he was put on the edge of the ship*, the branching ability of the X-bars allows for more room. Consider *I quietly yawn during a movie.*

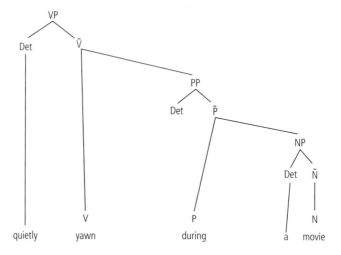

The verb *yawn* works the same as before, and the tree structure is the same for its verb status. The only difference is that an additional phrase, *during a movie*, is connected to the intermediate node $\overline{V}$. In turn, that Prepositional Phrase branches in the expected manner.

The next Verb Phrase is *eat the cupcake*, with *eat* as the transitive verb and *cupcake* as the direct object. The Noun Phrase of *the cupcake* is therefore a constituent of the Verb Phrase connected by the $\overline{V}$.

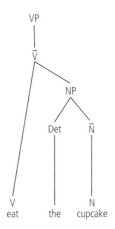

Remember, a constituent is any subunit of a dominant node. In the tree above, the NP is a constituent of the VP. If you keep the constituency clear in your head before you start drawing lines, making phrase trees will be easier. It is an important habit to develop when the sentences are simple; you will need it when sentences become more complex. As there are more layers of hierarchy, it will help to identify the constituent status of every part of the tree. As with intransitive verbs, transitive verbs can also be connected to other phrases, as we see in the following tree:

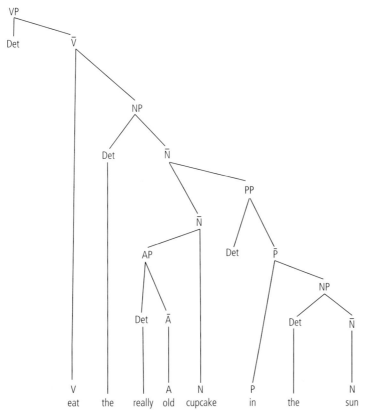

In this Verb Phrase, *eat the really old cupcake in the sun*, an Adjective Phrase clearly modifies the direct object *cupcake*; however, the Prepositional Phrase can modify either the verb *eat* directly or the noun *cupcake* (in other words, it is a direct constituent of the NP headed by *cupcake*). How could it modify either? Here is where some choices must be made in the constituency of the phrases. In drawing the tree structure for this Verb Phrase, the Prepositional Phrase must have a connection somewhere. Should it hook into the N̄ between the N of *cupcake* and its NP (as we saw in the previous tree)? Or should it connect higher up to the V̄ of eat. The V̄ acts as a pipeline, so other phrases hooked into it modify that node and all connecting nodes below it. Whether *in the sun* modifies the direct object or the verb is up to the speaker and audience, but since it is not all that ambiguous, we can simply choose one or the other. The one tree structure is above, and the other is below, but please note the difference in hierarchy and constituency between them:

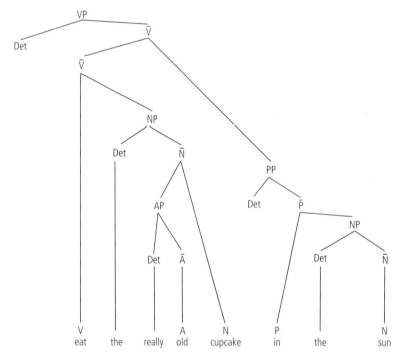

Now, try to work out the following Verb Phrases with an X-bar tree structure:

quietly rest
run quickly
recline in my chair
rake the yard
color the picture on the desk
shut the door in the kitchen
close the broken window
trim the plant in the yard

some hints for drawing the trees

With adverbs, remember that the Determiner slot of the VP (and all the branches) can swing around like a mobile: All the same machinery is there for *quickly run* and *run quickly* even though the adverb is on the different sides of the verb. The trees also do not change greatly for *recline in my chair*, except the phrase joined to the $\bar{V}$ is a Prepositional Phrase. For all the phrases, decide what you want the constituency of words and phrases to be before you start drawing lines and connecting nodes. For the Prepositional Phrases like *on the desk*, will *on the desk* modify the Noun Phrase *the picture* or will it modify the verb *color*? The meaning's change would be slight at most for these words, but for other words, it might be quite large (as it will be for structurally ambiguous sentences later on). For example, consider the last Verb Phrase above: *trim the plant in the yard*. It could be that the plant was originally in the house, but that you should take it into the yard to trim it: That meaning would arise from having the Prepositional Phrase *in the yard* attached to the $\bar{V}$ of *trim*. Or, it could be that the plant located in the yard is the one to be trimmed: That meaning would be achieved by having *in the yard* attached to the $\bar{N}$ of *plant*. With all trees, it is best to decide the constituency before you start drawing.

ditransitive Verb Phrases

Ditransitive verbs present an extra quandary for hierarchical arrangement and constituency. As you might remember from Chapter 4, this kind of verb is called *ditransitive* because the subject goes "across" the verb to two objects, conventionally called a direct object and an indirect object. In several varieties of English, the arrangement of the direct and indirect object can vary: For *give*, people produce either *Subject give <u>Direct Object</u> to* **Indirect Object** or *Subject give* **Indirect Object** *<u>Direct Object</u>*.

> *Give <u>the shrimp</u> to* **the octopus** or *Give* **the octopus** *<u>the shrimp</u>*
> *Pass <u>the ball</u> to* **Beckham** or *Pass* **Beckham** *<u>the ball</u>*
> *Put the cat on the table* or …? {The switch does not always work: Can you figure out when it does not?}

This pattern is called **dative alternation**. The forms alternate between a direct-object~indirect-object order to an indirect-object~direct-object construction. Several different factors influence whether people use the indirect-object construction or not, including whether the receiver is alive or not and the semantic category of the verb. Note that in the third line, *the table* is not alive, and it is more challenging to create *Put on the table the cat* as a possible, grammatical sentence.

The ditransitive verbs have some variable constructions. Some speakers in the United States allow for the indirect-object~direct-object construction, while others require the direct object and a Prepositional Phrase with the indirect object. How should we handle this variation of phrases with X-bar trees?

Sketch out the tree structure for *put the cat on the table* before reading further here. Decide upon the constituency of words before drawing out lines.

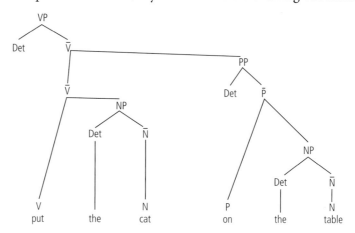

Why not have the Prepositional Phrase *on the table* come off of the N̄ of *cat*? This arrangement would make *on the table* a constituent of that Noun Phrase. Instead, because *put* is a ditransitive verb, both objects have to be visible and directly part of the hierarchy of the Verb Phrase through the intermediate-node pipeline of V̄. This situation is completely different from a phrase like *sat on the snow in the yard*, where *in the yard* could modify *snow* or the verb *sat*. With ditransitive verbs, both objects must be part of the V̄ structure.

For the Verb Phrase *give the octopus the shrimp*, the ditransitive verb works the same way for its hierarchy and constituency. The Noun Phrase *the shrimp* does not modify what kind of octopus we are talking about: It is the direct object of *give*. The tree structure must reflect these relationships for us to appropriately model what goes on in the mental grammar. Note that in this Verb Phrase as before, the V̄ is copied by virtue of the second rule of the X-bar format (which allows for infinite recursion). Then, consider what could go on with this Verb Phrase: *give the octopus the shrimp under the rock*.

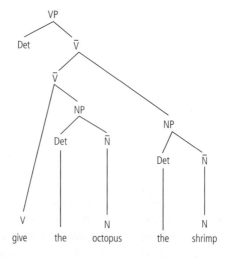

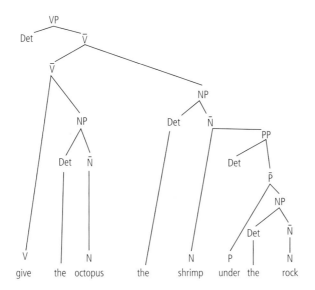

With this tree structure, the Prepositional Phrase *under the rock* is part of the Noun Phrase headed by *shrimp*, basically describing which shrimp is to be given. In the following tree structure, the Prepositional Phrase *under the rock* is attached to the V̄ and therefore modifies the act of giving, regardless of where the shrimp came from, be it the refrigerator or a separate tank.

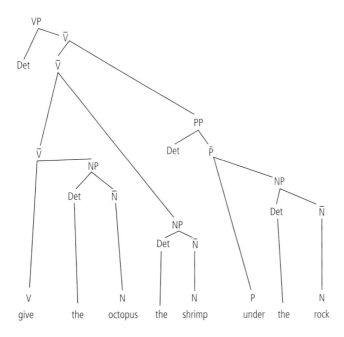

We deal more with such choices of hierarchy and constituency when we handle structurally ambiguous sentences. But before we can do that, we must first understand better what qualities make a sentence a sentence.

the motivation for Inflectional Phrases (IPs) ⎯⎯⎯⎯⎯⎯⎯⎯

What are the Verb Phrases in the phrases a-i? How can you tell they are Verb Phrases?

a.   the dog to sit
b.   the squid to sleep
c.   the goat to jump

d.   the dog to catch the Frisbee
e.   the squid to squeeze the clam
f.   the goat to bite my brother

g.   the dog to put the cat on the table
h.   the squid to give the octopus the shrimp
i.   the goat to pass Beckham the ball

Are the phrases a-i sentences? If not, then what kinds of units are they? There is obviously a Noun Phrase up front, but what follows afterwards? The division is clearest in a-c, where *to sit*, *to sleep*, and *to jump* follow the initial Noun Phrase. All of these *to* units are Verb Phrases (VPs). The other examples (d–i) also contain Verb Phrases starting with *to*. The Verb Phrases stretch from the *to* all the way to the last word in the phrase.

In a-i, the Verb Phrase form is the infinitive, meaning that the verb is not conjugated (e.g. *the teacher to write* vs. *the teacher writes*). In Old English, the infinitives were marked with a suffix, such as *acsian* for 'to ask,' but with the loss of suffixes in English, a preposition once again had to shoulder the task of marking unconjugated verbs. There is a Noun Phrase and a Verb Phrase in examples a-i, but they are a bit more buried under other words in d-f and even more buried in phrases g-i. Consider what kinds of verbs are in a-c, as compared with g-f, and try to remember our discussions of transitivity from Chapter 4.

The verbs in examples a-c are intransitive. The verbs in d-f are transitive and have a Noun Phrase working as a direct object. The verbs in phrases g-i are ditransitive and have two Noun Phrases attached, filling the roles as direct and indirect objects. So, we now know what is what inside these collections of words, but are they sentences? With no conjugated verb, these phrases cannot be sentences. Yet, are they ungrammatical? If you just shouted these out loud in the middle of a Wal-Mart, it might seem out of place (more on that in Chapter 9), but how about placing phrases of a-i in the frame "I want _____" so that we get "I want the dog to sit" and "I want the squid to sleep." These sentences work fine for native speakers. Their grammaticality is not in question.

Now figure out the differences for j–r:

j.   The dog sit<u>s</u>.
k.   The squid sleep<u>s</u>.
l.   The goat jump<u>s</u>.

m. The dog catch<u>es</u> the Frisbee
n. The squid squeeze<u>s</u> the clam
o. The goat bite<u>s</u> my brother

p. The dog put<u>s</u> the cat on the table
q. The squid give<u>s</u> the octopus the shrimp
r. The goat pass<u>es</u> Beckham the ball

All of these collections of phrases *are* sentences. Each one has a conjugated verb with an inflectional suffix. The transitivity works the same as before. The only difference is that they become sentences with the addition of the inflectional suffix -*s*. Of course you also realize that they would be sentences even with a different subject and a different verbal inflection. Ponder over these pairs:

s. Sit! ... ... The dogs sit.
t. Sleep! ... ... The squids sleep.
u. Jump! ... ... The goats jump.

v. Catch the Frisbee. ... ... The dogs catch the Frisbee.
w. Squeeze the clam. ... ... The squids squeeze the clams.
x. Bite my brother. ... ... The goats bite my brother.

y. Put the cat on the table. ... ... The dogs put the cat on the table.
z. Give the octopus the shrimp. ... ... The squids give the octopus the shrimp.
aa. Pass Beckham the ball. ... ... The goats pass Beckham the ball.

In the first halves of examples s-aa, the sentences have been placed in the imperative mood: The subject of each has been made second person, and the sentence is given as a command. The second part of the phrases in examples s-aa has the sentence with a third-person plural subject. The conjugation of the verb has changed, but we can still tell that the sentence is conjugated. In Modern English, there is no longer an overt (spelled or pronounced) verbal suffix for third-person plural subjects (perhaps *were* for *to be* is our last remaining marked verb). Yet, because there is no infinitive-marking *to* in front of the verb, it is clearly conjugated. These patterns of sentence/no-sentence work even with more irregular verbs such as *be*, *have*, and *do*:

bb. (I want) the teacher to be on time.
cc. The teacher is on time.
dd. The teacher was on time.

ee. (I want) the miner to have the best tools.
ff. The miner has the best tools.
gg. The miner had the best tools.

hh. (I want) the coach to do the best possible job.
ii. The coach does the best possible job.
jj. The coach did the best possible job.

In examples a-jj, what makes a sentence a sentence is not its size. More words does not a sentence make. The essential quality of a sentence is the verbal inflection, which is aligned with the subject. The Verb Phrases in examples a-jj are Verb Phrases whether or not they have an inflectional verbal suffix. Sometimes the Verb Phrases have other parts such as direct and indirect objects, but sometimes verbs are all alone inside their Verb Phrases.

the structure of Inflectional Phrases

In all English-speaking communities, children work through several different stages of subject-verb agreement. As Pinker notes in *Words and Rules*, often children learn exceptions to past-tense verb conjugation (e.g. buy → bought) and then learn a regular rule for past tense that is applied to every verb (e.g. buy → buyed) before relearning the exceptions. One pattern that emerges both with children and as a normal form in some communities is the transfer of the verbal -*s* to novel places.

For example, the form *got* comes from *gotten*, the original perfect participle of *get*. This relationship is not always clear to native speakers (or anyone else) because the form *gotten* has become increasingly rare in many varieties of English. It primarily survives not as a verb, but as an adjective in a form like *ill gotten gains*. As a perfect participle, *got* can be used in the perfect aspect with the verb *have*, so that many speakers can pull off *She has got three filters*. English speakers have their auxiliary (helping) verbs unstressed and often contracted so that *She's got three of them* is the norm. Some speakers, including children, take this unstressed, contracted *has* even further, to where it is fully absent: *She got three of them*. The next step children can make is to reanalyze *got* as the main verb itself and then to inflect it with a verbal -*s*, providing *She gots three of them*. The morphology of the third-person singular -*s* in English allows us to see the cognitive process of subject-verb concord working in the mental grammar of speakers. For languages with richer morphological marking, like Spanish, we can hear the agreement with every slot in the subject paradigm.

As we could see from our uninflected verb phrases in the previous section, a Noun Phrase and Verb Phrase combination does not a sentence make: *The dog to sit*. What does make the sentence a sentence? The inflection on the verb: *The dog sits*. What about subjects that do not demand any overt inflection in English, like third-person plural: *The dogs sit*? Although the verbs do not have any <u>overt</u> sound serving as the inflection, it is generally understood in linguistic study that they do have a verbal inflection that is phonetically null: *The dogs sit∅*. In this case, it is the present-tense marker that is phonetically null. In a sentence like *The dogs sat* the verb's vowel switch (ablaut) shows the past-tense marker. In a sentence like *She hit the wall*, the phonetically null marker shows the past tense. English has a diverse verb history.

In Old English, there were different markers for each person-number slot in the subject paradigm, but those have been gradually worn away over the years, mostly by phonological changes such as the schwa rule. For example the verb *to steal* was conjugated with one ending in the first-person singular, *ic stele* 'I steal,' another for third-person singular, *hē stilð* 'He steals,' and yet another for third-person plural, *hie stælon* 'They steal.' Despite the loss of such diverse forms, in Modern English, the verb in *I steal* is just as conjugated as the verb in *she steals* or *I stole*.

To analyze sentences with our three X-bar rules, we need to understand them as **Inflectional Phrases**, with an inflection as the head of the phrase. Many introductory books cast sentences as a type of entity unto themselves. They provide an S-node that breaks down into Noun Phrases and Verb Phrases. While not a dastardly decision, the choice to talk about sentences as an S-node obscures the role of the verb inflection in making sentences. It also destroys the symmetry between Inflectional Phrases, Noun Phrases, Verb Phrases, and the other phrases. All of them can be represented with a common plan, which includes recursion, in order to model the creative productivity of human language.

One point to note is how the division between the subject and the predicate is handled. The predicate will be in the VP. The subject is in the Determiner slot of the Inflectional Phrase. The Determiner slot modifies the rest of the phrase, and the subject modifies the rest of the sentence. In our sentences, we will almost always have Noun Phrases in the Inflectional Phrase's Determiner slots.

building Inflectional Phrases

To understand how to construct Inflectional Phrases, let us consider where to put the head of the phrase, the inflection. In previous chapters, we have seen that modals carry verbal inflection. In the following sentences, ponder what the modal verbs are doing. Remember, modal verbs have a slightly different conjugation paradigm from other verbs in Modern English:

This tired student <u>can</u> finish his homework.
This tired student <u>could</u> finish his homework.
This tired student <u>will</u> finish his homework.
This tired student <u>would</u> finish his homework.
This tired student <u>shall</u> finish his homework.
This tired student <u>should</u> finish his homework.
This tired student <u>may</u> finish his homework.
This tired student <u>might</u> finish his homework.

All of these should be compared with the same sentence where the non-modal verb receives the verbal inflection:

This tired student finish<u>es</u> his homework.

The key difference is of course the verbal *-s* (which is spelled *-es* since the final sound in *finish* is a sibilant). However, all the modals above carry the verbal inflection as part of their structure. We will start mapping our tree structure of sentences with modals to make the transition to these Inflectional Phrases easier, and we will start as easily as we can, with a single-word subject and an intransitive verb: *She will sneeze.*

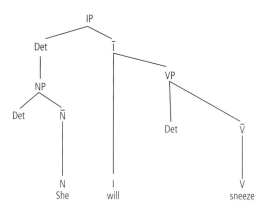

With the inflection, here carried by the modal, anchoring down the sentence, the IP is split between the subject and the predicate. For this simple sentence, the subject and the predicate each have one kind of phrase, and each phrase is one word long. Nothing complex to see here, but it is important to linger for a moment. Note that the Inflectional Phrase breaks down the same way as all other phrases. A different kind of template is not needed to handle this sentence or any other sentence. The same phrasal structures introduced in Chapter 7 allow for constituency and hierarchy to be described with larger, more complex structures. The sentences for this chapter fall neatly within this structure:

$$XP \rightarrow Det; \overline{X}$$
$$^{\diamond}\overline{X} \rightarrow \overline{X}; YP$$
$$\overline{X} \rightarrow X; YP$$

Although the *She will sneeze* sentence is simple, the structure can handle multiple expansions. Remember that the second rule above has a star named *infinite recursion*. Let us expand a few sentences to see how we can stretch this simple structure. A transitive verb allows us to make an addition to the Verb Phrase, and a few Adjective Phrases allow us to make additions to the subject's Noun Phrase and the predicate. Here is one with an expanded subject and an expanded predicate: *The wretched witch will destroy the gingerbread house.*

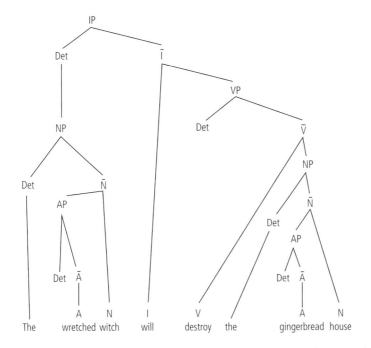

The adjectives fit neatly within the Noun Phrases (one in the subject and one in the predicate). The Noun Phrase in the predicate functions as the direct object and is a constituent of the Verb Phrase. The same structures from last chapter are preserved in this sentence.

Now work through the following sentences, all of them Inflectional Phrases. Parse them into subjects and predicates, with the modal verb dividing the two:

The younger bull would follow the rodeo clown.
A crafty documentarian could chase the solitary wolverine through the snow.
The shrewd shopper will quickly buy the recently expired cheese.

All of three of these verbs are transitive, with a direct object. Ditransitive verbs are a slightly different story. As detailed with the Verb Phrases earlier in the chapter, ditransitive verbs require two objects. These two objects must both be connected to the verb through the verb's intermediate nodes. Consider the following sentence:

The child could give the chicken to the cat.

And then the same sentence chunked out:

The child could give [the chicken] [to the cat].

In this original rendition, there is a Noun Phrase and a Prepositional Phrase as constituents of the Verb Phrase. But, with the alternative construction, there are two adjacent Noun Phrases:

The child could give the cat the chicken
The child could give [the cat] [the chicken]

In either case, the direct and indirect objects are constituents of the Verb Phrase and separate from each other. In the first rendition, the phrase *to the cat* does not modify *the chicken*: The *cat* is the receiver of the chicken.

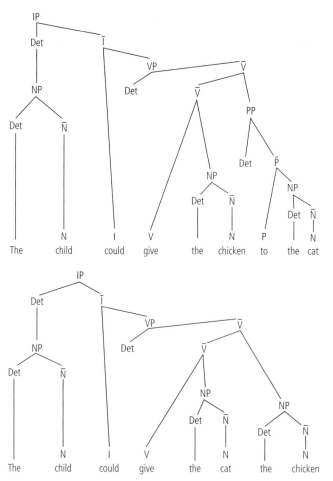

Before we move forward with verbal inflections other than just modals, we need to make one other stipulation. The *-s* verbal inflection and the past tense *-ed* are both bound morphemes (inflectional). Yet, they are both obviously suffixes, and they must attach to the verb to be grammatical in most varieties of English. Subject-verb concord does vary widely in English, but the variation is always in the direction of not having any overt verbal inflections (e.g. *he go everyday*), or at times, applying verbal *-s* to every possible verb (e.g. *we goes everyday*). Despite these two inflections being suffixes, as with the modals, we assume here that they are originally generated between the subject and the predicate and then moved into their suffixed position at the back of the verb. Consider how the conjugated item (which tells us the tense) moves around in the following sentences:

Figure 8.2   A wombat. Robyn Butler/Shutterstock.

The wombat <u>might</u> poop every morning.
The wombat poop<u>s</u> every morning.
The wombats poop__ every morning.
The wombat poop<u>ed</u> every morning.

The first three sentences are nonpast tense and the third is past tense. These inflected items present the phrase as a sentence because it has conjugation. Compare those with *the wombat to poop*. In the last three sentences above, the inflectional markers have been moved to the ends of the verbs because English morphology demands it.

Take a look at *The wombat poops every morning* in a phrase tree. Note what happens with the verbal suffix *-s*:

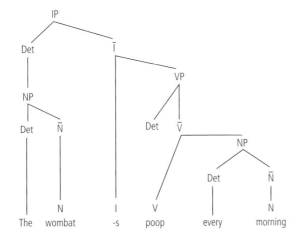

We would make the same kind of switch if there were an *-ed* like in *The wombat pooped*. If there is no phonetically overt inflection, then we will keep life simple by placing the word *past* or *nonpast* where the lexical item would normally go, as in this sentence: *The children finger-paint on Thursdays.*

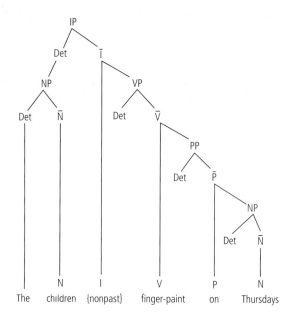

Just like with Verb Phrases, it is important to practice sketching out tree structure with Inflectional Phrases. The hierarchy of the tree structure and the constituency of the phrases will not jump off the page and slap you in the face. Although your mental grammar understands those qualities, it will not directly hand you answers. In the same way, if you were to have a biology quiz on the different metabolism processes cells work through to sustain life, your metabolizing cells cannot send you a memo explaining what is going on.

Try out the sentences below to test your hierarchy and constituent parsing skills. Remember to move the inflection from the verb if it is a suffix and splice it between the subject and the predicate. If the inflection is phonetically null, then just write *past* or *nonpast* under the Inflection (the head of the Inflectional Phrase) as indicated in a few examples below:

The dragon spit → The dragon [past] spit
The dragon spit fire
The bold dragon spit fire on my shoes
The bold dragon in the air spit fire on the house
The bold dragon in the air spit purple fire on the new house

The teacher answered the students → The teacher [-ed] answer the students
The tired teacher answered the bewildered students

The very energetic, young teacher answered the students after class
The very scared, confused teacher answered the frightening students before
the masquerade ball

meaning and ambiguity: part 2

At the start of the chapter we touched upon the meaning differences in sentences
with structural ambiguity, ambiguity in their phrase structure rather than just
in their word meanings. Now that we have worked through how to describe
Verb Phrases and entire Inflectional Phrases, we are ready to plot out how the
different meanings in a structurally ambiguous phrase correspond to different
constituency and hierarchical arrangements. Revisit the following sentences:

1. *One morning I shot an elephant in my pajamas.*
        (How he got in my pajamas, I don't know)
2. *We need more intelligent leaders*
3. *Umberto turned on the TV*
4. *Nature bats last*

What we need for these sentences are different tree structures for each structurally different meaning. Each of these four sentences has a different kind of solution than the others. The sentence *The toddler kissed the child with the Elmo
puppet* has the same type of ambiguity in its structure as *I shot an elephant in
my pajamas*; the meaning depends on the constituency of the PP. In each of
these, pay attention to what phrases are grouped under what other phrases. The
hierarchy and constituency are still important for resolving which meaning is
connected to which tree structure.

With the Groucho Marx joke of *I shot an elephant in my pajamas*, the one
meaning is that the shooter was in the pajamas, and the other meaning is that
the elephant was in the pajamas. Note that normal semantic boundaries are
forcing most people to reach for the first meaning. The punchline *How he got
in my pajamas, I don't know* forces the other meaning to arise. When that switch
in meaning happens, the hierarchy of the phrase structure changes in our minds,
to allow the other meaning. Take a few moments and sketch out what changes
in that hierarchy. What is the phrase that flips around to yield the humorous
meaning?

The Prepositional Phrase *in my pajamas* can modify one of two things. In an
innocuous sentence like *The cat could sit on the snow in the yard*, the Prepositional Phrase *in the yard* could modify the sitting, or it could modify the snow.
The Prepositional Phrase *in my pajamas* could either modify the shooting (and
hence, the shooter) or it could modify its adjacent Noun Phrase, *an elephant*.
As you can see in these phrase structure trees, for the pajama-wearing-shooter
meaning, the Prepositional Phrase is attached higher up on the intermediate
verb node. For the elephant-wearing meaning, the Prepositional Phrase is

attached under the direct-object Noun Phrase. This switch nicely illustrates that the linear order of the words does not strictly determine meaning. The hierarchical arrangement of the words ultimately does.

For *We need more intelligent leaders*, there is a different structural switch in play. The variation for the structural ambiguity is again in the Verb Phrase, but it does not involve the placement of a Prepositional Phrase. Can you tell what the difference in constituency is for this sentence? The one meaning involves a greater number of intelligent leaders (the intelligence level of those leaders, in that rendition, is unspecified). The other meaning involves an unspecified number of leaders who are more intelligent. The key question of meaning is whether *more* modifies the noun of *leaders* or whether it modifies the adjective of *intelligent*. Let us look at how these different meanings fall out with X-bar phrase structure:

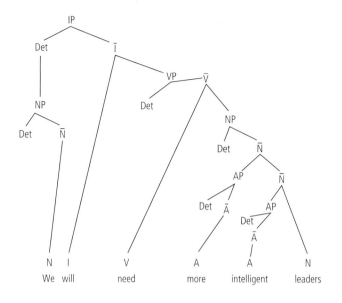

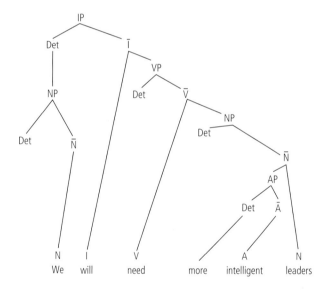

The greater quantity meaning has *more* as an Adjective in an Adjective Phrase, but note its constituency in that first tree. It is a constituent of the *leaders* Noun Phrase, but it is not a constituent of the Adjective Phrase *intelligent*. In the next tree, which represents leaders of greater intelligence, the word *more* acts as a determiner in the Adjective Phrase of *intelligent*. (It could also work as an Adjective in its own Adjective Phrase under the Adjective Phrase of *intelligent*, but considering the lack of meaning difference for this extra drawing, I opted to set it as a modifier in the Determiner slot of the *intelligent* Adjective Phrase.) This structural ambiguity is just like *the deep blue pool* of the previous chapter.

With *Umberto turned on the TV*, we have a real confluence of ambiguity. At least two of the meanings result from structural ambiguity, and those will earn separate trees. At least two other meanings result from lexical ambiguity, but those ambiguities do not get separate trees. We will be sure to label each tree with its different meanings.

To summarize from earlier in the chapter, the most common interpretation of *Umberto turned on the TV* is that Umberto activates the television by making it illuminate. The second meaning places Umberto on top of the TV while spinning. The third meaning involves sexually exciting the TV. The other possible meaning is 'to betray' in that Umberto is disloyal to the TV, perhaps by watching his programs on a computer instead. The important question is which meaning fits with which hierarchical arrangements?

Consider the point of variation within the structural ambiguity. With the meaning of 'send electricity to the TV,' what is the verb? With the meaning of 'spin,' what is the verb? Here is a different type of structural variation. With the first meaning, the verb is *turn on*; with the second meaning, the verb is only *turn* (and *on* becomes the preposition of *on the TV*). The first tree structure will have a transitive verb requiring a subject and direct object, and no Prepositional Phrase is involved. This is the tree structure:

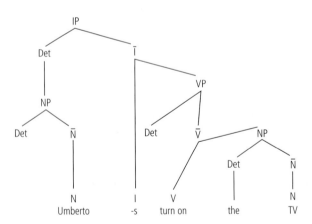

Flips the switch to power on the TV
Sexually excites the TV
Betrays/beats up the TV

For the spinning meaning, the verb will be intransitive with a following Prepositional Phrase. The tree structure will look like this:

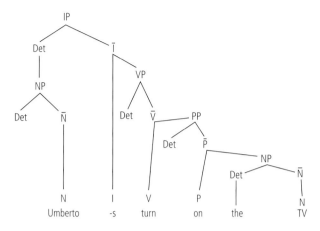

Spins while on top of the TV

These two trees take care of several meanings, with the key difference of the verb *turn on* in one tree and the verb *turn* in the other tree. Consider what the verbs are, since that is the point of variation for this structurally ambiguous sentence. With the meaning of sexually excite, the verb is *turn on*, fitting the structure in the first tree with Noun Phrase as direct object. The meaning of *betray* also fits with that tree structure: To replace that verb would render the sentence as *Umberto betrayed the TV*.

The last structurally ambiguous sentence is *Nature bats last*. With this collection of morphemes, the meanings fall into two structurally different tree types. To figure out what those are, you need to assess what grammatical jobs the different morphemes perform in the sentence. One meaning is that in the ball game of life, Mother Nature is up to bat last. With that meaning, what are the subject and the verb in *Nature bats last*? The other meaning is that a certain kind of bat, the nature bat, lasts a considerable amount of time. With that meaning, what is the subject, and what is the verb? Draw out both phrase structure trees before continuing further.

The possible point of confusion is the role of the *-s* on *bats*. When *bats* is a verb, what grammatical job is the *-s* doing? When *bats* is a noun, what grammatical job is it doing then? In both cases, the *-s* is an inflectional bound suffix; in the first case, it is the third-person singular verbal *-s*, and in the second case, it is the plural noun marker. Here we have suffixal homophony. In the first rendition with *bats* as the verb, to construct the Inflectional Phrase tree, the Inflection must be placed between the subject and the predicate. In the second rendition with *bats* as the subject, it remains part of the Noun, and the verbal inflection is simply *nonpast* (with no overt suffix marking it).

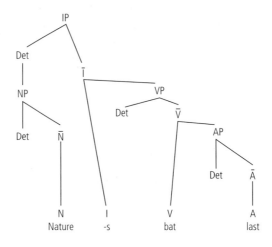

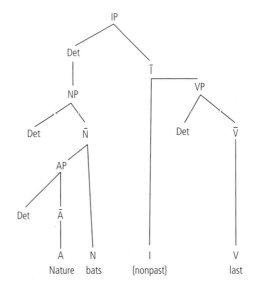

With only three words and a total of four morphemes, we have two different tree structures. The first has a two-word subject with a single word in the predicate. The second has a single-word subject with a two-word predicate. As this sentence shows, the complexity for syntactic structure is not in the words themselves for a language like English. The complexity results from the hierarchical structure ordering the levels of constituency to organize those words. With structurally ambiguous phrases, the hierarchical arrangement of the constituency can always be configured in at least two separate ways.

constituency in a different kind of phrase

What do we do with a phrase like the following?

The horse raced past the barn fell

This kind of sentence is called a *garden path* sentence because it leads you on a winding turn (around corners you did not see coming and where you may not have expected to end up). Where does the constituency trap us here? Most people start to read this phrase as the sentence *The horse raced past the barn*, where the subject is *the horse*, the inflection is *-ed*, and the verb is *race*. In that sentence, the non-garden-path version, the collection of *past the barn* is a Prepositional Phrase, and it is in the predicate and the Verb Phrase of *race*. It is much like our earlier Verb Phrase of *yawn during a movie*.

The tricky part comes about with *fell*. It is the past-tense form of the verb *fall* and is begging for a subject. Most readers start searching back for a subject (since there are no more following words). The first possible subject (having the semantic qualities of 'things that could fall') is the word *barn*. Having *barn* as a subject might work, but that would make the entire collection of words an awkwardly phrased run-on: *[the horse raced past] [the barn fell]*. The next possibility

Word to the Wise: A shift in style

Our knowledge of Old English is limited to the texts which have survived fires, humidity, mold, mice, and worms (book worms, which are really like book larvae, for example *psocoptera*). Those texts that do survive tell us about how complex the written sentences were in the Old English time period. We can only guess that their spoken forms were equally complex, especially since several of the written texts were intended to be spoken aloud at events. In comparing Old English phrases and sentences, it is clear that the complexity of sentences has changed for many genres of Modern English. Old English phrases were often arranged one after the other and connected by various conjunctions

Hē wæs ēadmōd and geþungen and swā ānræd þurhwunode …
He was humble and devout, and continued so steadfast. …
(from Ælfric's Life of St. Edmund)

This style of sentence construction is called *parataxis*, because the many connected parts are laid out parallel to each other. Modern written English, at least in legal, medical, and academic writing, no longer demonstrates parataxis but instead largely has a main phrase that has one or more subordinate phrases (like this very sentence). This style of writing is called *hypotaxis*. The *hypo* here is like *hypo* in *hypodermic needle* and *hypothermia*. It places some phrases "below" other phrases, attaching them with words like *which*, *because*, *while*, *after*. Although there has been a shift in style for written works in some genres, it is probably most accurate to describe spoken English as still generally paratactic, except of course for discourse that aims at highly educated models, such as class lectures and formal speeches.

back for nouns is *horse*, but how could *horse* not be fully occupied with the verb *raced*? The solution is that *raced past the barn* should be viewed as a subordinate clause. In other words, the full sentence would be *The horse that was raced past the barn fell*. This ellipsis of *that was* allows for the confusion.

How might we handle subordinate clauses so that there are Inflectional Phrases inside other Inflectional Phrases? We already have one kind of lexical item which can handle such embedded Inflectional Phrases. In the following sentence, what is starting off the embedded Inflectional Phrase? *The teacher kept her job after she won the lottery*. The Inflectional Phrase *she won the lottery* is connected to the first Inflectional Phrase by the preposition *after*. The X-bar tree for this sentence would look like this:

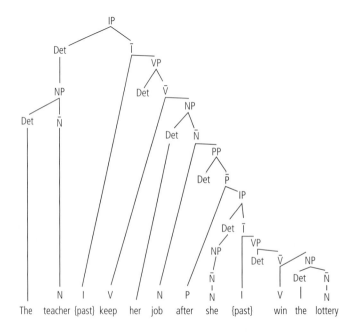

Here, the preposition *after* is leading into another subject (e.g. *she*) and predicate (e.g. *won*). What should we do with the hierarchical structure? The intermediate node of the Prepositional Phrase can attach to an IP as well as it can an NP, so there is no reason why another Inflectional Phrase should be banned. With the extra Inflectional Phrase, there is of course a head of phrase, I.

For many other phrases, another step is necessary. To handle this extra layer of complexity, we need an extra element to generate other X-bar trees. This element is called a **complementizer** (C). It works for words like *that*, *which*, and *who* in the following sentences:

> The light <u>that</u> I bought at the pet store was blue.
> The pen, <u>which</u> I dropped, lasted until Friday.
> The president <u>who</u> waved to us was convicted of treason.

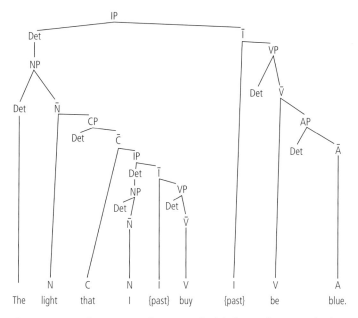

The Complementizer Phrase is a frame to hold the Inflectional Phrase; it provides a docking station for it. The embedded Inflectional Phrases can themselves be longer than the phrases in which they are embedded. In this realm of life, size does not matter. Since the second rule allows for infinite expansion, even the internal, embedded Inflectional Phrases can expand as needed.

English and other languages

Language works through a great deal of variation of sound, words, phrases, and discourse. On some other planet, there might be creatures who have a different type of language: Sounds could be combined in any order, with no limits of syllables or phonotactic constraints. Morphemes might not have any categories to distinguish them; they could be combined randomly as the speaker saw fit. Words could be combined into only one kind of phrase, which itself could be ordered in all possible ways with the same meaning. This other possible planet is not Earth, and these possible unearthly creatures are certainly not human.

Our languages do not fall from our lips and hands helter-skelter. We are not like the hypothetical fleet of typing monkeys who randomly hit keys to produce not only mountains of garbage-strings of alphabetical characters but also the complete works of Shakespeare (and Isaac Asimov!). We are human. As humans, the possibilities of our language require boundaries.

We have seen these boundaries in syllables, where sounds are chunked into an organized unit containing an onset, nucleus, and coda. We have seen them in morphemes, where lexical categories are attached as roots and affixes in hierarchical layers. We have seen these boundaries in phrases, where lexical categories form heads of phrases under intermediate and top-shelf nodes. After all this complexity, could there possibly be more layers of order to the immensity of human language? But, of course.

Word to the Wise: Acquiring language by any means necessary

When we think of acquiring a spoken language, most of us conjure up ideas of babies hearing their parents and then babbling for months on end. Yet, it seems that babies will do whatever they have to do to acquire language. Researchers have found that infants, from four to twelve months of age, pay attention to how people move their lips while listening to them speak. The infants were shown videos of women speaking in their home language (English) or in Spanish (which they had not been exposed to previously). The researchers, David Lewkowicz and Amy Hansen-Tift, used an eye-tracker to carefully detail where the infants looked. At four months of age, the babies visually tracked the women's eyes. Between six and eight months, the infants switched over to focusing on the speakers' lips. This period is also when children begin to babble, checking out how their own lips and tongue and jaws work. The infants continued to focus on lip movements during speech until about ten months of age, when they shifted their gaze back to the eyes of the person talking. For the infants who were shown speakers of a language they did not know, they continued to focus on the lips longer, as late as twelve months of age, presumably to work out what was going on with the new kind of speech.

As a study of how humans develop, this finding indicates that we use several different kinds of information to build our mental grammars. Importantly children who fall outside these ranges, perhaps not refocusing after ten months on a parent's eyes when hearing a native language, might be more likely to be later diagnosed with learning disabilities.

The ordered complexity of human language starts early in our infancy, and whether it be with the Universal Grammar or emergence from the combination of other mental skills, our genetic code guides us to build a functioning mental grammar. The ordered complexity pervades every part of our linguistic system.

As young infants, we experience language in every way possible, acquiring sounded language or signed language as it is available. During this period, we make choices, although "making" here is a grand overstatement. Our brains are making choices. Our brains are hardwiring certain pathways according to data in the environment. There is a lot of noise in both visual or sound signals, and there are a lot of opportunities for human babies to mix up language information. Amazingly though, within 36 to 48 months, almost all children have most of the basics down. How do we pull off this daunting computational trick in such a short time when we cannot perform so many other basic skills as infants? We seem to have a language advantage.

Steven Pinker calls it a language instinct. We know how to acquire a language because basic blueprints are hard-wired in our brains as part of the human genetic code. What is the best way to characterize that knowledge? How do we best describe it? It is still an open question, but Mark Baker describes our acquisition advantage through our command of the atoms of language. Just as atoms of chemical elements combine to form all known molecules and substances, atoms of language are qualities that, when combined in certain ways, produce all the observable languages on Earth. Whereas atoms of elements are very small, atoms of language are very abstract. Abstract here does not mean they are vague. They are actually quite specific. It means they cover a wide range of events in a wide range of languages, and only through comparison of languages were linguists able to discover them.

These atoms of language are the principles and parameters discussed in Chapter 7. These are the qualities and trends human language follows, and every general theory of human language needs to account for them. We delve further into the headedness parameter here and investigate another parameter to show how they affect sentence structure and how they pattern across languages. For a more involved argument, with full justification of these parameters and the story of how these atoms of language were discovered, interested readers should go to Baker's *The Atoms of Language*.

The first parameter deals with subjects. In some languages, a subject of a sentence must be overtly expressed. In English, to talk about the weather requires a subject...*It's raining; It's snowing*. In Italian, to talk about the weather does not require a subject...*Piove; Nevica*. Those conjugated verbs are grammatical in their subjectless state, whereas if an English speaker tried *raining* or *snowing* as complete sentences, they would seem a bit odd. Spanish works much like Italian, where subjects for such weather verbs are not required: *está lloviendo; está nevando*. French on the other hand requires a subject like English does. For French, the convention is to use the third-person singular, masculine form as "it" for these weather statements: *Il pleut; Il neige*.

Languages like Italian and Spanish allow **null subjects**: The slot is phonetically empty, but the verb is still conjugated as if there were an overt subject in the sentence. Languages like English and French do not allow null subjects; these languages require there to be some word in the subject slot, be it a pronoun like *it* or an existential like *there*. In French, *There is a set of teeth* can be translated as *Il y a un ensemble de dents*, with *il* working as the subject. In Spanish the phrase would be rendered as *Hay un conjunto de dientes* with no overt subject.

After looking through enough languages, some linguists have ventured that human babies have a choice to make when they experience language: *Is the language I am hearing a null-subject language or not?* Of course no infant verbalizes such a question, but this kind of question is what their highly active brains are trying to figure out. If children experience subjectless sentences like *Hay un libro*, then it is a null-subject language. However, by experiencing short, existential expressions like *There is a book/Il y a un livre*, babies find out that all sentences have something in the subject slot, thus learning that the language requires overt subjects. Consider this parameter like a toggle switch. Either it can be flipped to one position (null subjects) or to the other position (filled subject slots).

This parameter allows for many other patterns to fall out with subject variation. In Italian, *Egli verrà* 'He will come' and *Verrà* 'He will come' both work fine. In forming questions from declarative (indicative) sentences, Italian allows for different constructions from English. A phrase like *Credi che egli verrà* '(you) believe that he will come' can be used to form this question <u>*Chi*</u> *credi che* _____ *verrà?* '<u>Who</u> do (you) think that ____ will come?' That question does not translate well into English when done on a word-to-word basis. English speakers would need to render it as 'You think that who will come,' ditching the inversion of the subject and verb at the start of the phrase. Or, English speakers would need to drop the *that*, leaving just 'Who do you think _____ will come?' where the blank represents a slot from where *who* has been moved.

From all these comparisons, we can see that Italian has different settings than English. This particular parameter affects all instances where null subjects may arise in a language. Baker (2001:58) characterizes the null-subject parameter in the following way:

"In some languages every tensed clause must have an overt subject noun phrase."

"In other languages tensed clauses need not have an overt subject noun phrase."

The term 'tensed clause' refers to phrases with conjugated verbs: Phrases like *the dog to walk* do not qualify as tensed, but *The dog walks* does. The null-subject parameter is one toggle switch that allows children to figure out how to understand and produce a language. As children, we do not consciously ponder such choices any more than we ponder *how* to send signals to our brains when we are learning to walk. We just play with our legs, and we play with our words.

Another parameter in this model of the Universal Grammar was introduced in Chapter 7, and it deals with how heads of phrases are arranged: the headedness parameter. With the phrases you have worked through so far, you have positioned the X carefully in relation to the rest of the lexical slots of the XP. And as you know, this head of phrase and phrase structure can swing around like a mobile:

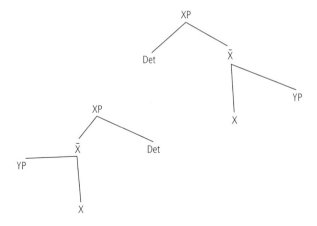

With this ability, there are many different options for how to order words in phrases.

For phrases that mark location, the locative can come before the accompanying Noun Phrase (prepositional) or after the accompanying Noun Phrase (postpositional). It so happens that the **pre**positional languages have some other qualities in common: Their auxiliaries (e.g. *will run*) come before their verbs, and verbs come before their objects (e.g. *hit the ball*). Even that would be only mildly remarkable, but the languages with **post**positional phrases have auxiliaries which follow their main verbs and direct objects which precede their verbs. At a surface level, it would seem that objects of locatives, direct objects, and auxiliaries are unrelated, but consider their structure in an X-bar tree with these English and Tamil phrases:

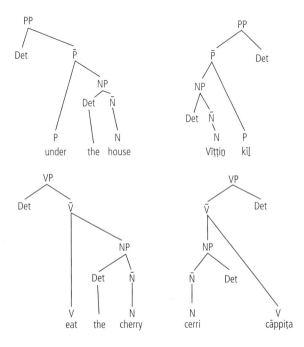

Here, the heads of the phrases are switched. The structure is the same between both Prepositional Phrases and Postpositional Phrases, except for the location of the heads.

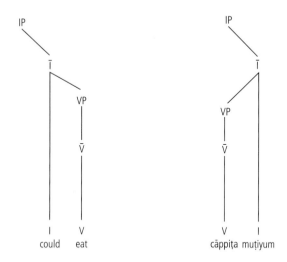

The same goes for the auxiliaries and their main verbs. For a language like English, the inflection heading the Inflectional Phrase comes before the main verb; for languages like Tamil, the inflection comes after the main verb (e.g. I could eat vs. Nān cāppiṭa muṭiyum).

How might linguists have discovered these differences? By comparing different languages, it became clear that the organization of phrases showed strikingly similar patterns. Here is a small demonstration of Baker's (2001:60) analysis of (romanized) Japanese and English:

Japanese order		English order	
direct object	verb	verb	direct object
sushi-o	taberu	eat	sushi
sushi	eat		
noun phrase	locative	locative	noun phrase
Tokyo	ni	in	Tokyo
Tokyo	in		
main verb	auxiliary	auxiliary	main verb
tabe	rareru	be	eaten
eaten	be		
embedded clause complementizer		complementizer embedded clause	
Gwen-wa Kim-ga yuusyuuda to omou		Gwen believes that Kim is excellent	
Gwen Kim excellent that thinks			

Source: *The Atoms of Language*, Mark C. Baker, copyright © 2001. Reprinted by permission of Basic Books, a member of The Perseus Books Group.

There are other phrase patterns that fall out in the same way for these two languages. For example, in a Verb Phrase in English, any Prepositional Phrases come after the main verb (e.g. *I sleep on the floor*). However, these are reversed in Japanese, and the head of the Verb Phrase comes last (e.g. *Watashi wa yuka de nemuru* 'I floor on sleep.' The heads of the phrases are reversed. In the Universal Grammar, there appears to be a parameter with a switch that can either be flipped to head initial (like English) or head final (like Japanese and Tamil). You might protest that if there were such a switch, there would be a lot of similarity in the world's languages regarding how they build phrases. Phrases would be built either like English or like Japanese.

To investigate this possibility, let us take a look at the order of Subjects, Verbs, and Objects in the world's languages, as given by Baker (2001:128):

Basic word order	Percentages of languages	Example languages
Subject-[object-verb]	45	Japanese, Turkish, Quechua
Subject-[verb-object]	42	English, Edo, Indonesian
Verb-subject-object	9	Zapotec, Welsh, Niuean

Source: Baker (2001).

There are some other combinations that make up the other 4% of the world's languages, but as you can see, 87% of the world's languages have their inflected verb either first or last in the Inflectional Phrase. Were this distribution of patterns random, the percentages would be much more like this next table:

Basic word order	Percentages of languages
Subject-[object-verb]	17
Subject-[verb-object]	17
Verb-subject-object	17
Verb-object-subject	17
Object-subject-verb	16
Object-verb-subject	16

However, that is not the case. Not even close. The distribution we do have in the first table shows that a strong constraint directs how the heads of phrases fall out.

variation today

subject-verb concord

On the Outer Banks of North Carolina and in the Appalachian Mountains, there is a fading feature of rural varieties of English. This feature is called the Northern Subject Rule (*northern* as in Scotland). An example of this feature is *The birds pecks at the crabs*. With plural nouns like *birds*, the verb *peck* gets an inflectional *-s*. This paradigm for conjugating a verb works differently than most other places. For most dialects across the United States, verbs get conjugated according to the following pattern:

I walk	We walk
You walk	You walk
The cat walks	The cats walk

In other words, only verbs with third-person singular subjects receive an *-s* suffix. On the Outer Banks, in the Appalachian Mountains, and in Scotland, at least in earlier times, the verbs conjugated with third-person plural subjects also received an *-s*:

I walk	We walk
You walk	You walk
The cat walks	The cats walks

The exception to this pattern fell with pronouns. As you could tell from our tree diagrams, pronouns like *she* and *they* operate differently than the lexical category of noun. For example, they are not involved in Determiner Phrases: **the she*. With this subject-verb concord pattern, the pronoun *they* also does not trigger the verbal *-s*: Sentences like **They pecks at the crabs* do not happen for speakers with this pattern. Interestingly, even this exception to the rule has an exception to it. *They* only blocks the verbal *-s* if it is directly adjacent to the verb. In a sentence like *They quickly pecks at the crabs*, there is an intervening adverb and the verbal *-s* can appear. This pattern is no longer robust in Appalachia or on the Outer Banks. At the end of the twentieth century, this third-person plural verbal *-s* appeared less than 6% of the time on Ocracoke, NC.

It is no accident that both of these dialect areas have traces of the same subject-verb concord pattern. It originates in the English-speaking areas of Scotland. Speakers then carried it to the plantations in Ireland (like Ulster, Ireland) and from there to the United States. These Scots-Irish migrants brought over their dialect patterns and settled in both the Outer Banks and the Appalachian Mountains. Both areas had less in-migration from surrounding regions than other areas. Neither one was fully isolated, although some areas of the Outer Banks only received modern conveniences, such as daily mail service, in the last half of the twentieth century. Consequently, they have shared a few features, such as this one and *a*-prefixing (e.g. *she was a-running*), which other varieties of English abandoned earlier. This subject-verb concord pattern has been a part of the English language for over 600 years, starting back in the Old English period. The following example comes from Scots-Irish English of the seventeenth century (Montgomery 1997).

Al sic termis procedis of fantastiknes ande glorious consaitis.
'All such terms proceeds from fantastic and glorious consensus.'

Several kinds of subject-verb variation still occur in English, but standard patterns are so thoroughly imposed throughout the English-speaking world that they are often chastised.

the verb "need"

From West Virginia throughout the Midwest, there exists a construction which drives people from other parts of the country a bit batty. Consider the sentence *The plates need washed*. Can you guess the dialect variation? For other areas of the country, the verb *to be* would be required after the verb *need*: *The plates need to be washed*. There is no difference in meaning between *the plates need washed* and *the plates need to be washed*, so what is going on? Many scholars see this variation as a syntactic feature, but it probably has a simpler explanation.

The verb *need* is itself different in its lexical listing. For some dialects of English, the verb *need* requires a following Verb Phrase like *to be washed*. For other dialects, the verb *need* requires a following past participle or adjective: *The board needs washed* or *The board needs washing*. This variation is not syntactic in that there is some constraint across verbs; there is no general rule where all transitive verbs requiring Verb Phrases in some dialects are transformed over to past participles. The lexical listing for the verb *need* seems to be specified in some dialects to have certain slots and different slots in other dialects.

---

chapter summary

In human languages, more complex thoughts are represented by building words into phrases, like seeds growing into trees with many branches. This chapter concentrated on the Verb Phrase and the Inflectional Phrase. Using the same X-bar templates as the previous chapter, we laid out how both kinds of phrases are arranged, including their hierarchical organization. By having the Inflection (I) of a sentence as the head of both the subject and the predicate, the same kinds of structure can be used to build every phrase. The transitivity of verbs comes into play as a ditransitive verb will require different structure within the Inflectional Phrase than a transitive or intransitive verb, just as oak trees branch differently from maples. Structural ambiguity in sentences can be resolved by drawing two different tree structures to represent the different hierarchical and constituency patterns. When viewed as units of subject, verb, and object, disconnected languages show amazingly similar patterns. The organizational connections found between languages, such as Subject-Object-Verb languages greatly preferring postpositions, are attributed to the choices from the parameters of the Universal Grammar, the biological blueprints for building the mental grammar. The parameters of headedness and null subjects were illustrated to show their far-reaching effects.

key concepts

- Complementizer
- Dative alternation
- Ditransitive
- Hypotaxis
- Indirect object
- Inflectional Phrase
- Lexical ambiguity
- Null subjects
- Parataxis
- Predicate
- Structural ambiguity
- Subject
- Transitivity
- Verb Phrase

references

Baker, R. (2002) *The Atoms of Language: The Mind's Hidden Rules of Grammar*. Basic Books.

Lewkowicz, D.J. and Hansen-Tift, A.M. (1997) "Infants deploy selective attention to the mouth of a talking face when learning speech." *Proceedings of the National Academy of Sciences 109*, no. 5 (2012):1431–1436.

Montgomery, P. (1997) "Making the trans-Atlantic link between varieties of English: The case of plural verbal -s." *Journal of English Linguistics 25*:122–141.

further reading

An Introduction to Syntactic Analysis and Theory. Hilda Koopman, Dominique Sportiche, and Edward Stabler. 2014. Wiley Blackwell.

This book is designed for students with no background in the study of syntax. It is both readable and workable in the sense that it provides plenty of exercises to practice new-found syntactic knowledge. Syntactic understanding is not gained passively, but instead students must actively construct it. This book works both morphological and syntactic ends of building grammatical phrases, starting with simpler concepts and leading up to more complex ones. With its recent publication date, *An Introduction to Syntactic Analysis and Theory* is also up-to-date in its syntactic ideas.

Foundations of Language: Brain, Meaning, Grammar, Evolution. Ray Jackendoff. 2002. Oxford University Press.

This book provides a wonderful perspective on the linguistic study of grammar. It is approachable by new explorers in grammar studies and offers insights to the human mind. By working through an interdisciplinary approach, Jackendoff establishes a theory of how both syntax and semantics work in the human mind.

A User's Guide to Thought and Meaning. Ray Jackendoff. 2012. Oxford University Press.

Jackendoff's earlier *Foundations of Language* was a grand *opus* of Jackendoff's thoughts on syntax and semantics and should be read by all serious students of syntax. This shorter work takes a much more informal approach to explaining how phrases are built and meaning is rendered. This book is specifically geared towards nonspecialists and allows a careful overview of consciousness and thought.

Syntax: A Generative Introduction. 3rd edition. Andrew Carnie. 2013. Wiley Blackwell.
This well-written and accessible introduction to syntax in the generative tradition is a textbook that reaches out in many different ways to describe the syntactic properties of English. In this chapter, a single, simplified approach was presented to demonstrate hierarchy and constituency, but Carnie deploys a full arsenal of analysis to illustrate the graceful complexity and beauty of human language syntax.

exercises

individual work

1. Identify and label all of the phrases in the following sentences. Also, label the subject and predicate from each sentence and the inflection (even if it is {past} or {non-past}). For example, in the sentence *The teacher dropped the phone on the table* the divisions would be the following:
   Subject: the teacher
   Predicate: drop the phone on the table
   NP: the teacher
   I: -ed
   VP: drop the phone on the table
   NP: the phone
   PP: on the table
   NP: the table

   Intransitive verbs:

   a. A cat sits.
   b. The cat sits in the yard.
   c. The black cat sits on the snow in the yard.
   d. The very black cat in the yard sits on the very white snow.
   e. The children run.
   f. The trees fell outside our property line.

   Transitive verbs:

   g. A cat eats a chicken.
   h. An old yellow cat eats a chicken in the yard.
   i. The children run the dog.
   j. The dog trees the cat.

   Ditransitive verbs:

   k. The child gives the chicken to the cat.
   l. I passed David the ball.
   m. David threw the ball to me.

n.   You should exchange the vacuum for a blender.

    o.   I put the garage door opener in the right shoe of the pair of shoes in the box outside your back door.

2. For the preceding sentences, draw an X-bar tree for each Inflectional Phrase.

First, as with the exercises in Chapter 7, please use enough space to draw them. A single landscape page per sentence is ideal.

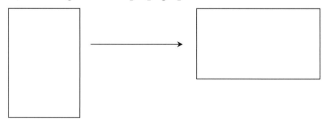

Second, put the words flat across the bottom. Making the words carousel up and down will really confuse you while trying to figure out the constituency relationships of these sentences. Let us try *Those pesky dragons on her roof had a barbecue* as an example sentence.

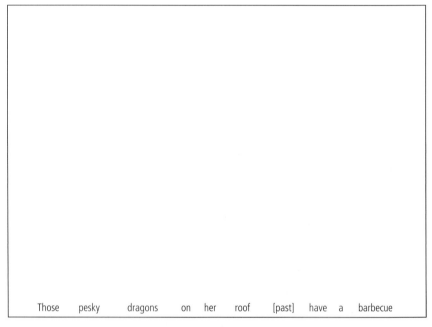

Those   pesky   dragons   on   her   roof   [past]   have   a   barbecue

Third, identify the heads of phrases. In *Those pesky dragons on her roof had a barbecue* there are the Adjective *pesky*, the Noun *dragons*, the Preposition *on*, the Noun *roof*, the Inflection [past], the Verb *have*, and the Noun *barbecue*. Note that the word *her* in this phrase functions as a Determiner and not as a Noun. It just so happens that because of the history of English, the possessive form is *her* and the object form is also *her*.

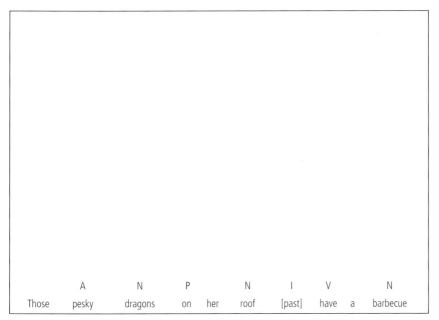

| | A | N | P | N | I | V | N |
| Those | pesky | dragons | on | her | roof | [past] | have | a | barbecue |

Fourth, draw the top level node and follow Rule 1 for that node.

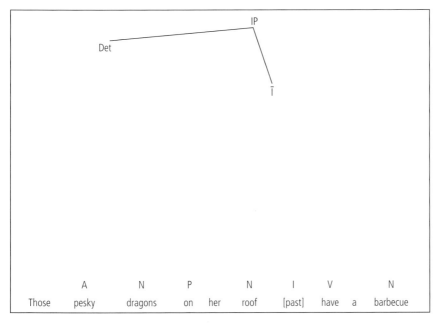

| | A | N | P | N | I | V | N |
| Those | pesky | dragons | on | her | roof | [past] | have | a | barbecue |

Fifth, from this point on, consider each node to be a hill you just climbed. You could not see beyond the hill until you got to the top of it, but now that you are there, you have to decide what constituents to take care of next. How many nodes can you see from the one you are standing on? In these exercises, Inflectional Phrases will be the standard. Accordingly, each IP will start out in exactly the same manner.

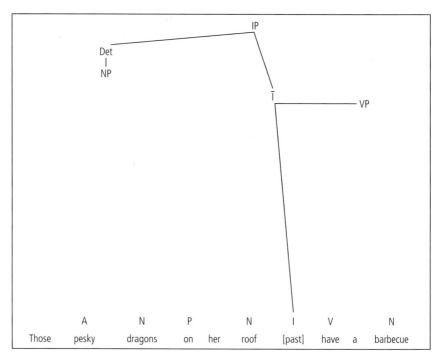

Sixth, continue following Rules 1, maybe 2, and 3 until you reach the head of each phrase and connect every word to a slot in the tree.

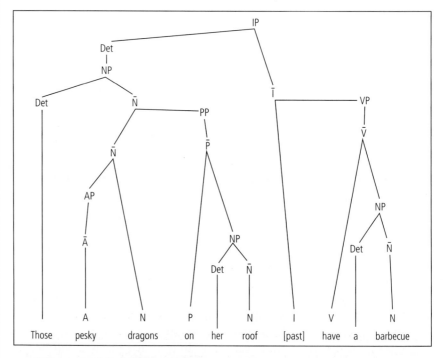

Be sure to label all the nodes.

3.   Identify the different meanings for each of these structurally ambigu-
     ous sentences. What is the place where the structural ambiguity arises?
     a.   Herbie saw the star with the telescope.
     b.   The toddler kissed the child with the puppet.
     c.   She bought the dog toys.
     d.   The British left waffles on the Falklands Islands.
     e.   They are hunting dogs.
     f.   Time flies like an arrow.
     g.   A dictionary fell on the modern novel reader.
     h.   The striker hit the referee with the water bottle.
     i.   He gave her gecko food.
     j.   The deep blue pool was cold.
     k.   The current information technology is better.
     l.   We saw that gas can explode.
4.   For each of the preceding ambiguous sentences, draw two X-bar trees.

group work

1.   For the following phrases, parse each one and separate each phrase
     off with brackets. Also, identify the subject and the predicate. For
     example, in the phrase *Their tall camel stepped on her zucchini*, the
     subject would be *their tall camel* and the predicate would be *step on
     her zucchini*. The Inflection for this sentence is the past-tense mor-
     pheme, *-ed*. With brackets, this Inflectional Phrase comes out as the
     following (empty DETs are not shown):

     [IP [DET [NP [DET *their*] [$\bar{N}$ [AP [$\bar{A}$ [A *tall*]]] [N *camel*]]]]

     [$\bar{I}$ [I-*ed*] [VP [$\bar{V}$ [V *step*] [PP [$\bar{P}$ [P *on*] [NP [DET *her*]
     [$\bar{N}$ [N *zucchini*]]]]]]]]]

     You might be wondering why there are so many brackets at the right
     side of that parsing. Each one ends a different constituent. You can
     label the end of each one if it makes it easier to see:

     zucchini N] $\bar{N}$] NP] $\bar{P}$] PP] $\bar{V}$] VP] $\bar{I}$] IP]

     Each of those phrases had not stopped until the end of the line. The
     word *zucchini* was embedded in each one. This nested quality of
     phrases is a basic part of human language and a shared responsibility
     between morphology and syntax. In English, it is mostly syntax's job.
     For the following phrases, remember that modals (e.g. *can, may,
     might, will, should*) will act as the Inflection of the Inflectional Phrase.

    a.   The wind will blow.

    b.   Some rain should fall.

    c.   My pug snores.

    d.   That cute pug eats like a pig.

    e.   This adorable pug with the injured eye might trip.

    f.   Our sugar-glider really likes us.

    g.   Those low-flying griffins over the forest seem terribly friendly despite their claws.

    h.   Stark sunshine floated through the window in the family room this afternoon.

    i.   A dragon ate my couch.

    j.   Our favorite squid in the backyard pool deftly retrieved the couch from the gullet of the dragon.

2. Which of the following are lexically ambiguous, and which are structurally ambiguous? How do you go about figuring that out?

    a.   Sneaking carefully across the room, she peered into the lampshade and saw a bug.

    b.   The head fell out of the window.

    c.   Gretchen went through the door.

    d.   The Viking thought it was a very fancy club.

    e.   After the poker game, the gravedigger found the missing spade.

    f.   During the parade at the beach, she saw the biggest wave she had ever seen.

    g.   We disliked the striped chair and couch.

    h.   Umberto turned on the speaker.

    i.   The craft had been going downhill for some time now.

    j.   Swimming in the river, the programmer realized he didn't know how much money he had left, so he headed for the bank.

3. Develop five structurally ambiguous sentences and five sentences with lexical ambiguity.

4. For the following garden path sentences, discern where the break is between the different potential meanings. Between the potential reading (the unfulfilled one) and the only complete reading, is there a change in the heads of phrases? What causes the switch? These come from the linguist John M. Lawler, who delivers some intriguing garden path sentences (http://www-personal.umich.edu/~jlawler/).

    a.   The prime number few.

    b.   Fat people eat accumulates.

    c.   The cotton clothing is usually made of grows in Mississippi.

    d.   Until the police arrest the drug dealers control the street.

    e.   The man who hunts ducks out on weekends.

    f.   When Fred eats food gets thrown.

    g.   Mary gave the child the dog bit a Band-Aid.

    h.   The girl told the story cried.

    i.   I convinced her children are noisy.

    j.   She told me a little white lie will come back to haunt me.

    k.   The man who whistles tunes pianos.

    l.   The old man the boat.

    m.   The raft floated down the river sank.

5. In the two examples below, what is different with the verb from your dialect variety?

> In the following sentence from an Australian documentary on kangaroos, an Australian said: "I never thought kangaroos to use an underpass."

> Sir Alex Ferguson, revered former manager of Manchester United, said: "… as long as humans are humans you hope something stupid to happen."

---

study questions

1. Does the form of the word change with lexical ambiguity? What does happen with lexical ambiguity?

2. Do structurally ambiguous phrases require different phrase trees? If so, why?

3. What does the $\bar{V}$ do in relation to other phrases?

4. How is the Determiner slot of an XP like a mobile?

5. What should you do before you begin drawing lines and connecting nodes in a phrase tree, and why should you do this?

6. What are ditransitive verbs, and what do they require in the VP?

7. What is dative alternation?

8. What makes a sentence a sentence?

9. What is the head of an Inflectional Phrase?

10. Where, in a phrase tree, does the subject of an Inflectional Phrase go?

11. Where, in a phrase tree, does the Inflection of an Inflectional Phrase go?

12. What determines meaning in a structurally ambiguous sentence?

13. What does a garden path sentence do?

14. Can there be more than one Inflectional Phrases in a sentence?

15. What is the role of a complementizer?

16. What is a null subject?

17. What are some qualities that prepositional languages have in common?
18. What are the most common orders of Subjects, Verbs, and Objects in the world's languages?
19. Why do the dialects of Appalachia and the Outer Banks have traces of the same subject-verb concord pattern?
20. How does the verb *need* exhibit variation in the United States?

 Visit the book's companion website for additional resources relating to this chapter at: http://www.wiley.com/go/hazen/introlanguage

9

From Phrases to Meaning

An Introduction to Language, First Edition. Kirk Hazen.
© 2015 John Wiley & Sons, Inc. Published 2015 by John Wiley & Sons, Inc.

chapter overview

In the last chapter, we focused on the construction of phrases, combining smaller phrases to make sentences. Yet, sentences are only part of what we do every day. The realm above the sentence is called discourse, and one of the basic parts of discourse is the utterance. This chapter focuses on how people construct, manage, and interpret discourse through utterances. We create discourse with different levels of information, and interpreting that information requires attention to context and possible meanings. As we learned in the previous chapters, some of the information comes from language: Morphemes combined into words combined into phrases then flows through phonology. Yet, a lot of interpretation comes from the discourse context. After all, sometimes it is not what you say, but when and how you say it. Much of this chapter explores the conversational rules we follow when talking with friends and random people we meet: The rules that direct the *what, when,* and *how* of our conversations. The rest of the chapter focuses on our use of pragmatic knowledge to figure out what people actually mean in conversations.

meaning and ambiguity

Chapter 8 focused on Verb Phrases and sentences in the form of Inflectional Phrases. We examined the structure of sentences, working through their constituency and order via hierarchical trees. In this chapter, we put sentences to work rather than treat them like specimens for dissection. Yet, they are not employed as just *sentences*. Technically, sentences are simply those Inflectional Phrases with a subject and predicate. When people write sentences on a page or say a sentence out loud, those are no longer *just* sentences: They become **utterances**. An utterance is any bit of language produced in a social context. This chapter focuses mostly on spoken language, but social context is equally as relevant in writing. Utterances are not restricted by size, so they could be any unit of language, including smaller phrases, single words, and sounds.

To illustrate how widely the meaning of utterances can swing, we will work through two different contexts for a simple sentence: "The door is locked." The sentence itself has a subject and predicate, and its verb is set up as non-past, neutral, and indicative. The sentence has four XPs for its hierarchical structure and six morphemes (if you count *is* as two). Perhaps it would be uttered with four syllables. All that information gets processed in our brains, and at this point in the book, hopefully there is nothing overwhelming about that information. Yet, when that sentence gets spoken out loud in some kind of social context, it becomes an utterance, and we have even more information to process.

In the first context, imagine two roommates who are at their apartment and exhausted both from their day of rigorous studying and from a party they have just hosted and closed down. The one roommate is a constant worrier but is too tired to get off the couch. That roommate keeps saying, "People are going to try to come back....too tired." The other roommate, tired from both the party and the first roommate's worries, replies, "The door is locked," and then heads to bed.

In the second context, imagine an adventure movie where the hero is running through a large house in an attempt to escape a pack of vicious, mutated poodles. The hero makes it down a long narrow hallway in the basement to a steel exit door. From the other side of the door, the dastardly bad guy shouts, "The door is locked!"

What are the various meanings in these contexts? First, ponder for a moment the act of speaking. Choosing to speak, rather than remain silent, is a meaningful act in itself. As we all know, even silence can hold meaning. For each of these speakers, the utterance is a **speech act**, such as a statement, a request, a threat, or a command. It is a decision to engage and influence the discourse. The utterances we wield are often speech acts, and those acts contribute to the meaning of the sentences.

What meanings can we dig out of "The door is locked"? For the first context, several clues contribute to the interpretable meanings: The roommates' day has been long; they have just finished a party; other people attended the party; the roommates are tired and are finished with the day; and they do not want to continue the party. As the worrisome roommate carries on with potential problems, the other roommate closes down the conversation and the long day with the utterance: "The door is locked." That speech act provides at least the following meanings:

1. *The entrance to the apartment is secured and not easily openable.*
2. *The party people will not be re-entering the apartment.*
3. *You should not worry about this topic.*
4. *This conversation is done.*
5. (Possible) *Stop whining.*

With the second example, we have the same sentence with all the same linguistic characteristics. The vocal qualities of the utterances, like its intonation and loudness, might be different, and those qualities can influence meaning although they will not be analyzed here. With this same sentence, we have a different utterance because it is in a different context. For this second scene, the contextual clues are radically shifted from the first scene: The hero is in danger; the hero is in a hurry to escape; the danger comes from a pursuing pack of hounds;

physical distance is the key to safety (rather than a bomb or virus inside the hero); and the hero is trying to find an exit. Against these background facts, the bad guy provides the utterance, "The door is locked." The following meanings could be derived from this speech act:

1. *The exit to the house is secured and not easily openable.*
2. *The hero's current plans must change.*
3. *The bad guy really is in control.*
4. *The bad guy wants to exert knowledge of that control* (hence the speech act).
5. *The hero's hope of escape is probably dashed.*
6. (Possible and the source of the heightened conflict) *The bad guy is going to win this fight.*

In our daily lives, we do not make such examinations of basic facts. We do not list the background knowledge when we enter a restaurant and work our way through ordering, receiving, eating, and paying for lunch. But, and it is a big *but*, our minds do. In this chapter we detail the kinds of decisions our minds make with utterances and pragmatic knowledge. Rarely do we become consciously aware of the decisions we make in conversations and the logic we follow. Yet, comedians do make use of all of these decisions by violating them. Humor is created through contrast, and comedians contrast expected speech acts with wildly unexpected ones to create humor. While we are not always aware of these basic language decisions, we all have some knowledge of discourse context and utterance, and with this chapter you now have terms to analyze that knowledge.

A different way we rely on both language and context everyday is through pronouns. We have dealt with pronouns in previous chapters, and they have a quality unique to human language. **Deixis** is the ability to have a meaning but point to other entities for reference. The pronoun *I* means 'first-person singular' but does not refer to only one person. It points out any person who uses it. The meaning of first-person singular is stable, but the reference switches from user to user. The language quality of deixis requires contextual information to complete a pronoun's meaning.

Imagine a scene where six women are lined up by police as potential suspects for a bank robbery, and a bank teller is asked which woman held the gun. If the bank teller only says *she's the one* without pointing in any fashion, the statement is completely ambiguous. Yet, in this case the ambiguity is neither lexical nor structural. Instead, it is contextual. The pronoun *she* has no ability in and of itself to point at any particular person, but only picks out one female (usually animate but even that can be extended). If only one female is in the area being discussed, the process of elimination picks out who it is. Yet, if more than one female is present, then it is up to the speaker to make unambiguous the reference for *she*. Resolving contextual ambiguity with pronouns is such a normal part of our daily lives that we hardly notice the ways we resolve any potential confusion.

Word Play: Who's on first?

From 1936 to 1945, Bud Abbot and Lou Costello refined an older comedy skit they entitled *Who's on First?* It became a hit and has been reproduced many times since. The humor in the skit is created through lexical ambiguity between interrogative pronouns like *who, what,* and *why* and these same forms used as <u>names</u>: *Who, What,* and *Why.* As pronouns, they have the quality of deixis: They point toward some other identifiable agent. As names, they label a person directly.

> Abbott: I'm telling you. Who's on first, What's on second, I Don't Know is on third—
> Costello: You know the fellows' names?
> Abbott: Yes.
> Costello: Well, then who's playing first?
> Abbott: Yes.
> Costello: I mean the fellow's name on first base.
> Abbott: Who.
> Costello: The fellow playing first base.
> Abbott: Who.
> Costello: The guy on first base.
> Abbott: Who is on first.

http://www.youtube.com/watch?v=kTcRRaXV-fg

In a *Saturday Morning Breakfast Cereal* webcomic, Zach Weiner provides a 57-panel version of the *Who's on First* with the symbols of chemical elements. How is that possible? Weiner creatively used ambiguity between the sounds of the symbols and other words. Consider elements like No (Nobelium), Na (Sodium), K (Potassium), O (Oxygen), and U (Uranium). These can be confused with *no, nah, 'K, oh,* and *you.*

http://www.smbc-comics.com/index.php?db=comics&id=2349#

The skit discussed in Word Play: Who's on first? puts a different twist on pronouns. Instead of using contextual ambiguity as the foundation for a series of jokes, Bud Abbott converts pronouns with deixis to regular words without deixis. For example, a form like *Who* is being used as a label like *Rusty* or *Pedro.* With that switch, lexical ambiguity between the pronoun system and the regular noun system arises.

another realm of language structure

Consider the word "Wow." As a single word made of perhaps three sounds, it does not have a lot going for it. Yet, in the right context, it can be interpreted with plenty of meaning. Consider a clumsy friend getting an open-cup soft drink and walking back to your table. After she trips and spills the drink all over you and your lunch, you say, "Wow." What meanings could be associated with that utterance of "Wow"? In a different context, if you exclaimed "Wow" after getting back an *A* on a test you thought you had failed, what meanings might arise from that utterance? With the same word come different meanings in different contexts.

What triggers these various interpretations of "Wow"? In part, it is the context; however, from the context of the utterance, we use our **pragmatic knowledge** to figure out what the utterance means. *Pragmatic knowledge* refers to the information outside of language which influences its interpretation, including knowledge of physical and social facts. Different people have varying levels of skill, but as a species, humans are really good at using pragmatic knowledge to figure out language meaning. As speakers, we weave together all the utterances of a context into a single collection, called a **discourse**. As used by scholars, the term *discourse* could refer to a small collection of utterances in a context, such as a single conversation, or it could refer to many conversations in similar contexts, such as "medical discourse" or "legal discourse." The study of discourse and pragmatics are separate areas in linguistics, but they overlap in many ways. In this chapter, we use findings from both fields to better understand the complex patterns of utterances in our daily lives.

structure and constraints

People produce utterances just like they produce syllables, morphemes, words, and phrases. We will not draw hierarchical trees for conversations the way we did for these other units, but there are guidelines for utterances. People do not use them helter skelter. We follow several guidelines, and even when we violate them, most of us know we are violating them. The violating part confirms the shared social agreement we have about them.

The basic principle we usually follow in a discourse is called the **cooperative principle**. When people talk with each other, the normal understanding between them is that the things they say are supposed to help and that participants are communicating cooperatively. If someone says, "I'm really hungry," and another person responds, "There are a few places to eat on High Street," most of us normally believe that the second statement relates to the first statement because we assume the two people are cooperating. Imagine how weird our conversations would be if we did not have the cooperative principle as the foundation to understanding. Ponder the scenario in which one friend says, "Where's Jill?" and the other one replies, "Her car is over in Fred's driveway"; the first friend stares for a bit and then says, "Did I ask you where her car was? Why are you telling me about her car?" If we did not follow the cooperative principle, we would not be able to understand anything except for the most direct statements. We would not be able to catch any implications in a conversation from what was said, or what was left unsaid. The philosopher Paul Grice first named this idea and also proposed four maxims for conversations.

Any kind of maxim is a short statement expressing a general truth. These **conversational maxims** are not strict laws and neither is the cooperative principle. We violate them for all kinds of reasons, and when we do, someone in the conversation usually knows that a violation has occurred.

The first one is the **maxim of quantity**. Consider this scene:

A young girl is standing in the kitchen holding a mixing bowl:

Daughter: "How do I make a chocolate cake?"
Mom: "Use sugar."

There is something wrong with the Mom's answer. It does not have enough information. Although sugar could be part of the chocolate cake, it certainly will not be the only ingredient, and the orders for mixing and baking are also ignored. In fact, most of the important information is left out. Compare that scene with the following:

Coach approaches an athlete who is shivering during a late autumn practice:

Coach: "You cold?"
Athlete: "Cold is a sensation within our minds, a reaction of our nervous system's uptake of data from our skin to our brain, a series of neurochemical reactions propagated along shockingly small pathways, and although to what end it is difficult to say, I *can* say that those messages have been transferred between my outer layer and my inner layer."
Coach: "Moving more might warm you up. Move."

Here, the athlete's answer is much too long. A simple "yes" would have been a perfectly acceptable answer. The maxim of quantity handles both kinds of situation. It requires that the speaker provide enough information, not too little, not too much, just enough. What is actually appropriate will change from context to context: The appropriate answer with your friends might be a lot shorter than the appropriate answer in a college classroom, and learning those conventions is an important part of learning what is *appropriate* in those situations in those communities.

The next conversational maxim is the **maxim of quality**. It does not deal with how well the conversation is constructed. Instead, it handles the truth of the information. Ponder the following scene:

In a city market, a customer is shopping for art and stands in front of a painting:

Customer: "How much for this one of the sunflowers?"

Artist: "Three cents."
Customer: "What? Really?!"
Artist: "Just teasing! That is $300."

The artist here makes a statement, "three cents," which is untrue. The actual cost of the painting is $300. This utterance is wrong, and the artist, ever so briefly, has violated the maxim of quality. There are times when everybody knows the maxim of quality has been violated, but everybody plays along with that knowledge. When parents and funny uncles play "got-your-nose," pretending to pinch off a young child's nose and hold it between two fingers, the giggle factor for the child (hopefully) is that the utterance is so wrong, it is funny.

The next conversational maxim is the **maxim of relation**. Like the maxim of quality, it is a fairly simple rule for speakers to follow: Be relevant. Give utterances connected to the conversation at hand. Reconsider the example from above:

Standing outside their rental house:

Friend 1: "Where's Jill?"
Friend 2: "Her car is over in Fred's driveway."

With the maxim of relation as a basic tenet of the conversation, we must assume that Friend 2's response relates to Friend 1's question. If we do not make that assumption, the driveway response is just a random fact, like how many squid happen to be in the fish tank or the fridge. The same maxim of relation goes for every communication environment. Consider the text exchange below:

Texting between two roommates:

Roommate 1: "I stop by grocery store"
Roommate 2: "milk"
Roommate 1: "k"
Roommate 2: "beer"
Roommate 1: "enough"

Without the maxim of relation, such exchanges would be very odd. Imagine all the situations where uttering "milk" would be met with stares. Yet, with the constraints of texting and the context of grocery store, responses such as "milk" instead of "While you are there, please pick up some milk" are completely understandable.

The next conversational maxim is the **maxim of manner**. This maxim is slightly more complex, although its main intent is simply *be clear*. The trouble comes with all the different ways we could not be clear. In this first scene, the meaning is unclear not because of any one utterance. Why is the following scene unclear?:

Mother trying to explain how to make a chocolate cake over the phone:

Mother: "You have to mix the flour, sugar, and milk thoroughly."
Daughter: "Ok, I think it is, but it is all white."

Mother: "Pull it out of the oven."
Daughter: "What? I'm supposed to be stirring it in the oven?"

Here, the problem is the order of the utterances. At some point, pulling the cake out of the oven should take place, but not before all the ingredients are mixed. Since discourse deals with flocks of phrases, such problems arise in conversations. Another way speakers confuse their audience, therefore violating the maxim of manner, is by using terms the audience does not understand. Unfortunately, this happens all too often in dialogues between teachers and students:

Third grade classroom, during writing exercises:

Teacher: "We need to improve our spelling with our verbs in the past tense."
Student: "The past what?"
Teacher: "Too many people are orthographically representing the morphophonological alternation for weak verbs in English when it should simply be E D."
Student: [stunned silence]

Here, the terms are way outside the young student's grasp, even if the ideas are not. These terms confuse the listener because the audience cannot peg a meaning on the form. Audiences also have troubles with other kinds of form and meaning mix ups, as in the following example:

Two friends meeting in a public place, but one is in a hurry to get to class:

Friend 1: "Would you rather head downtown tonight or have people over to my place?"
Friend 2 (while rushing off): "Yeah!"
Friend 1: "Huh?"

Here, the response *yeah* is contextually ambiguous because it is unclear which Inflectional Phrase in the speech act is being chosen, or maybe either one would be fine for Friend 2. Either way around, Friend 2's response violates the maxim of manner by not being clear.

Figure 9.1 Some taboo words have complicated pragmatic knowledge, as in this *Boondocks* comic. THE BOONDOCKS © 2005 Aaron McGruder. Dist. By UNIVERSAL UCLICK. Reprinted with permission. All rights reserved.

With these four conversational maxims, the main idea is that they are assumptions about conversations, not enforceable rules. Later, we will explore how all of us exploit these assumptions.

structure of intent and effect

How do people use the cooperative principle and the conversational maxims to make successful conversations? We use these devices to pit two kinds of utterance meanings against each other. One kind is the most literal meaning we can squeeze out of the words in the utterance: the **locutionary** meaning. The other kind is the speaker's intended meaning: the **illocutionary** meaning. On the foundation of the cooperative principle, we choose whether or not to follow the conversational maxims and then emphasize either the locutionary or illocutionary meanings.

To see how this works, consider a discourse where one speaker, at first glance, appears to violate the maxim of relevance:

At a planning meeting for the homecoming parade:

Planner 1: "I think a float where we have a giant robotic arm shucking a giant ear of corn is a great plan. It can't possibly fail."
Planner 2: "Titanic"
Planner 3: "Good point"

We need to take a look at the utterance "Titanic" and its probable meanings on both the locutionary and illocutionary levels. On the locutionary level, it is simply a noun and a name of a famous boat. This kind of statement could be understood as a **non sequitur** (Latin for 'it does not follow'), as the name *Titanic* does not have any logical connection to corn, robotic arms, or homecoming parade floats. The choice depends on whether or not the people in the conversation want to abide by both the cooperative principle and the maxim of relevance in assuming that "Titanic" has something to do with the previous statement. In a small way, the audience has to force the possible meanings of the utterance to fit the context. If so, the story of Titanic, and its supposed invincibility and subsequent sinking on its first voyage, might be a warning and reminder about building something too big and being too confident about its prospects.

In a different approach, speakers might disconnect locutionary and illocutionary meanings to create sarcasm. Sarcasm is the use of irony to show contempt for someone. In the following scene, the audience should "read between the lines" of the speaker's meanings:

The brother is at the sink washing dishes while his sister is getting up from the table:

Sister: "I'm going to watch TV."
Brother: "Why don't you just leave your dishes on the table for me to get?"

Sister: "Thanks!"

Brother throws the wet dish cloth at his sister's head.

Here, the locutionary meaning of the brother's utterance derives from an interrogative, neutral, nonpast sentence with one conjugated verb and a nested Inflectional Phrase tucked inside the final Prepositional Phrase. The locutionary meaning is somewhere around *Is there any reason for you not to let the dishes remain on the table to be my burden?* We could imagine contexts where such an utterance would be intended nicely, perhaps if the person at the table had just gotten out of the hospital with broken bones and a concussion. In the context provided here, however, the illocutionary meaning is probably much closer to *Get your own dishes off the table and wash them yourself.*

Along with the locutionary and illocutionary meanings, many language scholars include **perlocutionary effect** as part of the utterance-analysis toolkit. The perlocutionary effect is the psychological outcome for the audience. In the imagined scenes above, we also have to imagine the perlocutionary effects. For the homecoming-float skit, Planner 3 shows the perlocutionary effect of recognizing the notice from Planner 2's "Titanic" warning. For the sibling skit, the sister's reaction of "Thanks" could either be the result of her only attending to the locutionary meaning and assuming the illocutionary meaning was the same, or the more likely explanation is that she recognized her brother's more sarcastic illocutionary meaning and chose to ignore it, turning his locutionary meaning back against him (taking the non-offer as an actual offer to leave her dishes on the table). The perlocutionary effect for the sister would differ depending on how the locutionary and illocutionary meanings play out for her.

The interplay between locutionary meaning, illocutionary meaning, and perlocutionary effect can be complex. All three of them are part of the conversations we encounter everyday. Part of becoming competent adults in a social community is learning the conventions for the interplay of these three realms of meaning. Not all communities employ sarcasm or humor equally often, and learning what is tolerated is part of the journey of growing up.

the interplay of the -locutionary trio

Although we have considered how the foundation of the cooperative principle and conversational maxims interact with meaning in a restrained view, many of our interactions are more complex. In a scene from the TV show *Foster's Home for Imaginary Friends*, a character new to the foster home, Cheese, is set next to one of the long-term residents of the home, Eduardo, at a dinner table with no one else around. The two have never met, and Eduardo is a super nice guy who is always ready to accommodate other people, but he is not ready for the conversation that comes next.

Cheese: "I like cereal." [Slurps]

Eduardo: "I like potatoes."

Cheese: "I like cereal."

Eduardo: "Si, and I like potatoes."
Cheese, emphatically: "I LIKE CEREAL!"
Eduardo, cautiously: "Si, and I like potatoes."
Cheese, yelling: "I like cereal!"
Eduardo, fearful and with rising, questioning intonation: "I like potatoes."
Cheese, with threatening, raspy voice: "I like cereeeeaaaal."

There is much more to the video of this exchange, because their facial expressions and body language convey other information, in addition to the sound effects and background music (Do an internet search for "best Cheese Foster's Home" for clips). The sum result is that the conversation was not one that Eduardo knew how to handle, and subsequently he puts Cheese with another imaginary friend. What did Cheese do that was so wrong? His sentence is the same in every utterance, but the utterances themselves are different from each other. It is important that you can figure out why the utterances are different, but the sentence remains the same.

With his first statement, Eduardo is trying to abide by the cooperative principle and all the conversational maxims, especially the maxims of relevance and manner. Eduardo continues to try to follow this profile of the good conversational partner, but with Cheese's second and third utterances, the connection between Cheese's locutionary and illocutionary meanings become unclear. The locutionary meaning stays the same throughout. What the intended meaning might be seems to change with each utterance. At first, it could be a simple declaration of what Cheese happens to like in the world; Eduardo responds in turn by sharing what he likes in the world. The illocutionary meaning drifts away to other realms when Cheese repeats the sentence in a new utterance, and the voice qualities provide ominous overtones to whatever Cheese's meaning is. I highly recommend you try leading a conversation astray like this at some point in your life (for the comic effect it will hopefully create).

the structure of implicature

As you can tell from how the cooperative principle interacts with the maxims and the potential contrasts between locutionary meaning and illocutionary meaning, we do a good bit of work to figure out meaning. The meaning we derive from these different parts of the conversation is called the **conversational implicature**. There are several types of conversational implicature, but we discuss only three types here. The first one, and perhaps the most obvious, is centered on the actual ordering of phrases in sentences, which we can call the **time-order implicature**. When we say a sentence like, "Lily ate lunch and went swimming," the word order of *lunch* before *swimming* implies that one happened before the other: The chronological ordering in the sentence mirrors the chronological ordering of the story. Unless there is some information to the contrary, most of us will understand that Lily's lunch happened before she went swimming.

Figure 9.2 How does this comic from *A Softer World* play with the normal implication of someone saying "Go big or go home"? http://www.asofterworld.com/index.php?id=695. Rollover text: "If you can't stand the heat, turn the A/C on." © Joey Comeau and Emily Horne. asofterworld.com

The next kind of conversational implicature came up earlier, and we can name it now as the **fulcrum implicature**. Like with a see-saw (perhaps teeter-totter in your dialect), the center point allows for one side to rise up, and that fulcrum holds the entire board at its center point. In the following scene, what is implied relies on the maxim of relation for the full meaning to be understood:

On a college campus, a family taking a tour asks a university employee about where they can buy university paraphernalia:

Touring Mom: "Where could we buy a university sweatshirt?"
University Employee: "The student union is two blocks straight that way."
Touring Mom: "Thanks."

The implication is that the student union is a building where sweatshirts can be found for sale. The mom picks up this meaning, relying on the fulcrum implicature, and feels the question has been answered. If the employee actually provided that utterance, and knew that (for some reason) the student union actually did not sell sweatshirts, then most people would consider the employee to be either telling a lie or, at the very least, being quite impolite.

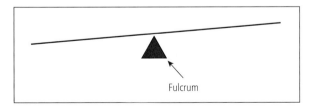

Figure 9.3 The fulcrum supports the lever where one side rises as the other side falls.

The last kind of conversational implicature might be best termed as the **diversion implicature**. For it to work and for the implication to actually get picked up by the audience, the speaker flouts one conversational maxim to supply the implied meaning through another. The word *flout* is not a common word, and it means to openly break a rule, often so others can notice you breaking it. To flout a maxim is to violate with the intent of making the violation noticeable to some audience. Consider the scene below:

A student is just getting back from an early morning organic chemistry class:

Student 1: "How was your o-chem prof?"
Student 2: "He enriched my soul with his well structured monologue."
Student 1: "That must fit well with the 8:00 AM start time."

Here, Student 2's utterance follows the maxims of relevance and quantity, but most likely violates the maxim of quality. The student's review of the organic chemistry professor is so out of line with a normal response, pressing on the maxim of manner, that the only feasible interpretation is to work from the idea that Student 2 is purposefully flouting the maxim of quality. Most likely, the professor rambled without direction from topic to topic. With this diversion implicature, speakers should be aware of how well their audience might tune in to which maxim they are intending to violate. Consider the following scene:

Two teenage friends randomly meet at the mall after one of the friends took an eight-year-old boy she is babysitting to a kid's action movie:

Friend 1: "What are you two up to?"
Friend 2: "We went to go see that new kids' movie."
Friend 1: "How was it?"
Friend 2: "It had sound and lights."
Boy: "Lots of explosions and big flashes and cars and crashing planes!"
Friend 1: "Good!"

The two friends are on a different wavelength of understanding than the eight-year-old boy. Friend 2 uses these differences in the audiences to make the diversion implicature work to satisfy both audiences and get her point across. With the utterance, "It had sound and lights," Friend 2 addresses the maxims of relevance, quality, and manner, but purposefully flouts the maxim of quantity: Informing the other friend that a movie had sound and lights is vastly undershooting the information given in a regular, casual review.

By employing the diversion implicature and sacrificing the maxim of quantity, it highlights the information that is not being said out loud, such as criticism on the quality of the plot or the acting. The young boy does not pick up on his babysitter's diversion implicature and interprets the utterance "It had sounds and lights" as an opportunity to enthusiastically expand further on the topic with exactly what was in those sounds and lights. The babysitting Friend 2 was able to successfully negotiate the conversation without being verbose because she knew how to play one meaning to one particular audience while playing another to a different audience. This kind of conversational work is what we all do, whether we reflect on our meaning making or not. In addition, as you may have noticed, some people are more adept at it than others.

Word Play: Fun with words

Here is another worth-while scene you should find in a video clip from *Foster's Home for Imaginary Friends*:

Scene: Bloo is an imaginary friend at Madame Foster's home, and Mac is his creator. Bloo and Mac are arguing about Bloo's supposedly new little brother, Cheese. Both are standing in the kitchen with Cheese. Mac is trying to get Bloo back into a good mood. Rather than staying away, Cheese keeps popping up between them.

Mac: "I have to take responsibility for him. It is only fair."
Bloo: "Figures."
Cheese: "I'm a cowboy."
Mac: "Look Bloo, things won't be any different. I promise."
Bloo: "Huh!"
Cheese: "Here's my horsee!" {Showing a toy purple rocking horse}
Mac: "Come on. Didn't you want to make that go-cart today? You've been talking about it all week."
Cheese: {Makes utterances of horse-galloping sounds and pistols shooting while pretending the horse is riding on Bloo's head}
Bloo: "Get out of here!"

In this scene, Mac is trying to appease Bloo and get him in a better mood. Cheese is neither engaging in their conversation, nor avoiding their conversation, nor starting a new conversation. He is simply making utterances. As with other kinds of humor, this contrast is stark enough to make people laugh. The contrast is between the expectations of the maxims of relevance and the cooperative principle and Cheese's actual utterances.

direct and indirect: getting the job done

When we do speech acts, such as requesting, demanding, or making a joke, all of us can choose a more straightforward approach or a more disguised strategy. If you are eating dinner with your family, you could say, "Pass me the salt," with the straightforward, imperative meaning of *pass me the salt*. For that kind of utterance, the illocutionary meaning matches the locutionary meaning, and when this happens it is called a **direct speech act**. Different people and different cultures have widely divergent opinions on the value of direct speech acts in certain contexts. In some social circles in England and the US South, direct speech acts are seen as rude. For natives of New York City, direct speech acts are seen as honest. Although not quite like lexical items, the discourse choice of a direct speech act is associated with social meaning because there was an alternative choice.

The other choice also involves locutionary and illocutionary meanings. Consider the same dinner-table scene: If at the table, you say, "Are you done with the salt?" with the intent of *pass me the salt*, the locutionary meaning does not match the illocutionary meaning. The literal *translation* of this utterance, the locutionary meaning, focuses on whether the salt-user has finished using the salt, but it goes no further and makes no demand concerning the speaker's potential future use of the salt. This kind is called an **indirect speech act** because the locutionary meaning does not match the illocutionary meaning. There are semantic degrees where some locutionary meanings match slightly more closely than other sets of meanings, but we maintain a binary label. It is important for you to realize that direct and indirect speech acts are choices speakers make in setting up and maintaining their relationships with others. Whether those choices are conscious or not is a question beyond the scope of this book. As we address politeness later in this chapter, these kinds of choices become important.

Words to the Wise: Interpreting indirect questions

Imagine if your boss asks you the following question at a future job: "Would you be able to finish this report by the end of the day?" Before you ever get to the report, you have to do some work to figure out the boss's intent. Is the boss laying out a work-plan and wanting to know where your report falls on the time line? Is the request really a command to finish the report by the end of the day?

Deborah Cameron (1998) argues that the use of indirect questions like these is guided by power relations, including those of gender and social status. With the workplace question from above, Cameron would argue that the boss is making a command, not asking an informational question. By making the command this way, we can tell that the boss assumes a certain level of authority. If the employee does not take up the interpretation of 'command,' but instead provides a yes/no answer such as "Yes, I would," then the employee is not granting the boss as much authority as the boss would like.

Cameron illustrates this interpretation of power and authority in indirect questions with a scene from a family dinner table: A husband asks a wife, "Is there any ketchup?" What is your interpretation of this question?

How could the interpretation of these questions vary?

Check out the difference between direct and indirect speech acts in these utterances below:

A brother who is moving out of the house makes a request of his sister who is watching TV:

Brother: "Grab the other end of this bookcase."
Sister: "Nope."

Here the brother went with the direct speech act. For this method to work, the brother would need to rely on either whatever authority he might have, or on sibling solidarity in order to compel his sister to comply. Contrast that with the indirect speech act in this version:

Brother: "Might my sweet sister be the best sister ever on her brother's last day in the house?"
Sister: "Ugh. Sure."

With the indirect speech act, the brother is not telling the sister to do anything, but he is letting it be known that he needs help and that he would really appreciate it. He is not asserting authority over her, but instead, he is appealing to her with a different rhetorical tactic. The sentence's only conjugated verb is *might*, allowing for possibility from the start. In the previous example the conjugated verb is *grab*. The difference highlights the contrast between command and request. Which tactic works better depends on how the two of them have negotiated their conversations over the years.

a special kind of verb: performative speech acts with performative verbs

With all of the meanings above, the different kinds of implicatures and speech acts, there were no restrictions in the smaller parts of language. Any utterance will have a locutionary, illocutionary, and perlocutionary component within a context. One specialized kind of utterance does have a specific requirement. A **performative speech act** is when uttering the words completes the action of the speech act. Making the utterance is the performance of the act. This is a specialized speech act because it requires a **performative verb**, such as *promise, damn, pronounce, christen,* and *sentence* (legal). As you might guess from this list, some performative speech acts are more common, such as these:

- I *promise* to come home on time.
- I *apologize* for riding my bike over your foot.
- I *accept* your apology.
- I *bet* you I can do it again.
- I *quit*.

Some performative speech acts might only be uttered in your immediate presence more rarely:

- *I hereby <u>pronounce</u> you man and wife.*
- *I <u>sentence</u> you to two years with no parole.*
- *I <u>christen</u> this ship Slocum.*
- *This meeting is hereby <u>adjourned</u>.*

The performative verbs are underlined in these examples, and as you should note, the subject is always first-person singular, except for the last example. The *doing* of the performative speech act must come from the speaker. The act of promising does not come from a third-person narrative point of view. A statement like, "He promises to come home on time," does not a promise make. The person making the promise has to utter the verb with non-past tense to make a performative speech act. The last example is a version of *I hereby <u>adjourn</u> this*

Figure 9.4   What do performative verbs do? T-Rex tries to explain in *Dinosaur Comics*: http://www .qwantz.com/index.php?comic=1262. Rollover text: "more accurately, t-rex would have easily won if he'd made the argument before the invention of written language. but then the punchline doesn't work! you can't just build the hms sinkytowne out of words!!" *Dinosaur Comics* by Ryan North. www .dinosaurcomics.com

meeting. Note that *hereby* is a good litmus test of the performative status of these sentences. The performative speech act is also dear to all fans of fantasy fiction. When a witch utters the right magic words and fire shoots from the ground, we can classify those words as a performative speech act. When Hermione Granger demonstrates the spell for levitation, she utters *Wingardium Leviosa*, words which actually make the action happen. Humans have been trying to make this kind of performative speech act happen for probably as long as we could utter words. Magic spells would be the ultimate performative verbs. And note that they are called *spells* to indicate the importance of language in the magic.

discourse markers

With many of the utterances people produce, there has to be some regulation to the flow of words, something like road signs controlling the flow of traffic. Few conversations are pre-thought-out, and we have to manage other people's attention as well as the topics and their rhetorical appeal. The attention which other people give to the speaker is called the **floor**. This term is one of several in this chapter where the popular understanding of the term overlaps nicely with its academic meaning. If someone has the floor while speaking, the other people should assume their role as audience and listen, even if they themselves were speaking previously. Not recognizing who has the floor is one of the areas where children generally fail compared to adults. Yet, there are also plenty of people who pay more attention to what they themselves are about to say than to the speaker who has the floor.

One of the tools at our disposal as we manage conversations is the **discourse marker**. As Fraser (1999) describes it, discourse markers are lexical items usually from the categories of conjunctions (e.g. *and, but*), adverbials (e.g. *consequently, therefore*), and prepositional phrases (e.g. *as a consequence, in particular*); discourse markers show a relationship between what has already been said and what is about to be said. They often direct the conversation like road signs, telling people to yield, stop, or merge in a lane. Consider this scene at a political fundraiser:

Supporter 1: "If we cut taxes any more, <u>well</u>, it will be a big problem for the budget."
Supporter 2: "<u>Actually</u>, sales taxes are steadily on the rise."

The underlined words function as discourse markers here. They provide some regular meaning to the phrases as sentences, but as utterances in context, they indicate that the speakers are about to speak more, that another utterance is to follow. Many different words and phrases can function as discourse markers, including *while, for example, however, and another thing*, and *actually*. Normally, discourse markers can be considered outside the boundary of the syntactic structure of the sentence. They are part of the order of the conversation, but they are not necessarily hierarchically embedded within the syntactic structure of a sentence.

In Canada, the expression *eh* can be used as a discourse marker, signaling either the end of a speaker's utterance or the turn all together. It is also a marker of communal agreement. One discourse marker that triggers a great deal of angst across all of North America is **discourse *like***. Discourse *like* involves inserting the word *like* into utterances for possibly many different purposes:

- With an example: *I normally get <u>like</u> a grilled chicken sandwich.*
- To give an approximate estimate: *We were headed out at <u>like</u> 7:00.*
- To link discourse topics: *This guy used to be a slob, and <u>like</u>, he is totally cleaned up.*
- To mark new information: *And <u>like</u>, the sheriff turned out to be his mom.*
- As a hesitation: *And after the meteorite, <u>like</u>, a lot of things happened.*

People can also use discourse *like*, and other words, when marking the start of their turn with no intent of adding meaning to the turn, but simply sign-posting where the turn starts. The hesitation role might seem like a completely insignificant part, but people use **fillers** to hold the floor in what otherwise would be silence while their mental grammar catches up with where they were headed in the conversation. For all the different discourse purposes, people will find lexical items to fill those slots. If discourse *like* truly becomes detested by everyone, a doubtful prospect, then people will find other words to take its place.

discourse scripts

When actors learn their lines for a movie, there is a script that provides words, but it also provides a routine for where to be and what to do. In our real lives, everyone develops scripts as part of living in society. **Discourse scripts** are just like lines for a play or movie. They direct us where to stand, when to wait, when to talk, what kinds of question to expect, and what the normal range of our response is expected to be. We learn them through repetition, and we are (slightly) surprised when we have to deviate from them. When we enter a restaurant where there is waitstaff and a hostess, if we have been through that kind of experience before, we know there is a routine: We enter; we are greeted; we inform someone, probably the hostess, of how many are in our party; we eventually get seated. Then we work through a routine for ordering: We are greeted by waitstaff, asked about drink orders, told about specials, and asked about food orders.

Many people in service industries have discourse scripts as part of their regular duties, and some of these are dictated by corporate policies. Once when I was in a serving-line behind two others in a university town, the person serving the food was a manager of the restaurant and greeted each customer in a friendly tone with some kind of address form before serving the burritos. The manager greeted the first fellow with "Hey buddy, wha'cha need," the second fellow with "S'up man, what're you hungry for," and me with "Sir, what could we serve you today?" With the first two greetings, the manager built camaraderie and socially informal greetings. With the third customer (me), the manager show heightened respect by building social deference {although all I could think was, "Wow, I am old as dirt"}. In all three, the manager was following a discourse script with variables to be determined by the addressee.

In most of these kinds of encounters, we pay little attention to the conversation itself. One of the difficult things about experiencing other cultures is that discourse scripts can differ. Some cultures might require short responses with no eye contact for ordering food, while others might require more personal greetings.

politeness

Although a discussion on politeness might appear better suited for a book about manners, utterances and politeness both rely on context. What we do with our language makes that context come to life, and our words are either threatening or comforting. The study of politeness is a cross-cultural field, as some of the most fascinating and revealing discoveries have been about the wide range of human behavior. Even within similar contexts, such as universities, different cultures treat language politeness differently. As Meyerhoff (2011:89) notes, students in Japan attach an honorific suffix -*sensei* to the teacher's last name. In Germany, university students address professors by their full academic titles: *Professor Doktor Schneider*. Contrast this level of expected formal politeness with US universities, where university professors regularly go by their first names. Although I leave it up to my students, and some do opt for Dr. Hazen, most of my students feel comfortable calling me Kirk. How can these three different strategies all work? With the Japanese and German approach, the formal titles put more social distance between the student and the teacher, and both sides feel comfortable with this social distance. With the first-name approach, both sides feel comfortable by building social ties of acceptance.

One of the ways we develop relationships in conversations is by manipulating what is called **face**. Like the term *floor*, several English-speaking cultures use a term *face* with a similar meaning to what we have here. If two boys are playing basketball, one player might taunt another player after a successful move with, "In your face!" Here, *face* means the realm of personal value you hold in the context of society. It is your social dignity and social prestige. You want to save face and not have others impinge on it. It is generally useful to distinguish between two kinds of face: positive face and negative face.

The descriptors of *positive* and *negative* are not about good or bad, but instead, they refer to desires everyone has. **Positive face** is the desire to be approved of by others and to be liked and admired. The following is a scene where the first speaker's positive face is addressed:

Speaker 1: "Hey Kevin."
Speaker 2: "Ross! Good to see you. How have you been?"

How is Speaker 1's positive face addressed? By respecting his prestige and his social persona, Speaker 2 is showing interest in Speaker 1. By attending to the speaker's positive face, many cultures view the act as polite and the proper thing to do (depending on social hierarchies). Consider the difference if Speaker 2 had *ignored* Speaker 1's initial engagement. Speaker 1's positive face would be threatened by the lack of recognition and affirmation.

To turn the other cheek, there is another kind of face useful for understanding how we manage discourse. The concept of **negative face** is our desire not to be impeded in what we do. With negative face, that desire triggers all kinds of **repairs** in conversations. Repairs are when we try to fix situations where we have impinged upon someone's negative face. Consider when you are walking down the street, headed to class. You are trying to get somewhere, but if someone stops you trying to catch your attention, you are being impeded.

You: [walking that walk]
Stranger: "Excuse me, could you tell me the time?"
You: [tells the time]

The stranger uses two strategies to lessen the impact on your negative face, thus repairing the conversation. Can you figure out what they are? Both involve social position through language, and in this particular case, the stranger is choosing a position less powerful than you. The stranger wants information from you and has to impose upon you to get that information. The first language strategy is for the stranger to ask for you to pardon the intrusion for threatening your negative face. Although the "excuse me" is in the form of an imperative command, it is functioning as a discourse marker to initiate a conversation. The second strategy is more subtle but probably equally effective. The stranger uses an indirect question. Note that the answer to the locutionary meaning of "could you tell me the time" is either *yes* or *no*, but the best assumption is that the speaker wants to be told the time. By using an indirect question, the stranger recognizes the social order of this small scene. The stranger is not in a position of power (teacher over student; boss over employee) and is unable to command you to tell the time. The stranger has to cajole it out of you.

With both positive and negative face, people in conversations are busy negotiating face-threatening acts. Some of these can be more mild while others can be more severe. Either the speaker or the audience could be challenged with a face-threatening act. For the listeners, the face-threatening act could be any kind of disagreement or criticism: If your teacher tells you that your personal essay "lacked detail," that utterance hits upon your positive face. If your friend says to you from the couch, "Get me a bowl of ice cream," that utterance hits upon your negative face by restricting your future actions: You have to choose to ignore, refuse, or accept the request.

Face threatening acts can also can affect *the speaker's* positive and negative face. Either on the large scale political world or in your romantic relationships, making an apology can be difficult. Why is it difficult? Certainly, utterances like "I'm sorry" and "I made a mistake" are not taxing in terms of syllables and morphemic boundaries. However, to make an apology to an audience, the speaker must reveal faults, imposing on the speaker's positive face. An apology might be the first step on the road to redemption, but it does require a hit to the speaker's public persona.

A speaker's negative face can also be threatened, but most people consider these kinds of threats to be much less damaging. Consider a scene where friends have taken you to the airport instead of you driving and paying for parking. As you get out of the car, you thank them for driving you: "I really appreciate you taking the time to drive me. Thank you." It may not seem like much, but you were socially obligated to thank your friends because you owed them at least that much attention. Contrast that social context with hiring a taxi to take you to the airport: You might say "thanks" to the driver, but you are also paying the driver and have little social obligation beyond making the proper payment. You are not paying your friends because they are doing you a favor, and you have picked up a social obligation. These are not grand slaps in the face, but they are small ways in which utterances and their contexts affect us. The system of face allows for the accounting of these relationships.

communicative competence

With the interplay of locutionary and illocutionary meanings, the choice of direct or indirect speech acts, the deployment of discourse markers, and the management of face, we do a lot of work in every conversation. Yet, rarely do we notice any of these features unless something goes wrong. Doing them does not usually feel like work. Part of the reason we barely notice all the conversational choices we make is because those choices are tightly ingrained in our mind. Think back to earlier chapters where we explored the structure of sounds, syllables, morphemes, and phrases. You most likely had never pondered the structure of these language units before reading those chapters, but with some focused attention, you were able to figure out layers of language knowledge in your mind. That knowledge is called **grammatical competence**. Grammatical competence encompasses all the knowledge in our mental grammar. With the relationships above the level of the phrase, the knowledge we have is called **communicative competence**. Although we of course must learn the community-specific rituals, scripts, levels of direct speech acts, and specific discourse markers, the need to manage conversations with all of these tools is part of every human culture. Developing communicative competence is part of what growing children do with language.

As a basic metaphor, we can view the difference between communicative and grammatical competence as the difference between our cultural knowledge of food and drink vs. our knowledge of digestion (knowledge in the sense that our body knows how to digest food and transfer water and nutrition).

variation in conversation

In conversation, speakers have many different parts to use and discourse markers to order them. Some of these end up as social trends. The evolution of discourse *like*, and quotative *be like* is an especially prominent social trend over the last 20 years. To be clear about the different parts here, the verb *to like*, as in *I like chocolate*, has always been a different word from comparative *like*, as in *She sat like Patience on a monument* (Shakespeare, *Twelfth Night*, 2.4.116). The comparative *like* came from an Old English adjective which also yielded *alike*, as in *these two are alike*. The evolution of discourse *like*, used as a discourse marker or filler, follows the comparative *like* lineage, as does the recent surge of quotative *be like*, as in *He was like, "Hey guys, watch this."* Similar to discourse *like*, quotative *be like* has proliferated greatly over the last few decades, and it has spread around the English-speaking globe.

Quotative *be like* has taken over from quotative *said*, as in *She said, "We will wait till tomorrow,"* in most English-speaking communities. Two researchers, Buchstaller and D'Arcy (2009), investigated quotative *be like* as a difference in conversational discourse between English, US, and New Zealand speakers. Although the trend in the United States is that middle-class females use quotative *be like* more often than males, they found that in England working-class men used quotative *be like* most often, whereas in New Zealand, middle-class men used it most often. This form is being exported from the United States to all over the world, but the social qualities attached to it by the adopting country vary. For an overview of the extensive reach of quotative *be like*, see Buchstaller (2014).

Social variation with discourse markers also arises for ethnic divisions. Lisa Green (2002:138) details different discourse strategies found in African American communities in the United States. One discourse script is called "playing the dozens," an event where two people in the same social circle dual with exaggerated claims about each other. Some examples Green cites from games of playing the dozens are the following:

"Your mother is so stupid, she thought a lawsuit was something you wear to court."
"Your mother is so old, she took her driving test on a dinosaur."

The discourse script of playing the dozens sets the two players at odds but builds a closer relationship between them by doing so. In addition, the wider audience for playing the dozens evaluates who the winner is, and this activity helps build the community through discourse. Other discourse strategies in African American communities include *loud talking*, where a line immediately intended for a nearby audience is spoken loudly enough for others to simultaneously hear. All social groups build their own discourse strategies, and ethnic divisions allow us to view their different paths.

Another realm of social variation is the different address forms used to label women and men. The most basic form for men is *Mr.*, but for women, there are traditionally two forms: *Miss* and *Mrs.*, with the latter going to mark married women. The address forms followed conventions, at least in the United States and a few other English-speaking cultures, where women were traditionally identified with their husband's names: *Mr. and Mrs. Stephen Kenton Snogglesworth*. As that system of renaming married women fell apart starting at the end of the 1800s, the confusion of the two titles for women helped to create a third title, *Ms.* As the *Oxford English Dictionary* records, this form was introduced in a 1901 Springfield, Massachusetts newspaper in this way:

> "The abbreviation 'Ms.' is simple, it is easy to write, and the person concerned can translate it properly according to circumstances. For oral use it might be rendered as 'Mizz,' which would be a close parallel to the practice long universal in many bucolic regions, where a slurred Mis' does duty for Miss and Mrs. alike."

Rarely do new forms of address, or any lexical item, get a direct written introduction. From the earlier discussion of politeness, you might be able to see that *Ms.* does not impose on the listener's negative face as does *Miss* or *Mrs.*, in that *Ms.* does not foreground the listener's marital status (which used to be an indicator of social status).

Words to the wise: The changing use of Ms.

According to Janet Fuller (2005), the term *Ms.* was used in the 1930s through the 1950s in business but never extensively replaced *Miss* or *Mrs.* Fuller notes that people could hold a two way distinction between grown-up females and males with *Ms.* and *Mr.* or a three-way distinction between *Miss* (young female), *Mrs.* (married female), and *Ms.* (grown-up, unmarried female). The traditional model is also still an option, where *Mrs./Miss* mark marital distinction only.

Fuller finds that education correlates with the use of *Ms.* She surveyed faculty and students at a Midwestern US university and found that those respondents with a doctorate were most likely to use *Ms.* It appears they use the term as a neutral (and safe) form of address. This safe, social use of *Ms.* was not common for one particular group: The ones who used it the least were the college-age female respondents. Fuller also found that women who defy traditional gender roles also were identified as *Ms.* more often.

A more recent change to discourse and the realm of politeness is the absence of context with certain kinds of communication. Consider texting over mobile phones, where the context is not always clear. In addition, the input for mobile phones is somewhat limiting, restricting people from always reaching the full maxim of quantity (leaving out explanations). The following exchange is a good example (from apocryphal stories on the internet):

Sent Text: "So Steve do you want to do it at your house or at mine?"

This text was meant for her baking buddy [as in actual cakes (Steve)], but the person who received it was her boyfriend.

Boyfriend's Response: "i cnt believe your cheating on me and your doing this on my birthday"

Here, the context of the text message is open to interpretation, and the boyfriend interpreted "do it" as sex, rather than the intended "bake a birthday cake." With *it* and its deixis, context is crucial. Text messages negate most contextual understanding. Note that the conversational principle and maxims still play a role in text messaging, but the lack of a clear context is not helping anyone out.

There are also the more direct mistakes of inputting text, not to mention autocorrect, which disturb many messages. Consider this text I once received: "what should expect u." Is that "what do you expect" or "what should you expect" or "when should we expect you"? After some other texting, it turns out it was a question of time, but the maxims of quantity and manner were getting slapped around with the first message. The importance of context and maintaining the conversational maxims applies to modern forms of communication as well as to others. At times we all forget to consider the pragmatic implications of what we write or say, but the same ground rules from this chapter apply to all those conversations.

chapter summary

This chapter explored the patterns humans create in flocks of phrases. The general realm for these flocks of phrases is called discourse, and the most basic unit of discourse is called the utterance. An utterance must have a context, which makes it different from the previous units of language we have studied, such as words and phrases. It is the interaction between the context and the language parts that creates meaning in the minds of the audience. The knowledge people use to maneuvre through a conversation is called communicative competence. Part of the knowledge we use is based on the cooperative principle, a baseline which allows us to meaningfully cooperate (or not) in a conversation. From such a foundation, we work with or against conversational maxims to create meaning. Each utterance we produce has a locutionary and illocutionary meaning along with some perlocutionary effect. These meanings can be foregrounded through direct speech acts, where the locutionary matches the illocutionary meaning, or indirect speech acts, where the locutionary does not match the illocutionary meaning. Some verbs are considered performative verbs when used in performative speech acts (e.g. *I promise*). As we juggle all those parts and meanings, we manage discourse with speakers' turns on the conversational floor and often signal our turns with discourse markers, such as discourse *like*. We also negotiate the social realm directly through the linguistic creation of politeness while we tend to speakers' and listeners' positive face and negative face. All of these parts play a role in our regular conversations.

key concepts

- Communicative competence
- Conversational implicature
- Conversational maxims
- Cooperative principle
- Deixis
- Direct speech act
- Discourse
- Discourse *like*
- Discourse marker
- Discourse scripts
- Diversion implicature
- Face
- Filler
- Floor
- Fulcrum implicature
- Grammatical competence
- Illocutionary
- Indirect speech act
- Locutionary
- Maxim of manner
- Maxim of quality
- Maxim of quantity
- Maxim of relation
- Negative face
- Non sequitur
- Performative speech act
- Performative verb
- Perlocutionary effect
- Positive face
- Pragmatic knowledge
- Repairs
- Situational context
- Social context

- Speech act
- Time-order implicature
- Utterances

references

Cameron, D. (1998) "'Is there any ketchup, Vera?': Gender, power and pragmatics." *Discourse & Society 9*, no. 4: 437–455.

Fraser, B. (1999) "What are discourse markers?." *Journal of Pragmatics 31*, no. 7: 931–952.

Fuller, J.M. (2005) "The uses and meanings of the female title Ms." *American Speech 80*, no. 2: 180–206.

Meyerhoff, M. (2013) *Introducing Sociolinguistics*. Taylor & Francis.

further reading

Introduction to Pragmatics. Betty J. Birner. 2012. Wiley Blackwell.

This book helps students find their way through the field of pragmatics. It focuses on the boundaries between meaning and pragmatics to show how important context is in human language. Although this book covers the foundation of pragmatics, it also explores new approaches, including those for Grice's conversational maxims.

Susan Ehrlich, Miriam Meyerhoff, and Janet Holmes (eds.). 2014. *The Handbook of Language, Gender, and Sexuality*, 2nd edition. Wiley Blackwell.

The study of language and gender is not a single field with a single methodology, but the study of discourse does play an important role in the study of language and gender. This handbook is the best place to find the many different ways to study the discourse of gender. This book is a collection of overviews by leading scholars. Accordingly, it has breadth of the entire field of study, as well as detailed examples of research.

The Handbook of Discourse Analysis. Deborah Schiffrin, Deborah Tannen, and Heidi E. Hamilton. 2003. Blackwell.

This book provides a full overview of the many different topics analyzed using discourse analysis. Various ways of analyzing discourse exist, and this book brings together scholars from those approaches to illustrate diverse sets of data, from literary texts to political speeches. For students interested in discourse analysis, this book provides a good glimpse of what is possible.

exercises

individual work

1. Label the maxim(s) violated in each of the following **bolded utterances**:
   a. Suffering from a bout of homesickness at summer camp, the young girl tells her counselor, **"I'm fine,"** before bursting out into tears.

    b.   At the check point, the state trooper asks the drunken motorist for his driver's license, and the motorist responds, **"I like your badge."**

    c.   While searching in the auto-parts store, a confused-looking man asks where the spark-plugs are located, and the clerk answers, **"On a shelf."**

2. For the following utterances and contexts, consider what interpretable meanings can be derived from them:

    a.   A student writes in an email, "I want to meet with you some time soon," and the instructor replies, "I should be in starting late next week."

    b.   On the first day of class, the instructor asks, "How many of you are taking this class again?"

    c.   On the first day of class, the instructor says while looking at the students, "So many familiar faces."

    d.   As the high schooler bounces excitedly into the house, Mom asks what happened on her date, and the she responds, **"OK"**, before dashing into her room.

    e.   You are asking for driving directions from a stranger in a gas station. He responds by saying, **"To make lasagna…"** and proceeds to provide you with a full recipe.

3. For the following scene, please **provide** an utterance and clearly **identify** the **situational context**, the **social context**, the locutionary and illocutionary meanings, and the perlocutionary effect. Also decide whether it is a direct or indirect speech act:

    In a clothing store where several customers are shopping, a sales clerk wants to ask one family to keep their children more quiet. What does the sales clerk say?

    Utterance:
    Context:
    Locutionary:
    Illocutionary:
    Perlocutionary:
    Direct or indirect speech act?

4. For the following scene, please **provide** an utterance and clearly **identify** the situational context, the social context, the locutionary and illocutionary meanings, and the perlocutionary effect. Also decide whether it is a direct or indirect speech act:

    In a classroom where students are taking a test, a professor wants to warn a student about cheating without pointing out that student individually. What does the professor say to the entire class?

Utterance:
Context:
Locutionary:
Illocutionary:
Perlocutionary:
Direct or indirect speech act?

group work

5. Develop at least three scenes where people use the discourse marker *well*. Each scene should prompt a different meaning of *well*. Brainstorm what those meanings might include. Be prepared to act them out in front of the class and to have the rest of the class figure out what those meanings are. Does your group have other discourse markers that are associated with as many different meanings as *well*?

6. Survey your group about whether their use of the word *right* is usually positive, ironic, or suggestive? Do people in your group use all three meanings, and would they use them all in the same context?

    Positive would be when you mean basically *yes*:
    Friend says: "I should serve you more ice cream?"
    You say: "Right."

    Ironic meaning is when you basically mean *no*:
    Friend says: "I am sure you want another piece of mince-meat pie."
    You say: "Riiiight."

    Suggestive meaning is when you are trying to get agreement, possibly another echoed *right*, out of someone else:
    You say: "You should to stop by to see your parents, right?"
    Friend says: "Yes."

7. Make a turn-by-turn analysis of the *Who's on First* skit. What meanings are at play as they move from position to position? How does the humor get created? If possible, view one of the original renditions by Abbott and Costello online.

8. Develop skits to break Grice's maxims. Perform the skits, but do not tell the others in your class which maxims you are violating. They must guess.

9. Personal scenes: Describe your most memorable moment of you being misunderstood? What was the language breakdown?

10. For the following scene, please read the utterance provided and clearly **identify** the situational context, the social context, as well as the locutionary, illocutionary, and perlocutionary qualities. Also, identify whether the utterance is a direct or indirect speech act:

   In line at the local coffee shop, a nonregular customer, who doesn't see the small line, steps directly up to the counter to be served. The clerk behind the counter says the following:

   Utterance: "These people were here before you."
   Context:
   Locutionary:
   Illocutionary:
   Perlocutionary:
   Direct or Indirect Speech Act?

study questions

1. How are utterances different from sentences?
2. How do utterances get their meaning?
3. What principle guides conversations?
4. What maxim asks speakers to tell the truth?
5. What maxim asks speakers to provide just the right amount of information?
6. What maxim asks speakers to present information clearly?
7. What maxim asks speakers to present information connected to the point?
8. What are the two levels of utterance meaning, and how are they different from each other?
9. How does the perlocutionary effect come about?
10. How do speakers use implications to get meanings across?
11. How are the three types of conversational implicature different from each other?
12. How does a direct speech act involve locutionary meaning?
13. How does an indirect speech act involve illocutionary meaning?
14. How is a performative speech act different from other kinds of speech acts?
15. What is the conversational floor?
16. In what ways do speakers use discourse markers?
17. What kinds of discourse scripts do you follow on a regular basis?
18. In terms of language study, what is politeness?

19. How is the social concept of face connected to language?
20. How can positive face be affected by language?
21. How can negative face be affected by language?
22. How is communicative competence similar to grammatical competence?
23. How is it different?

Visit the book's companion website for additional resources relating to this chapter at: http://www.wiley.com/go/hazen/introlanguage

10 The Winding Paths of Language in Education

An Introduction to Language, First Edition. Kirk Hazen.
© 2015 John Wiley & Sons, Inc. Published 2015 by John Wiley & Sons, Inc.

chapter overview

The previous chapters have explained how language works. For the most part, we toured the skills and knowledge people have in their heads. This chapter helps us understand how our language is treated in formal education, and how it could be used in the future. You probably remember times where teachers subjected you to "grammar" lessons. Why did they do that? By comparing teaching about language to the teaching of other subjects, this chapter illuminates basic assumptions and goals of formal language education, including those "grammar" lessons. With those goals in mind, we consider different approaches to teaching about language, including prescriptive and rhetorical approaches. We also turn to the spectre of correct English, sightings of it in the wild, and its connection with what actually gets taught, genre conventions. With the importance placed upon literacy in our modern world, knowledge of genre conventions are a central educational goal. This goal can be best achieved in an education that accurately explains how language works. All of us will keep our prescriptive pet peeves (e.g. how many commas in a list, prepositions at the end of sentences,...), but by the end of this chapter, you get to keep them in a larger perspective. In sum, this chapter explains how a rhetorical perspective can accomplish all the beneficial educational goals while fostering a better understanding of human language.

language in education

comparing different kinds of classes

Ponder the difference between a high-school biology class and a high-school English class. Despite both being topics in secondary schools, biology and English have some important differences in how they are taught. Biology is an academic field where researchers investigate life. To teach biology means to teach about how life works, but think about what it means to teach English. The secondary-school topic of English is a mash-up of different areas of scholarship and cultural history. There are academic fields within it, such as literary studies and composition. The topics of the English classroom are a mixed bag. In biology classes, students learn about the processes within and between organisms that result in life. Students study how the human digestive system converts food into energy or about the foraging trips of the King Penguin (who repeatedly makes deep dives in search of fish). In English classes in secondary schools, students learn literature such as allegorical fables of totalitarian governments (Orwell's *Animal Farm*) or composition skills such as how to write a five-paragraph essay. One side of the English language classroom is cultural, and the other side is about building skills within certain genres (e.g.

formal academic writing/poetry/drama). Yet in English classrooms, students rarely learn about how language actually works.

Consider this comparison: English courses are like physical education (PE or gym) courses. In PE, students learn different sports, including their rules. They practice their athletic skills while participating in those sports, such as football, ultimate Frisbee, or netball. In English classes, students learn different genres of writing, including their rules, and they practice their writing skills while participating in those genres, such as fiction, poetry, or business writing. In PE classes, students might play football for a few weeks and work on volleyball for the next few weeks. To learn these sports, students need to know the positions, the rules, and the strategies for success. Importantly, they need time to practice. In English classes, students might study drama for a few weeks and work on poetry for the next few weeks. To learn these genres the students need to know the parts, the **genre conventions**, and the successful models. Just like sports, the skills of writing and reading improve with practice. Imagine how hard it would be to learn about how to write an essay only by reading directions. There are genre conventions for every kind of writing. Here is an *xkcd* comic about road writing: http://xkcd.com/781/.

In English classes, you learn culturally invented genres with a culturally invented technology (writing), and you improve your writing skills through practice. Now, contrast a PE class with a biology class. In PE, you learn culturally invented sports and improve your athletic skills through the practice of those sports. In a biology class, you learn about naturally developed biological systems, be they separate organisms, organs, or individual cells. You do not practice with your biological systems. Imagine how wacky it would be to sit in a biology class, willing your central nervous system to relay signals faster or slower from your hand to your brain. Instead, you learn about how those signals actually get transferred. Linguistic classes in college work much the same way as biology classes: You learn about how language works.

Anybody who talks about language, including English teachers, should know about how language works. Imagine if a PE teacher did not know the basics of the human body, including why people sweat and the importance of hydration: "Quit sweating! And no water breaks." It would be like an English teacher not knowing why people have different pronunciations for spellings like <ea> (e.g. *great*, *meat*) or dative alternation between direct and indirect objects (e.g. *pass me the ball; pass the ball to me*).

After working through this book, you should know that language and writing are not the same thing. You also should know many of the qualities of language. Unfortunately, the modern state of linguistic knowledge for most people, at least in the United States, is about where the state of biological knowledge was around the end of the nineteenth century: We are just getting past the days of bloodletting. The goal of this chapter is to help us better understand how language knowledge can be used in education.

correct English

At my university, we had an accomplished teacher of British literature who would carefully mark her students' essays with a red pencil, checking for what she called "grammatical rules" (what we call *genre conventions*). She would allow students to redo essays when they wanted to improve their grades, but only if the students first corrected all their violations on a separate sheet of paper and cited the appropriate usage rule in the class's handbook. This situation involves a teacher who dedicated extra time for her students and helped lead them to better understanding of formal writing through the best avenues of motivation available. The points she emphasized are that genre conventions are important, and writers should adhere to these conventions to fulfill their rhetorical goals.

Having taught 27 college composition courses, I fully agree that genre conventions need to be followed to fulfill rhetorical goals. Yet because the chimera of correct English is sure to arise when talking about the role of language in education, it is best to address that topic directly. To do so, we must explore assumptions about correct English and the general desire people have to judge others, including their language. In commenting that a segment of talk or writing is good or correct, people might come from the **Prescriptively Correct Perspective**.

Here are some basic assumptions of the Prescriptively Correct Perspective (PCP):[1]

a.   Some forms of the language always work better (linguistically) than other forms of the language. For example, *She is not home today* always works better than *She ain't home today*.
b.   The correct form was chosen because it works better at all times.
c.   The correct form of today should be protected from corrupting influences that would cause decay.
d.   The correct form of today has already been corrupted by modern slovenly thinking and should be reformed to the standards of yesteryear.

The other approach is the **Rhetorically Correct Perspective**.

Rhetorically Correct Perspective (RCP) is associated with the following assumptions:

e.   Some forms of the language work better in certain contexts than other forms. For example, *She ain't home today* will work better than *She is not home today* in some contexts. As the context changes, so does the most rhetorically-appropriate form.
f.   No single set of standards exists to judge language production. Language production is judged by the rhetoric of the situation – the interplay of the agent's intention, the audience, and the message.
g.   The best form for any particular context will necessarily change because change is part of human language.
h.   The best form for any particular context will most likely be different from the best form of years past, but in no way can it be linguistically superior.

The Rhetorically Correct Perspective puts the emphasis on the social process of judgment and works better with our modern knowledge of language. These two perspectives are different from judging whether or not a phrase fits the descriptive grammar of a language: In English, *me griffin tree staring is the that in at* is a descriptively ungrammatical phrasing of *The griffin in that tree is staring at me*. Judging a phrase like *Who do you want to speak to?* is a different activity; PCP and RCP are about judging utterances that native speakers actually produce. By discussing these different perspectives of correct English, we gain a more accurate understanding of language and its role in education.

Consider these scenes. They have minimal details with them, but you can infer a lot from the details included. What do the assumptions of the Prescriptively Correct Perspective and the Rhetorically Correct Perspective have to say about each of these conversations?

In Texas, a customer in a local market tries to speak Spanish to a vendor at a tamale stand who replies in English. How would this conversation be judged?	
PCP	RCP
PCP does not have much to say about communication between languages, but if the customer's Spanish was not understandable, that could be treated as an error.	The customer made an assumption about the language and tried to accommodate towards the context and the vendor. The vendor made an assumption about the language preference of the customer. If they both understand each other and take the interaction as respectful, they are good to go.

A computer programmer is trying to explain a recent problem to a journalist friend, and she says, "This jimmy had put in Yoda conditions and had been refuctoring my previous work so that in the end it was just hooker code." The journalist friend looks baffled.	
PCP	RCP
There is nothing incorrect in the phrasing and construction of this utterance.	If the programmer actually wants to explain her problem, she needs to use words the journalist will understand. RCP would judge this utterance poorly as it is not well crafted for the audience.

At a pre-game tailgate party, you introduce a new acquaintance to a group of your friends. The new acquaintance says, without any sarcasm, "I am honored to make your acquaintance. I hope we can build a life-long relationship."	
PCP	RCP
There is nothing incorrect in the phrasing and construction of this utterance.	These utterances do not fit this context. In terms of RCP, this language is just weird.

At a pre-game tailgate party, you say to your friends, "We gonna rock this game."	
PCP	RCP
The phrase is missing the verb *are* and the progressive should be [gowĩŋ tu] and not [gənə]. It is incorrect and demonstrates a debasement of the English language.	For this context, this utterance works fine. The form [gənə] has been made into a modal verb like *will* in Modern English and has a style constraint related to the formality of the situation. This form fits this context well.

In an expository essay on economic changes in your home state, you write: "The property value gonna continue to rise through the end of the decade."	
PCP	RCP
The phrase is missing the verb *is* and the progressive should be [gowĩŋ tu] and not [gənə]. It would be even better if the modal verb such as *should* or *will* were used. It is incorrect and demonstrates a debasement of the English language.	For this context, this utterance does not work well. The form [gənə] is stylistically restricted to more casual contexts. The genre conventions of an expository essay in an academic setting prohibit the use of such casual forms. This use of *gonna* is a mistake.

From these examples, note that the Rhetorically Correct Perspective can make both positive and negative evaluations. It is not a perspective where anything goes, but instead it makes judgments according to the genre conventions of the context.

Often mentioned is the fear that chaos would reign for language and writing if the Prescriptively Correct Perspective were not upheld. Actual language chaos is not a possibility with our species' ability for regulated language variation, so we can rest easy about the potential doom of civilization.

Authors adhere to genre conventions all the time. Yet, even in writing, variation persists. When a New Zealand author writes *civilisation* and an American author writes *civilization*, the differences of their writing standards do not derive from editing troubles, slovenly work habits, or a lack of morality. The authors simply have different standards, not superior and inferior ones. The Rhetorically Correct Perspective can handle variation like these spelling differences and make judgments according to the context.

The cultural context also greatly molds the political powers of vernacular and standard varieties. The most stark contrast to the US dialect situation is that of Norway. Norway has two written standards, *bokmål* and *nynorsk*, both based on Norwegian speech. Vikør (1982:42) reports that, because of Norwegian ethnic pride, "forced speech standardization is forbidden by law" and writes that the Primary School Act reads: "In their oral training, pupils may use the language they speak at home, and the teacher must give due consideration to the speech of the pupils in his vocabulary and his manner of expression." This institutional respect for language variation has a long tradition dating back to a parliamentary motion in 1878. An important part of this tradition is the underlying belief that regional dialects reflect Norwegian cultural tradition. In the case of Norway, the Rhetorically Correct Perspective was taken up and codified in writing systems.

Genre conventions are an important part of formal education, and the Rhetorically Correct Perspective helps students learn them more effectively and efficiently than the Prescriptively Correct Perspective.

Words to the Wise: The ever urgent decline of reading

See if this sounds familiar:

"The need for better readers and speakers was never more urgent than now. Deficiency in expressive reading and effective speaking has been observed and deplored for many years."

The wording may seem a bit odd, but the sentiment is clearly recognizable. This statement is by Isaac Hinton Brown, written in the preface to *Common School Elocution and Oratory*. The year was 1897. It fits well with the Golden Age hypothesis of language, which claims that at some previous time, the state of language was better, and that currently things are worse. Our contemporary complaints about language are much the same, as will be future complaints. In 1712, Jonathan Swift wrote a *Proposal for Correcting, Improving, and Ascertaining the English Tongue*. Style guides, the touch stones of genre conventions, were not widely available for writers, and much consternation arose from all the variation at hand. In this particular proposal, Swift is not practicing satire, to the best of our knowledge. He writes:

…our Language is extremely imperfect; that its daily Improvements are by no means in proportion to its daily Corruptions; and the Pretenders to polish and refine it, have chiefly multiplied Abuses and Absurdities; and, that in many Instances, it offends against every Part of Grammar.

It was an age of super-cool spelling rules, when any word of import could be capitalized, so you should not judge Swift for his variations in spelling. These kinds of variation in style are a regular part of what humans do, and as styles change, certain conventions come in and out of style.

Complaining about language is always in style. Whether or not you want to join in depends on how much complaining pleases you and raises your own sense of self-worth. If you do complain about the supposedly deplorable state of some group's language, remember you are part of a long line of complainers. Previous complaints have not reduced the number of subsequent complaints since the time of Plato, but perhaps over the next 2,400 years, the added complaints will do the trick.

what roles does language play in education?

Students and teachers use language in every subject to communicate orally and in writing. Language forms the foundation for communication in sciences and mathematics, as much as in literary and cultural studies. Specialized terms abound. In mathematics and sciences, there are symbol systems that allow for tightly constrained communication. In mathematics, the symbols $+$, $-$, Σ, and $\int$ all have specific jobs. Chemistry has not only formulas but also an entire periodic table with highly ordered rows and columns of numbers and symbols, like 107 Bh (Bohrium with an atomic number of 107). In the same vein, any kind of command line with computers requires specific language: To run a linear model in the R statistical package, the correct notation of "lm(*formula*, data $=$ *data. frame*)" must be adhered to. For all these disciplines, they rely on language, but they have specific requirements and symbols which they have adopted to assure that their chances for communication are not hurt by ambiguity.

For these classrooms that focus on topics other than language, teachers teach about these symbols and complex systems. What should English classes teach? Most states require reading a wide variety of literature, writing in several different genres, and basic understanding of genre conventions of writing (often called *grammar*, as if there were only one kind). The knowledge of how language works as presented in this book should help all those goals.

Language is part of every component of testing in schools, and understanding how language variation can influence teachers and students will help the entire educational process. From history tests to algebra, the language of the test plays a role in the results. In the book *American English*, Wolfram and Schilling-Estes (2006) detail all the areas where language affects testing, including the definition of correctness, language as the testing tool, and the sociolinguistic context. These areas are especially important for tests of language achievement. If a teacher wants to lead students through a history lesson on the Black Death in Europe in the 1300s (when at least 30% of the population was killed by bacteria), the students could work through facts about the plague verbally and interactively in a game-show format, like *Jeopardy!*. Even though this activity will help the students to learn the required facts about this bleak period, if the testing is done through a formal written test, the quality of the students' writing and their ability to adhere to genre conventions of institutional essay writing will probably play as large a role as any student's command of the facts.

As Wolfram and Schilling-Estes detail, a crucial component to testing language is the **content validity** of the test. Content validity is the extent to which a test actually tests what it is supposed to test. Ponder the test questions below:

Which pairs of words rhyme?
A. ten~pin
B. great~meat
C. meat~sheet
D. caught~shot

What answer(s) would you provide for this question? Might it be A and C, or C and D? Does anyone in your class have A, C, and D? After you have figured out what pairs of words rhyme for you, ponder whether this kind of answer can be guided by the Prescriptively Correct Perspective. If you consider that many people hold pronunciations to a perspective much like the PCP, you will realize that those people would say there *is* one right answer. Traditionally, in terms of the history of American English, the prescriptively correct answer would be C. Every English speaker, since at least 1700, has *meat* and *sheet* rhyming. The pairs *ten~pin* and *caught~shot* were both historically unmerged and, hence, did not rhyme in any region of US English. Today, there are tens of millions of speakers with one or the other merger and at least a million with both. The Rhetorically Correct Perspective would take such factors into consideration when designing such a test question, and the decision about the "correct" answer plays a crucial role in the question's content validity.

With this question, the content validity lies in its ability to tease apart which test takers are from which dialect areas. Does *pin~pen* rhyme for you? For millions of Americans, along with a fair number of Australians and New Zealanders, they do rhyme, but for millions more English speakers, they do not. For *caught~cot*, probably the majority of North Americans have these two words rhyming. Is there a single right answer for this question?

It depends on what population the test was normed. When tests are normed, the scores, and sometimes the answers, are adjusted according to the normal range of scores for a certain population. If this question were normed on a northern California population, (D) would be one of the correct answers. For other English-speaking areas, (A) would also be a correct answer. The answer (C) would be correct for all English-speaking communities. If this kind of question is used to determine a student's verbal ability or metalinguistic skills, then the test would violate the purported content validity because it simply divides the test-taking population into dialect regions.

What is the following question meant to test?

What is the correct way to phrase the following question?
A. Who do you want to give the job to?
B. Whom do you want to assign the job to?
C. You want to give the job to whom?
D. To whom would you want to assign the job?

Before you read on, consider the question from our two perspectives of correct English. From the Prescriptively Correct Perspective, there is only one right answer. To figure it out, analyze the four choices to see what varies between them. There are four key variations. The first is the distinction in case for *who* and *whom*. From Chapter 5, remember that Old English marked all nouns with case, but that system has dwindled so that only pronouns have case in Modern English: *I* is the subject and *me* is the object. This distinction has mostly faded for the interrogative pronoun *who* (the subject) and its object form *whom*. The PCP views this older distinction as the only legitimate way to use the forms.

The second variation is that of the verb carrying the Inflection of the question. In A and B, the verb is *do*, and it is carrying the present tense Inflection. In C, the verb *want* is carrying the Inflection. In D, the modal verb *would* is carrying the Inflection. For many Americans, there is a distinction in politeness where a modal verb introduces conditionality (remember mood from Chapter 4) and thus seems less direct. The third variation is between *give* and *assign*. For many people, *assign* seems more official, often related to formal schooling or business; these two words have different historical origins, with *give* coming from Old English and *assign* coming from Latin through French. The Latinate etymology grants *assign* a more formal tone. The fourth variation is that of the placement of the preposition *to*. As discussed in Chapter 4, preposition placement in English has always been variable, but some writers of the seventeenth and eighteenth centuries argued to arrange English like Latin to give it more prestige.

All of the variations for this question deal with scales of formality, and the Prescriptively Correct Perspective would see these as simple divisions between the supposed right answer, D, and the other supposed wrong answers. Answer A is the most informal of the answers, with its statistically normal *who* and its sentence final preposition. Answer B is a nod toward prescriptive expectations of *whom*, and a switch of the infinitive verb from the Anglo-Saxon *give* to the Latinate *assign*. Answer C puts all the parts in order according to prescriptive expectations, but answer D combines all the formal elements and maintains the more prominent preposition fronting. For the Rhetorically Correct Perspective, a context would need to be provided to allow an answer to be given. The RCP takes up a more complex view of the world. All of the answers work according to descriptive rules of English, although D might get you odd looks in some social contexts.

If a test using such a question explicitly directed the students to determine correctness based on the highest levels of formality, so that more formal means more correct, then it would have decent content validity. If instead correctness is vaguely defined or if the test only assesses a student's supposed verbal ability, then the test would be violating content validity.

Try to discover the focus of the next test question:

Which of the following sentences is correct?
A. The basement needs to be cleaned, and there's three of you lined up to do it.
B. The basement needs cleaned, and there are three of you lined up to do it.
C. The basement needs to be cleaned, and there are three of you lined up to do it.

With these answers, there are two variables to consider for the Rhetorically Correct Perspective. The first is the lexical selection of the verb *need*. In some

Figure 10.1   In this comic from *Saturday Morning Breakfast Cereal*, what meaning of grammar is being used? http://www.smbc-comics.com/index.php?id=1079. Votey: " 'Please Help' is not a complete sentence!" © *Saturday Morning Breakfast Cereal*, by Zach Weinersmith. www.smbc-comics.com

dialects in the Midwest of the United States, the verb requires a following past-participle (e.g. *cleaned*), but in other dialects, the verb *need* requires an infinitive verb phrase (e.g. *to be cleaned*). In the post-comma part, an alternation exists between *there is/there are*. In regular conversations, at least half of speakers use *there is* and *there was* almost exclusively. The Prescriptively Correct Perspective holds that only C would be right, but for many speakers, A or B would work fine in most conversations. If a test using such a question directly states that it is asking students to discern between dialect varieties, it would be valid. Otherwise, its content validity would be questionable.

analyzing "grammar" advice

As we discussed in Chapter 1, the term *grammar* carries more baggage than perhaps any other term in language study. It is such a loaded word that we must divide its various meanings into five different terms to make our meaning clear: *teaching grammar, prescriptive grammar, descriptive grammar, mental grammar, and Universal Grammar*. The first three of those terms can describe books, and the last two are more abstract ideas about how humans acquire and do language. In most educational programs and almost all school systems, these distinctions are not made. Without clear definitions of these different kinds of grammar, teaching writing will never be as effective as it could be. In addition, students will not actually learn about how language works.

To disambiguate a traditional usage of *grammar*, let us consider an example from a manual of genre conventions and prescriptive advice. *The Chicago Manual of Style* is in its 16th edition and has been one of the more successful handbooks. As a style guide, it is a set of conventions to which writers can subscribe or not. There are different style guides, and in following one, you are choosing not to follow others. For the most part, these kinds of style guides uphold the Prescriptively Correct Perspective.

The conflated use of the term *grammar* is common in style guides. As advice is dispensed, prescriptive conjecture is mixed with genre conventions and descriptive observations. To illustrate this conflated flux, we dissect an example from the subsection on "Good usage versus common usage" (5.220), although numerous sections would make an equally good illustration. This particular advice is about the use of *that* and *which*. Here it is in its entirety:

> **that; which**. These are both relative pronouns (see 5.54–63). In polished American prose, *that* is used restrictively to narrow a category or identify a particular item being talked about [any building that is taller must be outside the state]; *which* is used nonrestrictively—not to narrow a class or identify a particular item but to add something about an item already identified [alongside the officer trotted a toy poodle, which is hardly a typical police dog]. *Which* should be used restrictively only when it is preceded by a preposition [the situation in which we find ourselves]. Otherwise, it is almost always preceded by a comma, a parenthesis, or a dash. In British English, writers and editors seldom observe the distinction between the two words. See also 6.22.

Before going further, read back over the passage and distinguish between prescriptive advice and descriptive observation.

Which statements are used with a sense of obligation? Of course this section is in a book concerned with providing style advice: The author's duty is to provide a suggestion about this topic. What exactly is the advice?

We can figure it out by working through these sentences:

1. I dropped the computer that I bought last Tuesday.
2. I dropped the computer which I bought last Tuesday.
3. The dog that I saw swimming had a collar.
4. The dog which I saw swimming had a collar.
5. Any building which is taller must be outside the state.
6. Any building that is taller must be outside the state.

And then, consider these sentences:

7. Next to the patio is a rose, which is one of my favorite flowers.
8. Next to the patio is a rose, that is one of my favorite flowers.

In all the sentences, *that* and *which* have a job to do. The important distinction between 7 and 8 is the roles *that* and *which* play. In English, the form *that* is tied to several jobs, including one as a relative pronoun and one as a demonstrative pronoun (i.e. *this, that*; *these, those*). In 8, the *that* of *that is one of my favorite flowers* functions as a demonstrative pronoun and does not subordinate the sentence (read the sentences out loud to check). It is just the subject of the second sentence. Most writers would probably separate the two Inflectional Phrases of 8 with a period or a semicolon. People do create combinations like 8, but we understand that they are two separate sentences.

In 1, 3, and 5, *that* is also a function word, but in those cases it is a relative pronoun, as is *which*. I purposely included no internal punctuation to these sentences, but how does *The Chicago Manual of Style* suggest that the two be distinguished? The advice is that if the relative pronoun uniquely identifies the noun to which it is attached, the relative pronoun *that* should be used. This advice has a notable exception: If the relative pronoun is preceded by a preposition, then the relative pronoun has to be *which*. This exception is part of the descriptive grammar of English. It is not normal for English speakers to have *that* in phrases like * *The house in that we kissed burned down*. Between both sets of sentences, check out whether or not the *that/which* forms the subject of the Inflectional Phrase to which it is attached. The regulation about *which* coming after prepositions relates to its status as a nonsubject.

The prescriptive advice does not, however, jive with normal usage in many varieties of English (spoken or written). British English, including Australian English and New Zealand English, do not make the distinction between the "restrictive" distinction of *that/which*. It is not a natural distinction, and no one else except some Americans have tried to enforce it as social fashion. *The Chicago Manual of Style* uses the phrase "seldom observe the distinction" as if the distinction were natural and a couple of hundred million of users happen to have missed it.

To be clear, following the Prescriptively Correct Perspective and this style guide's advice, this next sentence would be wrong:

• *I am sad about the ice cream which I dropped.*

Its supposed transgression comes from using *which* with *I dropped*, as that phrase uniquely identifies the noun to which it is attached. According to this style guide's advice, this sentence is right:

• *I am sad about the ice cream that I dropped*

As general advice, it has the ring of rigor and logic to it, marking off one type from another. This appeal is why it was proposed as a potential future rule in 1926 by H.W. Fowler in *A Dictionary of Modern English Usage*. It was a suggestion then, and it is still a suggestion today in the 16th edition of *The Chicago Manual of Style*.

In summary, the advice is two-fold: (1) Use a comma before *which* when it is used to introduce an aside and (2) use *that* when uniquely identifying a preceding noun. The first is advice about writing, as commas play no role in spoken language and all rules of writing are part of the genre conventions of writing. The second is an advised constraint about what people should do with themselves. Linguists note that descriptive accounts show that there is a lot of flux between *that* and *which* in English (as there is in this book). The style guide's retort is that in "polished prose" this advice is followed, and therefore you should follow it also. The trouble is that there is a lot of polished prose which does not take up this distinction. We can be aware of such advice, and if the publications we write for use *The Chicago Manual of Style*, then we know what to do.

Unfortunately, in the United States one of the favored pet peeves of the prescriptively inclined is exactly this bit of advice. Geoffrey Pullum has dubbed it **which** hunting. The Language Log post "A decline in which-hunting?" (http://languagelog.ldc.upenn.edu/nll/?p=5479) details a lot of the history of *which* hunting and notes some famous authors, including the advice-giving George Orwell, who are prolific users of restrictive *which*.

There are plenty of other examples like *which* hunting in advice from the Prescriptively Correct Perspective. Some of the advice is descriptive, accounting for what people actually do in writing, but a good deal of it is simply prescriptive. The different motivations and nuances of prescriptive advice are explored in this next section.

prescriptive approaches to language

When connected to language study, the term *prescriptive* carries a lot of cultural baggage. For people who would self-identify as *prescriptivist*, the term carries connotations of 'discipline', 'rigor', 'standards', and 'correctness'. For people who would denounce prescriptivists, the term carries connotations of 'intolerance', 'ignorance', and 'snob'. *Prescriptive* is a loaded term. Unfortunately, it is difficult to have a decent and educated discussion about language teaching when people simply want to demean others.

The term *prescriptivist* is a recent one, not being recorded in writing until 1952. In the *Oxford English Dictionary*, the term *prescriptive* (from Latin roots) itself is first recorded in 1663: "He proposes the Laws of Government, as founded upon the Law of God, Nature, and Nations, to be prescriptive of all virtue, accumulated in the fear of God." In this first context, it was designed to impose moral authority and is often invoked with the same attitude today. The term *prescription* is even older. It originally dealt with the legal rights of titles, but eventually, it began to be used in the modern sense of a doctor's instructions for medicine: From 1568, "Quhairin I am constrynit of necessitie to vse the prescriptioun of sum medicinis in Latine." As both a linguist and a teacher, I still see the metaphor of "sick language" when I encounter advice packaged as *prescriptive rules*. The trouble is that the *sick language metaphor* ignores the concepts of genre conventions and language variation. There is a difference between teaching prescriptive rules and teaching genre conventions, and the term *prescriptive rules* has as its foundation a false assumption about how language works.

A large part of the goal here is to distinguish between mythology and accurate knowledge. For the future teachers among you, please realize that I am not trying to dictate how you teach what others have decided you must teach. As a teacher and textbook writer, I want to provide tools for your teaching tool bag. As a linguist, I want you to teach about how language actually works. Future teachers should learn the most effective, efficient, and accurate ways to teach genre conventions. As teachers, you will deal with pressures from many different groups. Understanding the history of these pressures will prepare you to respond reasonably and professionally.

The prescriptivist tradition is most likely as old as human language. One of the earliest, and perhaps most dire, citations of dialect discrimination based on prescriptivist standards is the story of **shibboleth**. The term *shibboleth* itself meant "ear of corn" in the Old Testament story of Judges (xii.4–6), but variable pronunciation was the telling feature. Soldiers of Gilead were defending the fords of the Jordan River against deserting Ephraimites. To check for those disguised Ephraimites trying to sneak through their defenses, the Gileadites tested a particular dialect feature:

> "Whenever one of the fugitives of Ephraim said, 'Let me go over,' the men of Gilead would say to him, 'Are you an Ephraimite?' When he said: 'No,'[6] they said to him, 'Then say Shibboleth,' and he said, 'Sibboleth,' for he could not pronounce it right. Then they seized him and killed him at the fords of the Jordan. Forty-two thousand of the Ephraimites fell at that time." (xii.4–6)

The linguistic difference between *shibboleth* and *sibboleth* is in the two sounds [ʃ] and [s], the same as that between <shoe> and <Sue>: The tongue is slightly further back on the roof of the mouth in the <sh> form. Death awaited those who did not make the proper choice of tongue placement.

This story contains the basic themes of the prescriptivist approach. First, there are separate social groups, be the separation tribal, ethnic, socioeconomic, or some other form. Second, the basis for judgment is social, not linguistic: The Ephraimites were not killed because [s] was painful to hear; certainly the Gileadites had <s>s [s] in their language. The Ephraimites were killed because they were Ephraimites; the [s]-form of *shibboleth* was simply a dialect feature used to identify a social group. Third, the standards of the prescriptive judgment are not questioned.

Modern prescriptivism has taken up all three of these elements since its current social rules were formulated between 1600 and 1800. Many prescriptivist doctrines of today were established in those centuries, often in erroneous but well-intentioned comparisons between English and Latin: Do not split

Word Play: Spelling wrecks

In 2012, Ms. Jerri Peterson had the honor to carry the Olympic torch in England. To commemorate the event, she got a tattoo back home in Atlanta, GA. Unfortunately, the Georgia tattoo artist forgot to turn on spellcheck. Ms. Peterson received a tattoo that reads "Oylmpic torch bearer." Ms. Peterson laughed about the mistake, and took it in good stride, yet spelling is important, especially with something as indelible as a tattoo. From the Rhetorically Correct Perspective, it is important to get these spellings right.

With tattoos, Chinese logographs are a popular choice, but all too often they are printed backwards or upside down. Such symbols are simply art for most English readers, but having a misspelled "I'M AWSOME" (an actual tattoo) on your back is worth a laugh for any English reader. The same goes for the "Sweet Pee" tattoo. Homophones are a beast that way.

Twitter and Facebook are of course hotbeds of spelling errors, aided by correction software, and those that cross up one word for another are a great source for humor:

Missouri loves company	{Missouri instead of Misery}
I am a force to be record with	{record vs. reckoned}
She betta pay amish	{amish vs. homage}
Can sex be good without an organism?	{organism vs. orgasm}
Who paid off the damn jewelry	{jewelry vs. jury}
Are you having a sarcasm?	{sarcasm vs. orgasm}
Your dairy air looks rather ravishing	{dairy air vs. derrière)

It might not possible for teachers to make students understand all the ways that misspellings can bite their reputations, but the fear should prompt more proofreading. Rhetoric does not sleep, and these kinds of spelling mistakes really impede the intended message. For teachers themselves, when we write up handouts and make copies, if we have a spelling mistake, every copy we make just replicates that mistake.

infinitives (e.g. Our mission is <u>to boldly go</u> where no one has gone before); Do not strand prepositions (e.g. We have much to be thankful <u>for</u>).

The pedagogical trouble with traditional prescriptive doctrines is not the need to follow genre conventions, but rather the assumptions about language and the *holier-than-thou* attitude often used when the advice is delivered. A bland genre convention for writing is 'capitalize the first letter in a sentence.' It is fine advice for adhering to normal practice in the genre of formal writing. But it would be wrong to assume that if such capitalization did not occur language would be broken or communication would fail. A social fashion would not be followed, but the communication functions of language would continue on unhindered in the face of this written variation (see e.e. cummings's "the Cambridge ladies who live in furnished souls" from *Tulips and Chimneys* (1923)).

Rather, a primary problem with prescriptivism is its assumption about language, and the most basic assumption has no empirical support. It is the foundation of language miseducation: a single, supreme form exists. People throughout written history have used this assumption for discriminatory goals. In every instance, the supreme form is chosen for social reasons, and any linguistic pseudo-justification comes after the choosing. The Greeks and Romans named the Germanic tribes *barbarians*, specifically pointing out a language criticism in that name. Throughout the Middle English period, English was seen as unsophisticated and useless for prose, verse, or intellectual work while Latin reigned supreme. With both the Germanic peoples and earlier Englishes, the languages were fine, but these judgments were based on social decisions. Within any one language, different varieties are associated with social relations. In contrast to this long tradition, future teachers should understand the natural linguistic equality of all language varieties and establish teaching tactics that incorporate a sound view of language. The Rhetorically Correct Perspective allows for this modern teaching approach while upholding genre conventions.

prescriptive peeves

All too often, judgments about language variation patterns can be harbingers of hatred. A reoccurring theme surrounding prescriptive advice is the indignation exuded through **peeves**. Some pet peeves are more innocuous, as with the desire to maintain the space in the word *a lot* (vs. *alot*). Others are uttered more fervently, such as the denouncement of *be* in *She be laughing all the time*. To claim that something like habitual *be* is an abomination of the English language is to fail to understand how it works in traditional African American Vernacular English. In parts of rural North Carolina, habitual *be* is still a regular part of even younger speaker's language. In the summer of 2013, a young store clerk and I were talking about what things people ask for in the grocery store. He said, "People be asking for all kinds of crazy things." This use of *be* is an aspect marker and indicates that the asking occurs on a regular basis, in the same way that "have asked" indicates the perfect aspect. That is the descriptively grammatical usage. It would be ungrammatical to say, *"She be calling me right now," because the time aspect of the sentence is punctual. The Prescriptively Correct Perspective cannot handle this kind of language complexity. It simply claims it is wrong.

As Rickford and Rickford (2000:208) document, even an established writer such as William Raspberry has made the claim that African American Vernacular English is "a language that has no right or wrong expressions, no consistent spellings or pronunciations and no discernible rules." For many commentators, the fear is a supposed chaos, and the claim for a single variety of correct English calms the fear. Yet, a language feature like habitual *be* clearly demonstrates the rule-governed language variation all humans have: *She be laughing all the time* is grammatical, but *she be laughing right now* would be ungrammatical for native speakers. As with all language varieties, African American Vernacular English has rules. Additionally, understanding this kind of language variation does not vacate genre conventions of written language.

Word Play: Malapropisms

One kind of spelling mistake is called a *malapropism*. Malapropisms are a category of miscues. A malapropism is a wrong word choice (whether made on purpose or not). The name of this category is taken from Mrs. Malaprop, a character in the play *The Rivals*, written in 1775 by Richard Brinsley Sheridan. This character substituted similar sounding words for the intended choices, yielding humorously wrong meanings. Her name, Mala-prop, is taken from the French for 'ill-suited.' The character herself has the substitution *illiterate* for *obliterate*: "…forget this fellow – to *illiterate* him, I say, quite from your memory" (*The Rivals*, Act I Scene II Line 178).

 Malapropisms are often used for comic effect, in comics and elsewhere, as the audience is supposed to catch the contrast between the intended meaning and the delivered meaning. Sometimes however, malapropisms are not so carefully crafted, but are simply mistakes, as in the headlines about voters being *weary* of a newly elected president rather than being *wary* (http://languagelog.ldc.upenn.edu/nll/?p=4054).

As a linguist, I occasionally have people show me examples of language variation they find to be funny or ridiculous or offensive. One of my favorites was a woman who showed me a letter from her county government concerning some property the woman owned. In the letter was a sentence with the line, "If it be relevant to your particular situation …". The woman complained to me about how the author, an African American county employee the woman knew personally, could make such a mistake. She also complained about the state of the county's school system (as if the school system were somehow responsible for a letter written by a middle-aged county employee). Take a moment to ponder the line in question. The complaint was made about the verb *be*, and the woman argued that it was broken English and typical of so many African Americans in the community. I would have explained how habitual *be* works, but the line in question is an example of the subjunctive in English, not invariant *be*. The subjunctive can be used when expressing a conditional situation, wish, or desire. Perhaps the most famous example is the possibly apocryphal quote from Patrick Henry: "If this be treason, make the most of it." The subjunctive is often reserved for formal writing, such as this letter from the county government. This woman had taken her quick judgment about African Americans and combined it with her incomplete knowledge about the English language to form a complaint where she enjoyed her indignation. This combination of social prejudice, linguistic ignorance, and self-indulgence often provides the motivation for prescriptive judgments found in public realms such as internet blog posts and comment areas.

When you correct someone's grammar, try to remember

those rules are like the stars you see through a telescope,

just pretty echoes of the long dead.

Figure 10.2   From A Softer World, a reflection on pet peeves and grammar: http://asofterworld .com/index.php?id=1003. Rollover text: "Beautiful, but gone." © Joey Comeau and Emily Horne. asofterworld.com

descriptive grammar and genre conventions

Language variation is an important part of every human society, but students are rarely taught about it. By learning three basic facts of language variation, we can better understand many of the mysteries of language we regularly face. All of us should understand the following: (1) Language variation is natural and useful, (2) living languages change over time, and (3) language use is linked to social identity.

Our minds create language variation. The language variation, in daily use, leads to language change over time. For people who live in the same geographical area or share the same social identity, they organize their language variation so that they share language norms; in other words, they speak the same dialect. Although dialects differ geographically and socially, no dialect is better structurally than another. They all work with the same mental machinery. While many people believe there to be only one correct form of a language, what is considered standard actually varies from dialect to dialect. For example, a normal, Southern US pronunciation of the word *pin* does not differ from the pronunciation of the word *pen*. Other dialects make a distinction between the vowels *i* and *e* preceding the nasal sound /n/, and speakers of those dialects may assess the Southern pronunciation as wrong instead of simply different.

Descriptive approaches also work well for explaining modern spelling, variations in national spelling norms, and the rich history held in modern spelling. One benefit of our spelling system is the easy availability of language change examples. A diachronic comparison can yield differences (e.g. between older and modern pronunciations of *knight*) or similarities (e.g. the use of vowel alternation in *foot/feet* to mark plurality in both Old English and Modern English). English spelling preserves letters well beyond their usefulness in representing pronunciation. It is a conservative system: Changes to the form of spoken words are most often not reflected in their written representation.

One concise example of conservative spelling is the word *knight*. In earlier times, its form contained the [k] sound upfront, the high-front vowel [i] like in *meet*, and a voiceless velar fricative [x] like that of German *Bach* or Dutch *Van Gogh*. The pronunciation for this earlier *knight* would have been [knixt]. Its modern form for many English speakers is [naɪt]. Three different changes in English affected this word. First, word-initial [k] was lost before [n] in words such as *knot, knee,* and *knob*. Second, the long-vowels in English played musical chairs for most speakers during the Great Vowel Shift; the [i] vowel in words like Middle English *flight* and *bite* became, eventually, the [aɪ] vowel for most English varieties. For most English speakers, the <gh> of *right, flight,* and *might* represents no sound; *right* rhymes with *rite* in modern English, but this was not true in earlier times. The [x] sound was never frequent in English and eventually fell by the wayside for many communities. All three of these changes eventually yielded our modern, and transformed, pronunciation of *knight*. Words like *knight* contain entire history lessons because of conservative spelling, and a descriptive account can reveal that detailed history.

Too often, history lessons of this type are not of interest because they do not have the verve of rancorous debate. Within public debates about language, people treat language as a moral battlefield. It is difficult to imagine political groups arguing about the latest trends in computer languages. However, such groups weighed in with heated debate about Ebonics (see Rickford and Rickford, 2000). This kind of background makes talking about English tricky. In this tradition, many people simply have been taught that there is good language and bad language. In general, people do not like to be told of gray areas.

Genre conventions of spelling, composition, and rhetoric are part of every school system. Language scholars in no way want to overturn these conventions, but we do want teachers and students to understand that their languages, regardless of the social stigmas stacked against them, are beautifully complex, rule-governed systems. The Rhetorically Correct Perspective enhances all of the genre conventions schools need to teach by allowing for an accurate description of how language works. This chapter and the next should help students to better understand language variation as both a normal quality of being human and an important aspect of who they are in society. Hopefully, both chapters will lead teachers and students to discuss the language variation of their own communities, since it is with self-study that effective educational practices continue.

Importantly, if both teachers and students understand language variation, genre conventions should become less arduous for all involved. Genre conventions are socially driven; they are not laws of linguistics. A choice of forms, such as *knelt* vs. *kneeled*, is a social choice. If language variation is better understood, then everyone in the educational process will be more willing to openly discuss such topics.

Some genre conventions are easier to spot than others. Within literature, there are many different forms of poems, each with their own conventions. Ponder the small outcrop of poetry called the cinquain. In its most frequently-used modern poetry form, the cinquain has a regimented structure that controls both the number of lines and the length of lines. Read through the following cinquain from the Flashkids' *Summer Study Daily Activity Workbook 5th grade* (2007:38).

Baby
Soft, cuddly
Cooing, gurgling, smiling
Tiny toes and fingers
Infant

This poem has the following structure:

The topic (one word or two syllables) in the first line
Adjectives (two words or four syllables) in the second line
Progressive participles (three words or six syllables) in the third line
A descriptive phrase (four words or eight syllables) in the fourth line
The topic rephrased (one word or two syllables)

This structure convention is specific and directs the poet to work the imagination within that form. Yet, the form itself has changed over time. As genre conventions themselves are trends within a craft, they are apt to change and do so at the whim of social fashions. Earlier, the cinquain was made more popular by Adelaide Crapsey (1878–1914). Consider the structural differences of her work in the poem "Amaze" (http://www.poetryfoundation.org/poem/175528):

Amaze

I know
Not these my hands
And yet I think there was
A woman like me once had hands
Like these.

Here, the previous topic structure is not present, and the lines are not as restricted. The genre conventions changed between the start of the twentieth century and the start of the twenty-first. Poets both work within genre conventions and work against them, eventually changing them. Even earlier, George Herbert (1593–1633) in "The World" wrote a different kind of cinquain:

Love built a stately house, where Fortune came,
And spinning fancies, she was heard to say
That her fine cobwebs did support the frame,
Whereas they were supported by the same;
But Wisdom quickly swept them all away.
(https://www.poets.org/poetsorg/poem/world)

In Herbert's poem there is an *abaab* rhyme scheme, but the line size is more open to variation. This five-line construction differs from the "baby" cinquain from the 5th-grade workbook, either in topic or structure. The different genre conventions between the poems and centuries do not make the one right and the other wrong (although we can certainly have our personal choices about which we prefer).

Too often, students learn that language variation falls between supposed "good" and "bad" language. When this happens, then students who have the "bad" form consider their own language and themselves deviant. Besides simply being based on false information, this attacking method is not a decent way to encourage analysis and attention to detail. One of the difficulties in explaining language variation to students or the general public is that teachers might encounter unwieldy challenges, including widespread misperceptions about how language works and intolerance toward disempowered groups. Teaching about language variation might mean questioning some widely held views about language. While popular views are not always inaccurate, they need to be re-examined at times. In the same way, many people believe that there is a single set of standards for English, but linguistics shows that a standard English in one part of the country is different from a standard English in other parts of the country, as well as from standard Englishes in other English-speaking countries. Debate about which one is "correct" can become a cultural and moral battlefield in which individuals argue the merits of language use and language instruction according to absolute standards of right and wrong.

Hate towards different ethnic and cultural groups still runs rampant in our society. The teacher can directly address implicitly biased forms (e.g. "The lady doctor" vs. "The doctor"), but to what extent the teacher is responsible for changing the audience's attitude towards others is a vastly different question.

responsibility, outreach, and education

One of the goals for linguists should be to teach about how language variation works, especially for vernacular communities whose language might be slandered. During the 1960s, sociolinguists were at the forefront of language scholars in arguing that vernacular dialects, especially African American Vernacular English, were different yet legitimate varieties of English. Such a claim is too often seen as ludicrous, but this argument must be faced directly in order for the public understanding of language to improve. Recognition of language variation as normal and legitimate helps students understand how language works while requiring them to reflect on their own language patterns and prejudices.

Future teachers might ask how can they mark misplaced commas if language variation is such a natural quality and eliminating it is neither a possible nor desirable goal of education. The answer lies in understanding the role of language in institutional English education. The key element of that understanding is to maintain the distinction is between genre conventions, such as comma placement, and language variation, such as vowel pronunciations. Genre conventions, from spelling and commas to paragraph structure and essay outlines, must be explicitly taught. No child naturally acquires literacy. All skills and bits of knowledge that must be explicitly taught and learned are open to evaluation as genre conventions. Any language variation patterns acquired by students that conflict with genre conventions should be especially emphasized. For example, numerous dialects in the United States, including English in Appalachia and African American Vernacular English, have consonant cluster reduction, so that both *past* and *passed* are sometimes realized as [pæs]. In most conversations, contextual clues keep everyone well informed, but in writing, the genre conventions of spelling require the <t> and <ed> to be there. As William Labov has shown in numerous publications, educational materials often fail to focus on such patterns. In response, he has developed a program to do that: Labov's PORTALS is an intervention program for grades 4–8 and is being used in several states to help children from different dialect backgrounds master genre conventions of English literacy. A primary goal of such a program is to guide the students to develop the metalinguistic skills needed to edit their own writing to meet existing genre conventions.

A program in California has taken these ideas and put them into practice at several different high schools. The SKILLS program run by University of California Santa Barbara has developed a curriculum where they lead students in analyzing and describing their own language variation patterns and those of their community. Class work involves several different projects: (1) Interviewing an elder member of their family or community and analyzing that person's language; (2) compiling and defining slang terms within their high school; (3) a community assessment of language use; (4) a practice policy debate about language topics. For example, students have studied bilingual practice in a Future Farmers of America club and then researched bilingual school policies in order to engage in a mock debate on the topic (www.skills.ucsb.edu). This kind of comprehensive program helps students develop their metalinguistic skills. With those skills, they will excel in any field where detailed analysis is required.

Talking to students about language variation does not kill good writing. High expectations for genre conventions should be a standard for every educational institution. The key to any piece of writing, monologue, or conversation is its rhetoric. It is important to emphasize that good writing is a crucial goal for students. High standards for reading and writing should be the corner stone of every educational institution, and teaching the truth about how language works will only make that process more efficient and effective.

chapter summary

In this chapter we applied the previous chapters' knowledge to domains in which all students have vested interests: language variation and language education. Language variation can be an efficient and effective way to teach about language, especially considering the importance of genre conventions for a society dependent upon literacy. Of the two possible ways to understand how language judgments get made, the Prescriptively Correct Perspective and the Rhetorically Correct Perspective, only the Rhetorically Correct Perspective handles the reality of language variation and how language works. The prescriptive tradition has a long history, and our modern form of it dates back centuries; however, its assumptions about language are outdated and wrong. Many pet peeves are based in that tradition and are sometimes used with social indignation. In contrast, by taking into account context and intent, the rhetorical perspective allows for more straightforward judgments. This chapter explains how the Rhetorically Correct Perspective can accomplish educational goals while fostering an understanding of human language.

key concepts

- Content validity
- Definitions of correct English
- Descriptive
- Descriptive grammar
- Genre conventions
- Mental grammar
- Pet peeves
- Prescriptive grammar
- Prescriptively Correct Perspective
- Prescriptivism
- Rhetorically Correct Perspective
- Shibboleth
- Standard Englishes
- Teaching grammar
- Universal Grammar
- *Which* hunting

note

1   It is mere coincidence that PCP is also an abbreviation for a drug. Yet…as The Partnership notes for PCP (drugfree.org): "Its sedative and anesthetic effects are trance-like, and patients experience a feeling of being 'out of body' and detached from their environment. Use of PCP in humans was discontinued in 1965, because it was found that patients often became agitated, delusional, and irrational while recovering from its anesthetic effects."

references

Crapsey, Adelaide (1878–1914) http://www.poetryfoundation.org/bio/adelaide-crapsey
cummings, e.e. ([1923] 2006) "The Cambridge ladies who live in furnished souls," in *Tulips and Chimneys American English*. New York: Thomas Seltzer.
Fowler, H.W. (1965) *A Dictionary of Modern Usage*. 2nd edition. New York, Oxford: Oxford University Press.

Green, L.J. (2002) *African American English: A Linguistic Introduction*. Cambridge: Cambridge University Press.

Henry P. http://en.wikipedia.org/wiki/Patrick_henry

Herbert G. (1593–1633) "The World": http://www.poetryfoundation.org/bio/george -herbert

Hood, C. and Stead, J. (2012) *Summer Study Daily Activity Workbook 5th Grade*. Flashkids. New York: Sterling Publishers.

http://xkcd.com/781/

University of Chicago (2010) *The Chicago Manual of Style*. 16th edition. Chicago: University of Chicago Press.

Vikør, L. (1989) "The position of standardized vs. dialectal speech in Norway," *International Journal of the Sociology of Language 80*: 41–60.

Wolfram, W. and Schilling-Estes, N. (2006) *American English*. Oxford: Blackwell.

---

further reading

The Story of Ain't: America, Its Language, and the Most Controversial Dictionary Ever Published. David Skinner. 2012. Harper.

This wonderfully-written book tells the story of the mammoth controversy surrounding *Merriam Webster's Third New International Dictionary* in 1961. Skinner sketches the intellectual climate of the twentieth century leading up to the publication of the dictionary and its subsequent firestorm. As part of that sketch, Skinner details linguists' (often failed) attempts to change opinions about language, prescriptivism, and dictionaries.

Understanding Language Variation in U.S. Schools. Anne H. Charity Hudley and Christine Mallinson. 2010. Teachers College Press.

Dialects in Schools and Communities. C. Adger, W. Wolfram, and D. Christian. 2007. Routledge.

If you are looking for sources to begin exploring work on language and education, consider Adger, Wolfram, and Christian (2007) and Charity Huddley and Mallinson (2010). In these books, the authors detail language variation in the United States, the nature of variation in linguistic systems, cultural effects on language variation, the concept of standard English and language difference, techniques of oral language instruction, techniques of written language instruction, the interaction of language variation and reading, and dialect awareness programs for student investigators. Both books include further reading and exercises, and hence this book would work well as a teacher training textbook or a reference for scholars.

Spoken Soul. John Rickford and Russell Rickford. 2000. Wiley.

All future teachers should read *Spoken Soul*. This book provides the best nontechnical account of African-American English available. Its educational implications are sweeping, and it is firmly grounded in linguistics. It also provides a detailed explanation of the firestorm surrounding the Ebonics controversy. For an academic discussion which is both concise and accurate, also see Lisa Green's (2002) *African American English*.

English with an Accent: Language, Ideology and Discrimination in the United States. 2nd edition. Rosina Lippi-Green. 2011. Routledge.

For many sociolinguists, this book makes the most direct and clear argument of why and how people discriminate using dialect variation. Lippi-Green explores topics such as discrimination against Latino English and Asian American English, but perhaps this book is most famous for the way it tackles Disney's use of dialect in popular movies.

Anyone professionally working with language and education should know about ERIC Digests such as the following:

Vernacular Dialects in U.S. Schools (ERIC Digest). D. Christian. 1997. ERIC Clearinghouse on Language and Linguistics. http://www.cal.org/resources/digest/christ01.html

exercises

individual work

1. For each of the following bits of advice, describe how it is prescriptive and/or descriptive. Create two sentences for each bit of advice: one to fit it and one to violate it. Then design a context for each sentence you created: Explain why each sentence works (or not) according to the Prescriptively Correct Perspective and why each sentence works (or not) according to the Rhetorically Correct Perspective. Also for each bit of advice, on what linguistic level does the advice operate (e.g. phonological, morphological, syntactic, lexical, semantic, orthographic)? It will probably help to search for example sentences.

   For example: Do not use *can* as a verb to indicate permission.

Sentence ignoring advice		Sentence following advice	
Can Jack come over to my house?		*With the river full to its banks, we can float the supplies across.*	
Context: A 10-year-old asking a friend's mom if Jack is allowed to play		Context: A team of explorers trying to make it to their next camp site	
PCP	RCP	PCP	RCP
The use of *can* should be reserved for questions of logical possibility and not permission. The verb *may* should be used for permission.	In this context, the verb *can* is not ambiguous. Whether intending permission or possibility, this question is perfectly normal in this context.	This usage of *can* clearly portrays the logical possibilities of moving the supplies. Permission is not an issue.	This use of *can* is descriptively grammatical and semantically transparent. It fits well.
Area of linguistic advice			
Lexical and semantic			

a. Do not end a sentence with a preposition.

b. Do not split an infinitive.

c. Use *who* as a subject and *whom* as an object.

d. Do not use *and, but,* or *so* at the start of a sentence.

e. Use *these* and *this* for things close to you and *those* and *that* for things further away.

f. Do not use *I* or *me* in formal writing.

g. Use *an* before a vowel and *a* before a consonant.

2. *Like* vs. *as*:

In the following sentences, which do you prefer, *as* or *like*? Prescriptively, some advice manuals prefer *like* in some of the sentences but *as* in the others. Make your own assessment and then check a style guide to see how well your judgments match up with prescriptive advice.

a. Teachers sometimes see themselves as heroes [as, like] Odysseus.

b. The widow in that old picture looks [as, like] my mom.

c. Nothing happened just [as, like] I thought.

d. He's searching around [as if, like] that lost ring were actually made of gold.

e. She wants to run [as, like] she has never run before.

f. It sank [as, like] a rock.

g. In the end, they made mistakes, [as, like] all teenagers do.

h. At the club, we danced [as if, like] we were on fire.

i. We were silent [as if, like] our mouths were sewn shut.

j. [As, Like] the dweeb we all thought he was, he had put gelatin in all our drinks.

3. *Might* vs. *may* and modals:

For the following sentences, make a choice between *may* or *might*. Which one would sound better? Are the meanings the same for you with each choice? If there is a meaning difference between *may* and *might*, does it show up in every sentence?

a. She [may, might] head down the slope.

b. It [may, might] not be possible to release the injured prisoners?

c. The wording [may, might] seem a bit odd.

d. This kind of discussion brings the teacher and the students into an awareness of how terms [may, might] be used in different senses.

e. Students [may, might] use a different language at home.

f. You [may, might] want to go to the party.

g. Classroom visitors [may, might] be escorted out of the building.

h. Get the dog leash, and I [may, might] take her for a walk.

i. If you really want dessert, you [may, might] get a bowl of ice cream.

j.   The librarian said we [may, might] be able to get a larger study room.

Grammar Girl (http://grammar.quickanddirtytips.com/) argues that *may* indicates certainty and that *might* indicates more doubt. Do you agree with that assessment? Grammar Girl also argues that *might* is the past tense of *may*, but that has not been true for a few centuries. Consider *She might want to go.* Is there any past-time reference indicated? The Oxford English Dictionary also lists *might* as the past tense of *may*. Can you find a modern usage to substantiate that claim?

With *may* and *might*, some speakers draw a distinction between the two based on a scale of permission distinction. I once gave a paper at a conference that had the title "What may bidialectalism be?" One of my colleagues from New Zealand laughed out loud and asked who would grant it permission to exist? For her, *may* strongly indicated permission and *might* just sheer possibility.

In the following sentences, is there any difference in meaning between the *may* sentence and the *might* sentence?

k.   *Her parents said she may go to the party.*
l.   *Her parents said she might go to the party.*

The modals like *might, should,* and *would* are called preterit present verbs because they used to be the past tense forms of *may, shall,* and *will* but have themselves shifted to the present tense.

Are there present-time/past-time distinctions to be made with the other preterite-present verbs we use as modals?

m.   We [shall/should] finish that pitcher.
n.   The snow conditions [shall/should] hold up better next time.
o.   My favorite player [shall/should] have scored that goal.
p.   The car [will/would] roll down the hill if you take the brake off.
q.   Visitors [will/would] have in mind the kind of nightmare scenes that took place here last year.
r.   The children [will/would] remember only the bad moments of our vacation.

4.   *Fewer* or *less*:

With all the synchronic variation in language, it sometimes happens that the norm at one point in time is different from an earlier point in time. This variation can happen in small cubbyholes of the language. For example, consider how English speakers mark a comparison of quantity. On the positive side, they can say *more* in phrases like

I want more water
I want more shoes.

For English speakers, *more* works with both count nouns and mass nouns (Chapter 4). On the negative side, English speakers are a bit divided, both synchronically and diachronically. Consider the following sentences and choose which you feel would be the best choice.

    a.   It would be nice if the room had [fewer, less] flowers.

    b.   There were [fewer, less] opportunities to get to the beach than I had hoped.

    c.   [Fewer, Less] horses were on the island.

    d.   Six [fewer, less] cars finished the race.

    e.   There was [fewer, less] water in the bathtub than when he got in.

    f.   She drank [fewer, less] ginger-ale than before.

    g.   [Fewer, Less] snow fell on the Thanksgiving Day Parade this year.

    h.   I made [fewer, less] money off that sale.

After pondering a-h, consider what you would normally say in the following contexts.

    i.   The sign in the express lane in the grocery store reads "13 items or [fewer, less]."

    j.   We will deliver this pizza in 30 minutes or [fewer, less].

    k.   The contractor should finish the deck in 45 days or [fewer, less].

    l.   A lot of the gasoline leaked out so there is even [fewer, less].

5.   An article of transformation:

The words *a* and *an* have been used as indefinite determiners for a long time in English. The older form in all contexts was *an* because it originally came from *one*. Over time, the nasal *n* dropped off before consonants (e.g. *an book* → *a book*). That trend has continued, and some speakers of modern English have mostly *a* in their normal speech. For the phrases below, are some more acceptable than others for you? What phonological environments would you guess are more likely to find *a* before a vowel?

    a.   *a Inflectional Phrase* vs. *an Inflectional Phrase*

    b.   *a elephant* vs. *an elephant*

    c.   *a ant* vs. *an ant*

    d.   *a cat* vs. *an cat*

    e.   *a inquiry* vs. *an inquiry*

    f.   *a ostrich* vs. *an ostrich*

    g.   *a ukulele* vs. *an ukulele*

    h.   *a NSF proposal* vs. *an NSF proposal*

    i.   *a ESPN-televised game* vs. *an ESPN-televised game*

    j.   *a union job* vs. *an union job*

    k.   *a historic day* vs. *an historic day*

    l.   *a FBI informant* vs. *an FBI informant*

    m.   *a STD* vs. *an STD*

    n.   *a elf* vs. *an elf*

    o.   *a echo* vs. *an echo*

    p.   *a indelible mark* vs. *an indelible mark*

    q.   *a English teacher* vs. *an English teacher*

6. The prescription of the hyphen:
    Articulate what rules might exist for hyphens given the following forms, and compare your assessment with a modern style guide.
    In attributive, compound adjectives:
    a. well-trained falcon vs. African American English
    b. Judeo-Christian traditions vs. Asian American culture
    c. Irish English Resource Centre vs. Hiberno-English dictionary
    In compounds:
    d. cubby hole vs. cubby-hole vs. cubbyhole
    e. out-loud vs. out loud
    f. T-shirt vs. TV
    g. T-rex vs. Trex

7. Aspect: Progressive vs. neutral
    Can you find any prescriptive advice (internet or style-manual based) on the following synchronic variation in the form of verbs?
    a. The people who are conversing should look at each other.
    b. The people who converse should look at each other.
    c. The people who are conversing are saying things that help each other communicate cooperatively.
    d. The people who converse say things that help each other communicate cooperatively.
    e. I would expel all students who are throwing things.
    f. I would expel all students who throw things.
    g. An example would be a friend saying *ice cream* after hearing about last night's game.
    h. An example would be a friend who says *ice cream* after hearing about last night's game.

8. *Which* hunting revisited: *that* vs. *which*
    Read the following Language Log post and then search out, copy, paste, and label 10 internet instances each of restrictive and nonrestrictive *which*: (http://languagelog.ldc.upenn.edu/nll/?p=3934 or just search for *Language Log 3934*).

9. Epicene *they*:
    Singular *they* is an increasingly frequent trend: Read two of the Language Log posts on singular *they* and then search out, copy, and paste 15 internet instances of singular *they*: (http://languagelog.ldc.upenn .edu/nll/?cat=27 or search for *Language Log singular they*).

10. Consider the following texts, including their genres, and decide how they would be judged by both the Prescriptively Correct Perspective and the Rhetorically Correct Perspective. Explain and justify your decisions.

    Toni Morrison (1987): *Beloved*
    I got a tree on my back and a haint in my house, and nothing in between but the daughter I am holding in my arms. No more

running – from nothing. I will never run from another thing on this earth. I took one journey and I paid for the ticket, but let me tell you something, Paul D Garner: it cost too much! Do you hear me? It cost too much.

(15)

…

The picture is still there and what's more, if you go there – you who never was there – if you go there and stand in the place where it was, it will happen again; it will be there for you, waiting for you. So, Denver, you can't never go there. Never. Because even though it's all over – over and done with – it's going to always be there waiting for you.

(36)

Mary Ann Samyn (2005): *Purr*, "Cabin Fever in the Gray World"

My overture. Her sugary.
My overture. Her ferocity.

It's a toss-up.

Ring. Ring. Ring. Ring. Ring.

In her voice, when I hear it if I do,
a pivot:

    Don't you / worry / about / me.

This is tone, boys and girls. Inflection.

All day the day snows down around
each of us separately.

No, the day's debris----

group work

11. Malapropisms:
     What linguistic contrasts are in malapropisms that make them funny for so many people? If they are not funny for you, what linguistic contrasts are missing? What level of language is being contrasted? Consider the following malapropisms as part of your answer.
     a. Sheridan: Mrs. Malaprop: "…she's as headstrong as an *allegory* on the banks of the Nile." (i.e. *alligator*; *The Rivals* Act III, Scene III Line 195)

    b.   Shakespeare: "if she has been a woman *cardinally* given" (i.e. *carnally*; *Measure for Measure*, Act 2, Scene I)

    c.   Shakespeare: "I will tell her, sir, that you do *protest*, which, as I take it, is a gentlemanlike offer." (i.e. *propose*; Romeo and Juliet Act 2, Scene IV)

    d.   Archie Bunker: "A *Menstrual* show" (i.e. *minstrel*; *All in the Family)*

    e.   Archie Bunker: "In closing, I'd like to say *Molotov.*" (i.e. *Mazel Tov*; *All in the Family)*

    f.   Bart Simpson: "The *ironing* is delicious." (i.e. *irony*; "Lisa's Date with Destiny" from *The Simpsons*)

12.   Consider the following sets of words:

    a.   rise, mount, ascent
    b.   ask, question, interrogate
    c.   fast, firm, secure
    d.   fire, flame, conflagration
    e.   holy, sacred, consecrated
    f.   time, age, epoch

To figure out what meanings the different words evoke, construct a sentence to frame them and see which one fits best. For example, "The glue will hold the note [fast, firm, secure] to the frame." Alternatively, use a good dictionary to search out and copy down an example sentence for each word (noting how the diction and tone of the words differ).

The first word in each set has Germanic roots. The second has a French origin. The third is of Latin ancestry. How does the origin of the word line-up with your group's interpretation of the words' connotations?

13.   Within your group, come up with five prescriptive rules that are regularly ignored in most spoken conversations. Provide an example for each one. Does most of your group agree that they should be ignored?

14.   *Shibboleth* words:

What is a pronunciation of a word that is stigmatized in your hometown and is used to distinguish one group of people from another?

15.   For the following questions, discuss why all of the following statements are false.

    ~~True or~~ False:

    a.   Language is one of our most important cultural inventions.
    b.   Language change is a process of decay.
    c.   Grammar books used in schools cover most of the rules and processes of English.
    d.   Eskimos have many words for snow, and they "see" snow differently than others do.
    e.   Writing and speech are essentially the same thing.

    f.   Appalachian English is Elizabethan English.

    g.   Children require detailed instruction to learn language.

16. Overt or nonovert:

Complementizers do not always have to be pronounced in normal English conversations. Would most of your group produce the complementizer in these sentences?

    a.   Does most of your group agree [∅, that] they should be ignored?

    b.   The man [∅, that] I bought the pug from died.

    c.   I drive the minivan now that my partner has the car [∅, that] we bought last week.

    d.   Those hawks [∅, that] we saw in the state park are on the news.

    e.   The oldest tortoise [∅, that] I know of lives on St. Helena.

What is different about this next sentence?

    f.   Did you see the sugar glider [∅, that] was in that man's pocket?

study questions

1. How are English courses similar to PE courses?

2. Why is learning about language different from learning about writing?

3. What is prescriptivism?

4. What is the prescriptive basis for judgment?

5. What are three basic facts about language variation?

6. In what ways is English spelling a conservative system?

7. Is there only one standard English?

8. What are genre conventions?

9. What is PCP?

10. What is RCP?

11. How does content validity work with standardized testing?

12. What is the difference between a descriptive grammar and a prescriptive grammar?

13. Explain and give an example of a pet peeve.

14. What is a shibboleth?

Visit the book's companion website for additional resources relating to this chapter at: http://www.wiley.com/go/hazen/introlanguage

11 The Life Cycles of Language

An Introduction to Language, First Edition. Kirk Hazen.
© 2015 John Wiley & Sons, Inc. Published 2015 by John Wiley & Sons, Inc.

chapter overview

In this chapter, we discuss the different life cycles of language: From babies babbling their first words, through language change in our individual lives, to language change across centuries. Through all of these different stages, we create variation, and the current result of 1,500 years of English variation is the diversity of national and regional Englishes we see spanning the entire globe. We start the chapter where you started, by acquiring language through three stages all humans pass through on the way to having a language. We also check out the kinds of language changes you might go through in your lifetime. After starting with you, we investigate the range of synchronic and diachronic variation other English speakers have created after they acquired language. We also review some examples of language variation that have been described in the previous chapters in order to illustrate what is possible for us to produce. With all the different patterns of variation, we seamlessly weave together our daily language as part of our social lives. Even after all the change we make, we continue to communicate with our languages as (in)efficiently as we ever did. Our daily language is part of the fabric of language history, and our word choices and pronunciation twists decide what patches go into the quilt that will be the future history of English. In this chapter, you get to explore the kinds of changes that have come before and can envision the kinds of changes English will undergo in the next 100 years.

language acquisition

Babies are adorable. As I write this, a baby sits in his mom's lap at my local coffee shop (the Daily Grind), looking around his world, drumming the table, fascinated by the service dog sitting on the floor near him. As he drums the table and looks for attention with exploratory smiles, he hears all kinds of noise around him: music, traffic from outside, the cling-swoosh-chink of the kitchen and espresso machine. He is happy and inquisitive. He is also learning. He is learning at an amazing rate; I would call it work, but he looks too joyful (now chewing on his mom's iPhone). For students in high school and college who have to learn a language, it certainly seems like work. How does the baby enjoy what he does so effortlessly, but the older we get, the more difficult it is to learn a language?

This contrast between children and adults learning language was a mystery that was often ignored throughout centuries of language study. With the advent of modern language science, we have added greatly to our understanding of how we develop languages. The field of study is normally called child language acquisition. This academic field studies how children build a mental grammar and develop the skills needed to become a competent adult language user.

A key distinction to remember from Chapter 1 is the difference between **language acquisition** and language learning. To open a textbook and memorize

Spanish verb conjugations is an example of language learning. It involves formal instruction and a conscious effort to practice pronunciations and memorize grammatical rules.

Language acquisition is where a baby uses its biologically-encoded instructions and the language information in the environment to build a mental grammar of the language. Words and other lexical items are memorized easily, and the lexicon expands to many thousands of words. We do not remember the effort we put into language acquisition; it was a natural part of being human.

One of the nifty things about babies and language is that all of us, regardless of geographical location, race, or gender, go through the same stages of language acquisition. It is such a regular process across our species that when children fail to reach certain language milestones, parents and doctors start to diagnose possible problems, such as autism and hearing impairment. With language acquisition, like with most human skills, individuals differ from each other. Some people burst through the stages at a rapid run, while others take a more leisurely pace. At times, parents will brag on their children for learning new words and making new sounds, and certainly they should be proud. Still, normally developing children who acquire language slower than other children end up as fluent as those who acquire language faster. On the other hand, children who have been exposed to more words end up performing better on a wide range of standardized tests in their adolescence.

The overlapping stages of language acquisition include the following:

- sound stage
- word stage
- phrase stage

These stages are broad, overlapping categories. These stages are also over-simplifications. Building mental grammars is one of the most complex things we do as children, and these stages broadly describe only some major activities.

The first stage of language acquisition is the **sound stage**. Studies suggest that this stage starts before birth. Its end depends on what we consider to be the end of language acquisition. Infants face the challenge of hearing a lot of sounds in the world. It is a challenge because the language sounds have to be distinguished from music and barking dogs and noisy toys. As part of our innate knowledge of language, very young children identify language sounds because they are extraordinary listeners. More so than at any later part of their lives, babies younger than 6 months of age can distinguish all human language sounds. Remember, babies come equipped to acquire any of the 6,900+ languages on Earth and any of the previously-living languages. Starting at around 6 months, children narrow their listening range down to just those sounds that are part of the languages they hear on a regular basis. Different languages have different numbers of sounds, and babies pick up some sounds earlier than others (see Word Play: Baby sounds).

To learn language sounds, babies play with them. We call it babbling, but it is important and necessary to acquire a language. Babbling is the natural way to work out what sounds are part of the language and how to make them. Babies themselves do not have any formal training about where to move their tongues or how to shape their mouths. They must babble and play with the tools they have to figure it out. Babbling is so natural that even children acquiring a signed language babble with their hands. Children work on pronunciations of certain sounds for years, and of course, words like *spaghetti, significantly,* and *circum-navigation* can give all kinds of troubles, as do pairings in a sentence like *The committee members deliberate very deliberately.*

Word Play: Baby sounds

What sounds are hard for babies to learn, and what sounds are easier? It might be more useful for them to cry, and it might be more fun for them to laugh. But, language sounds get special treatment by babies.

The easiest language sounds for them to make are vowels. With vowels, they only have to shape their mouths and make voiced air blow over their vocal folds. What vowels they carve out is the question. Babies do not find vowels like lost change in the couch. They start with all the vowels sounds mushed together, like a giant block of soap. Their job is to carve out the vowels which match the ones they hear adults produce and throw the rest of the material away.

Consonants have more constriction and more definite places of articulation, yet some are easier than others. Bilabials like [m] and [p] are relatively easy. Other sounds are more tricky. For sounds like [s] and [z], it helps to have teeth first. Sounds like [θ] and [ð] take even longer. These two interdental fricatives are not part of many languages, and children acquire them later than most other consonant sounds. The leading guess is that their rare presence in human language results from the trouble babies have making them a part of the language.

Part of what children must learn are the syllable patterns for their languages. The one they learn first is also the one that is most common in the world's languages: Consonant Vowel (CV). Syllables like *mama* and *dada* are some of the first produced by many children, and some languages like Hawaiian or Japanese have almost exclusively CV syllables. If you take a Japanese word like デスク (desuku) 'desk' you will see an English loan word borrowed into Japanese. Compare the syllable structures of the Japanese and English words:

English: C V C C   Japanese: CV CV CV
            \<d e s k>   \<de su ku>

Figure 11.1 Baby signing. © Pop! Studio Photography/Corbis.

The English syllable structure, with its double consonant coda, would not be pronounceable in Japanese, so *desk* was modified with extra vowels to make it fit the CV template. When all human children are developing syllables, they start with basics like (CV) and (V), and if their language requires it, they move on to more complex onsets (CCV like *sky*) and complex codas (CVCC like *paste*). It is important to emphasize that languages with less complex syllable structures are neither inferior nor more primitive than other languages: They can be as technical, scholarly, and romantic as their speakers need them to be.

Most children have almost all their sounds and syllable patterns down by age 10, but starting after age three, children begin a different kind of sound project. They begin the transition away from sounding like their parents and towards sounding like their friends. It is a gradual process, but by 18 or so, the observable influence from parents is slight.

Within the realm of sound systems (phonology), the influence from parents is weakest. For example, my dad from rural Florida has the *pin~pen* merger, and my mom from Pittsburgh, Pennsylvania has the *caught~cot* merger. Growing up outside Detroit, Michigan, I picked up neither of those mergers, but I did join in with the vowel shifts of all the other suburban Detroit kids. Teenagers especially use sound differences to mark social cliques, and their communicative competence grows mightily as they figure out their identities.

One of the debates about the sound stage of acquisition is the use of "baby talk" or "motherese." This general category of language is called child-directed speech, and researchers have found that differences do exist between speakers' child-directed speech and their speech to others. One of the differences is in

Word Play: Extreme language learners: Ken Hale and how many languages?

Most people are exposed to at least two languages as children, but after puberty, picking up another language becomes much more difficult. A few people seem not to lose their ability to acquire a language. It is as if their Universal Grammars have not shut off, and they are able to build mental grammars of any language to which they are sufficiently exposed. These people are known as **polyglots**.

One of these rare humans was Ken Hale, and the linguistics profession had the good fortune to have him as one of our own. He studied many different kinds of languages and championed endangered languages. He acquired numerous languages, including English, Spanish, Tono O'odham, Jemez, Hopi, Navajo, and Warlpiri. He did not just learn a few words in each; rather, he sounded like a native speaker to other native speakers. If all of us had polyglot brains, learning other languages would be much easier. Yet, such skills are very rare.

how they distinguish their vowels. If you remember back to Chapter 2 and 3, we map differences between vowels in vowel space. The distinctions come with categories like high, front, tense [i]. For child-directed speech, vowels are made more distinct, so that vowels like [i] in *sheep* and [u] in *flute* are further apart from each other and the vowel [a] in *hot*. Not all kinds of child-directed speech show such differences, so it is tough to tell if such distinctions are *necessary* to acquire language. Many different kinds of language environments allow for language acquisition.

Child-directed speech with different intonation and volume-levels does draw infants' attention, and parents like to feel they are making a difference. As Levine and Munsch (2013) document, child-directed speech in no way deters or slows down language development. Yet, only some societies use it. They cite the Kaluli of Papua New Guinea who do not talk directly to their children until they can speak back, a habit found in several African communities. The Kaluli have no baby talk. The unusual trait for the Kaluli is that they speak *for* their babies to others, lending their children their voice until they can find their own. Despite these variations between how people speak to or do not speak to their infants, the babies themselves acquire language in the same stages the world over. This uniformity starts with the basic genetic instructions our species uses to acquire language. Because children build their mental grammars from the data around them, they sometimes come up with different pronunciations from their parents, as in this *Natalie Dee* comic: http://www.nataliedee.com/071813

The second stage of language acquisition is the **word stage**. Using the arbitrary connection of form and meaning as a starting point, children have the monumental task of learning tens of thousands of form/meaning pairs (words).

Remember that children do not start with words in their heads, but they seem to start with a lexicon that contains slots for nouns and verbs and possibly other lexical categories. Between one and one and a half years old, most children will start saying single words: The forms will be attached to specific and repeatable meanings (e.g. *toe* will mean *toe* every time it is spoken). All that babbling they started in the sound stage will be increasingly directed toward making repeatable sound combinations, in syllables, and then hooking those up with meanings. Plus, there are clear orders by which children learn words. Content categories – the nouns, verbs, and adjectives – are learned before function words like conjunctions, prepositions, and determinatives. Most children who acquire English probably learn the form *dog* as a noun (e.g. *the dog*) before they learn it as a verb (e.g. *The tax collector dogged me*), if they ever do. The syntactic and semantic context of the word provides clues as to what words fit in what slots.

Children are amazing word collectors, learning thousands of words every year. As we studied in Chapter 5, teenagers create slang words to mark where they fall socially, but learning those lexical items is part of a process they started when they were quite small. As an added bonus to the word stage, this ability to learn new words and create them when needed is one of the few skills we carry forward into our adult lives.

The third stage of language acquisition is the **phrase stage**. The start of this stage overlaps with the word stage for an obvious reason: We must have morphemes to build phrases. Usually the phrase stage starts off modestly around age two, and it starts logically enough, with most children using two word combinations to get the job done:

- *Pig play*: 'I want to play with the guinea pig'
- *More juice*: "Could you get me some more juice' (with an aside of 'I promise more sugar will not make me act like a maniac')
- *No tickle*: 'Please stop tickling me' (with an aside of 'That way I will not bash myself on the table')

Children then build up over the next months, creating three- and four-word phrases (e.g. *Give me more juice*). The following step in the phrase stage is the "all-hell-breaks-loose" period, as Stephen Pinker in *The Language Instinct* describes it. Children go from condensed short phrases to as many words as they see fit; there is no clear transition from a five-word stage to a six-word stage. Once children are able to designate hierarchy and constituency among their morphemes, once they are able to embed those phrase trees, they can build phrases as long as they please. It is this later part of the phrase stage that children start to add function morphemes to their phrases. A sentence like *Pig play* at age two can be *I want to play with the pig* at age four, adding in the pronoun *I*, the verb inflection, the preposition *with*, and the determinative *the*.

Between two and 12, all three stages work to construct the mental grammar. The sound stage might add templates for more complex onsets in syllables (CCCVC like *strike*) while the word and phrase stages are churning to help with complex constructions like perfect aspect (e.g. *I had cleaned my plate; I don't know why there is still salad on it*). As children make progress in the word and sound stages, sometimes parents think their children are going backwards. Early on in the word stage, children learn to memorize forms like *tooth~teeth* and *teach~taught*. These are irregular forms of nouns and verbs. Later in the word stage, children begin to learn morphological patterns. For example, they pick up skills with function morphemes to make nouns plural: *duck~ducks*. When they then begin to apply those patterns to every singular noun, the result is that their plural patterns are completely regular, but their memorized forms are wiped away. Previously memorized forms like *tooth~teeth* become regularized as *tooth~tooths*. This step means they are learning the patterns of the language and are developing normally. These children have transitioned from purely memorized forms to a rule of the mental grammar. After this point, they begin to learn that there are exceptions to the rules, both for plurals like *foot~feet* and *tooth~teeth* as well as irregular verbs like *swim~swam* and *teach~taught*.

The challenges facing children attempting to acquire language are as varied as the languages themselves. In plenty of languages, there is morphological marking on nouns, but in some of those, the subject itself is able to be absent. Carmel O'Shannessy (2014) has worked on Warlpiri, a language spoken by a few thousand people in the northern territory of Australia. In this language, the thing doing the action can be marked with a suffix, here *-ngku*.

1. Jarntu-<u>ngku</u>   ka-ø-jana   wajilypi-nyi   kurdu-kurdu.
   dog-ERGATIVE   IMPF-3SGS-3PLO   chase-NONPST   child-REDUP
      'The dog is chasing the children.'

2. Kurdu-kurdu   ka-ø-jana   wajilypi-nyi   jarntu-<u>ngku</u>.
   child-REDUP   IMPF-3SGS-3PLO   chase-NONPST   dog-ERGATIVE
      'The dog is chasing the children.'

As O'Shannessy describes, the two Warlpiri sentences have the same meaning. The *-ngku* suffix marks the dog as the chaser in each case. What makes acquisition for this trait especially tricky is that sometimes the subject in Warlpiri can be absent: Children have to figure out this kind of case marking from clues that variably occur. And amazingly, they do.

The acquisition of sounds, words, and phrases is part of the linguistic competence. Cultural competence is also acquired early in life. All of us had to sort out the cultural values of the varieties around us, the formal and informal registers people use in different contexts, and the styles associated with different places, jobs, and social classes. Children have as their models the adult conversations they hear around them. For example, English-speaking children ages six and older know to use [in] for words like *walking* in more fun, casual situations and [iŋ] more in serious, formal situations. Although a great deal of the acquisition of cultural competence is unconscious, not all of it is. Often, caregivers teach children traits of social registers: Inside a store, all parents have had to ask their children to speak more quietly; children have to use their "inside voice" because the shopping register does not include yelling as a polite language choice.

The leading hypothesis about how the human brain orchestrates the sound, word, and phrase stages along with the complexities of cultural competence is that our brains are wired from birth to acquire language. Exactly what the infant's brain knows about language is still up in the air, but humans acquire language as easily as they learn to run. This means that it is as natural for a human being to talk as it is for a bird to sing or for a spider to spin a web. In this sense, language may be like walking: The ability to walk is an instinct, and children develop the ability to walk whether or not anybody tries to teach them to do so. In the same way, children develop the ability to talk whether or not anybody tries to teach them. For this reason, many linguists believe that language ability is genetically coded. Researchers believe there is a **critical period** (lasting roughly from birth until puberty) during which language acquisition is the effortless, natural response to a language environment. The leading understanding is that changes occur in the structure of the brain during puberty, stopping the effortlessness. After that point, it is much harder to learn a new language. Unfortunately, that is exactly when most second-language education begins in the United States.

synchronic variation

Innovations in language can start with speakers of any age, but teenagers in many cultures advance them to new levels. Despite parents' protestations, teenagers are not a different species (although I cannot disprove that aliens traded out their sweet, docile children for hellions from another planet). Teenagers' reactions to authority and social constraints are part of their story. Another part is their masterful skills of social assessment. Although they may never admit it, teenagers are socially aware to extreme extents. With their social skills, they deploy and take note of a wide variety of language variation. They can quickly discern slight differences in vowels and assign social attributes to those. Of course, they are not consciously telling themselves, "Her [æ] in *fat* is really raised and on the periphery of vowel space. She definitely must be a burnout." The association of some linguistic quality and a social group is automatic and does not require special vocabulary or conscious attention to be processed.

Adults have been complaining about teenagers' language for at least 2,400 years. In 360 BCE, Plato wrote the dialogue *Cratylus*. Within this work, Socrates develops a philosophy of language based on a simple question: Are names inherent to their objects or are they conventionally associated? At one point, Socrates (wrongly) sides with a natural connection and decries that "the present generation care for euphony more than truth." This protest is one of the earliest extant complaints of language variation in western civilization. Socrates contends that the contemporary youth are changing the sounds of the 'true' names, hence ruining what has been given by gods and legislators. Many people have complained about language variation since Socrates, but all living languages change.

As change sweeps through a community, even some of the adults can get caught up in the change and participate in what is called **lifespan language change**.

This term refers to language change, mostly phonological change, after the critical period of language acquisition has ended. Gillian Sankoff introduced this term and studied how it plays out for speakers in Montreal, Canada. She focused on a pronunciation difference in Rs, where an older, alveolar variant of R has given way to the European norm of a uvular variant, which is made at the back of the mouth. Sankoff (2005) described the transition of some speakers from the alveolar R to the uvular R across their adult lives to be lifespan change. In other words, as teenagers, these Montreal speakers would have the alveolar R in words like *rouge* and *partir* in their youth but the uvular R in those words as they got older. It is not the most common phenomenon, but it is not exceedingly rare either. Lifespan change does appear to be restricted: Adult speakers only change in the direction the community is headed. Lifespan change does not refer to changes in a speaker's lexicon since we are all able to add words throughout our adult lives. It refers instead to phonological and morphological patterns like R-dropping and -*ly* variation (e.g. *She runs quick* vs. *she runs quickly*).

Synchronic variation is natural and forms the basis for language change. One of the things that helps it along towards language change is contact with other varieties. In the United States, there are 381 languages other than English according to the US Census, with 169 of them being Native American languages (http://www.census.gov/hhes/socdemo/language/). Unfortunately, despite their long-standing status on the North American continent, those speakers only number about half a million. In comparison there are 60 million speakers of the other 212 languages (combined). The map in Figure 11.2 shows there are few Native American languages in the eastern United States, a result of forced migration programs and educational restrictions disallowing such languages to be taught. This *xkcd* comic is titled "National Language" and comments on conflicting opinions: http://xkcd.com/84/.

In 2007, according to American Community Survey of the US Census, there were seven non-English languages in the United States with more than a million speakers. Spanish had the largest number, with 34.5 million speakers. Check out the US Census's Language Mapper, where you can find the distribution of these languages and zoom into to local communities: http://census.gov/hhes/socdemo/language/data/language_map.html. The other languages were Chinese (with varieties grouped together), French, Tagalog, Vietnamese, German, and Korean. In the maps of Figure 11.3, drawn from an American Community Service report in 2010, it is easy to see that these languages are distributed in a few different places in the United States. German- and Spanish-speaking populations do not overlap with each other, nor do they greatly overlap with the Slavic languages, although there is a bit of overlap between French and Spanish in Florida. All of these areas have the possibility for contact between speakers of different languages, especially English, and the synchronic language variation of that contact can lead to different paths of diachronic variation over time.

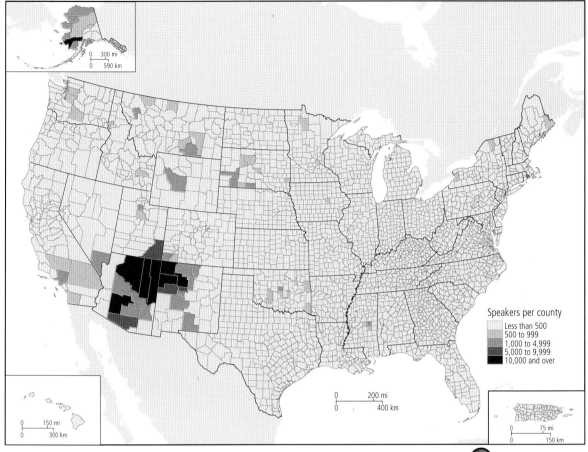

Figure 11.2   Number of speakers of Native North American languages, by county: 2006–2010. US Census Bureau. http://www.census.gov/prod/2011pubs/acsbr10-10.pdf

Although adults do not change dramatically in a particular language variety throughout their lives, all adults produce and take in language variation. Here we review some of the language variation patterns we have encountered throughout this book.

Language variation plays an important role for every human language. The variation of vocabulary, sounds, and syntax is why we have different languages. These should be considered nonmutually intelligible dialects of human language; the variation amongst them is enough to ensure we cannot understand each other. As discussed in Chapters 7 and 8, many linguists hypothesize that this kind of language variation is controlled by innate parameters set during the language acquisition process.

For both sounded languages and signed languages, there is variation in what people do. If you remember from Chapters 2 and 3, the R sounds in English contain a good deal of variation. To refresh your memories, try the following sentence out loud and note where your tongue is for each R sound: *The ho_r_se*

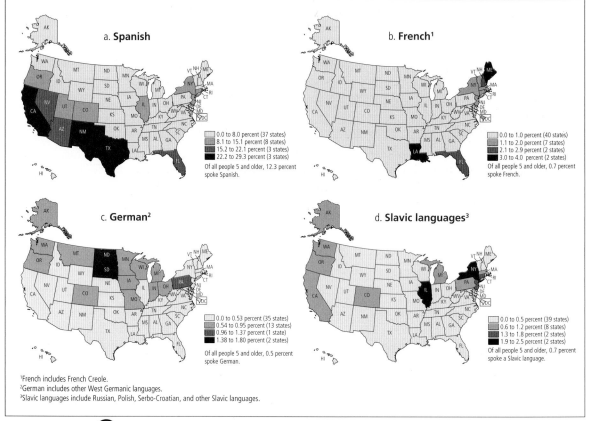

Figure 11.3   Percentage of the population 5 years and older speaking specified languages by state: 2007. US Census Bureau. http://www.census.gov/prod/2010pubs/acs-12.pdf

ran th<u>r</u>ough the wo<u>r</u>st puddle. For some people, their tongues during the R sound are bunched up in the back of the mouth, around the velar region where we pronounce the <k> of *kick*: a bunched R. For the other people, their tongues lie flat except for the tip, which is curled back slightly in the alveolar region of the mouth: a curled R. One way to test if you have a curled R or a bunched R is by saying the words *ho<u>r</u>se* and *wo<u>r</u>st*: If the <s> sounds more like an <sh> [ʃ] in *ha<u>rsh</u>* or *ma<u>rsh</u>*, then these Rs are probably curled Rs. Plenty of people report having both kinds of R. It is common for people to vary between bunched and curled Rs depending on the sound context of the R. Curled Rs are more likely in words like *rat, read, pry,* or *try*; bunched Rs are more likely in words like *bark, lager, poor,* or *quirk.*

As with the situation described above for Montreal, there are several different kinds of R in the world. Although the trilled Scottish R is socially different from the curled British R, the different Rs in the United States do not seem to have any social values attached to them. Since there is synchronic variation in the pronunciation of Rs, in the future some communities or social groups could take either the curled R or the bunched R and mark it in some social way. Were it to become a social marker of some group's identity, certain people would adopt it to identify with that group, while others would choose the other variant to distance themselves from that group.

Despite the variation of R across and within national varieties, some people will not vary between types of R. For the next sound, almost all US speakers produce synchronic variation. Like R, the L sounds can be produced either in the alveolar or velar regions of the mouth, depending on the phonological environment of the L. Try this sentence out loud to jog your memory about the feel of L-variation in English: *Leaves fall*. For *leaves*, the L sound will probably be in the alveolar region (the light L of Chapter 3); for *fall*, the L sound will probably be in the velar region (the dark L of Chapter 3). You should be able to glean this information from working through the following list of words and checking your own mouth to see where the Ls fall.

List 1: Different flavors of L
1.   a. leak
       b. bowl
2.   a. laugh
       b. cool
3.   a. probably
       b. control
4.   a. lift
       b. stall
5.   a. left
       b. pull

For most speakers, the light L will be in (a) and the dark L will be in (b). In some areas of the United States, for example parts of Appalachia and the South, speakers might not have any audible L in the (b) words. In other sets of L words, because language norms have changed over the centuries, English speakers vary widely on whether or not they produce L sounds: *palm, calm, balm, psalm, salmon, wolf, golf, chalk, stalk, talk*. Do you have any kind of L in those words? If so, what kind? These differences offer a good opportunity to highlight the concept of correctness in pronunciation. With these words, people have competing pronunciations of L, neither of which is more or less natural. In parallel, the pronunciation with or without the [l] may be judged as socially correct, but that judgment would be based on local social factors, not linguistic ones.

In varieties of English around the globe, another area of synchronic variation is happening with the sounds associated with [θ] and [f]: The [f] sound can replace the [θ] sound when pronouncing words like *birthday* → *birfday* and *bath* → *baf*. Like the R and L sounds, the [θ] and [f] sounds are closely related; switching [f] for [θ] is a simple and normal variation in the place of articulation. This synchronic variation is not seen as bad in all varieties, and in some it is completely unnoticed. In Australia, New Zealand, and England, it is common enough in some communities that it is socially unmarked. The same goes for areas of the Southern United States, but for the rest of the United States, it is heavily stigmatized. The variation between [θ] and [f] is a good illustration of how synchronic variation is used in social judgments: In some US communities, the [f] for [θ] variation is socially unmarked; in others, it is associated with disparaged social groups and is therefore stigmatized. In all these communities, the language variation itself is the same.

The small variations in language can appear and disappear without much notice or effect. They appear and disappear like so many bubbles rising and popping at the surface of boiling water. Yet, humans are really good at finding patterns. When given language variation, we often connect the dots to make a picture. If we grew up in the US South, we might notice that African Americans in our local area say [ɔnt] for *aunt* while other people say [ænt]. In areas of Philadelphia, we might consider the [ɔnt] for *aunt* pronunciation to be a fancy way of speaking, regardless of ethnicity. It will only take a few instances for us to set up the association between one pronunciation and one social group, but once we set it up, it is more difficult for us to dislodge it and re-establish a new association with those language variation patterns.

diachronic variation

what English was

Some of the synchronic variation we create every day does more than appear and disappear. Some of it affects the future. As social pressures pull and shove bits of variation about, some grow to be more common, becoming the new norm and eventually a regular part of the language. In this section, we trace some examples of diachronic variation in English to highlight snapshots of what English has been and what it has become.

Synchronic variation does not transform into diachronic variation overnight. With pronunciations, synchronic variation sometimes carries on for centuries, especially with consonants. When words like *which* were spelled in Old English, they appear to have been spelled according to their pronunciation, *hwich*. The first sound was a voiceless [h] with the lip-rounding of [w]. In varieties of English around the world, there has been variation between the innovative [w] and the original [hw] pronunciation. For most speakers in the United States, the [w] form in words like *which*, *where*, *whether*, and *whale* is probably the most common pronunciation. Yet, there is still disagreement about what the supposedly "correct" form for these <wh> spellings should be: The Oxford English Dictionary portrays *whale* as only having the [hweil] pronunciation. This more conservative form is receding but still present for a noticeable portion of the population. These two forms will probably be in competition with each other for at least another half century.

Synchronic variation also affects how lexical qualities change. In Old English, people used to have a form of the word *worthy* which allowed a following complementizer clause with "that":

- Old English: *ic ne eom wythe that ic thin sunu beo genemned.*
- Gloss: 'I not am worthy that I your son be called (named).'
- Translation: 'I am not worthy to be called your son.'

Today, *worthy* requires a following infinitive verb phrase: For example, *I am not worthy to be called your son.* The kind of complement the verb requires has changed, and this example is a small illustration of what kinds of changes have happened in lexical variation. This diachronic variation is similar to the synchronic variation for how the verb *need* in English has different lexical renditions in different regions of the United States. In some varieties, *need* requires an infinitive clause (e.g. *to be washed*); in other varieties, *need* requires a perfect participle (e.g. *washed*).

Other variation from previous centuries has picked up social meaning related to both social differences and differences in the formality of the context. The most prolific example is that of *-ing* variation. As was discussed in Chapter 6, the Old English suffix *-ende* (e.g. *wrīt-ende*) served as what became the progressive participle: "The scribe was *writing*." Early on, that suffix only had that one duty. A different suffix, *-inge* (e.g. *wrīt-inge)*, had a different job: It made verbs into nouns (e.g. *The scribe's writing confused me*). No social meaning appears to have been attached to either one during these earlier stages of English. As the two forms began to be confused, and their spellings were standardized as <ing> after the printing press was established in England (1476), social meanings began to be attached to the two suffixes. The [n] form came to be associated with lower social classes in England; thus, the [ŋ] form became associated with higher social classes. As a consequence, the social class markings were interpreted for all speakers as register variation, so that the [n] form is perceived as more informal and the [ŋ] form is viewed as more formal. Even young children today learn to shift their *-ing* to fit more or less formal contexts. What began as two separate suffixes in English has ended up as variation registering social class and formality. It has been a journey covering several centuries for these suffixes, but language variation continues on for English today. Future centuries may well look back at our current synchronic variation to find the birth of social markers for their times.

vowel shifts

Speakers pronounce vowels in lots of different ways for all languages. Everyone has a range of different pronunciations for what they treat as the same vowel. Plus the context around the vowel affects how it is pronounced. The /i/ vowels in *teen*, *meet*, *mead*, and *weed* will all be slightly different pronunciations, although native speakers recognize them all as "the same vowel." Because of the different phonetic environments, what is psychologically the same vowel (in other words, the same phoneme) ends up having the different pronunciations. Social factors, such as speakers' identities with their social class or their local clique, drive the different pronunciations further apart. Were vowels like cats, they would scatter randomly throughout vowel space. Yet, despite its relaxed attitude about place of articulation, vowel space is not ruled by chaos. There are clear paths to which vowels adhere when they move about in vowel space. We examine a major vowel shift, but many more exist, including some currently in the United States. Most likely, in your home community, several vowels are on the move.

Perhaps the most important vowel shift in English history is called the **Great Vowel Shift**. The Great Vowel Shift was so named for the same reason that World War I was named the Great War: It was such a massive event that it was unimaginable that it could ever be repeated. However, because of World War II, the Great War had to be renamed. Despite several major vowel shifts today, there are no plans to rename the Great Vowel Shift. It was a change in the pronunciation of long vowels over about two hundred years (roughly 1400–1600). There are several competing ideas of what triggered this change socially, but the linguistic happenings are well documented.[1]

Before the Great Vowel Shift, English had long and short vowels. As discussed in Chapter 2, since that time, we have had tense and lax vowels. The reason for the switch from a long/short system to a tense/lax system is that the pre-Great Vowel Shift vowel pairs were broken in the shift. The vowel chart in Figure 11.4 displays the arrangement of long vowels: The straight line on top represents long vowels (e.g. ī), and the short vowels are represented with the curved symbol on top (e.g. ŏ). In the pre-Great Vowel System, each long vowel had a short vowel counterpart.

The arrows in the next vowel chart illustrate that almost all the vowels pronounced with a Middle English long vowel moved to the next highest long-vowel pronunciation. Words with long vowels at the top of vowel space ended up, eventually, with diphthong vowels. So, the Middle English *pipe* and *hus* would have been pronounced [piːpə] and [huːs], respectively; in Modern English, they are pronounced [paɪp] and [haʊs]. A Middle English word such as *meet* and *boot* would have been pronounced as [meːt] and [boːt], respectively (note that the double-letter spellings were chosen to represent long vowels); in Modern English, they are pronounced as [mit] and [but]. The Middle English *hate* and *boat* would have been pronounced [haːtə] and [bɔːt], respectively; in Modern English, they are pronounced [het] and [bot].

Some of the words went up early for vowel reform, and some went up later. Therefore, we now have spellings which have split pronunciations. For example, the <ea> spelling of *meat* and *great* would lead us to believe that the vowels should be pronounced the same. At the start of the Great Vowel Shift, they were, but *meat* was an early adopter and hopped on the ē-train, the quickest way to the next stop. It was therefore able to make the connection to the ī-station with the rest of the ē-vowels. The vowel of *great* caught the later train to ē-station: When it arrived, the connection to the ī-station had already departed. The result is that in Modern English, *meat* is pronounced as [mit] while *great* is pronounced as [gret]. These various shifts added up to our modern system.

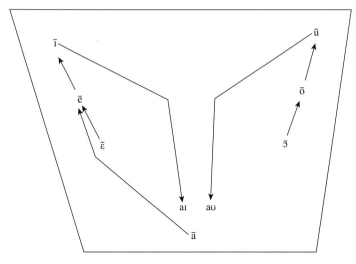

Figure 11.4   Some long vowel changes during the Great Vowel Shift.

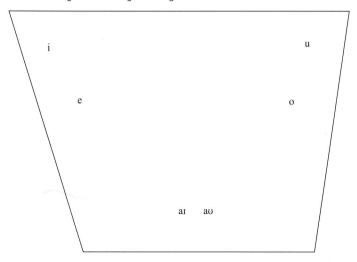

Figure 11.5   Modern English results of the former long vowel movements.

what English has become

If you remember back to Chapter 6, we worked through irregular verbs such as *find/found* and *seek/sought*. Some of the variations we have today in the English-speaking world come from synchronic variation over English's history. The memorized forms used to be regularly produced forms, but as the *-ed* method of making the past tense increasingly took over, the variation in past-tense forms was reduced. The different past-tense forms for the following verbs might have picked up social evaluations for you, but they remain normal instances of language variation. Which ones trigger social meanings for you?

- *Grow*: Over the summer, ivy _____ all over the shed.
- *Work*: Last week, I _____ hard to learn to be a blacksmith; I made a *wrought* iron gate.

- *Dive*: At the pool, she _____ five times in a minute.
- *Sneak*: Yesterday, I _____ into the game.
- *Hang*: Last month, Texas _____ three men. Last week, I _____ ten pictures.

In this set of irregular verbs, some have one form on which most people agree. Others might vary: Both *dived* and *dove* appear throughout the English-speaking world. These verb forms illustrate that what is "the norm" varies from area to area and from speaker to speaker. It is impossible to claim that the original form was the best, since for many verbs, the modern, socially-approved form is not the original form. Essentially, matters of correctness are contemporary social choices, not linguistic ones.

Consider these paths of variation. The verb *hang* has developed two accepted past-tense forms after more than a 1,000 years of variation: Often, *hung* is used for inanimate objects such as pictures and doors, but *hanged* is used for things being strung up by the neck and executed: For example, *They hung the picture but hanged the criminal.* The verb *dive* had the form *dived* for a few centuries, and this form is still normal in some English dialects. However, for most of the United States, the more normal form is *dove*; that change worked against the *-ed* trend because it was created by analogy with the verb *drive/drove*. The form *snuck* appears to be predominantly a US form which appears to have come about in the nineteenth century, but across even the United States, the original form of *sneaked* is still holding its ground.

For some of these forms, social valuations might be attached. Some of my students have argued that *snuck* is an ignorant form, only to be contradicted by other students who argue that *sneaked* is much worse. There is no linguistic argument for one over the other. The *snuck* form mirrors a previously productive way to make past-tense forms in English; however, that method went extinct, and only fossils from a previous time hang on. The *-ed* way of making past-tense forms was just one of several in Old English, but it kept converting verbs from other categories to join its pack. Now, it is seen as the "regular" way to make past-tense forms. Despite that 1,500 year history, the determination of "correctness" for any community is based on usage and fashion.

Our modern set of nouns in English still preserves forms originally crafted in the earliest day of English. Verbs are not the only parts of speech to have irregular forms. Nouns can have irregular or regular plural forms. In older forms of English, there were several different ways to make plural nouns; however, like irregular verbs, the numbers of ways to make a plural has dwindled over the centuries. Today, these irregulars are exceptions to the rule:

Irregular plurals
1. deer   deer
2. foot   feet
3. ox   oxen
4. focus   foci

These plurals have come to their modern form through different paths. The singular and plural form *deer* has been around as long as English itself; it belongs to a class of animal names which have always taken on the same form to represent the plural, like *sheep* and *fish*. The plural for *foot* used to be a larger class which changed the vowel to indicate plurality, as in the modern *mouse/mice* (though the plural for a computer *mouse* can be *mouses*). This class of vowel-changing plurals used to include *book*, the plural of which was something like *beek* (foot:feet::book:beek). Language change took place, and the plural of *book* took on its modern form, *books*. For *ox*, adding an <-en> on to a noun to make it plural used to be more common. In Chaucer's time (c. 1340–1400), nouns such as *eye* were still made plural this way:

> 551   That oon of hem was blynd and myghte nat see,
> The one of them was blind and could not see,
> 552   But it were with thilke *eyen* of his mynde
> Unless it were with those *eyes* of his mind
> 553   With whiche men seen, after that they ben blynde.
> With which men see, after they have become blind.
> (G. Chaucer, *The Man of Law's Tale, italics added*)

A word like *focus* is simply following its Latin pattern with its plural *foci*, although plenty of speakers prefer the English plural *focuses*. Variation is as normal in the creation of words as it is with the pronunciation of sounds. We have carried forward into Modern English the language variation of previous centuries. As you begin to see that even exceptions have regular patterns, you can better understand the difference between language variation and the social forces that put prestige or stigma on certain forms.

With synchronic variation feeding into diachronic variation, there are many moving parts to the English language. As some parts change, other components can be affected. Changes in the form of a word might provide opportunity for the meaning to change. One example is split between *mine* and *my*. In Old English, one form existed: *mīn*. The Old English form for *my son* would be *mīn sunu*. A sound change in the final consonant made the difference for this word. A diachronic trend affected final [n] sounds: They were susceptible to deletion. This trend is how English developed the indefinite determiner *a*, as in *a book*, from *an*, as in *an apple* (and *an* itself comes from the old form of the word *one*). With *a* and *an*, English speakers know that the beginning sound of the following word determines which one appears. The trick here is that, historically, *an* was the original form and its final [n] sound was dropped only before consonants, yielding *a* (e.g. older *an book* eventually became *a book*). Through the loss of the final nasal sounds, *mīn* became reduced sometimes to *my* in the Middle English period, but for a long time it only occurred when it preceded consonants in the following word (e.g. *mīn book → my book*). You can see the variation in phrases with *mīn*, such as *Ich ordainy min heize steward* 'I appoint my noble steward,' and phrases with *mī*, such as *To wite mi kingdom afterward* 'to keep my kingdom afterward.'[2] For a time, the [n] before vowels was not dropped, giving us such holdovers as "*mine eyes have seen the glory…*" from the Union US Civil War song "Battle Hymn of the Republic" (1862). From this change in the form of the word, a change in its function split this word into two words. The one form, *my*, took up the role of a possessive pronoun determiner and the other, *mine*, became a pronoun showing possession: *This one is my apple, and that banana is mine also.*

Another area of English where synchronic variation has fed into diachronic variation is negation in phrases. Negation in English is a process of morphology and syntax, and it too has evolved through variation over the centuries. English began with a system of multiple negation, and this system continues today despite the shift in its social status. Multiple negation has been part of English since the first Germanic invasions in 449 CE, and for the next 1,000 years, it was the standard form of negation. For example, from Chaucer's writing:

> "This world," quod I, "of so manye and diverse and contraryous parties, <u>ne</u> myghte <u>nevere</u> han ben assembled in o forme."

> "*This world,*" said I, "*of so many and diverse and adverse parts, <u>not</u> could <u>never</u> have been united in one form …*"
> (From Chaucer's translation of Boethius's *Consolation of Philosophy*)

Multiple negation has had bad press since the time of Robert Lowth, 1710–1787, one of the early self-appointed language surveyors who argued against it. The normal modern argument against multiple negation usually goes something like this: Since two negatives make a positive in math, then they must do the same in language. This prescriptive advice, however, only applies to multiplication, not addition, and it is hard to see why its proponents find it so convincing. Few stop to realize that human language is not like multiplication nor does it need to be.

The most accurate description of the stigma against multiple negation would have to include the distinction between negatives with an initial [n] and those without. Consider these two sentences:

BAD?   *I don't have no cookies.*
GOOD?   *I don't have any cookies.*

Is "any" positive or negative?

*I do have any cookies.

In linguistics, this use of *any* is a negative polarity item. From a syntactic perspective, it is clear that *I don't have any cookies* has as many negative elements as does *I don't have no cookies*. The key difference is with the word-initial <n>.

Modern languages, such as French, employ multiple negation as a regular part of their language. French originally had only the negative word *ne*, but after a while it added *pas* as a second negative marker. The cycle of change has come full circle for French, with many varieties and perhaps the majority of speakers only using *pas* to mark negation, as in the third sentence:

Je ne sais pas	'I do not know'
Il ne marche pas	'It does not work'
Il change pas	'It does not change'

Although the norm for 1,000 years, multiple negation in English has become socially stigmatized since the 1600s. Yet all told, our negation patterns for Old and Modern English are normal for human language.

Some things in English are perfectly average when compared to other languages, but a few things English speakers consider normal are actually quite bizarre for most languages. According to an Idibon research study on the rarity of certain language qualities (http://idibon.com/the-weirdest-languages/), English's way of devising yes/no questions appears to be odd. The majority of languages in that study used a suffix or separate word to mark the sentence as a question. Only 1.4% of the languages studied (13 of 954 languages) had phrases where verbs switch with subjects to ask a yes/no question (e.g. *He does drink* → *Does he drink?*). Five hundred and eighty-four of the languages studied (61.2%) had some kind of particle to mark a sentence as a question. So remember, just because something you do in English seems "normal" to you, that does not make it actually normal for human language. It just makes it possible. Still, a descriptive grammar of English has to account for our odd question formations, and an account of human language has to account for the synchronic variation of how languages ask such questions.

judging English variation

Variation in the construction of phrases is a hobgoblin for many teachers; they may be aghast about phrases like *They was at home* or *There was three hot dogs*. However, this kind of variation between national varieties is perfectly normal and not socially stigmatized. As with the previous instances of language variation examined in this chapter, variation in the construction of phrases might come under attack for social reasons. In looking at the synchronic variation of subject-verb concord across the sea, consistent differences in the evaluation of phrases arise.

In most varieties of English, nouns can have a singular form but still refer to a group of people or things: *government, corporation, flock*. These kinds of nouns are referred to as collective nouns. In the United States, most dialects use these nouns as if they were singular: *The government is working towards war*. In Australian English and other British dialects, these collective nouns can be used as plurals: *The government are working towards war*. In 2001, the unorthodox nature conservationist Steve Irwin (a.k.a. The Crocodile Hunter) did a public service message concerning the 9/11 attacks in which he said, "Animal Planet have set up a fund…" Although this may have seemed a bit bizarre to US ears,

Figure 11.6 Sometimes it is tough to know how and when to judge, even when you judge yourself. Consider this *Dinosaur Comics*: http://www.qwantz.com/index.php?comic=1025. Rollover text: "what i need you to imagine in panel 3 is a metal cowboy robot hand grabbing the crotch of a dinosaur, okay??" *Dinosaur Comics* by Ryan North. www.dinosaurcomics.com

this Australian was only doing what was perfectly natural for him. As a side note, the Croc Hunter also had consistent substitution of <f> for <th> sounds in words like *death* (*deaf*) and *birthday* (*birfday*).

For the construction of phrases, British and US English varieties both use *the* in the same way. But, these varieties use it with different words at times. In US English, it is most common to include the determiner in phrases like *to go to the hospital, to go to the university*; however, in British English the determiner can be absent. Without the determiner, *to go to hospital* or *to go to university* refers more to the event of being admitted to a hospital or a university; with the determiner, *to go to the hospital* or *to go to the university* refers either to being admitted to a specific hospital or university or to the physical act of going to the hospital building or university campus. Yet, in both British and US English, common forms which can exclude determiners are *to go to church* and *to go to college*. This synchronic variation in phrases is a result of different trends in the two varieties.

world Englishes

English has been transformed over the last two centuries. As it was spread to new lands, it was planted in different soils. It came in contact with many different varieties. As the English varieties prospered, their regular synchronic variation began to head in different directions, resulting in increasingly different varieties.

There are several different ways the varieties of English have been classified. Here, we use the metaphor of expanding circles, developed by Braj Kachru. The metaphor is that English has expanded around the world like waves expanding out from a rock dropped in a pond. There are normally three circles of Englishes, and the primary social division is the nation. It is good to keep in mind that every nation will have at least a few, if not hundreds, of varieties of English inside of it. The first circle is called the **inner circle**, and it contains all nations where English is the native language of a majority of speakers. This inner circle includes the Englishes in England, Scotland, Ireland, Northern Ireland, Canada, New Zealand, Australia, and the United States. The next level of division is called the **outer circle**. These are nations where English has become an important official language learned natively or formally. These include Englishes in India, the Philippines, Singapore, Nigeria, and South Africa. The last division is called the **expanding circle**, specifically varieties of English spoken in countries where English is learned as a foreign language to be used in business and academia. These include Russia and China. In addition to these three circles, English has become the main language at academic conferences around the world, as well as the language of air traffic controllers. We estimate that English is still expanding. Rough estimates place the population of the inner circle at 380,000,000 people; the outer circle has a population of at least 300,000,000; the expanding circle probably has a population twice that of the outer circle. It is a safe bet that there is twice the number of learners of English as a Second Language (ESL) as there are native speakers of English.

Beyond its massive native plantings, English has been broadcasted around the world for decades. In classroom settings, teaching English as a Second Language or English as a Foreign Language has become a worldwide profession. This section takes small samples from varieties in the three circles of English to show a simplified snapshot of the synchronic variation available in World Englishes. The main source for this information was *The Amazing World of Englishes* by Peter Siemund, Julia Davydova, and Georg Maier.

The inner circle varieties have been sampled throughout this book, especially English in North America. Two other realms of inner circle variation are those in Ireland and Scotland. Irish English, like many varieties, is transitioning from more insulated, local varieties at the start of the twentieth century to a state of vast change due to widely dispersed national and international varieties of English. As a result, some of the most talked about parts of Irish English are fading features. For example, the term *banjaxed* 'ruined, destroyed' is used as an adjective to describe the traditional English varieties of Ireland. Irish English had possible syntactic constructions like using *was* in the perfect instead of *had*: "I was gone" for "I had gone." A distinctive construction like "I am after eating my dinner" to mean 'I just ate my dinner' is lamented as a disappearing construction, yet there are still plenty of terms, including emerging ones, where Irish English is still distinctive. For example, "feckin' deadly mill" to mean 'an amazing fight.' With Scottish English, the same kinds of transitions are occurring. Both Irish English and Scots have words for 'young boy,' *gossoon* for Irish English and *loon* for Scots, but these kinds of forms are less frequently used. For English varieties in Scotland, language chroniclers do not have two separate bins for the differences between standard Scottish English and lowland Scots: Most likely there is a sliding continuum between the two idealized versions of Scottish English. Classic features of Scots might be considered to include words like *wee* for 'little' (e.g. *a wee lad*) and *does nae* for 'doesn't.' It would generally be considered that vowels in words like *house* and *mouse* would be pronounced in Scots with the [u] vowel like in the pre-Great Vowel Shift days. For the varieties in the inner circle, English is a native language with a longer history. For the varieties in the outer circle, English is a historically more recent language, and many other languages compete for status and speakers.

Two of these realms of the outer circle are varieties of English in India and Nigeria. We can use the terms Indian English and Nigerian English, but to be clear, inside those names are several varieties, just like American English covers many varieties. Ethnologue has wonderful statistics and maps of each country: www.ethnologue.com. The historical situations in Nigeria and India differ from the United States in several important ways, but for language purposes, the native population was not moved en masse by the English-speaking invaders. The indigenous languages of Nigeria and India continue to influence those varieties of English. In the United States, considering the long-standing contact between indigenous languages and English, there is shockingly little influence on English outside of place names (e.g. *Michigan* from the French form of the *Ojibwa* word *mishigamaa* 'large water'). Nigeria has just over 500 languages, and India has at least 400 languages. Those native languages influence the developing Englishes. In addition, Nigeria's languages come from three different language families. India's languages hail from two different language families: the Indo-Aryan languages and Dravidian languages. The official language of India is Hindi, but the secondary official language is English. In Nigeria, the official language is English, and it was chosen to help communication between different ethnic groups who speak several different languages, including Yoruba, Hausa, and Igbo. As a result of all the language contact, Nigerian English and Indian English have qualities not found in varieties of the inner circle. The most obvious are lexical items borrowed from indigenous languages. Nigerian English has words like *soja* 'soldier' and *katakata* 'confusion, trouble' derived apparently from English words but transformed by native languages' phonologies. With all varieties in the outer circle of Englishes, local phonologies influence the varieties of English that are spoken. The intonation of many languages native to India provide for different rhythms in Indian English than in other varieties, and often non-English varieties have fewer consonants, not adopting theta [θ] and engma [ŋ], resulting in new sets of homophones like *tin* 'thin' and *tin* 'tin' and *tin* 'thing.' Indian English has many words for items in Indian culture, including foods like *gobi* 'cauliflower,' *aloo* 'potatoes,' *ghee* 'clarified butter,' and *masala* 'dried spices.' Phrases are also affected in both Nigerian English and Indian English, in that the determinatives of English like *a* and *the* are more variable depending on other interacting languages. Verb tenses are used to mark aspect at times, so that in Indian English, a sentence like "I am here since today morning" can be taken to mean the perfect aspect: 'I have been here since this morning.' As these varieties progress, social elements will push some of them to become more like inner circle Englishes, but other local social pressures will push them to diverge away from inner circle Englishes.

The last circle is the expanding circle of Englishes. These include English-as-a-Foreign-Language varieties and result from formal instruction. In nations like Sweden, Denmark, Norway, and Finland, the English language is commonly taught from an early age. In Finland, more than 60% of the population know English to some extent, and upwards of 80% of the population know English in Denmark. Along with Germany, Spain, Russia, Italy, and France, these countries do not conduct politics or primary education in English, yet international relations and international business are often conducted in English. For US readers, consider how communication would happen if Texas, California, and New York had starkly different languages. In Europe, this situation makes English a **lingua franca**. This term refers to a language used amongst people working together who do not share a common mother tongue. It is an oddly humorous term when applied to English since the term originally was an Italian term for a mixed language used by merchants. From the 1600s to after World War II, the key international language was French. More recently, English has become the major international language.

The influence of English is stretching out to more corners of the globe, and it sometimes is adopted in unusual ways. A great example of its spread and innovation is one of the newest mixed languages on the planet, Light Warlpiri, mentioned earlier in discussing language acquisition. This new variety, probably created in the 1970s in Northern Australia, is spoken by a few hundred Aboriginal Australians. Carmel O'Shannessy worked with these speakers to reveal that they had built this language from three different sources: English, Kriol (a distinct English-based creole), and Warlpiri (an Aboriginal language). Below is an example of Light Warlpiri, drawn from O'Shannessy (2013).

Light Warlpiri:	Junga	mayi	nyuntu	**yu-m go**	wati-kari-kirl mayi?
	True	?	you	(nonfuture)-went	man other with?
	'Is it true that you went with another man?'				

Warlpiri:	Junga	mayi	nyuntu-∅-npa	**ya-nu**	wati-kari-kirli mayi?
	True	?	you	went	man-other-with?
	'Is it true that you went with another man?'				

Kriol:	Tru	indit	yu	**bin**	**go** la	otha-wan man?
	True	isn't it	you	been	go with	other-one man?
	'Is it true that you went with another man?'					

Pay close attention to the bolded parts, for in these parts are two rare innovations. Light Warlpiri has a nonfuture marker. The construction **yu-m go** is derived from a parallel with English's *I'm going*, but here the *'m* is used with the second person singular pronoun *yu* 'you'. The first innovation is that the verbs in Light Warlpiri are taken from English, but the nouns (like *wati* 'man') are taken from Warlpiri. Usually, new varieties have a single lexifier language supplying all the words. The second innovation is the nonfuture verb marker **-m** used with *you* as a verb marker. The three languages Light Warlpiri draws from do not have a nonfuture marker, but these speakers created one. This kind of innovation shows how English can be incorporated into many different languages over the next century.

communication with so many Englishes

Despite the increasingly large range of diversity in Englishes around the world, the principles of communication and rhetoric remain the same. The languages will change, but the species stays the same (or changes really slowly). Remember, the languages themselves do not cause miscommunication. People allow miscommunication to happen, and at times they even foster it.

Improvements in technology create ever-expanding areas for our languages. As there are more opportunities for us to communicate with others, we have more opportunities to mess up. What we might consider harmless fun can be taken by others as hurtful language. As communication increases, disapproval of utterances increases, and language judgments come under scrutiny. Take into consideration a series of utterances by Rio Ferdinand, a professional footballer with Manchester United, "I hear you fella! Choc ice is classic! hahahahahahha!!" This string of three utterances got Ferdinand charged by the English Football Association for improper conduct. He made them on Twitter, a troubled realm for any famous person: Twitter's lack of context rivals text messaging, and its speed means utterances can be widely broadcasted before being thoroughly thought through. In this tweet, Ferdinand was responding to another tweet that criticized a Black player who testified for a White player who had been previously charged with racial abuse for supposedly uttering a racial slur at Rio Ferdinand's brother. Professional football all too often plays out like a daytime soap opera.

Why was Rio Ferdinand charged? The English FA stated: "The allegation is that the player acted in a way which was improper and/or brought the game into disrepute by making comments which included a reference to ethnic origin and/or colour and/or race." With this charge, we have an issue about the interpretation of language, particularly slang. What does slang mean, and when is it offensive? The FA considered "choc ice" to constitute a "reference to ethnic origin and/or colour and/or race." Ferdinand begged to differ, unfortunately through the same conduit that got him in trouble in the first place, Twitter: "What I said yesterday is not a racist term. Its a type of slang/term used by many for someone who is being fake. So there." As everyone knows, utterances of "so there" make overwhelmingly convincing arguments. Yet, is Rio Ferdinand right? What does *choc ice* mean? As you know by now, all words have their meanings conventionally crafted by the people who use them thanks to the natural arbitrariness of form and meaning. He could well argue that he never intended a racial reference with the term *choc ice*. {By the way, the racial reference would be to someone who is Black on the outside (*chocolate*) yet White on the inside (*ice*)}. The FA could argue that the community of English Twitter users take *choc ice* to really refer to race, basing that argument on analysis of its usage in tweets or other media. Its meaning is negotiated in the community of speakers, and to discover its meaning, we would need to investigate its usage. Although Rio Ferdinand should ideally be able to speak his mind with whatever utterances he pleases, he represents several organizations who want to maintain a respectable social profile (plus, anybody who makes more in a week than most people do in a year should watch what they say).

Language disputes such as this one are common the world over. Despite our shared base of language acquisition, we naturally create language variation and use it for different ends. People disagree about language, and language reflects who we are. Language matters, to all of us. The best way we can help ourselves is to understand how language works, and I hope this book has helped you in that endeavor.

chapter summary

Language acquisition, synchronic variation, and diachronic variation are qualities unique to human language. Language acquisition is the natural process of building a mental grammar for a particular language. Most people build at least two mental grammars because they are exposed to multiple languages. The acquisition process proceeds through overlapping stages, including the sound stage, the word stage, and the phrase stage. Our mental grammars handle a wide variety of synchronic variation both productively and receptively, and we use it to locate each other on various social scales. By looking back at different stages of a language, we also observe diachronic variation, the echoes of synchronic variation over time. Every day that we speak and listen, we help change, in some small way, the history of English. Diachronic variation results from cumulative and directional synchronic variation, but not all synchronic variation results in diachronic variation. With English's age, a bit over 1,500 years old, and its expansion around the world thanks to the British Royal Navy and modern technology, English has changed a great deal since its start. In English's modern, global phase, the most accurate portrait is of World Englishes: national and regional varieties with unique histories. These national Englishes can be grouped according to a tripartite designation of inner circle, outer circle, and expanding circle varieties. With all of the variation now present in English, the need for clear communication is as important as ever.

key concepts

- Critical period
- Diachronic variation
- Expanding circle
- Great Vowel Shift
- Inner circle
- Language acquisition
- Lifespan language change
- Lingua franca
- Outer circle
- Phrase stage
- Polyglots
- Sound stage
- Synchronic variation
- Word stage

notes

1   The best website explanation of the Great Vowel Shift is here: http://eweb.furman.edu/~mmenzer/gvs/
2   Both from Sir Orfeo (cf http://en.wikipedia.org/wiki/Sir_Orfeo)

references

http://en.wikipedia.org/wiki/Sir_Orfeo
http://eweb.furman.edu/~mmenzer/gvs/
http://idibon.com/the-weirdest-languages/
http://www.census.gov/hhes/socdemo/language/
http://www.nataliedee.com/index.php?date=071813
Levine, L.E. and Munsch, J. (2013) *Child Development: An Active Learning Approach*. New York: SAGE.

O'Shannessy, C. (2013) "The role of multiple sources in the formation of an innovative auxiliary category in Light Warlpiri, a new Australian mixed language." *Language* 89, no. 2: 328–353.

Sankoff, G., and Blondeau, H. (2007) "Language change across the lifespan: /r/ in Montreal French." *Language*: 560–588.

Siemund, P., Davydova, J., and Maier, G. (2011) *The Amazing World of Englishes.* Cornelsen.

further reading

English Around the World: An Introduction. Edgar Schneider. 2011. Cambridge University Press.

The global expansion of English has had widespread linguistic, social, and cultural implications, affecting the lives of millions of people around the world. This textbook provides a lively and accessible introduction to world Englishes, describing varieties used in places as broad-ranging as America, Jamaica, Australia, Africa, and Asia and setting them within their historical and social contexts. Students are guided through the material with chapter previews, summaries, maps, timelines, lists of key terms, discussion questions, exercises, and a comprehensive glossary, helping them to understand, analyze, and compare different varieties of English, while applying descriptive terminology. The book is accompanied by a useful web site, containing textual and audio examples of the varieties introduced in the text, as well as links to related sources of interest.

The Handbook of World Englishes, ed. Braj Kachru, Yamuna Kachru, and Cecil Nelson. 2009. Wiley Blackwell.

The Handbook of World Englishes is a collection of studies on varieties of English around the world. The authors discuss all the major varieties, including those from Africa, Asia, Europe, North America, and South America. The handbook also explains the various sociolinguistic contexts of these languages, noting the differences between the circles of English. The authors also take up what role English plays in language policies and language planning.

First Language Acquisition. Eve Clark. 2009. Cambridge University Press.

For parents and anyone interested in how babies build their language skills, this book reports the most recent knowledge in the most readable manner. This second edition of Eve Clark's improves on her widely-read book on children's acquisition of a first language. It also synthesizes and presents research on the acquisition of two languages.

exercises

individual work

1. Research national varieties of English to find which one seems most different to you. What language features make it different to you? Here are some suggestions:

a.   Indian English
b.   Singaporean English
c.   Nigerian English
d.   South African English
e.   Irish English
f.   Scottish English
g.   New Zealand English
h.   Jamaican English
i.   Trinidadian English
j.   Ghanaian English
k.   Canadian English
l.   Kenyan English
m.   Puerto Rican English
n.   Cameroonian English
o.   Welsh English
p.   Guyanese English
q.   Bahamian English
r.   Thailand English (Tinglish)
s.   Burmese English
t.   Philippine English
u.   Liberian English
v.   Malaysian English (Manglish)
w.   Falkland Islands English
x.   Australian English
y.   Bermudian English
z.   Newfoundland English

2.   For the following exercises, go to http://www.arts.gla.ac.uk/stella/
     readings/ to see texts from the different historical periods of English.
     a.   Check out some Old English texts, reading both the translation
          and the original lines. Next, examine some Middle English texts
          by reading the Middle English lines and checking the glosses on
          the side for meanings of unfamiliar words.
     b.   What are three differences in spelling between the two texts?
     c.   What are some differences in vocabulary?
     d.   What are some differences in how the phrases are constructed?
3.   Read through some Early Modern English texts on the same site:
     a.   What has changed between Middle English and Early Modern
          English?
     b.   How does Early Modern English differ with your variety of
          English?
4.   In Singapore, the government has been very concerned about the
     public representation of English. Find some examples of Singlish on
     the internet, and make an argument as to whether the government
     action is justified. Here is a place to start: http://www.youtube.com/
     watch?v=cjoAiAV50ds or search for "Dr. Jiajia & BigBro Show."

group work

5. Which national varieties of English are most authentic to your group? (And yes, you have to figure out what *authentic* means to your group.)

6. Should spelling reform be implemented in English?

7. Should there be a worldwide standard English?

8. Would it be more accurate to talk about a single English language with multiple dialects, or multiple Englishes?

9. How long before some varieties of English become mutually unintelligible, or has it already happened? What would the criteria be for mutual unintelligibility?

10. Should governments try to reform national varieties of English to be closer to an American or British standard?

11. There are other realms of negation in English besides that of multiple of negation.
    Ponder the following words:
    a.   none
    b.   never
    c.   nought
    d.   nothing
    e.   nor
    f.   neither
    g.   nobody
    All of them were originally two forms and our modern words come from compounds. The first word in each original pair was the Old English word *ne* used to indicate negation. Do all of these function as negatives today?

12. Consider the following pairs of sentences. What kinds of multiple negation are allowed according to prescriptive advice and what kinds are not? How does the variation in the negation pairs play with the meaning?
    a.   I want neither strawberry nor vanilla.
    b.   I want neither strawberry or vanilla.
    c.   She doesn't want eggs nor bacon.
    d.   She doesn't want eggs or bacon.
    e.   Neither my bike nor my wheelbarrow are for sale.
    f.   Neither my bike or my wheelbarrow are for sale.
    g.   Neither grace nor beauty is to be expected in this movie.
    h.   Either grace nor beauty is to be expected in this movie.
    i.   What you decide to do is neither here nor there for me.
    j.   What you decide to do is neither here or there for me.
    k.   I like neither gobstoppers nor liquorice.
    l.   I like either gobstoppers nor liquorice.

Do any of the following seem descriptively ungrammatical to you? What part triggers that judgment for you?

m. Wouldn't you want either the float or the noodle?

n. Would you want neither the float nor the noodle?

o. Wouldn't you want neither the float nor the noodle?

p. Wouldn't you not want neither the float nor the noodle?

q. Would you not want neither the float nor the noodle?

13. The Great Vowel Shift: Historical dictionary work

As described above, the Great Vowel Shift was a change in the pronunciation of long vowels over a two hundred year period (roughly 1400–1600). The word classes of vowels changed pronunciations, and the long-vowel/short-vowel pairings were broken. For many of these vowels, their spelling representations were set before the vowels picked up their new pronunciations. Because of this change in word pronunciations, but not in spelling, the modern spelling of many words represents pre-Great-Vowel-Shift vowels. This mismatch provides an opportunity to examine the history of English within our regular spelling system. To do so, please find five words for each word class in the diagram below and complete the phonetic transcription in the table below. Are the groups able to find exceptions to the Great Vowel Shift pattern? Check out http://eweb.furman.edu/~mmenzer/gvs/ for more information.

Middle English Vowels	Middle English Phonetics	Modern English Spelling	Modern English Phonetics
ī <i>	14. [bitə] 15. 16. 17. 18.	19. <bite> 20. 21. 22. 23.	24. [baɪt] 25. 26. 27. 28.
ē <ee>	l. [met] m. n. o. p.	y. <meet> z. aa. bb. cc.	1. [mit] 2. 3. 4. 5.
ō <oo>	1. [bot] 2. 3. 4. 5.	1. <boot> 2. 3. 4. 5.	1. [but] 2. 3. 4. 5.

Middle English Vowels	Middle English Phonetics	Modern English Spelling	Modern English Phonetics
ā <a>	1. [makə] 2. 3. 4. 5.	1. <make> 2. 3. 4. 5.	1. [mek] 2. 3. 4. 5.

study questions

1. What is the difference between language learning and language acquisition?
2. What are the stages of language acquisition?
3. What work has to be done in the sound stage?
4. What is unique for humans about the phrase stage?
5. What is lifespan language change? When does it occur?
6. What is synchronic variation? Please explain an example.
7. What is diachronic variation? Please explain an example.
8. What changes have affected Modern English?
9. What is the metaphor of expanding circles? What are the circles of English?
10. Does English vary in the inner circle?
11. What is the difference between the outer and expanding circles?
12. How does technology help the expansion of English?

Visit the book's companion website for additional resources relating to this chapter at: http://www.wiley.com/go/hazen/introlanguage

Glossary

The number following the glossary term is the primary chapter in which the term can be found.

ablaut (6): A VOWEL alternation in a VERB to mark different VERB forms such as the past or the participle. The internal change in *ring, rang, rung*, would be an example of ABLAUT.

acronym (5): A WORD made from stringing together the initial orthographic letters of PHRASES or names. An ACRONYM is a process of WORD creation. NATO (North Atlantic Treaty Organization) and SCUBA (Self-Contained Underwater Breathing Apparatus) are both examples of ACRONYMS.

adjective (4): A LEXICAL CATEGORY that modifies NOUNS: In the PHRASE *the yellow house*, the WORD *yellow* is an ADJECTIVE modifying the NOUN *house*.

advancement (2): A quality of VOWEL sounds relating to how far front or far back a VOWEL is produced in the mouth. There are distinctions between back VOWELS, central VOWELS, and front VOWELS: [u] as in [bu] *boo* is a back VOWEL; [i] as in [bi] *bee* is a front VOWEL.

affix (5, 6): A BOUND MORPHEME that can be attached to a ROOT to form a new WORD. PREFIXES (e.g. *pre-*, *un-*), SUFFIXES (e.g. *-ly*, *-less*), and INFIXES (e.g. *-bloody-* as in *abso-bloody-lutely*) are all types of AFFIXES.

affricate (2): A single CONSONANT sound produced with the articulations of both a STOP and FRICATIVE: The [tʃ] in [tʃɹtʃ] *church*. It takes two combined PHONETIC SYMBOLS to represent the AFFRICATES [tʃ] and [dʒ].

alphabetism (5): A type of ACRONYM pronounced letter by letter: The ACRONYM FBI (Federal Bureau of Investigation) is pronounced [ɛfbiaɪ].

An Introduction to Language, First Edition. Kirk Hazen.
© 2015 John Wiley & Sons, Inc. Published 2015 by John Wiley & Sons, Inc.

alveolar (2): A NATURAL CLASS of CONSONANT sounds produced with the tip of the tongue touching the area behind the upper front teeth: The initial sounds of [ti] *tea* and [ni] *knee* are both ALVEOLAR.

ambiguity (1): AMBIGUITY arises when two or more meanings can be interpreted in the UTTERANCE; thus, the speaker's intended meaning might not match the audience's interpreted meaning. A WORD such as *bat* can have two meanings, and a PHRASE, such as *the deep blue pool* can have two meanings (is it a dark shade of blue, or is the volume of the blue pool deep?). The two types are LEXICAL AMBIGUITY and STRUCTURAL AMBIGUITY.

amelioration (5): On a scale of whether the WORD's meaning is good or bad, AMELIORATION is a SEMANTIC CHANGE where it becomes more favorable. For example, in Old English, the DENOTATION of the WORD *pretty* referred to sly and tricky actions, but *pretty* now refers to physical beauty.

analytic languages (6): Languages that have fewer MORPHEMES per WORD are ANALYTIC. These languages rely on SYNTAX to arrange FUNCTION MORPHEMES rather than MORPHOLOGY. An example is Mandarin Chinese.

arbitrariness (1): The natural relation between form and meaning. The meaning connected to any form is conventionally determined by a society. Meaning is not predictable from linguistic form, nor is form dictated by meaning. For example, nothing in the meaning of 'artificial, packaged, sweetened beverage' is naturally affiliated with the forms *pop* or *coke* or *soda*.

articulatory phonetics (2): The study of language sounds, concerning how those sounds are produced in the mouth. For CONSONANTS, there are three categories: PLACE OF ARTICULATION, MANNER OF ARTICULATION, and VOICE OF ARTICULATION.

aspect (4): Specifies the semantic quality of the VERB, indicating how complete, or not, the meaning of the VERB might be. PROGRESSIVE, PERFECT, and NEUTRAL are all categories of ASPECT.

aspiration (2): A quality of CONSONANT sounds pronounced with an audible release of breath: The initial sound of [tʰɪl] *till*.

assimilation (3): A PHONOLOGICAL process where speakers make one sound more similar to another sound. An example can be seen in the VOWEL difference of *bin~bid* [bĩn]~[bɪd] and *rung~rug* [ɹɤ̃ŋ]~[ɹəg], as the VOWEL before the NASAL CONSONANT is itself nasalized. Types of ASSIMILATION include PALATALIZATION, FLAPPING, DEVOICING, and NASALIZATION.

assumption of composition (6): The scholarly approach which conjectures that the WORDS people speak have been built from different MORPHEMES, as opposed to each WORD getting stored as a single chunk. For example: in the LEXICON, the WORD *unhappy* would be built from separately stored *un-* and *happy* instead of having a single memorized form, *unhappy*.

attributive (4): An ADJECTIVE that comes before the WORD it modifies. An example is the WORD *colorful* in the PHRASE *the colorful wallet*.

bilabial (2): A NATURAL CLASS in the PLACE OF ARTICULATION of CONSONANTS characterized by the use of both lips: The [b] in [bu] *boo* or the [p] in [pu] *poo*.

binary branching (6): A restriction of syntactic trees that allows each NODE to have a maximum of two branches. The assumption is that WORD trees or PHRASE trees can have one or two branches, but no more.

borrowed (5): WORDS that are brought into one language from another. For example, *government*, *dinner*, and *faith* were previously French words and are now part of modern English; therefore, these terms were BORROWED from the French language.

bound morpheme (6): A MORPHEME that cannot stand on its own in a PHRASE and must be attached to a FREE MORPHEME. AFFIXES are BOUND MORPHEMES. PREFIXES (e.g. *pre-*, *un-*), SUFFIXES (e.g. *-ly*, *-less*), and INFIXES (e.g. *-bloody-* as in *abso-bloody-lutley*) are all types of BOUND MORPHEMES.

case (4): A quality marking the grammatical role a NOUN plays. The only corner of Modern English grammar where CASE marking still survives is with PERSONAL PRONOUNS. The *I* in *I have a dream* is CASE marked for subject, but the *me* of *Give me a break* is CASE marked for object.

coda (3): A unit in the RHYME of a SYLLABLE. Like the ONSET, it could have one or more segments in it, depending on the PHONOTACTIC CONSTRAINTS in the language. It follows the NUCLEUS in the RHYME and is the final element. The CODA is less sonorous than the NUCLEUS: The [k] in [baɪk] *bike* is less sonorous than the VOWEL [aɪ].

communicative competence (9): The knowledge in the mind that guides people through conversations. It includes such information as when to talk and when to listen in a conversation, as well as regular routines in public places. Knowing to keep a quiet voice in a library would be part of COMMUNICATIVE COMPETENCE in many communities.

comparative (4): An ADJECTIVE form used to make a comparison: *Warmer* is a COMPARATIVE form in the PHRASE *the warmer blanket*. Some ADJECTIVES use *more* as the COMPARATIVE marker instead of the suffix *-er*: *more beautiful*.

complementizer (8): The HEAD OF A PHRASE used to generate a NODE that connects another PHRASE to a subordinate INFLECTIONAL PHRASE. A WORD like *that* is a COMPLEMENTIZER in the PHRASE *the ice cream <u>that</u> I dropped*.

compound (5): A situation where two free MORPHEMES are joined together into a new WORD: The WORD *basketball* is a COMPOUND of the WORDS *basket* and *ball*, and *editor-in-chief* is a COMPOUND of the WORDS *editor*, *in*, and *chief*. COMPOUNDS are considered single lexical items.

conditional (4): A MOOD that foregrounds the possibility of an event: The sentence *We could get there on time* is CONDITIONAL because the MODAL *could* indicates the possibility of the situation.

conditioned merger (3): A VOWEL MERGER that occurs in some environments while not occurring in others. For example, the FRONT-LAX MERGER is a CONDITIONED MERGER: It happens in *din∼den* [dĭn]∼[dĭn] but not with *bit∼bet* [bɪt]∼[bɛt].

conditioning environment (3): The phonological surroundings that trigger a PHONOLOGICAL RULE: The NASAL [n] in [bə̃n] *bun* triggers NASALIZATION of the [ə].

connotation (5): The secondary REFERENCE MEANING of a WORD. For example, the CONNOTATION of *social media* might be that it is evil and will destroy the art of conversation.

consonant (2): A NATURAL CLASS of sounds produced with greater constriction of the vocal tract than a VOWEL. Some CONSONANTS are more constricted (e.g. stops) while others are less constricted (e.g. liquids). CONSONANTS can be defined by their voice, place, and manner. The sounds [t], [d], and [g] are all STOP CONSONANT sounds while [ɹ] and [l] are LIQUID CONSONANTS.

constituency (7): The organizational quality of one unit being represented by another unit higher in the HIERARCHY. An XP represents constituents underneath it in the syntactic tree. For example, in the PHRASE *the deep blue pool* the two ADJECTIVES can be arranged into two different CONSTITUENCIES: Either *the {deep blue} pool* or *the {deep} {blue} pool*. All the WORDS are constituents of the NP.

content (4): LEXICAL CATEGORIES that carry most of the REFERENCE MEANING for our language. NOUNS, VERBS, ADJECTIVES, derivational SUFFIXES, and all PREFIXES in English are CONTENT MORPHEMES. For example, in *Coffee cups on the table*, the MORPHEMES *coffee*, *cup*, and *table* are CONTENT MORPHEMES.

content validity (10): A measure of the extent to which a test assesses the material it is supposed to test. For example, an English test that is comprised of biology questions would be a poor assessment of English language skills, and would therefore have poor CONTENT VALIDITY.

conversational implicature (9): This meaning is taken from the combination of LOCUTIONARY, ILLOCUTIONARY, and PERLOCUTIONARY elements of an UTTERANCE in DISCOURSE. The CONVERSATIONAL IMPLICATURE does not come from the lexical items themselves, but instead the meaning is taken from what the WORDS by that speaker suggest in that context. If you say, "I went home and played video games," the implication is that the events happened in the order presented. This meaning is plucked from the conversation as a whole.

conversational maxims (9): General tendencies people follow in conversations in order for the conversation to be successful. The maxims include the MAXIM OF QUANTITY, MAXIM OF QUALITY, MAXIM OF RELATION, and MAXIM OF MANNER.

cooperative principle (9): The basic assumption we generally follow in DISCOURSE. It is the normal understanding that people who converse say things that help each other communicate. For example: If you say, *"I am really bored,"* and your friend says, *"The basketball court is free,"* you will probably believe that the second statement relates to the first one because it is assumed that you and your friend are cooperating in the conversation.

coordinator (4): A LEXICAL CATEGORY of WORDS whose grammatical function is to connect two PHRASES together. *And, or,* and *but* are all COORDINATORS: *I caught the ball, <u>and</u> I threw it.*

count noun (4): A type of NOUN that takes a plural INFLECTIONAL SUFFIX. *Puppies, diamonds, children,* and *cities* are examples of COUNT NOUNS because they all have a plural SUFFIX. In *three glasses of water* the NOUN *water* is not a COUNT NOUN because a COUNT NOUN unit has to be made plural for it.

covert prestige (5): Admiration and praise coming from peers for activity that runs counter to institutional authority. Slang is often created to seek COVERT PRESTIGE from peers.

crash blossom (7): A newspaper headline that essentially encourages LEXICAL AMBIGUITY and/or STRUCTURAL AMBIGUITY. It often removes the relevant FUNCTION items, creating a pile up of NOUNS, ADJECTIVES, and PREPOSITIONS. For example, *Police help dog bite victim.*

critical period (11): The time period lasting roughly from infancy until puberty during which LANGUAGE ACQUISITION is the effortless, natural response to regular language around the child. This period ends for most people because changes occur in the structure of the brain during puberty. After that point, it is much harder to learn a new language.

dative alternation (8): Alternation of the order of the indirect and direct object in the VERB PHRASE. The patterns produced are either: Subject Verb <u>Direct Object</u> to **Indirect Object** as in *She gave <u>the shrimp</u> to **the octopus*** or Subject Verb **Indirect Object** <u>Direct Object</u> as in *She gave **the octopus** <u>the shrimp</u>.*

dead language (1): Any LANGUAGE that is not acquired by a community of native speakers: Ancient Latin is a DEAD LANGUAGE because it is no community's first language.

declarative (4): A grammatical MOOD of a simple statement where the SUBJECT precedes the VERB. Also known as *indicative*. The sentence *The sky is blue* is DECLARATIVE.

deixis (4, 9): The quality of referring to variable REFERENCE MEANINGS while maintaining a stable grammatical role. It allows for the specific reference of the

PRONOUN to change depending on the context of its usage. For example, the PRONOUN *I* refers to the speaker (as a subject), but its immediate meaning in any given context depends on who the speaker is. Most WORDS do not have this quality.

deletion (3): The PHONOLOGICAL process in which certain sounds in a WORD are not produced: The WORDS, *about* and *because*, are often rendered as [baʊt] *'bout* and [kəz] *'cause*. It is called *deletion* because linguists assume that the full form was stored in PHONEMES as /ebaʊt/ and /bikəz/ in the lexicon.

demonstrative pronoun (4): A set of PRONOUNS used to specify a NOUN. Modern English has four of them (prescriptively): *this, these; that, those*. The *them* form is also popular in some communities albeit often vernacular. For example: *these* folders vs. *them* folders. DEMONSTRATIVE PRONOUNS can also substitute for an entire NOUN PHRASE: *These* are the best.

denotation (5): The primary REFERENCE MEANING of a WORD. It is what most people consider to be the dictionary meaning. For example, the DENOTATION of *social media* is 'websites and applications used for social networking.'

denotation shift (5): A complete replacement of the basic REFERENCE MEANING for a WORD: The Old English word *clūd* 'rock or hill' yielded two modern WORDS, *cloud* and *clod*. While a clod of dirt might share some similar meaning to a hill, it is still different. *Cloud* has a completely different REFERENCE MEANING.

derivational (6): A BOUND and CONTENT MORPHEME. This group is in contrast to the INFLECTIONAL SUFFIXES in English. The DERIVATIONAL AFFIXES include PREFIXES like *pre-* and *non-* as well as SUFFIXES like *-ly* and *-ness*. A DERIVATIONAL AFFIX like *-er* in *teacher* is homophonous with *-er* in *the smarter squid*, which is INFLECTIONAL.

descriptive grammar (1): A linguistics book written to explain how a language works. It does not judge UTTERANCES in terms of social fashion, but it might explain the social norms and COMMUNICATIVE COMPETENCE in the LANGUAGE. Much of this book works from DESCRIPTIVE GRAMMAR knowledge. For example: a DESCRIPTIVE GRAMMAR of English should explain the usage of the WORD *ain't* as a negative, present-tense form of the VERB *be*, and it should note that the form is often stigmatized. It would also explain that English generally has ATTRIBUTIVE ADJECTIVES.

determinative (4): A LEXICAL CATEGORY that modifies the entirety of the NOUN PHRASE, including any ADJECTIVES or PREPOSITIONS that may be part of it. In the PHRASE, *the phone in her hand*, the word *the* is a DETERMINATIVE. They function as definite DETERMINERS.

determiner (4): A slot in a syntactic PHRASE whose function is to specify the remainder of the PHRASE. DEMONSTRATIVE PRONOUNS such as *this* can work in the DETERMINER slot, e.g. *this snake*. DETERMINATIVES, such as *the* and *a*, are commonly found in DETERMINER slots, e.g. *the dragon, a penguin*.

devoicing (3): A type of ASSIMILATION in which a sound is made VOICELESS. For example, DEVOICING happens when an aspirated CONSONANT comes before the /ɹ/ and /l/ sounds. The ASPIRATION bleeds through the LIQUIDS, bleaching them of their VOICE: *crypt* [kʰɹ̥ɪpt] has an example of DEVOICING.

diachronic variation (3): LANGUAGE VARIATION between two points in time: Through regular PALATALIZATION by speakers, the Old English form *kiken* 'chicken' [kikẽn] became the modern [tʃɪkẽn].

diphthongs (2): A NATURAL CLASS of single VOWELS with moving articulators. These VOWELS are initially made in one articulatory position and glide to another: The VOWEL sound in [bɔɪ] *boy* and [daɪ] *dye* are both DIPHTHONGS.

direct speech act (9): When the ILLOCUTIONARY meaning matches the LOCUTIONARY meaning of an UTTERANCE. If a sister says to her brother, *That shirt is ugly*, and she means to make the ugliness of the shirt known, then two meanings match.

discourse (1, 9): A collection of UTTERANCES. A single conversation, medical discourse, and legal discourse are all examples.

discourse *like* (9): Inserting the word *like* into UTTERANCES as a turn marker, a device to focus the listener's attention, an approximator, or another DISCOURSE job. It is a DISCOURSE MARKER that has triggered a great deal of angst in some communities. For example, *Like, I think we should meet at like 9:00 but that might be like too late.*

discourse marker (9): WORDS that are not part of the content of a conversation but direct the conversation. Like road signs when driving, they help us make turns in the conversation. WORDS like *well, actually, like, however,* and *for example* are used as DISCOURSE MARKERS.

discourse script (9): Common conversational templates that speakers follow based on often-repeated conversational exchanges. An example would be the process of ordering at a restaurant: There is a routine exchange of information between the customers and employees. Part of the COMMUNICATIVE COMPETENCE for a community is the DISCOURSE SCRIPT for such routines.

ditransitive (4): A type of VERB that requires a SUBJECT and two slots in the PREDICATE. In the sentence *She told him a secret*, the VERB, *told*, is DITRANSITIVE, because both *a secret* and *him* fill slots in the PREDICATE specified in the lexical listing of *tell*.

diversion implicature (9): A CONVERSATIONAL IMPLICATURE in which the speaker flouts one CONVERSATIONAL MAXIM to supply the implied meaning through another. For example, a student who says *My chemistry professor enriched my soul with his well-structured monologue this morning* diverts the focus to the manner of presentation and away from whether it is true or not. The MAXIM OF QUALITY is flouted here.

expanding circle (11): The circle of English that contains the countries where there is already a strong presence from a national LANGUAGE(s), but where English is learned as a foreign LANGUAGE to be used in business and academia (e.g. Russia and China).

expansion (7): The syntactic quality that allows for the possibility of an infinite addition of PHRASES. The INFLECTIONAL PHRASE *The natural Christmas tree beside the piano in the old house which sold last week* has undergone EXPANSION because it is made up of multiple embedded PHRASES.

face (9): The realm of personal value one holds in the context of society. Your dignity and social prestige are tied to your conversational FACE.

filler (9): WORDS used by speakers to hold the floor in what otherwise would be silence. Used while planning the next step in the conversation. For example: *Umm, I would like a salad instead of french fries.*

flap (3): A VOICED ALVEOLAR CONSONANT [ɾ] pronounced with a quick touch of the tongue to the alveolar ridge (without a full stop of airflow). Many Americans have a FLAP in the word *butter* [bəɾɹ].

flapping (3): A type of ASSIMILATION where a FLAP is produced from an ALVEOLAR STOP that comes before an unstressed SYLLABLE: *butter* /bətɹ/→[bəɾɹ] is an example of FLAPPING.

floor (9): This time period is the attention given to a speaker by a listener. In formal debates, such as in legislative bodies, a leader turns over the FLOOR to recognized speakers.

free morpheme (6): A MORPHEME that does not need to be attached to another MORPHEME to be part of a PHRASE. Some lexical categories, such as NOUNS, VERBS, ADJECTIVES, and PREPOSITIONS in English, are FREE MORPHEMES. The phrase *to go in the store* contains only FREE MORPHEMES.

fricative (2): A CONSONANT sound produced by breath forced through a constrictive passage. Airflow is pushed against the teeth, tongue, and lips to make turbulence in the forced air: The [f] and [ð] in [faðɹ] *father* are both FRICATIVES.

front-lax merger (3): This merger occurs when /ɪ/ and /ɛ/ are pronounced the same, predominantly before NASALS. For example, *bin*∼*Ben* [bĩn]∼[bĩn] would be merged but not *bit*∼*bet* [bɪt]∼[bɛt].

fulcrum implicature (9): A type of CONVERSATIONAL IMPLICATURE in which what is implied relies on the MAXIM OF RELATION for the ILLOCUTIONARY meaning to be understood. Lucy asks, "*Can anybody fix my computer?*" Zach says, "*There is a computer shop downtown.*" Zach's answer implies that the computer shop can fix Lucy's computer.

function (4): The LEXICAL CATEGORIES that establish grammatical relationships to help us figure out how the different parts are connected. PREPOSITIONS,

PRONOUNS, COORDINATORS, DETERMINERS, and INFLECTIONAL SUFFIXES are function morphemes. For example, in *coffee cups on the table*, the MORPHEMES *-s, on*, and *the* are FUNCTION MORPHEMES.

functional shift (5): This kind of lexical change involves the creation of a new WORD by moving an old word from one LEXICAL CATEGORY to another. The VERB *score* as in *I scored a goal* is a separate WORD as a NOUN in *Get up-to-the-minute scores*.

genre conventions (10): For any particular type of WRITING, there are a set of normal routines that authors follow. These normal routines are developed by the community of writers. For example, there are expectations for a text message to a friend that differ from those for an important academic paper. These expectations are the GENRE CONVENTIONS.

glide (2): A NATURAL CLASS of CONSONANT sounds that involve moving articulators during pronunciation. These are also SONORANTS: The first sound of [ju] *you* is the palatal glide [j], and the first sound of *wet* [wɛt] is the bilabial GLIDE [w].

glottal region (2): Contains the VOCAL FOLDS and the GLOTTIS and is found in the larynx.

glottal stop (2): A CONSONANT sound produced when the GLOTTIS closes, thus stopping airflow: The sound [ʔ] in the middle of *uh-oh* [əʔo].

glottis (2): The space between the VOCAL FOLDS located in the LARYNX. A GLOTTAL STOP is produced when the GLOTTIS snaps shut.

grammatical competence (9): All the LANGUAGE knowledge in our MENTAL GRAMMAR.

grammatical gender (4): A classification system for NOUNS. In languages with this kind of classification, the NOUNS fall into categories. Traditional grammarians picked names such as masculine and feminine, so these categories were called genders. Old English, modern German, and modern Spanish are examples of languages with GRAMMATICAL GENDER.

Great Vowel Shift (11): Perhaps the most important VOWEL shift in English history. It was a change in the pronunciation of long VOWELS over a two-hundred year period (roughly 1400–1600, although some changes stopped much later). It disrupted the long/short phonemic distinction of vowels, resulting in the modern TENSE/LAX distinction. Many modern VOWEL spellings (e.g. <bite>, <meet>) were set before the GREAT VOWEL SHIFT was complete, creating continuing confusion about vowel-to-spelling correspondence.

head of the phrase (7): The lexical category at the root which determines a PHRASE's syntactic type. For example, the HEAD OF THE PHRASE can be a NOUN, ADJECTIVE, VERB, or PREPOSITION. The HEAD OF THE PHRASE in a NOUN PHRASE is a NOUN: The word *dog* in *the small dog under the table* is the HEAD OF THE PHRASE.

headedness parameter (7): A variable constraint that allows the HEAD OF A PHRASE to come first or last within that PHRASE. For example, in some languages the DETERMINER comes before the NOUN, but in other languages the NOUN comes before the DETERMINER.

height (2): A distinctive quality of VOWEL sounds determined by how relatively high or low a VOWEL is produced in the mouth. Distinctions are made between high, mid, and low VOWELS: The VOWEL sound in the word [tuθ] *tooth* is higher than that in [boθ] *both*.

hierarchy (3, 6): The quality of organizing linguistic units into higher and lower levels so that some items dominate others. These units are nested inside of other units on higher levels. For example, the NUCLEUS and CODA are nested inside of the RHYME in the SYLLABLE.

homographs (4): Different WORDS that are spelled the same. These are sometimes HOMOPHONES, but not always. The WORDS *read* [ɹid] and *read* [ɹɛd] are pronounced differently, yet because they are spelled the same, they are HOMOGRAPHS.

homonyms (4): WORDS that are both HOMOPHONES and HOMOGRAPHS. *Skate* (VERB) and *skate* (NOUN 'type of fish') would be HOMONYMS.

homophones (2, 4): Different WORDS that have the same phonetic form. *Their, they're,* and *there* are HOMOPHONES.

idiom (5): An expression in LANGUAGE that does not obey the normal rules of adding up meaning from WORD to WORD, yet it is a LEXICAL ITEM particular to a variety: *My dogs are barking* is intended to mean that one's feet hurt, but its meaning is not composed out of the separate WORDS. Its meaning is conventionally applied to the entire form *<my dogs are barking>*.

illocutionary (9): This refers to the intended meaning of a speaker's UTTERANCE. For example, if a speaker intends to command a friend not to eat the speaker's frozen dairy dessert, the speaker could say *Do not eat my ice cream!* or *Eating my ice cream will be dangerous to your health* with the same illocutionary meaning.

imperative (4): A grammatical MOOD used to give a command: In English it is constructed in the non-past TENSE with the second-person subject implied (but not overtly stated). The IMPERATIVE sentence, *Do your homework*, is a command in which the subject, *you*, is implied.

indirect speech act (9): An UTTERANCE in which the LOCUTIONARY and ILLOCUTIONARY meanings do not match up. For example, while getting ready for a party, you are asked *Are you really wearing that to the party?* The LOCUTIONARY meaning could be *I am questioning whether or not you are wearing those clothes to the party*. The ILLOCUTIONARY meaning is probably closer to *That*

outfit is so hideous; you should not wear it. This UTTERANCE would be an INDI-
RECT SPEECH ACT.

infinite recursion (7): A syntactic quality that allows the hierarchical structure
to be repeated as many times as needed to allow for the expansion of the PHRASE.
The second rule in the X-bar phrase structure allows for INFINITE RECURSION.

infix (6): A BOUND MORPHEME that goes inside of another MORPHEME. In *un-
freakin-believable, freakin* is an INFIX.

inflectional affix (6): A BOUND and FUNCTION MORPHEME. This group is in
contrast to the DERIVATIONAL AFFIXESin English. Only nine INFLECTIONAL SUF-
FIXES remain in English, such as past-tense *-ed* and possessive *-'s*. A DERIVA-
TIONAL AFFIX like *-er* in *teacher* is homophonous with the INFLECTIONAL SUFFIX
-er in *The smarter squid.*

Inflectional Phrase (8): The syntactic term for a PHRASE with slots for the
SUBJECT and PREDICATE. The HEAD of an INFLECTIONAL PHRASE is the verbal
inflection, which is often phonetically null in English. *She will sneeze* is an
example of an INFLECTIONAL PHRASE with *will* functioning as the Inflection.

inner circle (11): The circle that contains all the nations where English is the
native LANGUAGE of a majority of speakers. Examples include the Englishes in
England, Scotland, Canada, and Ireland.

insertion (3): The PHONOLOGICAL process in which certain sounds may be
added to a WORD: The [p] sound is sometimes inserted in the WORD *hamster*,
thus making the pronunciation [hæmpstɹ].

interdental (2): A NATURAL CLASS of CONSONANT sounds formed by air flowing
over the tongue placed between the teeth. The first sound of [θɪk] *thick* is the
voiceless INTERDENTAL CONSONANT [θ].

interrogative (4): A grammatical MOOD used to ask a question. In English, the
INTERROGATIVE is produced when the SUBJECT and auxiliary are inverted from
their normal DECLARATIVE order: *Are you running late?* instead of *You are
running late.*

interrogative pronouns (4): PRONOUNS that are primarily used to ask questions. For example, the WORD *what* is an INTERROGATIVE PRONOUN in the
sentence *What is your favorite color?*

intransitive (4): A class of VERBS that requires only a SUBJECT in their lexical
listing. For example, the VERB *run* in the sentence, *She runs.*

jargon (5): A set of WORDS used in a profession, activity, or specialized group
with meanings particular to that population: For example, a *brace* is a term used
in soccer for scoring two goals in a game.

labiodental (2): A NATURAL CLASS of CONSONANT sounds made by pushing air
through the constriction of the top teeth and the bottom lip: The [f] in [fi] *fee*
is a LABIODENTAL FRICATIVE.

language (1): The species-specific, discrete combinatorial system humans acquire naturally and use for communication. Combinations start with small parts that are joined together to make larger parts. Language appears to develop naturally with the help of the UNIVERSAL GRAMMAR.

language acquisition (11): This refers to the process where babies use their UNIVERSAL GRAMMAR and the language information in the environment to build a MENTAL GRAMMAR of the LANGUAGE. This process includes a SOUND STAGE, a WORD STAGE, a PHRASE STAGE, and building COMMUNICATIVE COMPETENCE. Babbling, for example, is a natural way for babies to work through the sound stage.

language variation (1): Alternations, such as different pronunciations, words, and phrases, in a specific LANGUAGE. The level of language could be lexical, as in *pop* vs. *soda*; morphological, as in *-ly* vs. its absence in *She runs quick__*; phonological, like VOWEL variation; or syntactic, as in saying *pass the ball to me* vs. *pass me the ball*. LANGUAGE VARIATION can be identified with region, ethnicity, social class, gender, sexual orientation and many other social qualities.

larynx (2): The upper cartilaginous part of the respiratory tract containing the VOCAL FOLDS and the GLOTTIS.

lax (2): A quality of VOWEL sounds pronounced with the tongue and jaw muscles relatively relaxed in comparison with TENSE pronunciations. LAX sounds are closer to the center of the VOWEL space: The VOWEL sound in [bɪt] *bit* is LAX.

lexical ambiguity (4, 8): The concept that a WORD's phonetic form could be homophonous with another's and thus be associated with more than one meaning in a PHRASE: *A bat hit me in the face* could be interpreted two ways: *A wooden stick hit me*, or *a small, flying mammal hit me*. The two meanings would be connected to two different WORDS.

lexical categories (4): Classifications of WORDS based on their relations to other words in PHRASES. These categories are how the lexicon stores WORDS. VERBS and NOUNS are examples of LEXICAL CATEGORIES.

lifespan language change (11): This refers to mostly the phonological changes occurring after the LANGUAGE ACQUISITION period has ended. Any change that happens over the entirety of a speaker's life may be considered a LIFESPAN LANGUAGE CHANGE.

lingua franca (11): For people who do not share a common mother tongue, it is a LANGUAGE used to communicate together. Both English and French are common examples in Africa.

linguistics (1): The scientific study of LANGUAGE.

liquid (2): A NATURAL CLASS of CONSONANT of SONORANT sounds characterized by loose constriction in the oral cavity so that the air flows out of the mouth.

The [l] in the WORD [læb] *lab* is a lateral LIQUID because the air falls off the sides of the tongue.

living language (1): Any LANGUAGE acquired and used by a community of native speakers: Japanese and Portuguese are examples.

locatives (7): These are FUNCTION MORPHEMES used to locate NOUNS in time and space. For some languages, they consist of POSTPOSITIONS and PREPOSITIONS but for others they might be BOUND MORPHEMES. Examples from English include *after, on, by,* and *under.*

locutionary (9): This meaning is the most literal one that can be composed from the combination of WORDS in an UTTERANCE. During a championship basketball game, a player makes a last-second shot, but misses. His angry teammate says *Great shot.* The LOCUTIONARY meaning would be that the shot was highly superior. The ILLOCUTIONARY meaning probably contains criticism of the shot.

low-back merger (3): This merger occurs when the /a/ and /ɔ/ VOWELS are pronounced the same. These VOWELS were previously distinct for all speakers, but they are pronounced the same by many speakers today. For example, *caught* /kɔt/ and *cot* /kat/, for speakers with this merger, could both be said as [kat].

manner of articulation (2): The "how" in the way CONSONANT sounds are produced. How the tongue, jaw, and throat move when making consonant sounds determines the MANNER OF ARTICULATION. STOPS are a different manner than LIQUIDS.

maxim of manner (9): A CONVERSATIONAL MAXIM that asks for UTTERANCES to be clearly presented and unambiguous. For example, if you give driving directions that are out of order to someone, you are violating the MAXIM OF MANNER. This manner relates to how the UTTERANCE is said.

maxim of quality (9): This maxim requires the truth of a given UTTERANCE. For example: After a teacher assigns four pages of homework, a student might say *This will take forever.* This UTTERANCE is a violation of the MAXIM OF QUALITY because completing the homework will not really take forever.

maxim of quantity (9): This maxim requires the speaker to provide just enough information for the given context. It is the Goldilocks of CONVERSATIONAL MAXIMS. You do not want to give too much information or too little; you want it to be just right. For example, if a mother asks her child what he did in school that day, she will want to hear more than *nothing,* but she will not want to hear every single activity of the school day.

maxim of relation (9): This maxim requests the speaker to make the UTTERANCE relevant to the conversation. For example, if you ask a friend what time the movie starts, and your friend replies *7:30,* it is assumed that response is relevant to the question (and is not just some random set of numbers).

mental grammar (1): The place in the mind where LANGUAGE happens. Consider it as the software for language running on the hardware of the brain. Human babies create it from the interaction between UNIVERSAL GRAMMAR and language in their environment.

minimal pair (2, 3): Two WORDS that differ in form by one contrasting sound: The WORDS [mæt] *mat* and [bæt] *bat* are a MINIMAL PAIR because the sounds [m] and [b] mark a difference in meaning.

modal verb (4): A subclass of VERBS that work as auxiliaries and do not have a past-TENSE form in Modern English. In English, MODALS do not take the verbal *-s* for third-person singular: *She can sing* uses the modal verb *can*.

monolingual (1): Having the ability to understand and speak only one LANGUAGE with proficiency. Many Americans are MONOLINGUAL, but most people in the world are MULTILINGUAL.

monophthong (2): A NATURAL CLASS of VOWEL sounds with no moving articulators. The VOWEL sound in [mit] *meat* is a MONOPHTHONG.

mood (4): The relation of the speaker to the audience as represented by the arrangement or form of the VERB. DECLARATIVE, IMPERATIVE, INTERROGATIVE, and CONDITIONAL are all examples of MOOD.

morpheme (6): The smallest unit of LANGUAGE attached to a meaning or grammatical function. In the word *quickly*, both *quick* and *-ly* are MORPHEMES.

morphology: The part of the MENTAL GRAMMAR that combines MORPHEMES into larger units. For example, it would combine *un-happy-ness* into a WORD.

multilingual (1): Having the ability to produce and understand more than one LANGUAGE with proficiency. Most people in the world are MULTILINGUAL.

narrowing (5): A SEMANTIC CHANGE involving a shift from a broader range of reference to a more narrow range of reference: In Old English, *deer* referred to any hunted animal, but in Modern English, the word *deer* specifically refers to a species of ruminant mammal.

nasal (2): A NATURAL CLASS of SONORANT CONSONANT sounds produced by the passage of air through the nose rather than the mouth: The final sound in the word *sing* [sɪŋ] is a velar NASAL.

nasalization (3): A type of ASSIMILATION in which a VOWEL is followed by a NASAL CONSONANT, triggering air to be released out the nose (in the manner of a NASAL) during the VOWEL itself. The VOWELS of *bin* [bɪ̃n] and *rung* [ɹɔ̃ŋ] have NASALIZATION.

natural classes (3): Groups of sounds that are organized by a PHONETIC or articulatory quality. PHONOLOGICAL RULES make use of NATURAL CLASSES to organize patterns of sounds. For example, the divisions in the PLACES OF ARTICULATION, such as BILABIAL, ALVEOLAR, and VELAR, are all NATURAL CLASSES.

negative face (9): The desire not to be impeded in what you do. Imposing on someone's NEGATIVE FACE triggers repairs in conversations. For example, while sitting in a restaurant, a stranger walks up and says *Do you have a dollar I could have?* This act impacts your NEGATIVE FACE because your time and attention is redirected to the stranger.

nesting (7): A syntactic quality that allows one PHRASE to fit inside another. This quality is expressed with the YPs in the X-bar structure. In the NOUN PHRASE *the three cars in the parking lot* there is an ADJECTIVE PHRASE and a PREPOSITIONAL PHRASE, both of which are YPs within the NP.

neutral (4): The catch-all category of ASPECT for everything that is neither PROGRESSIVE nor PERFECT. The sentence *We eat the ice cream* is NEUTRAL, because it is neither the PROGRESSIVE *We are eating the ice cream* nor the PERFECT *We have eaten the ice cream.*

node (3): A point of organization in a HIERARCHICAL tree. The NODE is any point at which a branch terminates or joins another branch.

***non sequitur* (9):** An UTTERANCE that does not follow the flow of the DISCOURSE. An example would be a friend saying *ice cream* after being asked about last night's game.

nonce word (5): An invented WORD with form, but no conventional meaning. For example, *kepbleeg* had form, but no meaning (when it was created for this book) and would be a NONCE WORD.

noun (4): A basic LEXICAL CATEGORY where members can function as SUBJECT in a sentence or OBJECT OF A PREPOSITION. In the sentence *The boy on the couch is nice*, both *boy* and *couch* are NOUNS.

nucleus (3): The most sonorous segment that forms the basis of the SYLLABLE. The NUCLEUS is part of the RHYME along with the CODA. The VOWEL sound /æ/ in the word *pan* /pæn/ *pan* fills the NUCLEUS slot.

null subject (8): A SUBJECT that is phonetically empty, but the VERB is still conjugated as if there were an overt SUBJECT in the sentence. English is a language that does not allow NULL SUBJECTS, but Spanish does. In Spanish, *there is a set of teeth* would be translated as *Hay un conjunto de dientes*, and in that PHRASE there is no overt SUBJECT.

obstruents (2, 3): The non-ringing sounds that obstruct more air than SONORANTS, such as the [t] in *tile*. The NATURAL CLASSES of STOPS, FRICATIVES, and AFFRICATES make up OBSTRUENTS.

onset (3): A unit in the SYLLABLE. Like the CODA, it could have one or more segments in it, depending on the PHONOTACTIC CONSTRAINTS in the language. It is the segment or set of segments that start(s) a SYLLABLE and precedes the

RHYME. The ONSET is less sonorous than the NUCLEUS. The [b] is the ONSET in the WORD *bite* [baɪt].

onset maximization (3): A human language preference for making an ONSET in a SYLLABLE rather than a CODA. Given a CONSONANT and VOWEL combination of CVCV, ONSET MAXIMIZATION results in CV.CV (with two ONSETS) rather than CVC.V. This tendency is a basic component of human LANGUAGE. For example, babies make CV.CV sequences like *ma.ma* rather than *am.am* as their first SYLLABLES.

orthographic symbols (2): The written letters. Angled brackets are used to distinguish these from other kinds of symbols. For example <lab> is marked with angled brackets to highlight the ORTHOGRAPHIC SYMBOLS, in contrast to the PHONETIC SYMBOLS between square brackets [læb].

outer circle (11): The circle that contains the nations where English has become an important official language learned natively or formally by many residents. Examples include India, Nigeria, and South Africa.

overt prestige (5): Positive associations given by institutional authorities for activities seen as good, whether it is by school systems, organized sports, or social clubs. A student who avoids slang might gain OVERT PRESTIGE from teachers, but that student will earn no COVERT PRESTIGE from peers for this choice.

palatal (2): A NATURAL CLASS of CONSONANTS where sounds are produced with the tongue near or on the palate. For example, the [ʃ] of *she* [ʃi] is a VOICELESS, PALATAL FRICATIVE.

palatalization (3): A type of ASSIMILATION where a CONSONANT's PLACE OF ARTICULATION shifts to the PALATAL region because of influence from a PALATAL sound. A PHRASE like *It hit you* can be pronounced with a PALATAL AFFRICATE: [ɪthɪtju] → [ɪthɪtʃu].

parameter (7, 8): The forced choices infants must make while acquiring a LANGUAGE. These forced choices are supplied by the UNIVERSAL GRAMMAR. The HEADEDNESS PARAMETER provides the choice of having the HEAD OF PHRASE first or last.

parse (7, 8): Disassembling PHRASES to better understand their structure. A sentence like *My phone fell off the table* can be parsed into its CONSTITUENT parts, such as NOUN PHRASE, VERB PHRASE, and PREPOSITIONAL PHRASE.

peeves (10): Judgments made in frustration about LANGUAGE VARIATION patterns. For example, if a patient says to his doctor, *I got a cold*, and the doctor condescendingly replies, *No, you have a cold*. In this case, using *got* instead of *have* is one of the doctor's PEEVES.

pejoration (5): On a scale of whether the word's CONNOTATION is socially good or bad, PEJORATION is a SEMANTIC CHANGE towards a less favorable meaning. For example, in Old English, the DENOTATION of the WORD *silly* meant 'happy and prosperous,' but *silly* now means 'ridiculous.' The WORD's meaning has had a negative change.

perfect (4): An ASPECT in English where the auxiliary VERB *to have* and the perfect participle of a VERB are used together. For many VERBS, the PERFECT indicates that the action is completed. The sentence, *We have walked a lot*, is in the PERFECT ASPECT.

performative speech act (9): Uttering the WORDS completes the action of the SPEECH ACT. For example, *I promise not to eat all your Nutella*. Using the VERB *promise* in this context completes the action of promising.

performative verb (9): The VERBS required for a PERFORMATIVE SPEECH ACT. They complete their action as they are spoken. Examples include *promise, accept, bet, damn, christen*, and *pronounce.*

peripherality (2): A distinctive quality of VOWEL sounds determined by their placement as being closer towards the center of the vowel map or more on the edge, with those VOWELS closer to the edge of the map being TENSE VOWELS and those closer to the center being LAX VOWELS. For example, the VOWEL sound [i] in the WORD *these* [ðiz] is TENSE, but the VOWEL [ɪ] in the word *this* [ðɪs] is LAX.

perlocutionary effect (9): This result is the psychological outcome of an UTTER-ANCE for a listener. For example, if a teacher tells a student, *Great essay*, the student will probably feel positive about the work.

personal pronouns (4): These are a set of PRONOUNS that represent different grammatical persons. For example, in the sentence, *I want you to go to sleep, I* is in the first person and *you* is in the second person. Other qualities can also be shown in PERSONAL PRONOUNS, including number (e.g. plural *we* vs. singular *I*), possession (e.g. *her book*), CASE (e.g. subject *he* vs. object *him*), and gender (e.g. *she* vs. *he*).

phoneme (3): The mental representation of sound in the LEXICON. It is the smallest unit of LANGUAGE in the LEXICON that makes a difference in meaning. It is symbolically represented between forward slashes. The PHONEMES /t/ and /k/ in English trigger differences in meaning for English speakers: *tan* /tæn/ has a different meaning than *can* /kæn/.

phonetic symbol (2): The written representation of a spoken sound. These are shown in square brackets. For example, the word *squid* is phonetically transcribed as [skwɪd].

phonetics (2): The scientific study of sounds. For example, acoustic PHONETICS studies the physics of sounds in the air.

phonological rules (3): These rules transform PHONEMES into actual pronun-ciation. They operate in the MENTAL GRAMMAR. They work with groups of NATURAL CLASSES. For example, VOWELS can be transformed by a phonological rule of NASALIZATION: *bin* /bɪn/ →[bɪ̃n].

phonology (3): The component of the MENTAL GRAMMAR that handles the external realizations of LANGUAGE. PHONOLOGY transforms the output from the LEXICON, MORPHOLOGY, and SYNTAX into organized sounds and signs. PHONOLOGY also transforms incoming LANGUAGE to be processed by the other units of the MENTAL GRAMMAR.

phonotactic constraint (3): Regular patterns in a language that set restrictions on sound combinations. Native English speakers, for example, do not acquire a form such as /ŋa/ and thus feel that WORDS starting with [ŋ] are foreign. In addition, PHONOTACTIC CONSTRAINTS put limits on normal SYLLABLES for a language. For example, some languages allow ONSETS of CV (e.g. *toe*), but others allow CCV (e.g. *stow*) and even CCCV (e.g. *strow*).

phrase (1): A combination of WORDS in a structured pattern: *The whale* is an example of a NOUN PHRASE.

phrase stage (11): The third stage of LANGUAGE ACQUISITION. This stage overlaps with the WORD STAGE. It is when children begin to combine WORDS and MORPHEMES to form PHRASES. For example, a small child might form the PHRASE, *more juice*.

place of articulation (2): The location in the VOCAL TRACT where CONSONANT sounds are produced. The lips are the PLACE OF ARTICULATION for BILABIAL CONSONANTS like [b].

polyglot (11): People who do not lose their ability to natively acquire a LANGUAGE; they therefore are able to build MENTAL GRAMMARS of any LANGUAGE to which they are sufficiently exposed.

positive face (9): The desire to be approved, liked, and admired by others. Greeting a friend with *You look great today* would be an example of playing to the friend's POSITIVE FACE.

pragmatic knowledge (9): Information outside of LANGUAGE that influences interpretation. We use this information to figure out the meaning of UTTERANCES. Examples include knowledge of physical and social facts of a conversation.

predicate (4, 8): Sentences normally contain SUBJECTS and PREDICATES. The PREDICATE contains the VERB PHRASE and any other PHRASES dominated by the VERB PHRASE within the same INFLECTIONAL PHRASE. For example, in the sentence, *The coffee in the cup will soon be gone*, the PHRASE *will soon be gone* is the PREDICATE because it not the SUBJECT *The coffee in the cup*.

predicative (4): An ADJECTIVE that is part of the PREDICATE but modifies the SUBJECT. In the sentence, *This music sounds awful*, the ADJECTIVE *awful* modifies the SUBJECT *this music* through the VERB *sounds*.

prefix (6): A BOUND MORPHEME that attaches to the beginning of the STEM. *Un-*, *anti-*, and *non-* are all examples of PREFIXES.

preposition (4): PREPOSITIONS in English are free, FUNCTION MORPHEMES that connect PHRASES. They are part of a set of FUNCTION MORPHEMES called LOCA-TIVES, which also include postpositions. Semantically speaking, LOCATIVES locate physical objects in relation to each other and are extended metaphorically to many other NOUNS. In the sentence, *Shovel the snow on the sidewalk*, the WORD *on* is a PREPOSITION.

prescriptive grammar (1, 10): A collection of social fashion advice for GENRE CONVENTIONS. This advice is provided to enforce certain stylistic choices. The underlying assumption is that some LANGUAGE is sick and needs to get better, so advice is prescribed. For example, "Do not end a sentence with a preposition."

Prescriptively Correct Perspective (1, 10): This outlook on LANGUAGE assumes that any UTTERANCE should be judged against a single, unwavering set of con-ventions. In making a judgment, it assumes that one certain form of the LAN-GUAGE always works better and that this form must be protected from variation. For example, in this perspective, the PHRASE "I am not going" will always work better than "I ain't going" no matter what the context might be.

principles (7): The basic qualities that all human languages share. These are part of the UNIVERSAL GRAMMAR. For example, all human languages have systems for the LEXICON, PHONOLOGY, and MORPHOLOGY/SYNTAX.

progressive (4): An ASPECT that semantically indicates the ongoing quality of the VERB. In English, the PROGRESSIVE is produced with a form of the VERB *be* and the *-ing* SUFFIX attached to another VERB: *We are walking home.*

pronoun (4): A free, FUNCTION MORPHEME, in English, with DEIXIS that refers to another WORD. Consider this sentence: *Why does he love to eat it?* The WORDS *why*, *he*, and *it* refer to other WORDS. *Why* is an INTERROGATIVE PRONOUN while both *he* and *it* are PERSONAL PRONOUNS.

reference meaning (2): The most direct meaning for a memorized set of sounds in the LEXICON. Many people refer to the REFERENCE MEANING as the dictionary meaning. This meaning is distinct from SOCIAL MEANING. The REFERENCE MEANING for *necklace* most likely consists of a *string-like piece of jewelry worn around the neck.*

repair (9): A REPAIR is made when we try to fix a threat to someone's FACE. For example, if you ask someone for the time of day, you might say *Excuse me* at first to mitigate the face-threatening act.

Rhetorically Correct Perspective (1,10): The viewpoint of judging LANGUAGE as good or bad based on how well that language works for a speaker in a specific context. For example, while informally speaking to a friend, it is fine to say "I *will* call you later," where it might be better to say, "I *shall* call you later," in a more formal situation where different GENRE CONVENTIONS are in play.

rhyme (3): A unit in the SYLLABLE that groups together and dominates the NUCLEUS and CODA. It is the NODE of the SYLLABLE that follows the ONSET. For example, [aɪt] is the RHYME in the WORD *bite* [baɪt]. Linguists borrowed the term as the part of the SYLLABLE that rhymes.

root (6): A morphology term for the most inner-layer in a multi-morphemic word. The ROOT is the most basic STEM. For example, in the WORD *dehumidifier*, the SUFFIX *-ify* attaches to the ROOT *humid*.

schwa rule (3): The PHONOLOGICAL process where an unstressed VOWEL is transformed to the mid-central LAX VOWEL SCHWA [ə]. The WORD *about* /ebaʊt/ is often pronounced with a schwa sound as [əbaʊt].

semi-weak verbs (6): VERBS that are not quite either regular or irregular, having both an ABLAUT change between forms and an ALVEOLAR ending. Examples would be *sweep~swept* and *deal~dealt*.

sentence adverb (4): A WORD that modifies the meaning of an entire sentence, rather than solely the VERB: The word *hopefully* in the sentence, *Hopefully, we will ace our linguistics final*, modifies the sentence *We will ace our linguistics final* and not just the VERB *ace*.

shibboleth (10): A stigmatized pronunciation associated with a disfavored group. For example, pronouncing *birthday* as [bɹ̩fde] is a SHIBBOLETH in the US North but not in areas of the US South. This pronunciation is stigmatized in the North because it is associated with socially disparaged groups. In some areas of the US South, all speakers have it, and this pronunciation receives no stigma.

situational context (9): The physical surroundings that contribute to the PRAGMATIC KNOWLEDGE of a DISCOURSE. Talking in a quiet room with a few people is different from talking to a large audience in an open field.

sibilant (3): A NATURAL CLASS of hissing sounds. There are six of them in English: [s z ʃ ʒ tʃ dʒ]. The [s] in *silly* and the [tʃ] in *chin* are SIBILANTS.

social context (9): The relations between the speakers and audience in a DISCOURSE. Does one person have more authority than another or are they peers? Do the people belong to the same social groups? Is the DISCOURSE in a public place or a private space? Are there implications for these relationships in the DISCOURSE?

social meaning (2, 3): The counterpart to REFERENCE MEANING. SOCIAL MEANING is the connection between LANGUAGE and social groups. Many lexical items are associated with social groups or certain SOCIAL CONTEXTS, and those social connections are part of those lexical items' meanings. For example, WORDS like *automobile*, *wheels*, and *whip* can all have the same REFERENCE MEANING but probably have different SOCIAL MEANINGS.

social minimal pair (3): A pair of pronunciations that triggers a difference in SOCIAL MEANING rather than REFERENCE MEANING. The pronunciations of *bed* can vary between [bɛd] and [beəd], with the second one being marked for many as Southern, rural United States.

sonorant (2, 3): A NATURAL CLASS of ringing sounds that obstruct the air flow less than OBSTRUENTS. An example would be the [l] in *lip*. This set of sounds is made up of four other NATURAL CLASSES: LIQUIDS, NASALS, GLIDES, and VOWELS.

sonority (3): A sound's degree of resonance in comparison to other sounds. Consider that [l] has more ring (resonance) to it than [t], but that [a] has the most. [t] is least sonorant, [l] is more sonorant, and [a] is most sonorant. As a group, SONORANTS have more SONORITY than OBSTRUENTS.

sound stage (11): The first stage of LANGUAGE ACQUISITION in which infants must differentiate between human speech sounds and other non-human sounds, such as barking dogs and loud toys. This stage begins before birth, narrows to the languages' relevant sounds starting at six months, and continues to build the sound inventory for the next few years. Children learn not only the sounds but also the patterns of those sounds.

speech act (9): An UTTERANCE with a purpose. Saying *Could you help me?* is to make a request, and saying *You are on fire* is to inform.

standard~vernacular continuum (1): The range of judgment on LANGUAGE VARIATION in a community, with certain language patterns considered more stigmatized than others. These are opposite ends of the spectrum of judgment. For example, having the *pin-pen* vowel merger in the Southern US will be much more standard than in the North, where it is more rare.

stem (6): A morphology term for an inner-layer in a multi-morphemic word. The STEM is what the AFFIXES attach to. For example, in the WORD *dehumidifier*, the SUFFIX -*er* attaches to the STEM *dehumidify*. In the same way, the PREFIX *de-* attaches to the STEM *humidify*.

stop (2): A NATURAL CLASS of sounds produced with complete constriction of the airway in the VOCAL TRACT: The [d] in the WORD *mad* [mæd] or the [p] in *pie* [paɪ] are both STOPS.

strong verbs (6): VERBS that use ABLAUT to mark the past form. An example would be *bought*. It contains the VERB *buy* and the past-TENSE morpheme in the form of the ABLAUT.

structural ambiguity (7, 8): The concept that a string of WORDS can have more than one meaning because of the different possible HIERARCHAL organizations of its parts. The units therefore have different CONSTITUENCIES. *She kissed the boy with the puppet* can have two different syntactic trees corresponding to the two different meanings.

subject (8): Traditional grammar deems the SUBJECT to be the part of the sentence that is not the PREDICATE. The SUBJECT is the part of the INFLECTIONAL

PHRASE which coordinates with the verbal inflection, but the SUBJECT does not contain the VERB PHRASE. For example, in the sentence, *The coffee in the cup is cold*, the PHRASE *The coffee in the cup* is the SUBJECT because it is not the PREDICATE *is cold*. The third-person singular form of the VERB is used in coordination with this SUBJECT.

suffix (6): A BOUND MORPHEME that attaches to the end of the STEM: *-ed*, *-ing*, *-s*, and *-ly* are all SUFFIXES.

superlative (4): A state of an ADJECTIVE where it is the highest ranked along some scale: *warmest* is in its SUPERLATIVE form in *the warmest blanket*. Some ADJECTIVES take *most* to form the SUPERLATIVE: *The most beautiful*.

suppletion (6): A historical process where two or more previously distinct MORPHEMES are combined into one lexical item. For example, the modern WORD *bad* has *worse* and *worst* as its COMPARATIVE and SUPERLATIVE forms. These were added in the late Middle English period through SUPPLETION.

syllable (3): The template for sounds consisting of a RHYME, and possibly an ONSET. The RHYME is composed of at least a NUCLEUS and possibly a CODA. The two WORDS [e] *A* and [stɹẽŋθs] *strengths* both contain one SYLLABLE.

synchronic variation (3): Variation in a language at one point in time. The variation could be between different regions, different age groups, or any other social division. For example, parts of the United States use *trash can* while others use *garbage can*. In England, the same object might be a *rubbish bin* or *dustbin*. These are examples of lexical SYNCHRONIC VARIATION, but it can occur with any level of LANGUAGE.

syntax: The component of the MENTAL GRAMMAR that combines WORDS into PHRASES. It would take *tank*, *in*, and *the* and combine them into *in the tank*.

synthetic languages (6): Languages with more MORPHEMES per word than other languages. These languages usually rely more on MORPHOLOGY than SYNTAX to combine FUNCTION MORPHEMES. Spanish is more synthetic than English; it marks VERBS distinctively with SUFFIXES so we can figure out the person-number of the subject: *comemos* 'We eat' vs. *como* 'I eat'.

teaching grammar (1): This kind of text is an explanation of the patterns of a LANGUAGE, designed for non-native speakers. TEACHING GRAMMARS explain language regulations like "adjectives come before their nouns" and "objects come after their verbs," as well as supplying a limited vocabulary and exercises to practice. The textbook you use to learn a second language would be an example.

tense (vowel) (2): A quality of VOWEL sounds pronounced with the muscles relatively constricted. TENSE VOWELS are located closer to the edges of vowel space than LAX VOWELS. The VOWEL [i] in the WORD [ðiz] *these* is TENSE.

tense (verb) (4): The quality of a conjugated (finite) VERB form, usually denoting the range of time. There are two TENSES in Modern English: past (e.g. *walked*) and non-past (e.g. *walk*).

time-order implicature (9): A type of CONVERSATIONAL IMPLICATURE that suggests the chronological ordering of UTTERANCES mirrors the chronological ordering of a story. For example, *Jaclyn studied, took her test, and played video games*. This order of UTTERANCES implies that Jaclyn did these events in that specific order.

transitive (4): A quality of some VERBS where a SUBJECT and a direct object are logically required. In the sentence *He stabbed the vacuum*, the VERB *stab* is TRANSITIVE because the direct object, *the vacuum*, is part of the lexical listing for *stab*.

transitivity (4): The TRANSITIVITY of VERBS is a tricky subject, and scholars do not agree on how many there should be. In this book, we keep the situation simple in two ways. First, we only talk about three categories of TRANSITIVITY: INTRANSITIVE, TRANSITIVE, and DITRANSITIVE. Second, we stipulate that each VERB is lexically specified for TRANSITIVITY. In other words, when you memorize a VERB, such as kiss, you memorize its form, meaning, LEXICAL CATEGORY, and (since it is a verb) that it requires both a SUBJECT and object (that it is TRANSITIVE): In the sentences *She kisses him all the time* and *She kisses all the time*, the VERB is TRANSITIVE in both cases. The object in the second sentence is simply not expressed.

Universal Grammar (1, 8): The species-specific, biological endowment for building a MENTAL GRAMMAR. It supplies the basic blueprints for the MENTAL GRAMMAR, including both PRINCIPLES and PARAMETERS. To acquire a LANGUAGE, the baby must experience enough data from that language. The combination of that triggering experience and the UNIVERSAL GRAMMAR results in the MENTAL GRAMMAR.

utterance (9): This unit can be any bit of language produced in a SOCIAL CONTEXT. Shouting "Sacrilege!" in a cafeteria or spray painting "Free the elf!" on a bridge are both UTTERANCES.

velar (2): A NATURAL CLASS of sounds formed at the back of the roof of the mouth, behind the PALATAL region but in front of the pharyngeal region. The [g] of *gut* [gət] is a VELAR STOP.

verb (4): A basic LEXICAL CATEGORY that contains the framework for a sentence. VERBS have TRANSITIVITY and come in either infinitive or finite (conjugated) forms. The VERB *run* has a slot for the subject in its lexical listing and is INTRANSITIVE.

vernacular (1): In terms of LANGUAGE VARIATION, it is any form that is stigmatized. An example is saying *y'all* in New York City.

vocal folds (2): The two flaps of tissue within the LARYNX that gives us voice. VOICED sounds have more vocal fold vibrations. The VOICELESS sounds have few vocal fold vibrations. The GLOTTIS is the gap between the VOCAL FOLDS.

vocal tract (2): The airway associated with the production of speech, consisting of the throat, the mouth, and the NASAL cavity.

vocalization (3): Turning a CONSONANT sound into a VOWEL sound because the process makes the sound more *vocalic*. The terms *R-dropping* and *L-dropping* are both types of this process. The pronunciations *bar* [baː] and *coal* [koː] are examples.

voice of articulation (2): The binary choice between the VOCAL FOLDS vibrating or not. This is one of the primary characteristics distinguishing types of CONSONANTS. The [dʒ] in the WORD [dʒok] *joke* is a VOICED CONSONANT, meaning the VOCAL FOLDS vibrate in order to produce it.

voiced (2): A quality of sounds made with vibration of the VOCAL FOLDS: The [m] in the WORD [mi] *me* is VOICED, as is the VOWEL.

voiceless (2): A quality of sounds, in English usually CONSONANT sounds, made with little vibration of the VOCAL FOLDS: The [k] in the WORD [ki] *key* is VOICELESS.

vowel (2): A SONORANT sound produced with uninterrupted airflow in the vocal tract: [o], [i], and [æ] are all vowel sounds. VOWELS have a less constricted passageway than do CONSONANTS.

vowel space (3): A map that locates where a VOWEL is produced in the mouth. This space is divided into regions much the same way a geographic map can be ordered by longitude and latitude. The VOWEL [i] would be produced in the high-front region of VOWEL SPACE, while [u] would be produced in the high-back region of VOWEL SPACE.

weak verbs (6): VERBS that take an *-ed* to mark the past-TENSE form. Examples are *talked* and *shopped*.

weakening (5): A SEMANTIC CHANGE where the impact of the WORD, or its rhetorical force, is diminished over time. The diachronic semantic shift moves toward diluting the force of its meaning. *Quell* is a modern word for to 'quiet down' or 'make calm,' but its ancestor was the Old English word *cwellan* 'murder.'

***which* hunting (10):** A PEEVE in the United States arguing against *which* as a restrictive COMPLEMENTIZER. For example, according to the prescriptive advice, in the sentence *She wishes she had the ice cream cone which she dropped*, the WORD *which* should be replaced with *that*.

widening (5): A SEMANTIC CHANGE involving a shift from a narrower range of reference to a broader range of reference. The WORD *barn* used to refer to a storage building on a farm used only for barley. Now a lot of things are stored in a barn, such as tools and animals. The meaning of *barn* has undergone WIDENING.

word (1): A free-standing LANGUAGE unit containing both form and meaning: The WORD *coat* has the form [kot] and the meaning of 'an item of clothing for the upper body used as outerwear.' It can contain one or more MORPHEMES: For example, *squid* has one MORPHEME, but *squids* has two.

word stage (11): The second stage of LANGUAGE ACQUISITION in which children begin to obtain and comprehend whole WORDS and fit them into their appropriate LEXICAL CATEGORIES.

writing (1): A human technology invented to represent LANGUAGE. There are many different types around the world, and these different WRITING systems have been invented by many different people over several thousand years. For example, these letters are WRITING.

zero forms (4): A type of irregular plural NOUN that does not require a plural SUFFIX: *Deer, fish*, and *sheep* are all examples because their forms remain the same for the singular and plural.

Index

The numbers in parentheses are the primary chapters for the terms. For frequent terms, the page numbers are not exhaustive, but instead provide the pages where the term is a central point. Page numbers in bold refer to figures, and those in italics refer to tables.